**DATE DUE**

| | | |
|---|---|---|
| 1 2 MAY 1993 | | |
| JUL 2 4 '95 | | |
| AP 1 6 '02 | | |
| OC 8 '02 | | |
| OC 2 3 '02 | | |
| JA 1 3 '06 | | |
| FE 1 2 '09 | | |
| MR 3 0 '12 | | |
| NO 0 1 '14 | | |
| MY 2 6 '15 | | |
| | | |
| | | |
| | | |

# The Photographic
# Encyclopedia
# of
# WILDFLOWERS

*Wyethia amplexicaulis*

The Photographic
# Encyclopedia
## of
# WILDFLOWERS

TERESA FARINO

SMITHMARK

**For my grandmother, Mary Joan Copus**

| | |
|---|---|
| **Text**<br>Teresa Farino | **Editorial**<br>Valerie Noël-Finch |
| **Photography**<br>Planet Earth Pictures<br>Teresa Farino | **Production**<br>Ruth Arthur<br>David Proffit<br>Sally Connolly<br>Andrew Whitelaw |
| **Design**<br>Jill Coote | **Director of Production**<br>Gerald Hughes |
| **Senior Commissioning Editor**<br>Andrew Preston | |
| **Publishing Assistant**<br>Edward Doling | |

CLB 2424
© 1991 Colour Library Books Ltd, Godalming, Surrey, England.
All rights reserved.
This edition published in 1991 by SMITHMARK Publishers Inc.,
112 Madison Avenue, New York, NY 10016.
Color separations by Art Color Offset, Italy.
Printed and bound in Italy by Fratelli Spada, SpA.
ISBN 0 8317 2806 X

SMITHMARK books are available for bulk purchase for sales
promotions and premium use. For details write or telephone
the Manager of Special Sales, SMITHMARK Publishers, Inc,
112 Madison Avenue, New York, NY 10016. (212) 532-6600.

# CONTENTS

Previous pages: *Agapanthus sp.*
Left: *Papaver rhoeas*

# INTRODUCTION

Flowering plants, known to botanists as angiosperms, are thought to have evolved about 120 million years ago. By the end of the Cretaceous period, some 80-90 million years ago, they had become the dominant group of vascular plants on Earth, occurring in all habitats except the ocean deeps.

## FEATURES OF FLOWERING PLANTS

The main difference between angiosperms and other types of vascular plants, such as ferns, horsetails, cycads and gymnosperms (conifers), is that they possess true flowers.

Each flower has four parts arranged in whorls. The outer whorl, known as the calyx, consists of leaf-like bracts called sepals which are usually green and protect the flower in bud. Within the sepals is the corolla, which consists of more leaf-like bracts called petals that are often brightly coloured to attract pollinators. The male reproductive organs of the flower are the stamens, which bear pollen-producing structures at their tips called anthers. The female reproductive organs are the carpels, which contain ovules that later become the seeds. The ovules are enclosed in an ovary topped by a style and stigma, the latter receiving the pollen grains. The male reproductive organs of the flower are known collectively as the androecium, while the female parts are the gynaecium.

The main function of flowers is to produce seed to ensure the survival of the species. This may be achieved either by self-pollination (the stigmas receiving pollen from the stamens of the same flower) or by cross-pollination (the stigmas receiving pollen from a different flower of the same species). In some species the pollen is carried from flower to flower by the wind (or by water in some aquatic plants), while the majority of flowering plants have coloured petals or produce strong scents to attract pollinators, usually insects, birds or bats.

## HOW PLANTS ARE CLASSIFIED

All living things are classified in accordance with international scientific rules, using formal Latin names to group like with like and transcend language barriers. All flowering plants belong to the class Angiospermae, which is divided into two subclasses: the Dicotyledoneae and the Monocotyledoneae. Further subdivisions split these subclasses into orders, families, genera and species.

The basic unit of classification is the species, which may be broadly defined as including all individuals able to interbreed and produce fertile offspring. For example, gentians belong to the family Gentianaceae and the genus *Gentiana*, while the species known in English as the great yellow gentian, in Spanish as *genciana amarilla* and in French as *grande gentiane*, is identified internationally by the Latin name *Gentiana lutea*. At present about 250,000 species of flowering plants are known to man, although many others undoubtedly await discovery in the less well explored regions of the Earth. This is particularly the case in the tropical zone, where some two-thirds of all flowering plant families are found.

As more research is carried out into the alliances of the world's flowering plants, so new classification schemes are devised. The system used in this encyclopedia is that developed by Cronquist in 1981. The book is divided into nine chapters, each of which covers one of the major habitats and describes some of its more characteristic flora. Most of the genera featured are herbs, that is, non-woody plants, in keeping with the word 'wildflowers' in the title. Because of space limitations, groups with less conspicuous flowers, such as grasses, sedges and rushes, have been excluded.

Within each chapter the entries are arranged alphabetically by generic name. Using information from Mabberley's *The Plant Book* (Cambridge University Press, 1989), the family to which the genus belongs, as well as the number of species in that genus, are given after every entry. English names are used in addition to the scientific Latin names wherever possible.

## GUARDING OUR HERITAGE

It is hoped that this book may increase awareness of the beautiful and often bizarre world of flowering plants, a world of fundamental importance to the survival of man but increasingly threatened by the burgeoning human race.

Over half the food eaten by humans is currently derived from just three plants – wheat, rice and maize – although it is estimated that some 75,000 species are edible and many of these highly nutritious. More than 40 per cent of modern medicines are derived from natural sources, mostly from flowering plants, and over 75 per cent of people living in rural areas of the world rely on traditional herbal medicines. Just as important is that flowers, both wild and cultivated, are objects of great beauty, finding a place in the cultures of western civilizations and ancient tribal peoples.

Yet the human race continues to spread across the face of the Earth, bringing with it problems of habitat destruction, urbanization and pollution on an unprecedented scale. Natural ecosystems are rapidly being altered and once pristine areas of wilderness, particularly the tropical forests, are fast disappearing. It is estimated that between 10 and 15 per cent of flowering plants are threatened by this tide of human destruction, a figure that almost certainly includes many species of potential foodplants or sources of valuable drugs. And with the disappearance of every species, the world is undoubtedly a poorer place.

*Balsamorhiza sagittata*

# CHAPTER ONE

# MOUNTAINS

The principal high mountain ecosystems of the world, which range in heights from 2,000 m to over 8,000 m (6,600-26,200 ft), are the Rocky Mountains of western North America, which are duplicated in South America by the spine of the Andes, the Himalayas and associated ranges in Asia and the East African highlands and isolated volcanic peaks. Mountains are also a dominant part of New Zealand's landscape, while Europe boasts a number of isolated ranges including the Pyrenees, Alps, Carpathians and Caucasus.

The harsh climate of mountains results from the fact that air O temperatures decrease by 0.5°C (0.9°F) with every 100 m (330 ft) increase in height. Much of the annual precipitation falls as snow and in many high-mountain areas permanent snowfields occur. At the high altitudes above the limite where trees are able to grow the growing season for other plants is limited to about three months of the year, but during this time plants must also cope with high levels of infrared, visible and ultraviolet light, low oxygen levels and strong winds.

Most flowering plants in montane regions are herbaceous perennials whose overwintering buds are close to ground level so as to receive some protection from the winter snow cover. Annuals are rare, as they are usually unable to complete their life cycles in one short growing season, and account for less than 4 per cent of the high mountain flora. The long-lived perennial species commonly form cushion-like growths within which the temperature is considerably higher than that of the surrounding air, serving to protect the delicate buds during the winter. Low temperatures, high levels of ultraviolet light and strong winds have a dwarfing effect on many species. Many plants are evergreen and are thus able to start growing as soon as temperatures rise, when the snow melts and light is once again available for photosynthesis. Mountain flowers are typically large and brightly coloured to attract the few insects which live in these habitats.

Because of the discontinuous distribution of mountains across the Earth, many essentially arctic flowering plants which found themselves in montane habitats after the glaciers retreated during the last Ice Age were unable to spread through the lowlands and were effectively isolated in these mountain refuges. As a result many species of modern flowering plants are confined to but a single range of mountains.

Facing page: *Aconitum lamarckii*

Alpine meadow, Ecrins, France.

## ACIPHYLLA

These spiny rock plants are confined to Australasia. Apart from a single species in Australia and one in the Chatham Islands, they occur only in New Zealand and are typical of the alpine zone. They have the characteristic pinnate leaves of the carrot family, although these are usually stiff, spiny and erect. The flowers are arranged in dense yellowish or white clusters, with male and female flowers on separate plants. The larger plants of this genus are commonly referred to as speargrass or spaniard. It has been suggested that the erect, dagger-like leaves and stipules which characterize this genus evolved to protect the plant from grazing moas (although these massive flightless birds, unique to New Zealand, are now long extinct).

Among the larger species are *Aciphylla horrida*, in which the spectacular flowering stems may reach 1.5 m (5 ft) in height, and *A. scott-thomsonii*, the tallest plant in the genus, which is distinguished by its 1 m (3.3 ft) long glaucous leaves and 3 m (10 ft)

inflorescences. By contrast *A. divisa* is a much smaller, tufted plant with pale yellow, globose flower heads which grows in snow tussock grassland at higher elevations, although in areas of heavy grazing it is restricted to inaccessible bluffs and rocky outcrops. High alpine species occurring at heights of up to 2,000 m (6,600 ft), include *A. leighii, A. dobsonii, A. simplex, A. congesta* and *A. kirkii*.

**Umbelliferae; 39 species**

## ACONITUM

A genus of herbaceous perennials, mainly confined to the northern hemishpere, many of which occur in montane areas in Europe, Asia and North America. All species have the characteristic hooded flowers (formed by the sepals, the petals being reduced to nectaries) and palmately divided leaves.

Plants of this genus are commonly known as monkshoods, wolfbanes or aconites. The generic name, and its English equivalent of aconite, are thought to have been derived from *akontion*, a dart,

since certain tribes poison their arrows with the juices of these plants. The name wolfsbane is derived from an old belief that arrows or baits treated with these juices would be capable of killing wolves (or even werewolves!), whereas that of monkshood refers to the shape of the flowers, which supposedly resemble the headress of Mediaeval monks.

Aconites are a source of medicinal drugs as all parts of the plant contain high concentrations of alkaloids. Most important is a group of extremely toxic chemicals known as aconitines, used particularly in the treatment of heart disease. Aconitine, however, is one of the most deadly poisons to have been discovered, more powerful than prussic acid, and any treatment with this drug entails a certain risk.

The Himalayan region boasts a large number of aconites, including those with blue or purple flowers such as *Aconitum hookeri* and *A. violaceum*, found in open, rocky country between 3,600 and 4,800 m (11,800-15,800 ft) and Indian aconite *A. ferox*, perhaps the most deadly of all species, a twining plant which

medicine, and the very similar *A. compactum*. Both occur in damp meadows in the Alps and Pyrenees. Variants of common monkshood, however, extend to the British Isles, Scandinavia and the Urals and Caucasus. *A. paniculatum* is a species of the Alps and Apennines; *A. variegatum*, sometimes with pure white flowers, occurs only in the central Alps; *A. tauricum* is confined to the eastern parts of the same range. A northern European monkshood with hairy violet coloured flowers is lousehat *A. septentrionale*, which grows in birch forests and willow thickets at lower elevations in southern Norway.

Of the 15 North American species, western monkshood *A. columbianum* has dull blue flowers and grows in wet meadows in the Rocky Mountains up to 2,700 m (8,900 ft) and at lesser altitudes in California's Sierra Nevada, while *A. delphinifolium* has sky-blue flowers and grows in alpine meadows in Alaska and northeastern Siberia. *A. noveboracense*, the northern wild monkshood, is listed as a threatened species by the United States Fish and Wildlife Service (1985).

**Ranunculaceae; about 100 species**

### ADONIS

A small genus of annual or perennial herbs with red or yellow flowers which usually open before the leaves are fully developed. Characteristics of the genus, which is distributed across temperate Eurasia, are finely divided leaves and showy solitary flowers with more than eight petals and no nectaries. The genus is named after the ill-fated Adonis, from whose blood the plant sprang, according to Greek legend. The roots of some species contain a powerful cardiac drug called adonidin, which has a similar action to digitalin (derived from the plant genus *Digitalis*) in the treatment of heart and kidney disease but is said to be several times more potent. Plants in this genus are commonly known as pheasant's-eyes.

Several species are confined to montane regions. The yellow-flowered Pyrenean pheasant's-eye *Adonis pyrenaica* is an infrequent denizen of rocky ground in the French and Spanish Pyrenees up to 2,400 m (7,900 ft) (also found at Mont Pelat in the Alps) Maritimes. The very similar *A. vernalis*, has larger flowers and grows at lower altitudes from Scandinavia to the central and eastern European mountains. Apennine pheasant's-eye, *A. distorta* also has yellow flowers and grows in limestone habitats in Italy's central Apennines.

Himalayan species include the golden-flowered *A. chrysocanthus*, which occurs from Pakistan to

grows in forest clearings between 2,100 and 3,600 m (6,900-11,800 ft). Other species vary in flower colour. The small, cylindrical-hooded flowers of *A. laeve*, a forest plant found up to 3,300 m (10,800 ft), may be white, pale yellow or dull purple, whereas those of *A. gammiei*, a high alpine species growing at elevations of up to 4,800 m (15,800 ft), range from pale blue, through white to greenish yellow; *A. spicatum* has purple to greenish white flowers.

The mountains of Europe are also a stronghold for this genus. Typically the plants have yellow flowers, for example, *A. vulparia*, an extremely variable species occurring in woods, meadows and stony habitats up to 2,400 m (7,900 ft), and *A. anthora*, which grows in dry limestone meadows. Both species are found in the Alps, Pyrenees and Apennines, whereas the rarer *A. lamarckii* occur in the Pyrenees and southern Alps.

European aconites with blue or mauve flowers include common monkshood *A. napellus*, which is probably the best known and most widely used in

*Aconitum napellus*

*Adonis annua*

lobes of each basal leaf. It has noted astringent properties on account of the high tannin content of both leaves and roots, and was considered by herbalists to be one of the best remedies for inflamed wounds and bruises and particularly for stopping bleeding. In ancient times it was thought that placing the herb under the pillow promoted a peaceful night's sleep.

Alpine Lady's mantle, *A. alpina*, is common calcifuge of mountainous areas throughout Eurasia, but is also found on tundra herb slopes and scrub in the Arctic. It is distinguished by its leaves, which are divided almost to the base into 5-7 lanceolate lobes, toothed at the apex and silvery-hairy beneath. The yellow green flowers, each only about 3 mm (0.1 in) across, appear between June and August in dense clusters in a terminal inflorescence from 5 to 30 cm (2-12 in) tall. The leaves of *A. vulgaris* and *A. alpina* are eaten as a vegetable and are also the preferred food of the larvae of several species of moths, including the red carpet *Xanthorhoe munitata*, the dark marbled carpet *Chloroclystra citrata* and the rosy marbled moth *Elaphria venustula*.

Among a whole host of very similar and very variable Eurasian montane species are cut-leaved Lady's mantle *A. pentaphyllea* on acid soils in the Alps, often in melting snow patches, Hoppe's Lady's mantle *A. hoppeana* on limestone in the Alps and Apenr ines (also very rare in Britain) and *A. splendens* at elevations of up to 2,500 m (8,200 ft) in the Pyrenees, Jura and Alps. *A. trollii*, distributed from Pakistan to Kashmir between 3,000 and 4,100 m (9,800-13,500 ft), is one of three Himalayan species, while *A. sibirica* and *A. krylovii* are characteristic plants of the montane pastures above 3,500 m (11,500 ft) in the Tien Mountains of China.

The genus also contains several tropical African representatives, including *A. cryptantha*, widespread in East Africa, up to 4,000 m (13,100 ft), *A. fischeri* at lower elevations in the Aberdares and Masai region of Tanzania; *A. johnstonii* on Mount Kenya,

western Nepal between 3,300 and 4,300 m (10,800-14,100ft), especially on slopes on which the snow has recently melted; and the smaller but otherwise similar *A. nepalensis*, found at heights of up to 4,500 m (14,800 ft) from central Nepal to Sikkim.

Pheasant's-eyes are also found in woodland, and several annual species are typical of cornfields and disturbed wasteland. *A. amurensis*, for example, is a woodland plant particularly common in the Ussuri region of the eastern USSR and Japan. It is one of the earliest species to bloom, producing glossy yellow flowers in February and March. The red-flowered annuals include pheasant's-eye *A. annua*, *A. flammea* and summer adonis *A. aestivalis*, the latter growing in cornfields up to 3,000 m (9,800 ft) in the Himalayas, where its flowers are often yellow with purple centres rather than red.

**Ranunculaceae; 20 species**

## *ALCHEMILLA*

A large genus of mainly perennial herbs, particularly common in the northern temperate regions of Europe,

Asia and America, but also extending southwards into the tropical mountains. The flowers lack true petals, their role being played by the calyx and epicalyx, and are thus usually green and inconspicuous. The generic name *Alchemilla* is derived from the Arabic *alkemelych*, because of its supposed wonder-working properties. The leaves are furrowed so as to collect a droplet of rain or dew in the cup formed where the stem joins the leaf; this droplet was an ingredient of many mystic potions in ancient times. The collective common name, Lady's mantle was coined in the Middle Ages when the shallowly lobed leaves were thought to resemble the scalloped edges of the Virgin's mantle.

Common Lady's mantle *Alchemilla vulgaris*, an aggregate of over 20 very similar microspecies, occurs in mountainous regions throughout Europe, northern and western Asia, Greenland and eastern North America, although its range of habitats includes open woodlands, damp grasslands and Arctic tundra. One of the local names of this plant is 'nine hooks', due to the seven or nine broad, but shallow toothed

*Alchemilla alpina*

and Kilimanjaro and in the Virunga Mountains between 2,400 and 4,200 m (7,900-13,800 ft), and *A. rothii* in heath and bamboo zones of the higher East African mountains, including Ms Elgon and Kenya and in the Aberdares.

## Rosaceae; 250 species

### ANDROSACE
A genus of annual or tufted perennial herbs, commonly known as rock jasmines, which are distributed across northern temperate regions of the world. The leaves are usually confined to basal rosettes and the flowers are small pink, mauve or white (although *Androsace vitalina* has yellow flowers), either solitary or in clusters, usually with a yellow or orange throat. Many species are confined to montane habitats, especially the Himalayas and the mountains of central and southern Europe, where they typically form mats or cushions.

Over 20 species are found in the Himalayas, including *A. primuloides*, which has pink flowers and white woolly rosettes and occurs only in Kashmir where it is abundant on alpine slopes between 3,000 and 4,000 m (9,800-13,100 ft), and *A. lehmannii*, a common, pink or white-flowered cushion-forming plant in the humid alpine zone between 3,500 and 5,000 m (11,500-16,400 ft) in Nepal and Sikkim. *A. muscoidea*, with clusters of lilac flowers, *A. globifera*, with orange-eyed pink or mauve flowers, *A. rotundifolia*, with long-stalked pink flowers, and *A. sempervivoides*, with large, compact rosettes and pinkish flowers with a conspicuous yellow eye, are also common Himalayan species.

In Europe many rock jasmines have very limited ranges, such as the pink-flowered alpine rock jasmine *A. alpina* and the white-flowered Swiss rock jasmine *A. helvetica*, both of which occur only in the Alps. The white-flowered *A. hausmannii* has an even more restricted range, growing only in the eastern region, from the Gruppo di Brenta in the Alps of northeast Italy to the Salzburg Alps. In addition, Mathilda's rock jasmine *A. mathildae* is found only in the central Apennines, *A. cylindrica* and *A. ciliata* are both confined to the central Pyrenees, and *A. brevis* grows only in the mountains round Lake Como in the Italian Alps.

Other species have a much greater range, including milk-white rock jasmine *A. lactea*, which is found throughout the mountains of central Europe, pink rock jasmine *A. carnea*, a western European montane plant, *A. villosa*, whose distribution extends from the eastern Carpathians to the mountains of northern Spain, central Greece and Italy; and hairy rock jasmine *A. pubescens* which grows in both the Alps and Pyrenees.

## Primulaceae; about 100 species

### ANEMONE
A large genus with a more or less cosmopolitan distribution, centred on the northern temperate zone. Anemones have a characteristic whorl of three or four leaflets under the flowers, which are usually solitary and terminal, with 5-14 petal-like perianth segments and numerous stamens. The common name, which is the same as that of the genus, is thought to be derived from Anemos the Greek god of wind, who, according to legend, sends these flowers at the onset of spring as heralds of his arrival. Like most members of the buttercup family, anemones contain poisonous alkaloids, including anemonin, a poison of the central nervous system. American Indians value anemones for their powerful healing properties and formerly used the roots for treating wounds.

Several species are particularly associated with montane regions, especially in the Himalayas and the mountains of Europe, although a few high altitude representatives are also found in the southern hemisphere and North America. *Anemone tenuicaulis*, for example, is a delicate herb with pink or reddish brown flowers that occurs up to 1,500 m (5,000 ft) in snow tussock grassland in New Zealand, especially in the wetter South Island ranges. *A. thomsonii* is silky haired with solitary white or pinkish flowers and prefers boggy situations up to 3,900 m (12,800 ft) in the East African mountains, including Mts Kenya, Kilimanjaro and Elgon.

In the western mountains of North America grows *A. globosa*, a slender stemmed species with deep purple (rarely greenish yellow) flowers which occurs from Alaska through the higher valleys of the Rocky Mountains to California and New Mexico. It is one of 14 Rocky Mountain anemones, other common species being *A. parviflora* and the candle anemone *A. cylindrica*. *A. drummondii* is a hairy perennial herb with white, blue-tinged flowers which occurs further south in California's Sierra Nevada and the Coast Ranges between 1,500 and 3,200 m (5,000-10,500 ft).

About 17 species of anemone grow in the Himalayas. These can be divided into two groups according to whether or not the achenes are embedded in dense woolly hairs. Among those which protect the developing seeds in this way are *A. rupicola*, with large, showy white or pinkish flowers; *A. biflora*, with much smaller white flowers, bluish on the outside when young but becoming dull red with age; and the stout, silky haired *A. vitifolia*, with its distinctive loose clusters of large white flowers and heart-shaped, shallowly lobed leaves. *A. biflora* is one of the earliest plants to flower in the lower mountains of Kashmir, beginning in February, whilst the other species are found at higher altitudes from Afghanistan to southwest China and flower in late summer.

Himalayan anemones in which the achenes are not surrounded by woolly hairs include the white-, yellow- or blue-flowered *A. obtusiloba*, found up to 4,300 m (14,100 ft) from Pakistan to southeastern Tibet; the similar *A. demissa*, with clusters of white, blue or purple flowers, which grows on open slopes from western Nepal to southwest China; and *A. polyanthes*,

*Androsace villosa*

which has smaller white, red or mauve flowers and is particularly common in Nepal.

In Europe several species occur only on a particular mountain range, including *A. uralensis*, which has white, yellow, purple or reddish flowers and is found only in open coniferous woodlands in the central and southern Urals; the white-flowered *A. pavoniana*, which is confined to the limestone mountains of northern and central Spain; and the very similar Monte Baldo anemone *A. baldensis*, which grows in the Alps and the mountains of Yugoslavia.

**Ranunculaceae; 120 species**

### *AQUILEGIA*

The genus *Aquilegia* is confined to northern temperate regions and is distinguished by its drooping flowers (erect in *A. parviflora*), with their five, almost tubular petals, each of which terminates in an incurved, horn-like spur, and brightly coloured, petal-like sepals. The spurs secrete nectar to attract pollinating honey bees. The generic name is derived from the Latin *aquila*, meaning 'eagle', since the flower spurs are considered to resemble the bird's talons. The common name of columbine originates from the Latin *columba*, meaning 'dove' or 'pigeon', because the spray of flowers was thought to resemble a flight of doves. The ancient name of culverwort reinforces this theory, since *wort* is the Saxon word for plant and *culfre* means 'pigeon'.

In Britain, despite its possible introduction from Europe, the common columbine *Aquilegia vulgaris* was one of the badges of the House of Lancaster as well as of the earls of Derby. The leaves were once used in the treatment of sore mouths and throats, while the seeds are reputed to be efficacious in the treatment of yellow jaundice. The plant is sometimes also called granny's bonnet.

Columbines are found in most of the mountain

*Aquilegia vulgaris*

ranges of the northern hemisphere from the Himalayas to the Rockies. The blue columbine *A. coerulea* has deep blue to white flowers (depending on altitude and geographical location) and thrives in wet, rocky and shady situations up to 3,350 m (11,000 ft) in the Rocky Mountains, extending as far south as New Mexico. It is the state flower of Colorado.

Another very distinctive North American species is the Sitka columbine *A. formosa*, which has fiery red, petal-like sepals and yellowish petals. It is found in open coniferous woods from southern Alaska to California and as far east as Montana and Utah and its

seeds were formerly used to discourage headlice. *A. flavescens* is another Rocky Mountain species, with pale yellow flowers, while *A. pubescens*, which has white to yellowish flowers, is found in rocky habitats up to 3,650 m (12,000 ft) in the Californian mountains.

In the mountains of Europe, columbines are some of the most colourful members of the alpine flora. It can almost be said that each mountain range has its own species of *Aquilegia*, although the common columbine *A. vulgaris*, with its blue-violet flowers, is found at lower altitudes throughout Europe. The dark columbine *A. atrata* has dark purple flowers and

*Aquilegia coerulia*

occurs only in the Alps and Apennines; Einsel's columbine *A. einseleana* has blue-violet flowers and is confined to the Alps; and the bright blue flowers of the alpine columbine *A. alpina* are also found only in the Alps and Apennines.

The Pyrenean columbine *A. pyrenaica*, with its bright blue flowers, is found only in the Pyrenees, as is the similar *A. aragonensis*, while *A. discolor* has blue flowers with white-tipped sepals, and is confined to the limestone range known as the Picos de Europa in northern Spain. *A. cazorlensis* is another bright blue flowered species which occurs only on limestone slopes in the mountains of southeastern Spain, while the green-tipped flowers of *A. nevadensis* are only to be found in southern Spain's Sierra Nevada.

Four species of columbine are found in the Himalayas, including the handsome *A. nivalis*, which has solitary, blackish purple flowers and occurs up to 4,000 m (13,100 ft) from Pakistan to Himachal Pradesh; the white-flowered *A. fragrans*, whose sweet-scented blooms are common in meadows up to 3,600 m (11,800 ft); and two purple-flowered species *A. moorcroftiana* and *A. pubiflora*. Also in Asia are the pure white-flowered *A. flabellata*, a frequent species in the mountains of Japan, where it thrives in scrubland and damp woods at altitudes up to 1,500 m (5,000 ft) and the Amur columbine *A. amurensis*, which grows in woodland in Ussuriland in the eastern USSR.

**Ranunculaceae; about 70 species**

### ASTRANTIA

Known as masterworts, the species of this small genus of perennial herbs are distributed from central and southern Europe across the Caucasus into temperate Asia. The roots are often dark coloured and aromatic and the flower umbels differ from those of more typical members of the carrot family in resembling

*Astrantia major*

single, terminal blooms: the tiny, short-stalked flowers of the umbel look like hemispherical pincushions enclosed in a cup of papery, petal-like bracts.

Lesser masterwort *Astrantia minor*, a delicate plant of acid soils up to 2,700 m (8,900 ft) in the southwestern Alps, Pyrenees and northern Apennines, has greenish white umbels, while those of the large

*Astrantia major*

*Aquilegia chrysantha*

great masterwort *A. major*, also known as mountain sanicle, may be tinged with mauve or pink. *A. major* is found in meadows and woods, usually on calcareous soils, in the Pyrenees, Alps and Apennines, extending also to the mountains of northern Spain and Bulgaria; it is naturalized in northern and western Britain.

Bavarian masterwort *A. bavarica*, with whitish flowers and bracts, is confined to calcareous soils in the eastern Alps, where it may be found up to 2,300 m (7,500 ft) while the similar Carnic masterwort *A. carniolica* is found only at lower elevations in the southeastern Alps. *A. pauciflora* grows only on limestone soils in the mountains of Italy.

**Umbelliferae; 10 species**

*Celmisia monroi*

### CALLIANTHEMUM

Plants of this small genus are distributed across the mountainous regions of Europe and central Asia. *Callianthemum coriandrifolium* is a rare species of the Alps, Pyrenees, Carpathians and the mountains of the western Balkan peninsula, where it grows in dry grassy habitats on acidic soils at altitudes of between 1,800 and 3,000 m (5,900-9,800 ft). It has deeply lobed, blue-green leaves and flowers up to 3 cm (1.2 in) in diameter, each of which has 5-12 white or pinkish overlapping petals and yellow stamens.

C. *kernerianum* is found only in limestone habitats on Monte Baldo in northern Italy and the southern slopes of the Alps. It differs from C. *coriandrifolium* in having larger flowers with linear, widely spaced, whitish petals. A third European species is C. *anemonoides*, distinguished by its pale green leaves and white flowers with an orange central ring. It grows in open coniferous woodlands on calcareous soils in the northeastern Alps. The only species in the Himalayas is the very similar C. *pimpinelloides*, found from Afghanistan to southeastern Tibet, between 2,700 and 4,000 m (8,900-13,100 ft).

**Ranunculaceae; 10 species**

### CELMISIA

A genus of evergreen, perennial herbs or shrubs confined to the southern hemisphere. There are three Australian representatives, the remainder occurring only in New Zealand, where almost all species are found in alpine habitats. The genus is named after the Greek character Celmis, one of the attendants of Cybele, the Phrygian mother of the Gods. Commonly known as celmisias or cotton-daisies, these plants are characteristic members of the alpine vegetation, with distinctive whitish, daisy-like flowers, most of which have golden discs. The relative uniformity of the flowerheads means that the individual species are best identified by their vegetative form and leaf shape.

*Celmisia sessiliflora* is one of the more conspicuous species, the individual rosettes forming dense, hard, grey-green cushions up to 1 m (3.3 ft) in diameter. It is widespread in the mountains of South and Stewart Islands, where it grows in snow tussock herbfield and cushion bogs at altitudes up to some 1,800 m (5,900 ft). C. *argentea* is rather similar to C. *sessiliflora*, but distinguished by its silvery cushions; C. *clavata* is confined to Stewart Island, where it occurs in cushion bogs overlying peat; C. *laricifolia* is a South Island mat-forming species; and C. *major* is found only on Mt Egmont, North Island.

Other distinctive species include C. *bellidioides*, a creeping herb typical of wet rocks around waterfalls on South Island; C. *allanii*, a snow line species which grows between 1,300 and 1,700 m (4,300-5,600 ft); the silver-leaved, carpet-forming C. *hectori*, which is one of the most prominent plants of fellfield and snow banks in the high rainfall regions of Fjordland; and the largest celmisia of all - C. *coriacea* - a tufted

Alpine meadow, Switzerland.

herb which forms clumps up to 2 m (6.6 ft) across, with large leathery leaves, woolly beneath, and flowerheads up to 10 cm ((4 in) in diameter.

*C. vernicosa* is a densely tufted species native to the Auckland Islands, which is unique in the genus in having purple disc-florets, while the snow or silver daisy *C. asteliifolia*, is an Australian species with narrow, silver-hairy leaves and flowers about 5 cm (2 in) in diameter. It is common on the hill slopes of Kosciusko and other highland areas of New South Wales, Victoria and Tasmania. Two New Zealand species, *C. morganii* and *C. philocremna*, are listed as rare in the IUCN Plant Red Data Book (1980).

**Compositae; 61 species**

### CORTUSA

A small genus of perennial, often hairy herbs with a montane distribution from central Europe to northern Asia, including Japan. The only European species is alpine bells *Cortusa matthioli*, also known as bear's-ear sanicle, presumably on account of the leaf shape. It has almost circular but lobed and toothed, softly hairy leaves arranged in a basal tuft, from which arises a long stem with a terminal cluster of 3-15 nodding, rosy purple, bell-shaped flowers. It occurs in woods and damp places up of 2,200 m (7,200 ft), particularly on limestone in the Alps, Carpathians, Transylvanian Alps and the mountains of the southeastern Balkan peninsula.

*C. matthioli* is also found in similar habitats between 3,000 and 4,000 m (9,800-13,100 ft) in the Himalayas, although it is suspected that this plant may in fact be a separate species. Nowhere common, alpine bells becomes increasingly scarce to the west of its range and in some countries is protected by law. Similar species include *C. altaica*, an inhabitant of

*Erinus alpinus*

*Eryngium alpinum*

the mountains of the northern Balkan peninsula. As a result of over-collecting this species is now very rare in some parts of its range and is thus protected by law.

Confined to limestone habitats in the southwestern Alps is silver eryngo *E. spinalba*, named for its white flowers and ruff of greenish white bracts, which blooms earlier in the year and generally occurs at lower altitudes than *E. alpinum*. Pyrenean eryngo *E. bourgatii* has a wider distribution, being common in dry meadows and rocky habitats up to 2,000 m (6,600 ft) in the Pyrenees and mountains of northern Spain. It is distinguished by its steel blue flower bracts and white patterning along the veins of its deeply lobed, grey-green leaves.

Other montane species include the blue-flowered *E. duriaei* from the mountains of northern Iberia, glacier eryngo *E. glaciale*, a species found only above 2,500 m (8,200 ft) in southern Spain's Sierra Nevada and a few North African localities; and the splendid *E. amethystinum* of the Balkan peninsula, Italy and the Aegean. *E. giganteum* is a robust biennial or perennial species of the Caucasus, with silvery blue or greenish flowers.

Field eryngo *E. campestre*, also called snakeroot, is a characteristic species of dry grasslands in Europe, although in Britain it is now confined to Cornwall, Devon, Hampshire and Guernsey and is protected by law. The 1 m (3.3 ft) high, white-flowered button

the mountains of central Asia, and the yellow-flowered *C. semenovii*.

**Primulaceae; 8 species**

### ERINUS

The two members of this genus are typical inhabitants of the mountains of northern Spain, Pyrenees, Alps and Apennines, extending southwards into the Balearic Islands, Sardinia and North Africa. The best known of the two is the vary variable fairy foxglove *Erinus alpinus*. It is a small, tufted plant which thrives in rocky pastures, screes and cliffs, usually on limestone to heights of some 2,400 m (7,900 ft) throughout the range of the genus. The tiny rose-pink (rarely violet or white) flowers each have a two-lobed upper lip and three-lobed lower lip, although the five lobes are arranged so as to appear almost radially symmetrical. Several subspecies have been described and the plant is protected by law in some countries.

**Scrophulariaceae; 2 species**

### ERYNGIUM

This large genus of perennial herbs with spiny toothed leaves is widely distributed across both temperate and tropical regions of both hemispheres. In contrast to the broad umbels typical of the Umbelliferae, the tiny, stalkless flowers are arranged in dense hemispherical or cylindrical heads, subtended by a ring of spiny bracts. Although only a few species are typical of montane habitats, they form an important part of the alpine flora, especially in Europe.

The generic name may be derived from the Greek word eruggarein, meaning 'to eructate', which refers directly to the plants' supposed efficacy in treating flatulent disorders; alternatively the name may come from the diminutive of *eerungos*, 'the beard of a goat', possibly an allusion to the spiny appearance of most species. In Europe, the larvae of the dingy skipper butterfly *Erynnis tages* feed on the foliage of *Eryngium*.

Alpine eryngo *Eryngium alpinum*, also known as queen of the Alps, is a bluish green, hairless perennial with magnificent terminal umbels consisting of a compact, egg-shaped cluster of tiny flowers subtended by a dense collar of spiny violet-blue bracts. Flowering between July and September, it is a common plant of limestone grasslands up to some 2,500 m (8,200 ft) in the Alps, Jura, western and central Yugoslavia and

*Eryngium bourgatii*

*Eryngium alpinum*

snakeroot *E. aquaticum* (*E. yuccifolium*), and coyote thistle *E. leavenworthii* are among several North American representatives of the genus. *E. vesiculosum*, with its creeping rooting runners and spiny, grey-green leaves, is native to New Zealand.

Sea holly *E. maritimum*, with its distinctive purplish blue bracts, is widespread on maritime sand and shingle around the coasts of Europe, North Africa and southwest Asia. It has also become naturalized on the Atlantic coast of the United States.

The roots of some species were formerly used to treat snakebite, hence the common name of snakeroot, while the root of *E. maritimum* was at one time candied and sold throughout Europe as an aphrodisiac.

**Umbelliferae; 230 species**

## GENTIANA

The 300 or so members of this genus, commonly known as gentians, have a distribution ranging from polar to temperate regions in both hemispheres and are particularly associated with montane habitats. The flowers have a funnel-shaped or cylindrical corolla which divides into five short lobes at the tip, often with smaller folds (lobules) in between, and many are pollinated by butterflies and bees. Gentiana lutea, the great yellow gentian of the Pyrenees, Alps and Apennines, is a commercial source of gentian root which is believed to have tonic properties and is widely used in the flavouring of liqueurs. The roots of other European species such as *G. purpurea*, *G. pannonica*, *G. punctata* and *G. acaulis* have similar

properties, the active principles being bitter glycosides known as gentiin, gentiamarin and gentiopicrin.

About 60 species are native to the Himalayas, most of which flower in autumn. Those with especially conspicuous blooms include *G. algida*, whose yellowish white flowers spotted with blue and blue-ribbed outside are found on dry open slopes to heights of 5,600 m (18,500 ft), *G. cachemirica*, a blue-flowered species which always grows in rocky habitats, *G. tibetica*, with dense clusters of greenish-white flowers; and *G. ornata*, distinguished by its solitary, widely bell-shaped flowers decorated with stripes of purple and creamy white. Gentoams with smaller flowers (less than 1.5 cm (0.5 in) long) include several annual species, such as the diminutive

*Gentiana verna*

*Gentiana purpurea*

G. *argentea*, with narrow silvery leaves and dense leafy heads of tiny blue flowers, G. *carinata* and G. *marginata*, both of which also have clusters of blue flowers.

Although the European mountains boast only some 26 species of gentian, these attractive plants are among the most typical of high altitudes. Most are small blue-flowered plants, flowering from spring to summer. The great yellow gentian G. *lutea*, G. *burseri* and spotted gentian G. *punctata*, however, are robust plants with predominantly yellow flowers, while purple gentian G. *purpurea* and brown gentian G. *pannonica* have clusters of reddish purple flowers.

More typical gentians of the European mountains include the trumpet gentian G. *acaulis*, with large (4-7 cm (1.6-2.8 in)) usually deep blue flowers spotted with green inside, and the very similar Pyrenean trumpet gentian G. *occidentalis*. Trumpet gentians occur from the Alps and Carpathians to northeast Spain, central Italy and central Yugoslavia and are usually found on acid soils, while the Pyrenean trumpet gentian is confined to the Pyrenees and northern Spain's Cordillera Canta 'brica, preferring base-rich soils. Other similar species are the southern gentian G. *alpina*, which grows on and soils in the Alps, Pyrenees and the Sierra Nevada of southern Spain, and G. *clusii*, found on limestone soils in the mountains of central Europe.

European gentians with less conspicuous blooms include the Pyrenean gentian G. *pyrenaica* with violet-

*Gentiana romanzovii*

*Gentiana acaulis*

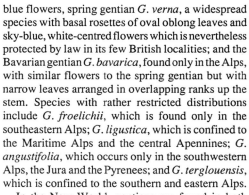

blue flowers, spring gentian *G. verna*, a widespread species with basal rosettes of oval oblong leaves and sky-blue, white-centred flowers which is nevertheless protected by law in its few British localities; and the Bavarian gentian *G. bavarica*, found only in the Alps, with similar flowers to the spring gentian but with narrow leaves arranged in overlapping ranks up the stem. Species with rather restricted distributions include *G. froelichii*, which is found only in the southeastern Alps; *G. ligustica*, which is confined to the Maritime Alps and the central Apennines; *G. angustifolia*, which occurs only in the southwestern Alps, the Jura and the Pyrenees; and *G. terglouensis*, which is confined to the southern and eastern Alps.

In the New World, gentians are found in both North and South America. Two conspicuous Andean species are *G. regina*, known locally as 'challengando', which has tall spikes of pale lilac flowers, and *G. flavido-flamea*, with flowers alternately striped with red and yellow. In the eastern United States, especially the Appalachian Mountains but extending southwards to northern Florida and Louisiana, grows *G. saponaria*, a tall herbaceous perennial with clusters of blue-violet flowers in the axils of the leaves.

About 20 species of gentian occur in the Rocky Mountain, including mountain gentian *G. calycosa*, with solitary, deep-blue flowers found at heights of around 3,000 m (9,800 ft) and the western fringed gentian *G. thermalis*, a bluish purple-flowered annual

*Gentiana lutea*

*Leontopodium alpinum*

species of wet montane meadows and warm springs in the Yellowstone National Park, where it occurs from the foothills to around 4,000 m (13,100 ft). Other Rocky Mountain species include the pleated gentian *G. affinis*, *G. strictiflora* and the arctic gentian *G. romanzorii*, whose distinctive creamy white flowers are streaked with purple or black.

Further south in the mountains of California, grows the alpine gentian *G. newberryi*, a perennial species with greenish white flowers often streaked on the outside with purplish bands which occurs between 2,100 and 3,600 m (6,900-11,800 ft), and the Sierra gentian *G. holopetala*, a blue-flowered annual species of wet meadows up to around 3,000 m (9,800 ft) in the San Bernardino Mountains and the Sierra Nevada.

In the southern hemisphere New Zealand possesses 19 native species of gentian, most of which occur in the alpine zone where, flowering from late January to April they are among the last of the high altitude flora to bloom. The New Zealand gentians have deeply lobed often white flowers. Typical high alpine species include *G. bellidifolia*, a widespread plant of both North and South Islands; *G. vernicosa*, a creeping South Island plant, *G. montana*, another creeping plant with reddish leaves and flattened clusters of up to 10 flowers, found only on South and Stewart islands; *G. divisa*, a South Island species whose dense, almost spherical clusters of flowers resemble snowballs when in full bloom, and *G. corymbifera*, also confined to South Island. All these occur at altitudes in excess of 1,500 m (5,000 ft) on snow tussock grassland and herb slopes.

**Gentianaceae; about 300 species**

### HABERLEA

The sole member of this genus *Haberlea rhodopensis* is one of several tropical plants of the Gesneriaceae (see *Jankaea* and *Ramonda*) found in European mountains, all of which are relics of the Tertiary geological period, when the climate of the region was markedly warmer. It has a basal rosette of broad, fleshy leaves from which arise numerous flowering stems bearing large, hairy, pale lilac flowers with yellow-orange centres. *Haberlea rhodopensis* is typically found on cliffs and in rock fissures, usually on limestone, and is confined to the Rhodope Mountains in Bulgaria and northeastern Greece.

**Gesneriaceae; a single species**

### HACQUETIA

Commonly known as hacquetia, *Hacquetia epipactis* is the only plant in this genus and is found only in the eastern Alps and northern Carpathians. It is a low, creeping perennial, with shiny, bright-green, 3-5 lobed leaves and small umbels of yellow flowers surrounded by a spreading collar of 5-6 large bracts similar to the leaves. *Hacquetia epipactis* prefers damp, shady habitats in open woodlands and scrub up to around 1,500 m (5,000 ft) and flowers in April and May.

**Umbelliferae; a single species**

### HELICHRYSUM

A large genus of annual, biennial and perennial herbs or shrubs found mainly in the warm regions of the Old World, especially in South Africa and Australia. The genus is typified by flowers with enlarged, brightly coloured, shiny and persistent bracts, and for this reason the plants are commonly known as 'everlasting flowers'; the dried flowerheads are often used in winter floral decorations. Over the range of the genus many species are found only in the high mountains, notably six alpine representatives in New Zealand and about 80 species above 1,500 m (5,000 ft) in the alpine zone of the volcanic peaks of East Africa.

Examples of African alpine everlasting flowers are *Helichrysum cymosum*, with yellowish woolly leaves and yellow-brown flowerheads arranged in terminal spheres, which is widespread in the stony grasslands of East Africa between 1,200 and 4,700 m (3,900-15,400 ft); the similar but less common *H.*

*kilimanjari*, found in the lower alpine zone of Mts Elgon, Mt Kenya and other East African mountains, and *H. meyeri-johannis*, with white woolly leaves and pinkish flowerheads, which occurs in damp grasslands between 2,800 and 4,100 m (9,200-13,500 ft) on Mt Elgon, Mt Kenya and Mt Kilimanjaro.

Other African species include *H. brownei*, a white-flowered species of high altitude shrubby vegetation above the heath zone on the Aberdares and Mt Kenya, and *H. setosum*, which has golden-yellow flowerheads and is locally abundant in grassy clearings in the montane rainforest of the East African mountains between 1,350 and 3,000 m (4,400-9,800 ft). *H. stulmanii* is found above the snow line of Mt Speke in the Ruwenzori Mountains, while *H. whyteanum* is confined to Malawi's Mulanje massif.

The New Zealand everlastings include the prostrate, creeping everlasting daisy *H. bellidioides*, which has large papery bracts and occurs up to 1,600 m (5,200 ft) in open vegetation in the mountains from East Cape and Mt Egmont southwards. Other species are the highly branched, yellow- or white-flowered *H. selago*, *H. coralloides* and *H. plumeum*, all of which are very similar and grow only in crevices in rock outcrops on South Island.

The genus is also common in the mountains and island cliffs of southern Europe, although individual pecies have very narrow ranges. For example, *H. frigidum* is found only in the mountains of Corsica and Sardinia, *H. doerfleri* is not known outside the mountain cliffs of eastern Crete, *H. saxatile* is unique to cliff faces in Sardinia and Pantelleria, *H. heldreichii* is confined to cliffs in western Crete and *H. ambiguum* endemic to calcareous rocks and cliffs in the Balearic Islands.

**Compositae; about 500 species**

### HOMOGYNE

A tiny genus of low, creeping perennials with erect stems confined to the mountains of Europe. The best known species is alpine coltsfoot *Homogyne alpina*, which has distinctive kidney shaped basal leaves, often purplish and hairy beneath, and solitary reddish-purple, goblet-shaped flowerheads, with tubular florets. Alpine coltsfoot prefers damp places, growing by streams, in meadows or in open woodland up to about 3,000 m (9,800 ft). It is fairly common throughout the mountains of western, central and southern Europe and is naturalized in Britain.

*H. discolor* is very similar, but with leaves white woolly beneath and bright purple florets with long, protruding styles. This species is confined to calcareous soils in the eastern Alps and the mountains of central Yugoslavia. Some authors distinguish a third species *H. sylvestris,* which occurs in woods and scrub over a similar geographical range to H. discolor.

**Compositae; 2 species**

### HORMINIUM

The sole member of this genus dragonmouth *Horminium pyrenaicum* is found only in the mountains of southern Europe. It is a perennial with corrugated leaves in a basal rosette from which arises a more or less leafless stem bearing stalkless clusters of bilaterally symmetrical, violet-blue flowers, usually arranged in a one-sided spike. Dragonmouth grows in a variety of base-rich habitats, especially on limestone, ranging from pastures and dry meadows to stony places and open woodlands, between 1,000 and 2,500 m (3,300-8,200 ft). It is widespread in the central Pyrenees and the central and eastern Alps, but very rare in the western Alps.

**Labiatae; a single species**

### HUTCHINSIA

A genus whose sole species is chamois-cress *Hutchinsia alpina,* one of the most typical plants of the high screes of northern temperate regions. It is a tufted perennial with deeply divided leaves and several leafless flower stems, each bearing a terminal cluster of white, four-petalled flowers. Chamois-cress occurs in most of the southern European mountains, from the Pyrenees eastwards to the Alps, Carpathians and Apennines, usually between 1,700 and 3,200 m (5,600-10,500 ft). The subspecies *H. alpina* ssp. *alpina* is found mainly on limestone, although *H. alpina* ssp. *brevicaulis* will thrive on any type of subsoil, but is not found in the Pyrenees.

**Cruciferae; a single species**

### JANKAEA

Like the genera *Ramonda* and *Haberlea,* this genus belongs to the mainly tropical and subtropical family Gesneriaceae, whose European representatives are completely isolated geographically from their nearest relatives in southern and eastern Asia. Their isolation is thought to stem from Tertiary times, over 50 million years ago when much of Europe was clothed in subtropical vegetation, these species being 'left behind' when the climate later cooled to its present state.

The sole species is *Jankaea heldreichii,* which is confined to Mt Olympus in Greece where it grows in shady crevices in limestone cliffs. It is easily identified by the dense white hairs on the upper surfaces of the leaves and flower stems, and has pale lilac, funnel-shaped flowers with yellow anthers.

**Gesneriaceae; a single species**

### JOVIBARBA

A genus confined to Europe, closely related to the genus Sempervivum but distinguished from it by flowers composed of 6 or 7 keeled, fringed petals instead of 9-20 unfringed segments. Plants of the genus *Jovibarba* have bell-shaped, pale yellow or white flowers, the various species being best distinguished using rosette-leaf characteristics. The generic name translates literally as 'Jupiter's beard', referring to the massive clusters of flowers.

Hen-and-chickens houseleek *Jovibarba sobolifera,*

grows in sandy and grassy places, usually on acid soils, up to 1,500 m (5,000 ft) in the central and eastern Alps, with a range extending to the eastern Carpathians and northern central USSR. Other species include *J. allionii,* which is confined to rocks and screes in the southwestern Alps up to 2,000 m (6,600 ft), *J. arenaria,* which is very like *J. sobolifera* but is confined to the eastern Alps; *J. heuffelii,* found only in the eastern Carpathians and the Balkan mountains, and J. hirta, a species ranging from central Europe to the northwestern Balkan peninsula to altitudes of about 1,900 m (6,200 ft).

**Crassulaceae; 5 species**

### LACCOPETALUM

This genus contains but a single species *Laccopetalum giganteum* native to the Peruvian Andes at height in excess of 4,000 m (13,100 ft) where it is locally known as *pacra pacra.* It is a coarse herb with thick stems and large, yellow-green flowers up to 13 cm (5 in) in diameter. The widespread collection of the flowers by South American Indians for use in the treatment of coughs, lung disorders and to improve the fertility of their cattle, has resulted in the virtual disappearance of this plant from its natural habitat.

**Ranunculaceae; a single species**

### LEONTOPODIUM

A genus of tufted, downy woolly perennial herbs typical of Eurasian mountain regions but also occurring naturally in the Andes. Undoubtedly the best known member of the genus is the edelweiss *Leontopodium alpinum,* a tufted woolly herb with small, yellowish white flower heads crowded into dense clusters and surrounded by conspicuous, snow white, bract-like leaves giving the appearance of a single flower.

Edelweiss grows in stony places, crevices in rock

faces and occasionally in high-altitude grasslands between 1,700 and 3,200 m (5,600-10,500 ft). Although still relatively common in the Alps, Pyrenees, Carpathians and mountains of the Balkan peninsula, it is a protected species, having almost disappeared in the wild as a result of over-collection. The subspecies snow edelweiss *L. alpinum* ssp. *nivale,* which is confined to the Abruzzi (Apennines), Yugoslavia and the western Balkans and distinguished by its spoon-shaped leaves, is unfortunately rarer still.

Some nine species of *Leontopodium* occur in the Himalayas, including *L. himalayanum* and *L. jacotianum,* both of which are fairly common on open slopes from Kashmir to western China between altitudes of 3,000 and 4,500 m (9,800-14,800 ft).

**Compositae; 35 species**

### LEUCOGENES

This genus, found only in New Zealand, contains just two species, both of which are very similar to the European edelweisses of the genus *Leontopodium.* North Island edelweiss *Leucogenes leontopodium* is a trailing subshrub with ascending leafy branches and compound flower heads surrounded by 10-20 woolly, petal-like bracts. Despite its name it is found on both North and South Islands, between 1,200 and 1,800 m (3,900-5,900 ft), where it is often abundant on exposed rocky sites and fellfield. The second species is South Island edelweiss *L. grandiceps,* which is very similar to *L. leoutopodium* but confined to South and Stewart Islands, where it grows on rock outcrops to elevations of around 1,900 m (6,200 ft).

**Compositae; 2 species**

### LEWISIA

A small genus of highly drought resistant, perennial rosette plants with succulent leaves native to the

*Lewisia rediviva*

*Liliaceae*

*Lilium philadelphicum*

western United States and Mexico, extending south to Bolivia. The plants are able to tolerate long periods without water, in desert and high mountains. The leaves are flat or cylindrical and may die back completely during the 'resting' period. The flowers are often large and showy and vary in colour from white to deep pink or orange. The genus is named after Meriwether Lewis of the Lewis and Clark expedition to the Pacific Northwest at the beginning of the nineteenth century.

Perhaps the best known plant in this genus is bitter-root *Lewisia rediviva*, whose long, fleshy leaves appear almost as soon as the snow melts but have disappeared by the time the flowers open in May or June. Each flower is between 3 and 6 cm (1.2-2.4 in) in diameter, with 12-18 long pink petals which fade to white at the base. This species is widespread from southwest Canada throughout the Rocky Mountains to California, where it grows on crags and precipices and other rocky habitats up to 2,500 m (8,200 ft). The thick, starchy roots are edible and highly nutritious, but have a rather bitter taste, hence the plant's common name.

Other montane species of Lewisia include L. cotyledon, a many-flowered plant again with pink flowers, but distinguished from those of the former by their smaller size and the presence of only 8-10 petals, each with a series of darker pink lines and a clearly visible white border. It is endemic to dry rocky slopes between 1,800 and 2,000 metres in the Rocky Mountains, especially in southwestern Oregon and northern California. A closely related species, Lewisia cantelowii, occurs at low altitudes in the Californian mountains, L. disepala, a species with whitish flowers, is found at heights of up to 2,600 metres in the Sierra Nevada and L. pygmaea is a tiny, silver-pink species of the Rocky Mountains.

**Portulacaceae; about 20 species**

## LILIUM

A genus of bulbous plants with unbranched flowering stems and scaly bulbs (many of which are edible), widely distributed across the northern temperate regions of the world, extending as far south as the Philippines. Many are particularly associated with mountain regions.

One of the better known lilies is the yellow turk's-cap lily *Lilium pyrenaicum*, so called because of the strongly recurved nature of the perianth segments of the flower. It is an elegant plant, sometimes attaining a height of 1.3 m (4.3 ft), the stem bearing 1-8 large orange-yellow flowers with bright orange stamens. *L. pyrenaicum*, as its name suggests, is found only in the Pyrenees and the mountains of northern Spain, where it grows in grasslands and open woodlands to about 2,200 m (7,200 ft).

Another turk's-cap lily is the martagon lily *L. martagon*, which has deep pink-orange flowers and occurs sporadically in the Alps, Apennines, Carpathians, Pyrenees and mountains of northern Spain to altitudes of around 2,700 m (8,900 ft), although it is also widespread in the lowlands of Europe and western Asia, especially in woodland. Similar species of European montane areas include the red-purple-flowered red lily *L. pomponium*, found only in the Maritime Alps; Carnic lily *L. carnolicum*, which has either red, orange or yellow flowers and occurs in the southeastern Alps and mountains of the Balkan peninsula and the Greek species *L. chalcedonicum*, with orange-red flowers. *L. rhodopaeum*, distinguished by its bright lemon-yellow flowers, is found only in the Rhodope mountains of Bulgaria and Greece and is listed as a rare species in the IUCN Plant Red Data Book (1980).

Another European species differs in having huge flame-coloured, erect, trumpet-shaped flowers. The orange lily *L. bulbiferum* is widespread in central and eastern Europe, but is also found in the alpine zone of the Pyrenees, Alps and Apennines, where it grows in meadows, woodlands and rocky habitats to altitudes

*Lilium pyrenaicum*

*Lilium martagon*

of around 2,400 m (7,900 ft). This flower is the emblem of the Orangemen of Northern Ireland.

In the Himalayas lilies usually have erect funnel-shaped flowers, although some have slightly recurved petals. Large-flowered species include *L. nepalense*, with sweet-scented yellow flowers up to 15 cm (6 in) long, which occurs between 2,300 and 3,500 m (7,500-11,500 ft), *L. wallichianum*, a lower altitude, white-flowered lily, with narrow funnels and petals recurved in the lower third only; and the rare *L. sherriffiae*, from eastern Nepal and Bhutan, which has reddish brown flowers, the insides chequered with gold. Other species have much smaller flowers, including *L. nanum*, with drooping, dull purple flowers, and *L. oxypetalum*, which has solitary pale yellow or cream flowers with spreading petals, both species occur between 3,300 and 4,3000 m (10,800-14,100 ft) from Himachal Pradesh to southwest China.

The genus is equally diverse in the North American mountains, the Rocky Mountains being home to the magnificent red lily *L. umbellatum* which, by contrast, has goblet-shaped flowers up to 10 cm (4 in) long. These flowers, which may be solitary or in clusters of three or four, have reddish orange petals decorated with purple spots. The red lily grows in damp places, from the plains into the high mountains, and is unfortunately in danger of becoming extinct due to thoughtless collection of the flowers which prevents the plant from setting seed. A second Rocky Mountain species is *L. columbianum*, variously known as the tiger, Oregon or Columbia lily, which is identified by its yellow-orange flowers with distinctive recurved petals.

Further south, the cascade lily *L. washingtonianum*, which has waxy trumpet-shaped, white or pale pink flowers, often dotted with minute purple spots, occurs

in the mountains of northern California and the southern Sierra Nevada; the similar redwood lily *L. rubescens* of the Coast Ranges of central and northern California is distinguished by its smaller flowers which change from white to a rich red-purple as they mature. Other species of the Californian mountains include the alpine lily *L. parvum*, which has orange or dark red flowers about 4 cm (1.6 in) long and thrives in wet habitats to 2,700 m (8,900 ft) in the Sierra Nevada; and the sierra lily *L. kelleyanum*, which has orange or yellow nodding flowers of the turk's-cap design and occurs up to about 3,200 m (10,500 ft).

Several of other lilies are predominantly temperate forest plants, including such North American species as the Canada lily *L. canadense*, *L. superbum* and the Carolina lily *L. michauxii*. The tiger lily *L. tigrinum*, which has edible bulbs, is native to China, Korea and Japan but has been introduced to North America.

**Liliaceae; 100 species**

## LLOYDIA

A small genus of slender bulbous plants found throughout temperate Eurasia, with a single North American species. The best known plants in this genus is the alplily Lloydia serotina, also commonly called the Snowdon lily, as it grows in Snowdonia in Wales. A handsome plant, it occurs throughout the range of the genus, from arctic Soviet Europe into the Urals, Soviet Asia and northern Japan, the Rocky Mountains of North America from Alaska to New Mexico, and in the Alps, Carpathians, Caucasus and Himalayas.

*Lloydia serotina* is a small plant with linear, grasslike leaves and erect, cup-shaped flowers which are white with red-brown or purplish veins and are pollinated by flies. It thrives in dry grassy habitats, on rock ledges and in mountain heaths, particularly favouring acidic soils such as those produced by granite. However it is rare in Britain and is protected by law.

Several other species of *Lloydia* occur alongside the alplily in the Himalayas, including *L. longiscapa*, which has white flowers marked with brown or orange towards the base and is found between 3,600 and 4,500 m (11,800-14,800 ft) on alpine slopes from Kashmir to southwest China; and *L. flavonutans*, distinguished by its delicate, nodding yellow flowers with reddish orange patches at the base and greenish veins, which occurs from central Nepal to southeastern Tibet at similar altitudes.

**Liliaceae; 12 species**

## LOBELIA

A large genus of annual or perennial herbs, subshrubs and sometimes trees distributed across tropical and warm regions, especially in the New World, with a few representatives straying into temperate zones. A distinct subsection of this genus is found exclusively at high altitudes in East Africa, where they are known as giant lobelias because the individual plants attain massive proportions.

Although the possible advantages or such bulk to life in the mountains have not yet been fully ascertained, it is thought that giantism may be of benefit in areas where the daily temperature fluctuation is very high. The massiveness of such plants may act as a thermal buffer, while the hollow flower stems contain chemicals which cause ice crystals to form at fairly high temperatures, thus protecting the rest of the plant from frost damage. In addition, the leaves are able to close over the flower bud at night and in doing so provide a nocturnal haven for many invertebrate animal. The flowers of the giant lobelias are pollinated by birds and the foliage provides fodder for mountain gorillas.

Among the giant lobelias of East Africa is *Lobelia deckenii* of Mt Kilimanjaro, which occurs in wet moorland at altitudes of between 2,700 and 4,100 m (8,900-13,500 ft) and where stems may reach a phenomenal 8.5 m (28 ft) in height. This species is named after one of the botanical collectors who first discovered it, Baron Carl Claus von der Decken (1833-1865). As with most giant lobelias, the flowers are hidden among bracts, which are sufficiently rigid to provide perches for the sunbirds that feed on the nectar and pollinate the flowers in the process.

Several well-defined subspecies have been described, including *L. deckenii* ssp. *keniensis*, a 3m (10 ft) high plant with blue-violet flowers which is confined to marshlands on Mt Kenya where it occurs between 3,240 and 4,350 m (10,600-14,300 ft), and *L. deckenii* ssp. *sattimae*, a blue-flowered plant of similar size which is known only from the Kenyan Aberdares. Another giant African species is *L. telekii*, which grows to 4 m (13 ft) in height and is distinguished from *L. deckenii* by pendulous bracts which hang over and protect the small white and purple flowers. It occurs on wet stony ground to altitudes of around 3,000 m (9,800 ft) on Mts Kenya and Elgon and in the Aberdares.

Many giant lobelias are very restricted in their distribution, sometimes being confined to a single mountain. These include *L. bequaertii* in the Ruwenzori, *L. burtii* on Ms Hanang, Meru and Loolmalassin, and *L. elgonensis* on Mt Elgon. Since these very similar species differ only in such minor characteristics as the shape and hairiness of the floral bracts and the degree of splitting of the corolla, they are often considered to be subspecies of *L. deckenii*.

**Campanulaceae; 365 species**

## MECANOPSIS

Perhaps the most distinctive member of the poppy family, Mecanopsis is an essentially Himalayan genus of annual, biennial or perennial herbs which extends into western China. There is also a single western European species - the Welsh poppy *Mecanopsis cambrica* - a yellow-flowered plant which occurs in the Pyrenees, Cevennes and the British Isles, particularly Wales, as its common name suggests.

Seventeen species of *Mecanopsis*, commonly known as Himalayan or Tibetan poppies, occur in the Himalayas proper, including such yellow-flowered species as *M. villosa*, whose flowers are borne singly on long, drooping stalks, *M. paniculata*, a robust plant growing to 2 m (6.6 ft), which has long cylindrical clusters of yellow, or occasionally white flowers; and the similar *M. regia*, which has fewer and larger flowers in its terminal inflorescences and leaf rosettes over 1 m (3.3 ft) across which are covered with long silky hairs.

Among the other species flowers may be red, purple, blue or nearly white, the best known of which is undoubtedly *M. horridula*, a bristly haired plant with a spike of light-blue to reddish flowers that can tolerate the severe climatic conditions found at altitudes of almost 6,000 m (19,700 ft). Other species include the rare *M. bella*, whose blue, purple or pink flowers are borne singly on short stems arising from a rosette of basal leaves (although the same plant may produce many flowering stems); *M. latifolia*, which is confined to Kashmir, where its blue (rarely white) flowers decorate rocky slopes between 3,500 and 4,000 m (11,500-13,100 ft), and *M. grandis*, a blue or purple-flowered plant which often forms large colonies on open slopes from western Nepal to southwest China.

**Papaveraceae; 42 species**

## MEGACODON

The sole species of this genus *Megacodon stylophorus* is confined to the Himalayas, from eastern Nepal to southwest China. It is a robust plant with a few large (6-8 cm (2,4-3 in)), pale yellow, bell-shaped flowers chequered with fine green lines within, which are often paired in the axils of the upper leaves. It thrives on open slopes and among shrubs between 3,300 and 4,300 m (10,800-14,100 ft).

**Gentianaceae; a single species**

*Lobelia keniensis*

## NARCISSUS

A small genus of bulbous herbs, commonly known as daffodils or narcissi, largely confined to Europe with a high profile in the Mediterranean region. The predominantly yellow or white flowers are very distinctive, being composed of six free perianth segments which unite into a single tube above the ovary with shallow ring or deeper cup – the corona or trumpet – projecting outwards at the junction of the perianth segments and the tube. Most species are spring flowering, but several of the Mediterranean plants produce their flowers in the autumn.

The generic name is considered to be derived not from the name of the classical youth who met his death by vainly trying to embrace his image in a clear stream, but from the Greek word *narkao*, ('to benumb') on account of the plants' considerable narcotic properties. An extract of daffodil bulbs, when applied to open wounds, has been known to cause paralysis of the whole nervous system and the heart.

More useful medicinal applications involve the decoction of dried flowers, which is said to relieve congestion of the bronchial tubes in children and has also proved useful in the treatment of dysentery. The Arabians recommended an oil derived from the bulb as a cure for baldness and an aphrodisiac.

Several plants in this genus are particularly associated with mountain areas, including two tiny species from the mountains of northern Iberia. *Narcissus asturiensis* is only 6-12 cm (2.4-4.7 in) tall, while the hoop-petticoat daffodil *N. bulbocodium* has pale lemon flowers in which the perianth segments are reduced to narrow rays. *N. pseudonarcissus* is a much larger plant, with orange-yellow trumpets and pale yellow perianth segments. Commonly known as the wild daffodil or Lent lily, it produces prolific displays in mountain meadows and pastures in spring, especially in the Pyrenees, the mountains of northern Spain and in Scandinavia; it is also native to the British Isles. The lesser wild daffodil *N. minor*, very

*Narcissus bulbocodium*

like the Lent lily but with smaller flowers, deep yellow throughout, grows in grasslands to 2,200 m (7,200 ft) in the Pyrenees.

The aptly named pheasant's eye narcissus *N. poeticus* is distinguished by its large solitary flowers, with white perianth segments and short, cup-like,

orange-yellow trumpets. This sweetly scented plant is found in damp meadows to 2,300 m (7,500 ft) in the Pyrenees, Alps and Apennines, and also in northwest Greece.

The rush-leaved narcissus *N. requienii* is a much more delicate plant, with thread-like leaves and small

*Narcissus pseudonarcissus*

*Narcissus triandus*

deep yellow flowers and in clusters of two or three characterized by their cup-shaped trumpets. It prefers stony habitats to 1,600 m (5,200 ft) in the Pyrenees and is very difficult to distinguish from the slightly larger rock narcissus *N. rupicola* (although this species has saucer-shaped trumpets) which grows in similar habitats in the Pyrenees.

Several montane daffodils are confined to very restricted areas, particularly in western Europe. These include *N. cuatrecasasii*, confined to the acid mountains of central and southern Spain; *N. cyclamineus* from damp mountain pastures in northern Iberia; *N. bicolor* in the Pyrenees and the French Corbie 'res; *N. longispathus*, which grows in mountain streams in the Sierra de Cazorla in southeast Spain; and *N. hedraeanthus*, from southern central and southeastern Iberia.

**Liliaceae (Amaryllidaceae); 27 species**

### NIGRITELLA

The sole member of this genus is vanilla orchid *Nigritella nigra*, so called because of the strong vanilla scent produced by the black-red flowers. Reaching a maximum of 25 cm (10 in) in height, but often considerably less (especially in alpine areas), this orchid is not among the most conspicuous members of its family. The dense spike of flowers is conical when it first appears, becoming ovoid as it matures and elongates. Several of distinct colour varieties exist, among them var. *alba*, which has pure white flowers, var. *flava*, with creamy yellow flowers and var. *rosea* with pink flowers.

The vanilla orchid thrives in high mountain pastures, where it often occurs in large numbers, and also grows along woodland fringes. In the southern European mountains (Massif Central, Pyrenees, Jura Alps, Italian Alps, Apennines, Carpathians and mountains of the Balkan peninsula) it may be found up to 2,800 m (9,200 ft), but it grows at considerably lower elevations in Scandinavia. Some authors identify a second species -*N. rubra*, the rosy vanilla orchid - but this is usually considered to be either a hybrid with *Gymnadenia*, or at best a subspecies of *N. nigra*.

**Orchidaceae; a single species**

### PAEDEROTA

This tiny genus of perennial herbs and contains just two members is found only in the mountains of southern Europe. The species are easily distinguished from each other: *Paederota bonarota* has blue or pinkish flowers and leaves with not more than nine teeth on each side, while yellow veronica *P. lutea* has yellow flowers and larger leaves with at least 10 teeth on each side.

In both cases the flowers are arranged in terminal, leafy, spike-like inflorescences. Each flower has a tube-like corolla opening out to form two distinct lips, the lower of which is divided into three lobes. The distribution of both species is centred on the eastern Alps, although *P. lutea* is also found in the mountains of western Yugoslavia. Their preferred habitat is cliff faces and rock crevices in limestone, *P. bonarota* reaching a maximum altitude of some 2,500 m (8,200 ft).

**Scrophulariaceae; 2 species**

### PAPAVER

An almost cosmopolitan genus of annual, bennial or perennial herbs, distributed across Europe, Asia, South Africa, Australia and western North America. Commonly known as poppies, the short-lived flowers have two free sepals and four entire petals, crumpled in bud. Most poppies contain a milky juice (latex). Many species are found in the world's mountainous regions, although the only true alpine poppy of the Himalayas is *Papaver nudicaule*, which has solitary, reddish orange flowers up to 4 cm (1.6 in) across and grows on the rocky hillsides of Kashmir between 3,600 and 4,800 m (11,800-15,800 ft), extending westwards into Afghanistan.

Many more species occur in the mountains of Europe, although they are perhaps better known as arable weeds of the Mediterranean region. Formerly grouped together under the umbrella of a single name - *P. alpinum* - the poppies of the European mountains have since been divided into several distinct species. Among the better known are the Alpine poppy *P. burseri*, a small, tufted, white-flowered plant which grows in damp stony places usually on calcareous rocks in the northeastern Alps and Carpathians between 1,200 and 2,000 m (3,900-6,600 ft) and the Pyrenean poppy *P. suaveolens*, a bristly yellow-flowered plant which occurs in similar habitats in the Pyrenees and the Sierra Nevada in the Iberian peninsula.

Other montane poppies include *P. rupifragum*, which has brick-red flowers and grows only in rock crevices in the limestone cliffs of the Sierra de Grazalema in southern Spain; the white-flowered *P. sendtneri* of the central and eastern Alps; and two yellow-flowered species, *P. kerneri* of the southeastern Alps and mountains of central Yugoslavia and *P. corona-sancti-stephani*, which is confined to the eastern and southern Carpathians. Perhaps the most widespread of all the European alpine poppies is the Rhaetian poppy *P. rhaeticum*, which also has with yellow flowers (rarely red or white) and occurs in the eastern Pyrenees and the southwestern and eastern Alps.

**Papaveraceae; 50 species**

### PEDICULARIS

A large genus of hemiparasitic, usually perennial herbs of northern temperate regions with a single species in Andean Ecuador and Colombia. They are commonly known as louseworts. The flowers are two-lipped; the upper lip is hooded and often extended into a curved or straight beak, while the lower lip is broad and three-lobed. The tubular or bell-shaped calyx is usually four-lobed. Flower colours range from white to yellow, or pale pink to purple.

In the Himalayas, where there are almost 80 species, louseworts are conspicuous members of the summer flora of the high alpine zone and the clearings of high altitude forests. Yellow-flowered Himalayan louseworts include *Pedicularis bicornuta*, a robust plant whose flowers are distinguished by their spirally coiled, bilobed beaks, which is common on alpine slopes in Kashmir, and *P. hoffmeisteri*, with pale yellow or cream flowers, which occurs in damp, shady places between 2,500 ad 4,500 m (8,200-14,800 ft) from Himachal Pradesh to eastern Nepal.

*P. cheilanthifolia* is a Himalayan alpine meadow lousewort with pink or whitish flowers arranged in a very hairy cluster, while *P. mollis* is another woolly species with small dark red or purple flowers in long, crowded spikes, which occurs in the Ladakh range in Kashmir and from western Nepal to southeast Tibet up to 4,300 m (14,100 ft). *P. pectinata* is distinguished by the long, sickle-shaped beaks of its pink flowers; *P. elwesii* by its large (to 4 cm (1.6 in)), dark purple flowers arranged in dense, terminal heads, again with sickle-shaped beaks; and *P. bifida* by its entire rather than divided leaves and lax, leafy spikes of pink flowers.

More than 50 species of lousewort occur in Europe, and they are especially common in mountain areas. Many are confined to a particular range, such as stemless lousewort *P. acaulis*, which has red-tinged white flowers and is only found in the foothills of the Alps and the mountains of northwest Yugoslavia, and *P. orthantha*, whose purplish red flowers are found only in stony alpine pastures in the mountains of Bulgaria and southern Yugoslavia. Other pink- or purple-flowered species with restricted distributions include *P. asparagoides*, which occurs only in the eastern Pyrenees and adjoining ranges; *P. schizocalyx*, which is confined to the mountains of western Spain;

*Pedicularis verticillata*

*Papaver rhaeticum*

Pyrenean lousewort *P. pyrenaica* and *P. mixta*, which are found only in the Pyrenees and Spain's Cordillera Cant ábrica and *P. elegans*, which is confined to the Apennines.

Many species occur only in the Alps. These include Tauern lousewort *P. portenschlagii* and fern-leaved lousewort *P. asplenifolia*, both of which have pinkish red flowers and favour alpine pastures and screes, and ascending lousewort *P. ascendens*, *P. julica* and *P. elongata*, all of which have yellow flowers and grow on calcareous soils in montane grassland and screes. Beakless red lousewort *P. recutita*, also known as truncate lousewort, has greenish yellow flowers tinged with crimson and occurs in mountain meadows and damp, shady places.

Wider ranging montane European louseworts include the splendid leafy lousewort *P. foliosa*, whose tall yellow spikes are found from the Vosges to northern Spain and southern Italy, and the rather similar *P. hacquetii*, which occurs in the Alps, Carpathians and Apennines. The attractive pink or lilac flowers of pink lousewort *P. rosea* are found in the Alps and in two stations in the Pyrenees; deep pinkishb red spikes of *P. petiolaris* decorate alpine meadows and stony slopes in the mountains of the Balkan peninsula and the Apennines; and long-beaked yellow lousewort *P. tuberosa*, with pale yellow flowers, grows on acid soils in open woods and montane pastures in the Alps, Apennines and Pyrenees.

Louseworts also occur in North America, although here they are much less diverse than in Eurasia. In the mountains of western North America two particularly common species of high altitude are elephant heads *P. groenlandica* and *P. attolens*, both of which have pink flowers resembling tiny elephants' heads, with the beak curving forward and beyond the lower lip to form the 'trunk' and the lateral lobes of the lower lip forming the 'ears'. This flower structure is thought to aid pollination, and at the same time reduce the

chances of hybridization between the two species. *P. groenlandica* is found in wet meadows throughout the western ranges, but *P. attolens* is found only in the south from the Cascade Mountains in Oregon to California's Sierra Nevada.

Other North American species are sickletop lousewort *P. racemosa*, also known as parrot's beak because of the distinctive shape of the twisted pink or white flowers, which grows in coniferous woods and

dry meadows in the Rocky Mountains; towering lousewort or fernleaf *P. bracteosa* which has feathery leaves and yellow, purple or red flowers and occurs in damp montane meadows and woods, also in the Rockies; and dwarf lousewort *P. semibarbata*, whose purple-tinged yellow flowers may be seen between May and July in dry coniferous woods in the Oregon and Californian ranges.

**Scrophulariaceae; over 350 species**

*Pedicularis verticillata*

*Primula farmosa*

## PRIMULA

This large genus of perennial herbs is largely confined to the northern hemisphere, although some species are found as far south as Ethiopia and the mountains of tropical Asia, to Java and New Guinea, as well as in southern South America. Commonly known as primroses, these plants are characterized by an umbel of colourful flowers borne on a leafless flowering stem arising from a basal rosette of usually entire leaves. The flowers have five petals fused into a cylindrical tube at the base, with spreading lobes. Colours range from white to yellow, pink, purple, red and blue, with many intermediate shades. More than 30 species are found in Europe, many of which are particularly associated with the mountains, whilst the Himalayas boast an incredible 66 species.

Among the more distinctive of the huge variety of Himalayan primroses are *Primula glomerata*, which has nodding blue flowers and occurs up to 5,000 m (16,400 ft) from western Nepal to southeastern Tibet; *P. sharmae*, a purple-flowered primrose found only on dry slopes and rock ledges in western and central Nepal; and *P. rosea*, a plant of damp habitats, especially snow melts and streamsides, which is distinguished by its yellow-eyed rose-pink flowers. *P. floribunda* is a softly hairy plant with golden-yellow flowers which prefers damp shady situations, while the tiny *P. minutissima*, with stemless, bright purple flowers which are much larger than the leaves, is found up to 5,200 m (17,000 ft) in dry, stony places.

One handsome species, which grows only in rock crevices in central Nepal, is *P. aureata*. This plant has rosettes of broad, toothed leaves covered with a silvery white powder known as farina, from which arise clusters of creamy yellow flowers with a central flush of golden yellow. A primrose found at the incredible altitude of 5,600 m (18,300 ft), again beneath overhanging rocks, is *P. caveana*, a small

*Primula angustifolia*

plant with purple, yellow-eyed flowers which is fairly common in Rolwaling and Khumbu in Nepal. One of the white-flowered Himalayan primroses is *P. reidii*, which has fragrant, widely bell-shaped flowers in a compact nodding cluster.

As with many montane plants, the European primroses are often fairly localized in their distribution, although bird's-eye primrose *P. farinosa* is a widespread species in marshes and damp meadows, ranging from sub-boreal habitats in Scotland and southern Sweden to the mountains of Iberia and Bulgaria. It has lilac or pinkish flowers and, as its name suggests, farinose leaves. Long-flowered primrose *P. halleri*, which is powdered with yellow farina and has cluster of 2-12 lilac flowers, occurs in the Alps, Carpathians and mountains of the Balkan peninsula in alpine meadows and rock crevices, usually on calcareous soils.

*P. hirsuta*, which has flowers ranging from lilac to a deep purplish red, usually with white centres, grows in acid pastures in the Alps and the central Pyrenees, while the closely related Piedmont primrose *P. pedemontana* is found in similar habitats in the southwestern Alps and northern Spain's Cordillera Canta 'brica. The least primrose *P. minima* with its bright pink flowers, occupies a similar ecological niche in the mountains of eastern central and southeastern Europe, and bear's-ear *P. auricula* occurs in wet alpine grassland and rock crevices in the Alps, Carpathians and Apennines. The common name of this latter species is derived from its broad, thick leaves, which are used in the Alps as a remedy for coughs.

Primroses with very restricted distributions include *P. deorum*, in wet alpine grassland in southwestern Bulgaria, *P. glutinosa* on acid soils in the eastern Alps, spectacular primrose *P. spectabilis* and glaucous primrose *P. glaucescens* on calcareous rocks in the southern Alps, *P. kitaibeliana* in stony, calcareous habitats in western central Yugoslavia, *P. apennina* on sandstone cliffledges in the northern Apennines, and *P. tyrolensis* in shady rock crevices in the Dolomites.

Across the Atlantic, several species of primrose occur in the Rocky Mountains and at high altitudes in the Californian ranges, including the sierra primrose *P. suffrutescens*, a woody species with branched, creeping stems and erect flowering shoots up to 10 cm (4 in) tall bearing terminal clusters of magenta flowers. It grows in shady habitats beneath overhanging rocks to altitudes of over 4,000 m (13.100 ft) in California's Sierra Nevada. Parry or alpine primrose *P. parryi* has large, blood-red, bell-shaped flowers borne in clusters of 3-12 on stems up to 45 cm (18 in) tall. It grows in alpine and subalpine meadows in the northern Rockies between 2,400 and 3,600 m (7,900-11,800 ft), often on streamsides or at the edges of melting snowfields. Other Rocky Mountain primroses include *P. incana*, with lilac flowers and white mealy stems and leaves, and fairy primrose *P. angustifolia*, which has purplish flowers and no farina.

**Primulaceae; 400 species**

## PUYA

Centred in the South American Andes, this is a large genus of terrestrial herbs, many of which are thick-stemmed, drought resistant plants with spiny margins to the leaves. The flowers are borne in simple or branched spikes, the branches providing perches for hummingbirds which often pollinate the flowers..

Several species are giant plants, the best known being *Puya raimondii*, which is probably the largest member of the genus, reaching almost 10 m (33 ft) in height. It grows in the high plateau of the central Andes and is reputed to live for 100 years, flower once and die. Each flowering spike produces around 8,000 flowers. *P. alpestris* is native to Chile and has leaf rosettes over 1 m (3.3 ft) across and greyish blue flowers. Another Chilean species is *P. chilensis*,

whose leaves yield a fibre used to produce rot-resistant fishing nets. The extreme spiny nature of the leaves, however, means that sheep, birds and other creatures of the high Andes become entangled and die, leading to speculations that the plant may absorb nutrients from the dead animals through its leaves. As a result, many of the more spiny puyas have been grubbed up by local farmers and are becoming increasingly rare.

*P. gigas* from Colombia is another massive species, reaching a height of around 9 m (29.5 ft); the Chilean *P. berteroniana* has tapering leaves about 1 m (3.3 ft) long and metallic blue flowers; and *P. ferruginea*, widespread in northern South America, has greenish white flowers and leaves a phenomenal 2 m (6.6 ft) in length. Smaller species are *P. nana* from Bolivia and *P. medica* which has bluish flower and is confined to Peru.

**Bromeliaceae; 168 species**

## RAMONDA

Confined to Europe, this genus is often considered to be a relic of Tertiary times when the climate of Europe was markedly warmer (see *Jankaea* and *Haberlea*). The leaves, which are arranged in a flat basal rosette, are deeply corrugated with short white hairs on the upper surface and a dense covering of woolly orange hairs beneath. The showy flowers are borne on leafless stalks and have between four and six (usually five) broad, overlapping petals.

*Ramonda myconi* is perhaps the best known plants in the genus, having deep violet, yellow-eyed flowers up to 4 cm (1.6 in) in diameter with protruding yellow anthers. It is found only in the Pyrenees and the adjoining mountains of northeastern Spain, where it grows in shady crevices in limestone rocks and is particularly associated with the enormous glacial cirques, such as Gavarnie, where it grows to heights of around 1,800 m (5,900 ft). *R. nathaliae* has similar

*Puya sp.*

flowers, pale lilac or violet in colour, and is confined to southern Yugoslavia and northern Greece, while the flowers of *R. serbica*, species of the Balkan peninsula and northwest Greece, are distinguished by their dark blue-violet anthers.

**Gesneriaceae; 3 species**

### RANUNCULUS

A large genus of of annual or perennial herbs, some of which are aquatic, widely distributed across temperate and polar regions and extending into the tropical mountains. The generic name is derived from the Latin for 'small frog', probably referring to the swampy habitat of some species. Plants in this genus are commonly known as buttercups because of the bright yellow flowers of many species, although others have white or reddish flowers. The flowers possess petaloid honey-leaves, varying in number from 0 to 12, although 5 is the usual complement, protected in bud by 3-7 perianth segments acting as sepals.

Europe is home to 131 species of Ranunculus, many of which are inhabitants of the mountains, often restricted to a single range. For example, the yellow-flowered Gouan's buttercup *Ranunculus gouanii* and *R. ruscinonensis* are confined to the Pyrenees, while the amplexicaule buttercup *R. amplexicaulis*, a white-flowered species, also extends westwards into the mountains of northern Spain. Buttercups found only in the Alps include yellow-flowered species such as *R. venetus* and *R. grenieranus* and the white-flowered *R. traunfellneri*. Examples of buttercups confined to other European ranges include Ranunculus acetosellifolius, a white-flowered species with arrow-shaped leaves from southern Spain's Sierra Nevada, and the yellow-flowered *R. carpaticus* from the Carpathians.

More widespread European buttercups of high altitudes include the yellow-flowered *R. oreophilus*, from the mountains of central and southern Europe; *R. demissus*, common in the mountains of southern Europe; and Thore's buttercup *R. thora*, found in the Pyrenees, Jura, Alps, Carpathians and mountains of the Balkan peninsula. White-flowered montane buttercups in Europe include the alpine buttercup *R. alpestris*, found in the Pyrenees, Jura, Alps, Apennines and Carpathians; *R. crenatus*, with a more easterly distribution, extending from the Alps and Apennines into the Carpathians and the Balkan peninsula; Pyrenean buttercup *R. pyrenaeus*, which despite its name is found in both the Pyrenees and the Alps; and parnassus-leaved buttercup *R. parnassifolius*, which has white or reddish flowers and again occurs in both the Alps and Pyrenees.

About 30 species of buttercup occur in the Himalayas, although many are plants of the foothills; the majority of the alpine species have small yellow flowers. Both *R. pulchellus* and *R. brotherusii* are commonly found on dry, open slopes and rock ledges at altitudes of up to 5,000 m (16,400 ft), while *R. involucratus* occurs among frost-shattered rocks and screes at heights in excess of 5,000 m (16,400 ft). Lower altitude species include *R. adoxifolius*, which grows in damp meadows from central Nepal to southeastern Tibet, and *R. hirtellus*, a buttercup of alpine slopes from Afghanistan to southwest China.

Buttercups are also found in the mountains of the New World. North American species include *R. alismaefolius*, a tall, yellow-flowered plant growing to heights at around 3,600 m (11,800 ft) in the Coast Ranges, the Sierra Nevada and the Rocky Mountains, and the splendid alpine buttercup *R. adoneus*, whose glossy yellow flowers are found only at high elevations in these western mountains, blooming as soon as the snow melts. The leaves of the latter species provide food for deer, elk, pikas and rockchucks, and the seeds are eaten by mice and chipmunks. Further south in the central Andes, two striking red-flowered buttercups found at high levels are *R. weberbaurii* and *R. guzmanii*, the latter clothed in dense golden hairs.

Also in the southern hemisphere are the buttercups of New Zealand, of which 17 species reach the alpine zone. Perhaps the most memorable is the magnificent great mountain buttercup *R. lyallii*, named after Dr Lyall, the surgeon-botanist on the HMS Terror and Acheron expedition of 1840-1860. Reaching over 1 m (3.3 ft) in height, this buttercup has hairless leaves and branched stems bearing many creamy white flowers, each with up to 25 overlapping petals. It is restricted to South and Stewart Islands, where it grows in snow tussock herbfields to elevations of 1,500 m (5,000 ft). *R. buchananii* has large, many petalled, white flowers and is confined to rocky habitats between 1,500 and 2,400 m (5,00-7,900 ft), while *R. insignis* usually has 5-7 bright yellow petals and up to 1,800 m (5,900 ft) on both North and South Islands.

**Ranunculaceae; about 250 species**

### RAOULIA

A small genus of tufted or creeping herbs and subshrubs with minute leaves covered with woolly down, many of which form dense, woody, rounded cushions and, as such, are commonly known as 'vegetable sheep'. The flowers are almost stalkless, pale yellow or white, rarely exceeding 1 cm (0.4 in) across, and are enclosed by papery translucent bracts, thus resembling small everlasting flowers of the genus *Helichrysum*. The genus is native to New Zealand, while the genus *Ewardia* is a closely related Australian group of species. The genus is named after M E Raoul, surgeon-botanist to the French vessels *L'Aube* and *L'Allier* in the early 1840s.

Several species form loose mats of much-branched, creeping stems, including *Raoulia subsericea* and *R. parkii*, both of which grow up to 1,500 m (5,000 ft)

*Ranunculus adoneus*

*Ranunculus alpestris*

on South Island, as well as *R. hookeri*, which is distinguished by the dense silvery hairs which clothe both surfaces of the leaves and occurs to 1,800 m (5,900 ft) on both the main islands.

The best known species, however, are those which form compact cushions, especially *R. mammillaris* and *R. bryoides*, whose mounds reach 1 m (3.3 ft) in diameter, and the spectacular 2 m (6.6 ft) growths of *R. eximia*. All three species occur only on South Island, where they colonize the frost-shattered rocks in the fellfield zone between 1,100 and 1,800 m (3,600-5,900 ft). *R. goyenii*, which forms smaller whitish green cushions, is confined to Stewart Island.

## Compositae; 20 species

### RHODIOLA

A small genus largely confined to northern temperate regions, with centres of distribution in the Himalayas and North Africa. Perhaps the best known species is roseroot *Rhodiola rosea*, which has purplish stems bearing alternate succulent, grey-green leaves (said to be edible), topped with large, flat-topped clusters of dull yellow flowers. This species, in which the male and female flowers are found on separate plants, is also commonly known as midsummer-men. Roseroot is a particularly widespread plant, being found in most European mountain ranges, in meadows, rocks and screes, to altitudes of around 3,000 m (9,800 ft); its range also includes subarctic Alaska, Canada and Eurasia. *R. iremelica*, sometimes considered to be a subspecies of *R. rosea*, is confined to the Urals.

About 20 species of *Rhodiola* occur in the Himalayas. Some species have bisexual flowers, including *R. sinuata*, which has pink or white flowers and is often epiphytic on large boulders occurring up to 4,300 m (14,100 ft); and *R. wallichiana*, which is distinguished by its compact clusters of pale yellow flowers and is particularly abundant in the Kashmir region. Species with single-sexed flowers range from *R. himalensis*, which may have dark red, pinkish or yellow flowers, to the red-purple or almost black flower clusters produced by *R. bupleuroides*. Both species thrive at heights of almost 5,000 m (16,400 ft).

## Crassulaceae; 36 species

### SAUSSUREA

A large genus of perennial herbs native to Eurasia, with a centre of distribution in the Himalayas. The leaves are spineless and the flowerheads, composed of disc-florets only, are usually purple, bluish or pink. The genus also extends into the New World, with species such as *Saussurea viscida* (*S. angustifolia*) growing in the dry tundra and mountain regions in Alaska and the Yukon Territory.

Some of the high mountain species are densely covered with white woolly hairs as a protection from climatic extremes, including *S. graminifolia*, *S. gossypiphora*, *S. simpsoniana*, *S. tridactyla* and *S. gnaphalodes*, all of which grow up to altitudes of 5,600 m (18,300 ft) in the Himalayas. All have clusters of purple flowerheads except *S. graminifolia*, in which the flowerheads are solitary and *S.*

*gnaphalodes*, which has reddish blooms. *S. gossypiphora* has been likened to a snowball in general appearance, the plants being globular with even the flowerheads deeply embedded in the mass of woolly hairs.

Among the 30 or so species of *Saussurea* in the Himalayas, other high altitude plants include *S. bracteata*, distinguished by its often pinkish, papery, boat-shaped bracts and densely crowded purple flowerheads, and found from Pakistan to Kashmir between 3,600 and 5,600 m (11,800-18,300 ft), and *S. nepalensis*, quite common in Nepal to heights of 4,900 m (16,000 ft), which has solitary, dark purple flowerheads. *S. costus*, which occurs from Pakistan to Himachal Pradesh, has a strong, lingering scent for which it is being used in the perfume industry in Kashmir. It also has important medicinal properties and is cultivated as a field crop in the Himalayas. *S. involucrata* occurs at heights of over 5,500 m (18,00 ft) in the Himalayas, but at lower altitudes in the Tien Mountains of China.

By comparison the European mountains have relatively few species of *Saussurea*, the best known being alpine saussurea *S. alpina*, a sweetly scented, purple-flowered plant found throughout most of Europe, including Britain and Scandinavia at low altitudes, the Pyrenees, southern Alps and Carpathians. Dwarf saussurea *S. pygmaea* is found only on mountain rocks and screes in the eastern Alps and western Carpathians; *S. porcii* grows only in subalpine meadows in the eastern Carpathians; and hearty-leaved saussurea *S. disolor*, with bluish violet flowers, is confined to the Alps, Carpathians, Apennines and a single locality in Bulgaria, where is usually grows in dry montane habitats.

**Compositae; about 300 species**

*SAXIFRAGA*

This large genus is distributed across the northern hemisphere from the Arctic south into the mountains of northern Africa and South America. Commonly known as saxifrages, these delightful little plants are very typical of high altitudes throughout their range. Typically rosette plants, in many species the individuals clump together to form mats or cushions. Some saxifrages 'lime-secreting', in that the plant secretes a chalky solution which encrusts the edges of the leaves. The flowers are five-petalled and are usually white, cream or yellow; some species produce bulbils in addition to, or instead of, fertile seeds.

In North America, some 25 species of saxifrage occur in the Rocky Mountains. Leaving aside those already described in the chapter on flowers from polar regions, typical species include the brook saxifrage *Saxifraga arguta*, a plant of the San Bernardino mountains and the Sierra Nevada, extending northwards into the Rockies, which has large rounded basal leaves and an open few-flowered inflorescence; and diamondleaf or snowball saxifrage *S. rhomboidea*, distinguished by its oval-oblong basal leaves and dense terminal clusters of white flowers, which occurs in moist places from the sagebrush hills to above the tree line in the southern Rockies. Western saxifrage *S. occidentalis*, with tiny white flowers, sometimes yellow-spotted at the base of the petals, is found in moist meadows and rocky places from British Columbia southwards, while alpine saxifrage

*S. tolmiei*, another white-flowered species, occurs throughout the Rockies from Alaska to California.

Across the Atlantic, Europe boasts more than 120 species of saxifrage, most occurring in montane habitats. Among the more widespread species of high altitude are spoon-leaved saxifrage *S. cuneifolia*, whose distribution includes the Pyrenees and northern Spain, the Cevennes, Alps, Apennines, Carpathians and northwest Yugoslavia, where it usually occurs between 800 and 1,700 m (2,600-5,600 ft), and round-leaved saxifrage *S. rotundifolia*, a white-flowered species, often with red and yellow-spotted petals, found in damp shady montane habitats in central and southern Europe. Mossy saxifrage *S. bryoides* is a species with cream-coloured flowers which grows on acid rocks in most European ranges between the Carpathians and the Pyrenees, extending south into Bulgaria, while Piedmont saxifrage *S. pedemontana* prefers siliceous rocks in the mountains of southern Europe.

Other widespread European montane saxifrages include scree saxifrage *S. androsacea*, common in snow patches and on damp screes from the Pyrenees to the Carpathians; musky saxifrage *S. moschata*, a yellow-flowered species of the mountains of central and southern Europe; white musky saxifrage *S. exarata*, sometimes with reddish flowers, which occurs in the Alps, Jura, Apennines and mountains of the Balkan peninsula; *S. retusa*, which grows mainly above 2,000 m (6,600 ft) in exposed habitats in the Pyrenees, Alps, Carpathians and mountains of Bulgaria; and blue saxifrage *S. caesia*, with glaucous leaves, which is widely distributed in the mountains of central and southern Europe.

Iberia is a particular centre of distribution for

saxifrages, many of which are confined to a single mountain range within the peninsula. Among these are wood saxifrage *S. umbrosa*, of the western and central Pyrenees; *S. latepetiolata*, on limestone rocks in eastern Spain; *S. praetermissa*, in snow patches and shady screes in the Pyrenees and the Cordillera Canta 'brica, where the yellow saxifrage *S. aretiodes* also occurs; *S. cuneata*, on calcareous soils in the western Pyrenees and northern Spain, and hairless mossy saxifrage *S. pentadactylis*, on acid soils of the eastern Pyrenees and mountains of northern and central Spain.

*S. camposii* occurs only in the mountains of southeastern Spain, near Ronda; *S. trifurcata*, *S. conifera* and *S. canaliculata* are all found in the limestone mountains of northern Spain; *S. nevadensis* is found only above 2,600 m (8,500 ft) in the Sierra Nevada; *S. biternata* is restricted to the limestone turrets of Antequera in southern Spain and is listed as a rare species in the IUCN Plant Red Data Book (1980); while *S. moncayensis* is confined to the Sierra de Moncayo in northeast Spain and *S. vayredana* is confined to siliceous screes near Montseny, in northeast Spain.

Other European montane saxifrages with particularly restricted distributions include *S. irrigua*, found only in the mountains of Krym (Crimea); cobweb saxifrage *S. arachnoidea*, confined to limestone caves in the southern Alps near Lake Garda; awl-leaved saxifrage *S. tenella*, on calcareous soils in the southeastern Alps; *S. wahlenbergii*, from grassy slopes in the western Carpathians; *S. scardica* and *S. spruneri*, restricted to the mountains of the Balkan peninsula; and *S. italica*, confined to the Apennines of central Italy. *S. florulenta* is found only

Alpine meadow, Val d'Anniviers, Switzerland.

*Sempervivum arachnoideum*

found in Europe, most in montane habitats. Their flowers have 8-16 petals and are usually yellow or pinkish-red, while the fleshy leaves characteristically form tight rosettes. Yellow-flowered species include Wulfen's houseleek *Sempervivum wulfenii*, native to the central and eastern Alps, and large-flowered houseleek *S. grandiflorum*, which is found only on acid rocks to 2,500 m (8,200 ft) in the southern Alps.

Among the more widespread pink, purple, or red-flowered European species are the cobweb houseleek *S. arachnoideum*, found on acid soils in the Alps, Apennines, Pyrenees and the Cordillera Cantábrica of northern Spain; mountain houseleek *S. montanum*, which has larger flowers and also occurs in the Pyrenees, Alps and Apennines, but extends into the Carpathians; and common houseleek *S. tectorum*, which is distributed throughout the mountains of western, central and southern Europe.

Those with more restricted ranges include *S. nevadense*, confined to Spain's Sierra Nevada; *S. giuseppii*, confined to northwest Spain; *S. erythraeum* and *S. leucanthum*, both known only from the mountains of Bulgaria; *S. cantabricum*, found only on the limestone crags of Picos de Europa in northern Spain; and Dolomitic houseleek *S. dolomiticum* and *S. pittoni*, both of which are found only in the eastern Alps.

*S. tectorum* is a plant that has adapted well to the presence of man, adding rooftops to its natural habitats, and in so doing has acquired a wealth of local myth and legend. It is said that this plant will guard what it grows on from fire and lightning, and such was the belief in its effectiveness that Charlemagne ordered the common houseleek to be planted on the roof of every house. Welsh peasants

on cliffs in the Maritime Alps of France and Italy. Because it grows very slowly, flowering for the first time after 10-12 years, and also suffers from the attentions of overzealous collectors, this species is listed as a vulnerable species in the IUCN Plant Red Data Book (1980).

The Himalayas are also incredibly rich in saxifrages, with almost 90 species recorded there, some of which, such as *S. androsacea*, also occur in Europe. Yellow-flowered Himalayan saxifrages include several species that can grow in excess of 5,000 m (16,400 ft), such as the delicate *S. hirculoides*; the rare, but attractive *S. lychnitis*; the mat-forming *S. jacquemontiana* and *S. saginoides*, which forms cushions up to 0.5 m (1.6 ft) in diameter, studded in July and August with tiny flowers.

The white- or pinkish flowered Himalayan saxifrages can be divided into those which have lime-encrusted leaves and those which do not. Among the lime-secreting species are *S. pulvinaria*, which forms large cushions at altitudes up to 5,200 m (17,000 ft) and is common on stony slopes in Kashmir, and *S. roylei* and *S. poluniniana*, both of which are rare inhabitants of Nepalese rock ledges at medium altitudes.

**Saxifragaceae; about 300 species**

### SEMPERVIVUM

A genus of dwarf rosette-forming succulent perennials distributed across Europe, Morocco and western Asia. The generic name is derived from the Latin *semper* ('always'), and *vivo* ('I live'), which refers to the plants' incredible tolerance of these species to adverse conditions, and hence their 'evergreen' nature.

Plants in this genus were dedicated in ancient times to Jupiter or Thor and were once commonly known as Jupiter's eye or Thor's beard (see *Jovibarba*). Today they are better known as houseleeks, probably because of the Roman tradition of growing them as houseplants, although 'leek' derives from the Anglo-Saxon *leac*, meaning plant.

At least half of the known species of houseleek are

*Sempervivum montanum*

*Senecio elgonensis*

similarly believed that this species protected their houses from storms, and superstitious country folk in Wiltshire believed that the removal of a common houseleek from their dwelling would bring death to the inhabitants. In any event, a thick covering of common houseleek is useful for keeping slates in place!

In addition, juice extracted from the fresh leaves of *S. tectorum* and related species contains malic acid in combination with lime, and has both astringent and diuretic properties. Houseleek juice was formerly used in the treatment of burns, scalds and other inflammatory conditions of the skin, as well as for removing warts and corns. *S. montanum* is a preferred foodplant of the caterpillars of two montane butterflies: the apollo *Parnassius apollo* and the small apollo P. phoebus.

**Crassulaceae; 42 species**

### SENECIO

One of the largest of all plant genera, *Senecio* has a more or less cosmopolitan distribution, although it is absent from Antarctica. In the tropical mountains of central and eastern Africa, certain plants of this genus reach staggering proportions. These tree senecios, sometimes classified separately in the genus *Dendrosenecio*, are commonly found in the montane forests and above the tree line. They may be trees or shrubs, growing up to 9 m (29.5 ft) tall, with branched stems terminating in rosettes of large leaves which often persist when dead, and spectacular clusters of yellow flowers.

Kenya is the centre of distribution of tree senecios, which are also commonly known as giant groundsels. Although there are considered to be only three separate species of tree senecio, many subspecies have been described, each of which occurs in a distinct locality. *Senecio keniensis* ssp. *brassica*, for example, is a relatively small representative of this group, the stems reaching a height of 1.8 m (6 ft) when in flower. It is found only on open moorland on the slopes of Mt Kenya, between altitudes of 3,300 to 3,900 m (10,800-12,800 ft). By contrast, *S. johnstonii* ssp. *cherangiensis*, which is confined to the Cherangani Hills between 2,550 and 3,300 m (8,400-10,800 ft), attains a maximum height of almost 10 m

*Senecio elgonensis*

Senecio brassica

(33 ft).

Other African tree senecios include *S. keniodendron*, from Mt Kenya and the Aberdares; *S. johnstonii* ssp. *barbatipes* and *S. johnstonii* ssp. *elgonensis*, which are confined to Mt Elgon; and *S. johnstonii* ssp. *johnstonii*, which has been recorded only from Mts Kilimanjaro and Meru in Tanzania.

**Compositae; 1,500 species**

*SOLDANELLA*

A small genus of rock plants found only in the central and southern European mountains, commonly known as snowbells as they often grow up through and flower in the snow. These perennial herbs have evergreen leathery leaves arranged in a basal rosette and nodding, bell-shaped flowers, the petals of which are deeply divided and a fringelike.

Most snowbells have a very restricted distribution. Austrian snowbell *Soldanella austriaca* has pale lilac or white flowers and grows only in wet calcareous soils in the Austrian Alps; the very similar least snowbell *S. mimima* is confined to the eastern Alps and central Apennines; the violet-flowered *S.*

*Soldanella maxima*

Sani Pass between Lesotho and South Africa.

Grenadier Range, Colorado, USA.

*carpatica* is found only in the western Carpathians; and *S. villosa*, a hairy species, again with violet flowers, is known only from the western Pyrenees. *S. pindicola* is confined to the banks of mountain streams near Metsovon in northwest Greece and *S. dimoniei* grows only in the mountains of Macedonia, eastern Albania and Bulgaria.

One or two members of this genus have a slightly wider range and are thus better known. Dwarf snowbell *S. pusilla*, a species with reddish violet bells, prefers acid soils in the Alps, Carpathians, Apennines and mountains of southwest Bulgaria; alpine snowbell *S. alpina* has blue-violet flowers which decorate upland meadows from the Pyrenees to southwest Germany and south to Calabria in Italy,

Alpine meadow, Petit Mountet, Switzerland.

and *S. montana* is a widespread species of acid soils found in the woods and meadows of central European and Bulgarian mountains.

**Primulaceae; 10 species**

### TROPAEOLEUM

A New World genus distributed from southern Mexico to Brazil and Patagonia. Many species, commonly known as nasturtiums, occur in the Andes from the cloud forests up into the arid alpine steppes, and many have adopted a climbing habit.

*Tropaeoleum polyphyllum*, a herbaceous trailing annual or perennial with much divided grey-green leaves, has large bright-yellow flowers. It grows in the Andes to the south of Peru, through Chile and Argentina, between 1,800 and 2,500 m (5,900-8,200 ft), in montane pastures, rocky terrain and woodlands. Other montane species include Indian cress *T. majus*, which is native to Peru but was first introduced to Europe in 1684 as the garden nasturtium, the Andean *T. peltatum*, whose flower buds and young fruits are sometimes used as a substitute for capers; and *T. tuberosum*, another Andean plant from Bolivia and Colombia, known locally as *añu*, whose tubers are edible when boiled.

**Tropaeolaceae; 86 species**

### WULFENIA

Just two species make up this genus of southeast Européan rock-plants. *Wulfenia carinthiaca* is a short, almost hairless perennial with deep green leaves in basal rosettes and dark violet-blue flowers arranged in dense spikes. It prefers damp, acid habitats and is found only in the Carnic Alps and the southern Dinaric Alps (Montenegro region) between 1,500 and 2,000 m (5,000-6,600 ft). Because of its rarity this plant is strictly protected by law in the countries where it occurs. The second species is *W. baldaccii*, which is distinguished by its smaller size, hairiness and bright blue flowers. It is confined to northern Albania where it thrives on shady mountain rocks. Some authorities recognize distinct Himalayan species, such as *W. amherstiana*.

**Scrophulariaceae; 2 species**

# CHAPTER TWO

# POLAR REGIONS

Sometimes known as the polar deserts, the fringes of the Arctic Ocean and the continental landmass of Antarctica are two of the most inhospitable habitats on Earth. Although these polar realms are as distant from each other as any two regions of the world can be, they have several features in common, both being capped with ice and experiencing severe climatic conditions.

Antarctica accounts for almost 10 per cent of the Earth's land surface but is permanently swathed in a sheet of ice which is, on average, almost 2.5 km (1.6 miles) thick and contains about 75 per cent of the world's fresh water. At the opposite end of the globe lies an ocean of ice some 3 km (1.9 miles) thick at the centre, from whose shores radiate the continents of the northern hemisphere. At both poles flowering plants are unknown in the icebound region. However, in the Arctic the surrounding plains, known as tundra, support diverse open plant communities, as do the subantarctic islands. In both cases the diversity of such communities increases with distance from the pole.

Polar regions are unique in that they experience six months of almost total darkness followed by six months during which the sun is permanently above the horizon. Even during the polar 'summer' temperatures are always low, since the sun's rays strike the Earth at an angle and the ice-sheets reflect much light back into the atmosphere. In addition, precipitation is extremely low and strong winds blow constantly. Not surprisingly, the ground is permanently frozen below a depth of a few metres, although the surface layers thaw in summer, which often causes waterlogging.

Even in such inhospitable climates plant life still abounds, although the native flora of the subantarctic islands comprises less than 70 species and the entire arctic region contains only about 900 species of flowering plant. The plants adaptations to such harsh conditions include a strong emphasis on vegetative reproduction (i.e. without seeds), overwintering buds that can flower within three to four days of snow-melt; large, brightly coloured, cup-shaped or tubular flowers which attract insects and encourage them to stay within the flower to keep warm and thus effect pollination; dark pigmentation in the foliage to absorb the warming rays of the sun and to shield the plant from excess ultraviolet radiation; and a dense covering of hairs to decrease water loss by reducing air flow around the plant. Other adaptations are essentially the same as those found in mountain plants and are discussed in the next chapter.

Facing page: tundra, Ellesmere Island, Canada.

Artic tundra ponds.

Tundra, Pribilof Islands, Alaska.

Top right: tundra vegetation, Norway.

*Papaver radicatum*

*Antennaria dioica*

## ANDROSACE

A genus of annual or tufted perennial herbs, commonly known as rock jasmines, distributed across the northern temperate and arctic regions. Characteristic features are basal leaves and flowers borne singly or in umbels. Each flower has a bell-shaped or almost spherical calyx with triangular lobes and a rather inflated corolla tube, usually shorter than the calyx, the throat of the tube closed by a ring of scales.

Many species are found in the tundra, particularly in rocky or stony places. Rock jasmine *Androsace chamaejasme* is a white-flowered, rosette-forming plant particularly common in Alaska, but also found in discrete localities throughout the northern hemisphere. *A. triflora* is small, densely tufted and grows in gravelly tundra only in the Siberian arctic. It rarely exceeds 2 cm (0.8 in) in height, each short flowering stem bearing three tiny yellow flowers in a terminal inflorescence.

Species that form compact cushions include the spring flowering Ochotsk douglasia *A. ochotensis* whose foliage is almost obscured by bright pink, five-petalled flowers. It grows in eastern Siberia, north Alaska and the Yukon. Similar species, although less spectacular, are *A. gormanii* and *A. arctica*, typically found in the northwest North American tundra, while a whole range of rock jasmines thrives in alpine habitats further south.

**Primulaceae; about 100 species**

## ANEMONE

A large genus of perennial herbs with an almost cosmopolitan distribution. Commonly known as anemones or windflowers, many are found in the cooler regions of the northern hemisphere, especially in woodlands, montane grasslands and tundra, although far-flung representatives also occur in South America and South Africa. Distinguishing features are the presence of three or four leaflets in a whorl just under the flowers, forming an involucre, and showy, usually solitary flowers that have no true petals, but instead possess 5-14 petal-like perianth segments and numerous stamens.

The highly poisonous yellow or Richardson's anemone *Anemone richardsonii* is a conspicuous single-flowered species with slender creeping rhizomes which grows in tundra meadows in Alaska, Canada and the west coast of Greenland, as well as in mountain snow flushes. Each fruit has a hooked beak which aids seed dispersal by catching in the coats of passing animals. Another single-flowered species is the northern windflower *A. parviflora*, characterized by glossy leaves and cream flowers, which often forms conspicuous 'drifts' in meadows, on stony slopes and snow flushes in the low arctic regions of Alaska and northwestern Canada.

The narcissus-flowered anemone *A. narcissiflora* produces clusters of large white to pale yellow flowers, the outer surface of the perianth segments often tinged with pink or purple. Several arctic subspecies have been described, ranging from Alaska to Eurasia, and *A. narcissiflora* is also found in European and North American alpine habitats.

**Ranunculaceae; 120 species**

## ANTENNARIA

This genus of small perennial herbs or dwarf shrubs has representatives extending from the subarctic zone to warm temperate regions, especially in the mountains. The plants, which have basal leaf-rosettes and erect, leafy, flowering stems, are typically covered with whitish hairs. The small unisexual, tubular flowers are subtended by a collar of stiff, papery involucral bracts, which are often coloured and petal-like and clustered together in terminal heads. Male and female flowers are found on separate plants.

*Antennaria villifera* has purplish flowers and yellow anthers and is a typical species of snowpatches and other damp places, especially on base-rich soils in arctic Europe and the northern Urals. Greenland cat's-paws *A. canescens* is found in snow patches and on herb-slopes in Iceland and the southern part of Greenland. The flowering stems arise from creeping overground shoots and the flowers are capable of producing fruits without pollination. In the extreme north of Greenland *A. canescens* is replaced by the densely tufted Labrador cat's-paws *A. ekmaniana*. The very similar alpine cat's-ear *A. alpina* is found only on mountain rocks and heaths in north and west Fennoscandia and the adjacent part of the Soviet Union.

Cat's-foot or mountain everlasting, *A. dioica* is found in both Eurasia and North America, its range extending into the Arctic. It is especially abundant in the mountains of Europe, particularly in the British Isles, Scandinavia and the Caucasus. The female flowers have red or pinkish involucral bracts, while those of the male flowers are white or yellowish. The whole plant is widely used in homeopathic medicine and reputed to be an effective remedy for such diverse diseases as mumps and diarrhoea, and even for the bites of poisonous reptiles.

Other montane representatives of this genus include Carpathian cat's-foot *A. carpatica*, which grows on dry, stony slopes to heights of over 3,000 m (9,800ft) in the Pyrenees, Alps and Carpathians, and pussytoes *A. rosea*, which is distinguished by its rose-coloured involucral bracts and is one of about 20 species found in the mountains of western North America from California to Alaska, between 1,400 and 3,600 m (4,600-11,800ft).

**Compositae; about 45 species**

## ARCTOSTAPHYLOS

This is a largely North American genus of dwarf shrubs with short-stalked, alternate leaves, five-lobed, urn-shaped flowers in small terminal clusters and

*Azorella compacta*

edible fruits. The generic name is derived from a combination of the Greek words *arctos* ('bear') and *staphyle* ('grape'), as the berries are reputed to be a favourite food of bears. Two circumpolar species are black bearberry *Arctostaphylos alpina* and bearberry *A. uva-ursi*, both of which are also found in mountainous regions further south.

*A. uva-ursi* is a mat-forming, evergreen shrub with waxy greenish white or pale pink flowers. When ripe the berry-like fruits are bright red. The closely related *A. alpina* differs in having serrated, deciduous leaves, white flowers and black berries. In the autumn the leaves of this species turn bright red, covering large areas of dry tundra heath in a crimson carpet. *A. alpina*, which also occurs in the high mountains of Scotland, is the badge of the clan of Ross.

In North America *A. uva-ursi* is known as kinnikinnick, an Indian word applied to several tobacco substitutes. The leaves contain 6-7 per cent tannins and were once used in the tanning of leather in the USSR and Sweden. In addition, the glycoside arbutin is present in some quantity and an infusion of dried bearberry leaves is often given in the treatment of inflammatory diseases of the urinary tract. The foliage of bearberry provides food for the larvae of several moths, including the netted mountain carpet *Semiothisa carbonaria*, the northern dart *Xestia alpicola* and the small dark yellow underwing *Anarta cordigera*.

**Ericaceae; about 50 species**

### AZORELLA

This genus of cushion-forming or spreading perennials is widely distributed in the southern hemisphere from temperate South America to the Falkland Islands, New Zealand and the subantarctic islands, but more or less confined to the Andes further north. These plants grow so incredibly slowly that in southern Peru individual plants have been estimated to be

around 3,000 years old.

*Azorella gummifera* produces huge mounds of densely packed rosettes in rocky or shaly habitats in the Falkland Islands. The tough cushions are consolidated by a white gum which is exuded between the rosettes and hardens into reddish beads on the surface of the mound. Because of the fragrant, resinous smell of the gum the mounds are commonly referred to as 'balsam bogs'. *A. caespitosa* is another mound-forming species of the Falkland Islands, while *A. selago*, a densely tufted cushion-forming plant, is typical of subantarctic heaths.

Other species of Azorella are more characteristic of the high mountains. These include *A. incisa*, one of the early colonizers of the barren slopes of Chilean volcanoes, and *A. pedunculata*, which occurs in Ecuador and has white-flowers and dense tufts of tiny, dissected leaves. *A. yareta* is a mat-forming species of the Peruvian and Bolivian Andes whose tough woody stems are an important source of fuel in such treeless habitats.

**Umbelliferae; 70 species**

### BOYKINIA

A small genus of saxifrage-like herbs from eastern Asia (Japan) and North America. The Alaska boykinia *Boykinia richardsonii* is confined to Alaska and the northern reaches of the neighbouring Yukon Territory, although it is thought to have had a much wider distribution under different climatic conditions in the Tertiary period (c. 50 million years ago). *B. richardsonii*, Bear flower so called because it is reputed to be a favourite food of the bears, is an attractive plant with tall spikes of dark centred, pale pink flowers. It is commonly found along the edges of snowfields, sometimes in large 'drifts'. Recent research has revealed that it forms an important part of the staple diet of Dall sheep in Alaska's Brooks Range. The similar *B. jamesii*, which grows in cracks

in cliff faces in the Rocky Mountains, is eaten by elk and deer where it is not too inaccessible.

**Saxifragaceae; 8 species**

### BRAYA

A characteristic genus of mainly perennial herbs with undivided leaves and white or purple, four-petalled flowers, distributed across the northern circumpolar region, extending into the Alps and the Himalayas. The generic name commemorates the Franco-German diplomat and botanist Graf von Bray (1765-1832). Four of the 20 species grow in the high arctic.

*Braya linearis* is a loosely tufted perennial herb with small, purplish flowers and long narrow seed pods atop a leafy 20 cm (8 in) stem. It grows typically in calcareous gravel or mountain scree in high arctic regions. *B. purpurascens*, also found on limy soils, has a flower stem either leafless or bearing a solitary leaf, while the seed pods are somewhat shorter. One of the smallest species is *B. thurild-wulffii*, a tiny tufted annual of arctic Canada and eastern Greenland with flowering stems less than 7cm (2.8 in) tall. The fourth species, *B. humilis*, is noteworthy for its ability to overwinter with its flowers at any stage of development, growth continuing the following season.

**Cruciferae; 20 species**

### CALCEOLARIA

This large genus of rosette-forming herbs and small shrubs is characteristic of the neotropical regions, but extends to the subantarctic zone of South America. These plants are commonly called slipperworts, because of the distinctive shape of the flowers.

Some cultivated forms are especially popular as pot plants, notably *Calceolaria darwinii*, a subantarctic species which has bulbous yellow flowers with red spotted lips. As its name suggests, this plant was first collected by Charles Darwin from Elizabeth Island in the Magellan Straits. Here it is common along the shoreline, flowering in November and December. A second species, *C. fothergillii*, is an uncommon plant of coastal slopes in the nearby Falkland Islands and also occurs in Patagonia. It has hairy, spoon-shaped leaves in a basal rosette, from which rise predominantly yellow flowers, although each inflated lip sports a conspicuous white bar and red stripe around the margin.

Chilean mountain species include *C. arachnoidea*, which is densely covered with white woolly hairs and has dull reddish purple flowers, and *C. tenella*, with small yellow flowers only about 1 cm (0.4 in) long. *C. biflora*, whose larger yellow flowers appear from January to March in the high altitude steppes and pastures (2,500-3,000 m/8,200-9,800 ft), is a widespread in the Andes from northern Chile to Patagonia.

**Scrophulariaceae; about 300 species**

### CARDAMINE

This large genus of annual, biennial and perennial herbs is widely distributed in a variety of habitats throughout the cold and temperate regions of the world. The four-petalled flowers may be white, pink, purplish or pale yellow and each has four or six stamens.

There are several arctic species. *Cardamine bellidifolia* is a diminutive circumpolar arctic cushion plant with tiny white flowers and spoon-shaped leaves. The plant is probably more noticeable in fruit, when it produces a cluster of needle-like, upright, violet-brown seed pods. It is typically found on poor soils in exposed situations, venturing into high mountain regions further south.

Arctic bittercress *Cardamine nymanii* is a larger species with pale pink-violet flowers, characteristic of wet places in northern Europe and Iceland, extending westwards into the Soviet arctic. In the southern hemisphere the tiny *C. depressa* var. *stellata*, its minute white flowers almost hidden among the rosette of basal leaves, occurs on Campbell Island and the Auckland Islands in the subantarctic zone near New Zealand.

**Cruciferae; 130 species**

### CASSIOPE

A genus of low, creeping, evergreen shrubs found throughout colder regions of the northern hemisphere as well as in the Himalayas. The stems are either procumbent or ascending, the small, stalkless leaves may be alternate or opposite and the nodding flowers are borne either at the ends of the stems or in the axils of the leaves. Each flower has a five-lobed, bell-shaped or hemispherical corolla and 10 stamens.

Arctic bell heather *Cassiope tetragona*, also known as firemoss cassiope, is a shrubby circumpolar species which is also common in alpine habitats further south. It has scale-like leaves, arranged in four overlapping rows, and the white, bell-shaped flowers (6-8 mm 0.2-0.3 in) hang from slender, erect stems which rise above the leaves. This species is one of the most characteristic and conspicuous plants of dry, stony tundra in arctic Eurasia and North America and is reputedly used by Eskimos as a source of fuel.

Mossplant *C. hypnoides* is a dwarf shrub with tiny, needle-like leaves. As its name suggests, it resembles a moss when not in flower but it is unmistakable in summer when the broad white bells (sometimes with a pinkish tinge) appear, each with a distinctive crimson stalk and calyx. Like *C. tetragona* it is highly typical of both arctic and alpine tundra, but prefers wetter habitats, especially late snow patches.

*Cassiope tetragona*

Other plants in this genus include *C. mertensiana*, a white-flowered North American species, and *C. fastigiata*, typical of open slopes in the Himalayas at up to 4,500 m (14,800 ft).

**Ericaceae; 12 species**

### CERASTIUM

A genus of hardy low-growing herbs, sometimes woody at the base, with a more or less cosmopolitan distribution. The flowers have free sepals and usually white, bifid or notched petals, although in some species the petals are absent. The generic name is derived from the Greek *keras* ('horn') which refers to the seed capsule, this being tapered and, in some species, bent slightly to one side like a cow's horn. The common name of mouse-ear probably alludes to the rounded, softly hairy leaves.

Many plants in this genus are regarded as weeds but several species are particularly characteristic of the polar regions. Arctic mouse-ear *Cerastium arcticum* is a white-flowered, softly hairy plant found at high latitudes on both sides of the Atlantic, while polar chickweed *C. regelii* has a circumpolar arctic range and is one of the few species of flowering plant never to have been recorded outside the Arctic Circle.

*Cerastium arcticum*

Mountain chickweed *C. beeringianum* occurs in the Siberian-West American arctic zone and at high elevations in America's western mountains, and starwort mouse-ear *C. cerastoides* is a loosely matted perennial which grows in wet snow patches and herb slopes of Eurasian arctic and montane regions.

**Caryophyllaceae; 60 species**

### CODONORCHIS

A tiny orchid genus of tropical and temperate America, its range extending south into the Falkland Islands. The dog orchid *Codonorchis lessonii* is the commonest of the four orchids found in the Falkland Islands, where it grows in dwarf heathland. The stems are between 10 and 25 cm (4-10 in) in height, each bearing a whorl of three shiny green leaves around the midpoint. The fragrant white, sometimes purplish tinged, flowers differ from those of typical orchids in being more or less radially symmetrical, the three sepals arranged in an equilateral triangle around the fused petals of the lip.

**Liliaceae; 3 species**

### COLOBANTHUS

A genus of the subantarctic islands of the south Pacific also found in the Andes. The flowers lack petals. *Colobanthus quitensis* is a cushion-forming plant with the distinction of being one of only two flowering plants to occur on the continent of Antarctica itself (the other being the grass *Deschampsia antarctica*). These two species are also the only flowering plants on the subantarctic island of South Orkney.

**Caryophyllaceae; 20 species**

### DIAPENSIA

A small genus of the Himalayas and western China with one circumpolar, arctic-alpine species: *Diapensia lapponica*. This is an evergreen, cushion-forming dwarf shrub with tiny leathery, spoon-shaped leaves. The average height of the foliage is about 5 cm (2 in), above which whitish, saxifrage-like flowers are borne on short stalks. Commonly known as Lapland diapensia, since the species was first described there, it grows in stony, exposed situations throughout the Arctic, preferring rather acid soils. In Europe *D. lapponica* is found as far south as the mountains of Scotland, where it was not discovered until 1951 and is now protected by law.

**Diapensiaceae; 4 species**

*Colobanthus quintensis*

## DRABA

A genus of small annual and tufted perennial herbs of northern temperate regions and South American mountains, with many species extending into the Arctic. Characteristic features are entire or toothed leaves and flowers with four slightly spreading sepals and four white or yellow petals.

*Draba lactea* is a circumpolar species of high latitudes, whilst species such as the cream-flowered *D. daurica*, the white-flowered arctic bitterwort *D. fladnizensis* and the yellow-flowered alpine whitlowgrass *D. alpina* (also known as alpine bitterwort), are found both in the arctic zone and in alpine regions further south.

*D. subcapitata* and *D. oblongata* are confined to the high Arctic, having an almost circumpolar distribution, whereas the yellow-flowered *D. kjellmanii* is confined to high-arctic Eurasia. Species with a more restricted range include the eastern Siberian arctic-alpine *D. barbata*, *D. pilosa* of Siberia and North America, and *D. pohlei*, which is confined to the Siberian arctic.

The diminutive snow whitlowgrass *D. nivalis* and rock whitlowgrass *D. norvegica* are white-flowered species of arctic and subarctic Eurasia, the latter extending to the British Isles. An indication of the arctic preference of this genus is that no less than 19

Mountain sorrel, poppies and whitlowgrass.

*Dryas octopetala*

*Eritrichium elongatum*

*Dryas integrifolia*

distinct species of *Draba* occur in Greenland. The common name 'whitlowgrass' is shared with the genus *Erophila*, also a crucifer.

**Cruciferae, about 300 species**

### DRYAS

A tiny artic-alpine genus of procumbent, branched dwarf shrubs with simple leaves and solitary, axillary flowers which may be either hermaphrodite or unisexual. Commonly known as mountain avens, each flower has 7-10 sepals, usually eight (7-16) petals and numerous stamens and carpels.

There is some disagreement over the number of species, but most authors recognize two: *Dryas integrifolia*, which occurs from Greenland across North America to eastern Siberia, and *D. octopetala*, an almost circumpolar arctic-alpine species characteristic of limestone areas, which is apparently absent from the Canadian arctic. *D. drummondii*, with creamy yellow flowers that never open fully, is sometimes considered to be a distinct species native to North America, as is *D. punctata*, which has large glands on the upper surface of the leaves and occurs in the Soviet arctic.

Mountain avens *D. octopetala* is a mat-forming perennial with oblong, distinctly lobed leaves, white woolly beneath and dark green above, which

distinguish this plant from all other members of the Rosaceae. The leaves of arctic avens *D. integrifolia* are entire, without these characteristic crenellations. Both species produce large white flowers, up to 3.5 cm (1.4 in) in diameter, each with as many as eight oblong petals. The many achenes develop elongated, feathery plumes when ripe to assist wind dispersal of the seeds.

The roots of the various *Dryas* species have nitrogen-fixing nodules which provide valuable soil enrichment in a region where nutrients are in short supply. Impressions of *Dryas* leaves found in the fossil record indicate cool periods in the past climate of the Earth. Mountain avens is the official floral emblem of Canada's Northwest Territories.

**Rosaceae; 2 or 3 species**

### EPILOBIUM

A large genus of perennial herbs or subshrubs typically found in temperate regions in both hemispheres as well as in the Arctic and on tropical mountains. Western North America is a particular stronghold of this genus. The leaves may be opposite, alternate or arranged in whorls each flower has four erect sepals, four white, pink or purple petals and eight stamens. The generic name is derived from the combination of the Greek words *epi*, meaning 'upon', and *lobos*, meaning 'a pod', referring to the position of the flowers on top of the long, thin, pod-like seed capsules. Many species are commonly known as willowherbs because of their willow-like leaves.

Rosebay willowherb *Epilobium angustifolium* (*Chamaenerion angustifolium*) is a tall attractive plant with terminal spikes of large pink flowers. It is circumpolar in distribution but is also found in a wide variety of habitats further south. Rosebay willowherb typically occurs in moist riverside situations but it is also widespread in wasteground, especially places subjected to burning, for which reason it is known as fireweed in the United States. Despite attaining heights of over 2 m (6.6 ft) in the more temperate parts of its range, dwarfed specimens of as little as 10 cm (4 in) are more usual in the Arctic.

The leaves of *E. angustifolium* have long been used as a substitute for tea, especially in the USSR where the infusion is called Kaporie Tea. Ale and vinegar are made from the dried, boiled pith by natives of the Kamchatka Peninsula, although the intoxicating effects of the ale are heightened by the addition of the toadstool known as fly agaric (*Amanita muscaria*). Rosebay willowherb is the territorial flower of the Yukon (Canada). The larvae of several moths feed on the leaves, including the small phoenix *Ecliptopera silaceata*, the elephant hawkmoth *Deilephila elpenor*, the small elephant hawkmoth *D. porcellus*, and the bedstraw hawkmoth *Hyles galii*.

Several other species of willowherb occur in the tundra, the most spectacular being river beauty or dwarf fireweed *E. latifolium*, a north Asian and North American species which extends into Iceland. This plant differs from rosebay willowherb in its creeping habit and grey-green leaves and is the national flower of Greenland. Other less conspicuous species include alpine willowherb *E. anagallidifolium*, a creeping perennial with stems up to 10 cm (4 in) and a few, pale purplish flowers, which is also found in mountains further south; and *E. hornemannii*, an arctic and subarctic European species which resembles alpine willowherb but has subterranean rather than above-ground runners and larger, pale violet flowers. *E. davuricum* is a white-flowered species which, in arctic localities, may be as little as 2 cm (0.8 in) high. Its distribution is almost circumpolar but it is absent from parts of the Eurasian arctic.

**Onagraceae; about 200 species**

### ERIGERON

A cosmopolitan genus of annual, biennial or perennial herbs with entire leaves and erect flowering stems topped by one to several flowerheads in a loose

*Gentiana verna*

cluster. The daisy-like flowers have yellow, female disc-florets and usually white, pink or purple ray-florets which are usually hermaphrodite.

Typical tundra representatives of this genus include cut-leaved fleabane *Erigeron compositus*, a plant distinguished by its divided leaves and white ray florets. It is found in dry, rocky places in eastern Alaska, western Canada and scattered localities elsewhere, including Greenland. Arctic fleabane *E. hyperboreus*, with pinkish ray-florets and entire leaves, is confined to stony soils in the arctic regions of North America, whilst *E. humilis* is a North American/European species, found in tundra herb slopes and fellfield habitats as well as in mountain meadows.

Alpine fleabane *E. borealis* has purplish ray-florets and grows on calcareous soils in northern Eurasia, its European range extending to the mountains of the British Isles. Perhaps the most common arctic member of the genus, however, is *E. uniflorus* which is found in snow patches and stony slopes in northern Eurasia and alpine pastures in mountainous regions further south. Several distinct subspecies have been described, including *E. uniflorus* ssp. *eriocephalus*, which has densely hairy involucral bracts (the hairs being up to 2 mm (0.1 in) in length) and is particularly characteristic of arctic regions.

**Compositae; about 200 species**

### ERITRICHIUM

A small genus of tufted perennial herbs, sometimes woody at the base, distributed across northern temperate regions, extending into the Arctic. The flowers are arranged in terminal inflorescences and have violet, blue or whitish petals with spreading lobes and short tubes. The generic name is derived from the Greek *erion* ('wool') and *trichos* ('hair') referring to the densely hairy leaves and stems.

Arctic forget-me-not *Eritrichium aretioides* is a fragrant perennial of gravelly or sandy habitats in the High Arctic, from the extreme north of Canada to Siberia and arctic Soviet Europe. It forms large mats or cushions up to 25 cm (10 in) in diameter. *E. villosum* is an arctic-alpine Asian plant, extending west only as far as Soviet Europe. Both species have small violet flowers which turn bright blue as they age.

Other species of *Eritrichium* are confined to montane regions further south, the best known of which is undoubtedly the king of the Alps, *E. nanum* which has pale blue to brilliant azure flowers (rarely white) and grows between 2,000 and 3,600 m (6,600-11,800 ft) in the Alps and Carpathians and up to 5,000 m (16,400 ft) in the Himalayas. This rather rare plant seems to prefer acid rocks and screes but is occasionally found on limestone.

*E. argenteum*, *E. howardii* and *E. elongatum* are North American species very similar to *E. nanum*. Alpine forget-me-not *E. elongatum* occurs on exposed ridges between 2,700 and 3,700 m (8,900-12,100 ft) in the Rocky Mountains, from Montana to New Mexico. A species typical of the Himalayas is *E. canum*, which has tufts of linear leaves and tiny blue flowers and grows at altitudes up to 4,500 m (14,800 ft).

**Boraginaceae; about 30 species**

### EUTREMA

A small genus of perennial herbs found predominantly in the Arctic and central and eastern Asia. The leaves are simple and the flowers have four sepals and four white petals. *Eutrema edwardsii* is a typical circumpolar high arctic species with fleshy leaves, tiny white flowers and relatively large, winged seeds (3 mm (0.1 in) in diameter). *E. edwardsii* is one of the northernmost flowering plants in the world but is also found in alpine habitats further south.

**Cruciferae; 15 species**

## GENTIANA

A genus of hairless, mostly perennial herbs widely distributed throughout the temperate and polar regions of both hemispheres, and in montane zones elsewhere (although absent from Africa). Commonly known as gentians, the flowers may be blue (Europe), red (South America and New Zealand) or, more rarely, yellow or white. The corolla is funnel-shaped or cylindrical and divided into five short lobes at the tip. The generic name has its origins with Gentius, an ancient king of Illyria (180-167 BC) who apparently discovered the medicinal value of these plants; the roots contain valuable bitter glycosides. In the Middle Ages, gentian extracts were commonly used as antidotes to poisons

Several gentians extend their range into the subantarctic region, including *Gentiana antipoda*, which is confined to Antipodes Island and classified as a rare species by the International Union for the Conservation of Nature and Natural Resources (IUCN), and *G. concinna*, a slender gentian with white or pinkish, red or purple streaked flowers which is native to nearby Auckland Island, where it grows on exposed hills.

Glaucous gentian *G. glauca* is an American arctic-alpine plant which also occurs in eastern Asia and has rather substantial bluish green flowers. Small, snow or alpine gentian *G. nivalis*, bears delicate flowers of an intense blue (rarely white) on stems only 5-10 cm (2-4 in) tall. It is found throughout northern Eurasia, to Scotland's Breadalbane and Clora Mountains where it is protected by law, as well as occurring in the Pyrenees and southern Apennines.

Slender gentian *G. tenella*, a species with blue-violet often four-petalled flowers, inhabits calcareous river gravels and montane pastures in subarctic Eurasia. The northern or golden gentian *G. aurea*, with its pale yellowish flowers (rarely violet), grows around sea and lake shores in arctic Eurasia. Both of these species are commonly placed in the genus *Gentianella*.

**Gentianaceae; about 300 species**

## GUNNERA

A largely southern hemisphere genus of herbs with runners or underground stems particularly characteristic of tropical and subtropical Africa, South America, Malaysia, Tasmania and Hawaii, although several species range south to Antarctica. The alternate leaves have erect stalks and oval to circular, palmately lobed blades. The flowers consist of two sepals, two petals (or petals absent) and two stamens. Some of the largest leaves known to science belong to plants from this genus.

Pig vine *Gunnera magellanica* is one of the commonest plants of antarctic America, from the Andes to Tierra del Fuego and the Falkland Islands. It has kidney-shaped, rhubarb-like leaves and petal-less male and female flowers which, as in all members of the genus, are found on separate plants. The elongated feathery styles of the female flowers indicate that the species is wind pollinated.

Ten species are native to New Zealand, including *G. monoica*, *G. densiflora* and *G. dentata*, all three of which are small herbs and prefer wet habitats in the low alpine zone. Another small subantarctic species, Hamilton's gunnera *G. hamiltonii*, is found only in one coastal locality on Stewart Island close to the southern tip of New Zealand, where it forms solitary rosettes or compact cushions up to 1 m (3.3 ft) across. This species is threatened by the introduction of competitive alien plants on the one hand and overgrazing of domestic animals on the other. It is classified as endangered on international lists.

**Gunneraceae; about 40 species**

## KOENIGIA

A small genus of annual herbs with sub opposite leaves and flowers with three sepaloid perianth segments and three stamens which alternate with three gland rudimentarg like stamens (staminodes). *Koenigia* is characteristic of the Arctic, mountains of northern Europe and temperate parts of eastern Asia, with a single South American species.

Common or Iceland purslane *Koenigia islandica* is one of the few annual plants to occur in the Arctic, in fact having the dubious distinction of being the northernmost annual species in the world. It is a tiny plant, with prostrate reddish stems 1-5 cm (0.4-2 in) high, bearing fleshy leaves about 5 mm (0.2 in) long. The minute flowers lack true petals, having instead three yellow-green, sepal-like lobes, each only 1 mm (0.04 in) in length. *K. islandica* is a plant of bare ground, especially snow patches, in the extreme north of Europe and Asia, extending south as far as the mountains of Scotland.

**Polygonaceae; 7 species**

## LOISELEURIA

This genus contains but a single species – alpine, mountain or trailing azalea *Loiseleuria procumbens* – which has a circumpolar distribution in the northern hemisphere and also occurs in montane habitats as far south as the Pyrenees, Alps and Carpathians in Europe. It is a creeping evergreen shrub whose hairless branches form extensive mats, rooting freely for anchorage. The opposite leaves have inrolled margins and the small, reddish-pink, bell-shaped flowers are either solitary or arranged in small clusters, but do not rise far above the foliage. Each flower has five free sepals, a deeply five-lobed corolla and five stamens which alternate with the corolla lobes.

A noted lime hater of tundra habitats, *Loiseleuria procumbens* grows equally well in peat bogs, dry

*Gunnera sp.*

*Oxyria digyna*

heathlands or on exposed rocky slopes and fellfield. It is named after J.L.A. Loiseleur-Deslongchamps (1774-1849), a French botanist and physician.

**Ericaceae; a single species**

### LYALLIA

A tiny genus of herbs confined to the islands of the subantarctic region and named after Dr David Lyall, the surgeon aboard HMS *Terror* (captained by James Clark Ross) on the memorable Antarctic Voyage of 1839-1842. Male and female flowers are found on separate plants.

*Lyallia kerguelensis*, which is confined to the island of Kerguelen and is rare even here, is thought to have been much more widespread in Tertiary times (c. 50 million years ago), its range decreasing as the climate of Antarctica cooled. It has dense globular rosettes which may spread over considerable areas in exposed habitats, and minute greenish flowers. The other species in this genus is *L. caespitosa*, which is confined to South Island, New Zealand, where it grows in the high alpine zone between 1,300 and 2,000 m (4,300-6,600 ft). The rosettes cluster together to form unisexual cushions of over 20 cm (8 in) in diameter, the male clumps being much more conspicuous because the flowers have bright orange stamens.

**Portulacaceae (Hectorellaceae); 2 species**

*Papaver dahlianum*

## MINUARTIA

A widespread genus of annual, biennial or perennial herbs ranging from the Arctic south to the Himalayas, northern Africa and Mexico, with a single representative in Chile. The leaves are opposite and the flowers are either solitary or arranged in few-flowered clusters. Each flower has five free sepals and five entire, white, lilac or pinkish petals. Plants of this genus are commonly known as sandworts because of their general predilection for sand and gravel habitats.

A characteristic arctic species is *Minuartia arctica*, a densely tufted perennial herb with stems 5-9 cm (2-3.5 in) tall topped by solitary flowers, which occurs in the Soviet high arctic extending west as far as the Urals. The very similar *M. macrocarpa* has a comparable Eurasian range but is also found in western North America. Two-flowered sandwort *M. biflora*, with its larger pale lilac flowers, is a characteristic plant of snow patches, damp heaths and fellfield in northern Europe, Greenland and Iceland.

Mountain sandwort *M. rubella* is a circumpolar arctic-alpine species which favours basic soils, its range extending southwards to the mountains of Scotland. Teesdale sandwort *M. stricta*, which bears clusters of small white flowers, occurs in arctic and subarctic regions and more southerly mountains; it is rare in the British Isles, where it is protected by law.

**Caryophyllaceae; 120 species**

## MYOSOTIDIUM

The sole member of this genus is the giant or Chatham Islands forget-me-not *Myosotidium hortensia*, which is confined to the Chatham Islands to the east of New Zealand. It is a magnificent succulent perennial with a stout cylindrical rhizome which produces a crowded rosette of ovate to cordate, deeply grooved basal leaves 15-30 cm (6-12 in) long. The flowering stems may be 1 m (3.3 ft) or more tall, bearing oblong, stalkless stem leaves and topped by a dense inflorescence of sky-blue flowers. The saucer-shaped corollas vary from pale to dark blue and measure 12-15 mm (0.5-0.6 in) across, each having a short tube and five rounded lobes.

*Myosotidium hortensia* was formerly abundant along the rocky and sandy coasts of Chatham Island but has been seriously depleted in recent years as a result of grazing pressures from introduced animals. Today it thrives only in localities inaccessible to introduced pigs and sheep and is listed as a vulnerable species in the IUCN's Plant Red Data Book. It is considered to be one of the world's most threatened plants in its natural habitat, despite being quite common in cultivation.

**Boraginaceae; a single species**

## NASSAUVIA

This genus of shrubs and perennial herbs is distributed from the southern Andes into the subantarctic zone and contains two species found only in the Falkland Islands. *Nassauvia serpens* is typical of loose scree and boulder habitats in the montane areas, where its branching subterranean stems can reach lengths of over 2 m (6.6 ft). Where the stems surface they form tangled bushes up to 1 m (3.3 ft) in diameter, and are covered with overlapping, scalelike leaves. The terminal, club-shaped inflorescences are composed of small white flowers with violet stamens and give off a strong fragrance. *N. gaudichaudii* forms low cushions up to 1 m (3.3 ft) in diameter, usually in coastal regions on rocks or sand. The small leaves have spiny margins and the scented flowers are cream with brown stamens.

**Compositae; 40 species**

## OXYRIA

A genus of perennial herbs containing only two species. Mountain sorrel *Oxyria digyna* is confined to the Arctic and high mountain habitats as far south

*Pedicularis lapponica*

as central Spain, Corsica and Bulgaria, while the second species is found in California. The flowers consist of four sepal-like perianth segments arranged in two whorls of two, six stamens and two stigmas.

*Oxyria digyna* has distinctive kidney-shaped leaves on long stalks and loose clusters of tiny (3 mm (0.1 in)) reddish flowers which together form an elongated spike on the flowering stem. The fruit are broadly winged to aid wind dispersal of the seeds. The leaves of mountain sorrel are rich in vitamin C and can be used either in salads or for making soup, although they also contain oxalic acid which gives a rather sour taste.

**Polygonaceae; 2 species**

## PAPAVER

A genus of annual, biennial or perennial herbs which usually contain a milky juice (latex). The flowers have two free sepals and four entire petals which are crumpled in bud, both sepals and petals usually falling soon after the flowers open. The seed capsules

are cylindrical to almost spherical and open by means of pores below the stigmatic disc.

Over half of the 50 species in this genus, commonly known as poppies, are found in Europe, the remainder occurring as far afield as Asia, South Africa, Australia and western North America. A distinctive feature is that the flowers are nodding when in bud; the open flowers are upright. Many poppies contain alkaloids which are of considerable value in medicine.

Arctic poppies are among the most attractive of all species, their large, brightly coloured flowers being found even in the high Arctic. *Papaver dahlianum* (= *P. polare*) is one such species of the extreme north. It has an almost circumpolar distribution but is particularly frequent in the Soviet polar deserts and arctic Norway. *P. dahlianum* forms dense rosettes which send out strongly branching horizontal roots, each of which gives rise to a new plant.

Other arctic representatives include *P. lapponicum*, a very variable circumpolar species of open stony ground with yellow flowers, and its close relative *P.*

*Phyllodoce caerulea*

*radicatum*, which has yellow, white or pink flowers borne on long, slender stalks and is confined to northwest Europe (Iceland, the Faeroes, Norway and Sweden). *P. laestadianum* is another species with a restricted distribution, being confined to arctic Scandinavia.

North American arctic species include the white-flowered (rarely yellow) *P. walpolei* which occurs in arctic Alaska and the Yukon, as well as in a small adjacent area of Siberia, and *P. alboroseum*, a sprawling species with pale pinkish flowers and a similar distribution.

**Papaveraceae; 50 species**

### PARRYA

A genus of perennial herbs distributed across the northern temperate zone, the most widespread member of which is *Parrya nudicaulis*. This circumpolar species has long stout rhizomes, basal rosettes of spoon-shaped or linear-oblong leaves, sometimes with toothed margins, and flowering stems up to 40 cm (16 in) tall. The white or pink flowers have four petals 12-20 mm (0.5-0.8 in) long which develop into needle-like seed pods up to 6 cm (2.4 in) long. *Parrya nudicaulis* is one of the more attractive members of the Cruciferae and is a typical species of tundra herb slopes and marshy places, both American and Asian sides of the Bering Straits.

**Cruciferae; 25 species**

### PEDICULARIS

A genus of mainly perennial herbs, commonly known as louseworts, and found throughout the northern hemisphere, especially the mountains of central and eastern Asia, with a single species occurring in the Andes. They are brightly coloured hemiparasites, obtaining part of their food by photosynthesis and the remainder through parasitizing the roots of other plants. The leaves are usually alternate and are much divided, the lower stalked and the upper often stalkless. The flowers are arranged in terminal, bracteate spikes with tubular or bell-shaped calyces. The two-lipped corollas have beaked upper lips and three-lobed spreading lower lips and there are four stamens.

The generic name is derived from the Latin *pediculus*, meaning 'louse'. Both generic and common names refer to the belief that sheep eating these plants became diseased and covered with parasites (in fact, since many temperate louseworts grow in marshy habitats, sheep pastured in these areas are liable to contract foot diseases and flukes). In North America louseworts are also known as bumblebee flowers. The roots of many species are edible.

There are many arctic members of this genus: Lapland lousewort *Pedicularis lapponica*, is a circumpolar species with rounded clusters of fragrant, cream or pale yellow flowers which grows in heaths and dry tundra: hairy lousewort *P. hirsuta*, grows on damp, stony tundra, seashores and river banks on calcareous soils, and has distinctive rounded heads of pale pink flowers protected within a dense mass of woolly hairs deriving from the calyx and upper stem and leaves. *P. hirsuta* is a predominantly Eurasian species (extending to Greenland) and is probably parasitic on various species of tundra willow.

*P. oederi* is another more or less circumpolar arctic-alpine species which prefers wetter habitats, especially snow-flushes, and has a dense spike of yellow flowers each with a distinct crimson apex to the upper-lip. Flame-tipped lousewort *P. flammea*, found in the arctic region on both sides of the Atlantic, is very similar (except that most of the upper-lip is dark red), as is Labrador lousewort *P. labradorica*, an almost circumpolar species found in arctic Asia,
America and Greenland.

Another arctic representative is fernweed or Sudetan lousewort *P. sudetica*, a plant with short heads of bright crimson flowers which is widespread in the North American tundra and northern Asia, extending west to the Sudetan Highlands of Czechoslovakia. Woolly lousewort *P. lanata* is a densely hairy species with oblong spikes of bright pink flowers which grows in rocky tundra and mountains across Alaska and Canada, Greenland and northeast Asia. *P. capitata*, which is distinguished by its large cream, yellow or pink flowers, is common in the North American arctic and is also found in a few scattered localities in northeast Asia.

**Scrophulariaceae; over 350 species**

### PHYLLODOCE

A small genus of hardy evergreen shrubs of cold northern temperate, boreal and arctic regions. The virtually stalkless leaves are alternate and the five-lobed flowers are arranged in short, terminal spikes together with bracts similar to the foliage leaves. The sepals are almost free and the urn-shaped corolla falls soon after the flowers open.

Blue or mountain heath *Phyllodoce caerulea* is a dwarf circumpolar species with leathery leaves and lilac or pink-purple pendulous flowers. It is a common plant of tundra heaths, its range extending into the mountains of northwest Europe with isolated stations in Scotland and the Pyrenees. Blue heath is protected by law in Britain. Pink mountain heather *P. empetriformis* is found in the Alaskan tundra as well as in montane regions further south.

**Ericaceae; 6 or 7 species**

### PLEUROPHYLLUM

A tiny genus confined to New Zealand's subantarctic islands. *Pleurophyllum speciosum* is found only on

Macquarie Island, is another attractive species, but *P. criniferum*, which attains a height of almost 2 m (6.6 ft), has flowers which lack the conspicuous ray-florets.

**Compositae; 3 species**

### POTENTILLA

A large genus of perennial, rarely annual or biennial, herbs or small shrubs of northern temperate, boreal and arctic regions with a few representatives in temperate zones of the southern hemisphere. The leaves are digitate, ternate or pinnate and the flowers are either solitary or arranged in clusters. Each flower has an epicalyx topped by five (rarely four or six) sepals and petals and 10-30 stamens. Plants of this genus are commonly known as cinquefoils in Europe and fivefingers in North America. Many *Potentilla* species are found in arctic and subarctic regions.

Two circumpolar species more or less confined to the Arctic are arctic cinquefoil *Potentilla hyparctica* and *P. pulchella*, both of which are dwarf, yellow-flowered species of damp heaths, fellfield and scree. Another yellow-flowered species, *P. hookerana*, is almost circumpolar in distribution, occurring from arctic Asia to Greenland, but is absent from Europe. Auckland and Campbell Islands. It has broad, hairy plantain-like leaves, white woolly beneath, topped by a magnificent spray of purple flowers, each some

4 cm (1.6 in) in diameter, which consist of both disc- and ray-florets. *P. hookeri*, which is also found on

Eurasian arctic cinquefoils include snow cinquefoil *P. nivea* and the very similar *P. chamissonis*, both of which have yellow flowers and three-lobed leaves. Alpine cinquefoil *P. crantzii*, with five-lobed leaves, is a lime loving species of northern and arctic Eurasia, also found as far south as the mountains of south and central Europe. It is distinguished by its heart-shaped yellow petals, each of which often has an orange spot at the base. *P. sericea* of south-facing slopes on the Soviet islands of Novaya Zemlya and Vaygach is one of the most attractive of all cinquefoils, its golden flowers borne on stems up to 40 cm (16 in) tall contrasting strongly with its feathery grey-green foliage.

Two-flowered cinquefoil *P. biflora* and one-flowered cinquefoil *P. uniflora* both have shiny yellow flowers and are found in rocky habitats across the North American polar region and into northeastern Siberia. The three-toothed cinquefoil *P. tridentata* is a white-flowered species of dry, rocky or sandy habitats from northeastern Canada to Greenland.

**Rosaceae; about 500 species**

### PRIMULA

A large genus of perennial herbs, commonly known as primroses. Most plants of this genus are found in

the northern hemisphere, including Ethiopia and tropical Asian mountains, but several species occur across the equator in Java, New Guinea and cold temperate regions of South America. The leaves are confined in a basal rosette and the flowers are usually arranged in umbels but are occasionally solitary. The bell-shaped or cylindrical calyx is five-toothed and the corolla consists of a cylindrical tube opening out into five spreading lobes.

Dusty miller *Primula magellanica* (classified by some authors as a variety of the bird's-eye primrose *P. farinosa*, a species of northern temperate regions of the Old World) is distinguished by its spoon-shaped farinose leaves and hemispherical clusters of small, white flowers with yellow 'eyes'. It grows in short turf and dwarf shrub heath in the Falkland Islands.

Pixie eyes or wedge-leaved primrose, *P. cuneifolia* has large pink flowers with yellow centres and fleshy leaves. It is found in arctic Alaska, the Yukon and adjacent areas of northeast Asia where it grows in damp grassland, especially in flushes emanating from melting snow fields. Northern primrose *P. borealis* is a similar species with a comparable distribution.

A circumpolar arctic species is *P. stricta*, a small primrose characterized by lax clusters of pink-purple flowers, while the rare, pale lilac-flowered (sometimes

*Potentilla pulchella*

white) Greenland primrose *P. egaliksensis* has a more restricted distribution, growing in moist tundra grasslands near the sea in Iceland, Greenland, Canada and Alaska.

**Primulaceae; 400 species**

### PRINGLEA

The sole representative of this genus is the Kerguelen cabbage *Pringlea antiscorbutica*, which is found only on Kerguelen and Crozet Islands in the subantarctic zone of the southern Indian Ocean. It is a giant cabbage-like plant with huge leathery leaves over 40 cm (16 in) in diameter and a spiked inflorescence of tiny petal-less flowers. The absence of flying insects on these islands means that the plant need not waste energy in producing vivid-coloured or scented flowers; the species is probably wind pollinated, although flowers with between one and four tiny, pinkish petals have occasionally been found on plants growing in shady conditions, apparently visited by thrips. Like several other subantarctic species (see Lyallia), the Kerguelen cabbage is thought to be a relic of the Tertiary flora of these islands.

The leaves of the Kerguelen cabbage are edible and easily digestible, but it was undoubtedly its effectiveness in preventing scurvy which rendered it so valuable to sailors on their way to Australia from the South Atlantic.

**Cruciferae; a single species**

### PSEUDORCHIS

A tiny orchid genus which combines the genera *Leucorchis* and *Polybactrum* and has a range extending from eastern North America to Europe. Plants in this genus have palmately lobed tubers, leafy stems and spurred flowers arranged in a dense spike. The perianth segments converge to form a helmet and the lip is three-lobed, the lateral lobes shorter and narrower than the central lobe. The flowers are strongly scented to attract pollinating insects such as moths and butterflies.

The small white orchid *Pseudorchis albida* is a Eurasian species which occurs from Greenland to western Siberia, venturing northwards into subarctic and arctic herb slopes, heaths and willow scrub. The tiny (2-3 mm (0.1 in)) green-yellow or white flowers form a cylindrical spike 3-7 cm (1.2-2.8 in) long. The somewhat smaller Frivald's frog orchid *P. frivaldii* has white or pinkish flowers and is confined to montane pastures in the Balkan peninsula.

**Orchidaceae; 3 species**

### RANUNCULUS

A large, almost cosmopolitan genus of annual or perennial herbs distributed throughout the temperate and polar regions of both hemispheres with representatives in the tropical mountains. The flowers may be solitary or in loose clusters. The 3-7 perianth segments are sepaloid and the white, yellow or reddish 'petals' are in fact honey-leaves, up to 12 in number or sometimes absent.

Over half the species in this genus are found in Europe where they are commonly known as buttercups. There are many of arctic species and a few antarctic ones, including *Ranunculus pinguis*, a giant, golden-flowered buttercup with broad, glossy leaves. Glacier crowfoot *R. glacialis* occurs in the arctic regions of eastern Europe, western Asia and Greenland, as well as in mountains as far south as Spain's Sierra Nevada, but is never found very far from snow patches or glaciers. It differs from the majority of arctic buttercups in having white flowers often flushed with pink or purple.

Arctic circumpolar buttercups include *R. hyperboreus*, which grows in very wet marshes and tundra pools and has small yellow flowers, each with only three petals, and the snow buttercup *R. nivalis*, a robust species with kidney-shaped leaves, larger, cup-shaped yellow flowers (15 mm (0.6 in) in diameter) and spreading, roughly hairy sepals. As its name suggests it is often found in flushes emanating from snow patches. The sulphur-coloured buttercup *R. sulphureus*, which favours marshes and mossy bogs in the most extreme arctic conditions, is very similar to *R. nivalis*.

Common yellow-flowered species of arctic Eurasia and Greenland include Lapland buttercup *R. lapponicus*, which prefers wet habitats, pygmy buttercup *R. pygmaeus*, a tiny, perennial arctic-alpine species with small, greenish yellow flowers which is also found in the mountains of central Europe; and northern buttercup *R. affinis*, characterized by its deeply divided basal leaves. Other species have a more restricted distribution, such as the Spitzbergen buttercup *R. spitzbergensis*, which is found only in the Fjord district of Spitzbergen, and *R. sabinii* which grows in the northernmost vegetated regions of Siberia, Greenland and the Canadian arctic archipelago.

*Ranunculus lapponicus*

*Saxifraga caespitosa*

North American arctic buttercups include the Cooley buttercup *R. cooleyae*, a species confined to arctic coastal habitats in northwest America with unmistakable many petalled, large yellow flowers; *R. eschscholtzii*, also found in scattered localities in Siberia, *R. cymbalaria*, a plant with small, bright yellow flowers and kidney-shaped leaves which is also naturalized in Europe, and *R. pedatifidus*, also found on Spitzbergen.

### Ranunculaceae; about 250 species

#### SAGINA

A genus of small annual or perennial herbs, commonly known as pearlworts, found throughout the northern temperate and arctic regions, extending into the tropical mountains. In some species the petals are absent, while in others there are four or five minute, white petals.

Arctic or alpine pearlwort *Sagina saginoides* has stems up to 7 cm (2.8 in) in height, each bearing a solitary flower 4-5 mm (0.2 in) in diameter. This species occurs in arctic and subarctic Eurasia and in mountains south to Iberia and central Greece. The flowers of the circumpolar snow pearlwort *S. intermedia* have four petals, whereas those of tufted pearlwort *S. caespitosa* have five. The latter is essentially a plant of montane regions of Greenland and northern Eurasia, descending to the lowlands only in the arctic zone.

### Caryophyllaceae; about 25 species

#### SAXIFRAGA

A genus of mostly perennial herbs, sometimes woody at the base, and known as saxifrages or rockfoils. They are cosmopolitan in distribution but are especially diverse in temperate and cold regions of the northern hemisphere. The flowers have five sepals and petals and 10 stamens and are usually arranged in clusters, although in some species they are solitary in the leaf axils.

Saxifrages are is essentially mountain plants, but more than 20 species are also found in the Arctic, many of which have a classic arctic-alpine distribution. The generic name is derived from the Latin *saxum* ('rock') and *frangere* ('to break'): a good indication of the crevice-hugging habits of many species. The predominant flower colours are white, cream or yellow.

One of the best known of all arctic-alpine plants is the purple saxifrage *Saxifraga oppositifolia*, also known as French knot moss, which is unusual in the genus in having vivid pink-purple flowers. Its tiny lime-encrusted leaves are arranged in pairs on stems which form mats or cushions and the small flowers are among the first to appear at the onset of favourable conditions. Another wide-ranging arctic species with lime-secreting pits on its leaves is livelong saxifrage *S. paniculata*, although the bluish green foliage is more typically organized as hemispherical basal rosettes. The petals are white or cream, sometimes decorated with small red dots.

Saxifrages with yellow flowers are not uncommon in the arctic tundra, typical species including the

*Saxifraga groenlandica*

aptly named yellow saxifrage *S. aizoides*, a Eurasian arctic-alpine with bright yellow-orange, often red-spotted flowers; yellow marsh saxifrage *S. hirculus*, an almost circumpolar species of bogs and wetlands in both the tundra and mountains further south; and thyme-leaved saxifrage *S. serpyllifolia*, an arctic-alpine plant confined to eastern Siberia and western America. The whiplash saxifrage or spiderplant *S. flagellaris* is another yellow-flowered species, although more distinctive is its method of vegetative reproduction: a series of overground 'whips' extends in many directions from the basal rosette, each producing a new plantlet at its extremity. It grows in scattered localities in North America, Siberia and on Spitzbergen, but the very closely related *S. platysepala* has a circumpolar high arctic range.

Spotted saxifrage *S. bronchialis* is an American-northeastern Siberian arctic-alpine species with pale yellow or cream flowers, while the spiked saxifrage *S. spicata*, with pale greenish yellow petals and large heart-shaped leaves, is found only in Alaska and a small adjacent area of the Yukon Territory. Not unlike the latter in having a spike of flowers and broad basal leaves is stiff stem or rusty saxifrage *S. hieracifolia*, an almost circumpolar arctic-alpine species distinguished by its tiny greenish red flowers; it typically grows in moist meadows and snow flushes.

Several arctic saxifrages depend on the production of bulbils rather than sexual reproduction by means of flowers. The flowering shoots of nodding or drooping saxifrage *S. cernua* often bear a single terminal flower, beneath which clusters of reddish bulbils are produced in the axils of the stem leaves. Despite the occasional flower, seeds are unknown in this circumpolar species. Drooping saxifrage is also common in mountains to the south of the arctic region, including those of the British Isles, although here it is a rare plant which is protected by law. The circumpolar arctic-alpine *S. foliolosa*, like *S. cernua*, produces a single terminal flower and bulbils.

*Saxifraga cernua*

White flowers, sometimes tinged or veined with pink, are produced by the majority of arctic saxifrages, including alpine saxifrage *S. nivalis* and slender saxifrage *S. tenuis*, both of which are stout-stemmed circumpolar species with leaves confined to a basal rosette. Species with finely divided foliage and white flowers include mossy saxifrage or Dovedale moss *S. hypnoides* which is confined to northwest Europe, including Iceland, and three-toothed saxifrage *S. tricuspidata*, an American species with spiny leaves also found in Greenland. Starry saxifrage *S. stellaris* has attractive white petals decorated with yellow spots at the base and contrasting pink anthers. Preferring wet rock alongside mountain streams it is found only in lowland areas in the Arctic.

Three more widespread circumpolar species are tufted saxifrage *S. caespitosa*, with dull white flowers, highland saxifrage *S. rivularis*, with pink-tinged white petals, and the very similar *S. hyperborea*, in which the whole plant, including the flowers, has a reddish tinge. Tufted saxifrage is protected by law in Britain, where it is on the southern edge of its range.

Yellow saxifrage *S. aizoides* is the foodplant of the larvae of the small apollo butterfly *Apollo phoebus*, as well as several moth species, including the red carpet *Xanthorhoe munitata*, the yellow-ringed carpet *Entephria flavicinctata* and the northern rustic *Standfussiana lucernea*.

**Saxifragaceae; about 300 species**

### SIBBALDIA

A small genus of perennial herbs distributed across the northern temperate and arctic regions. The best known species is *Sibbaldia procumbens*, a sprawling perennial with distinctive hairy, three-lobed leaves arranged in rosettes. The unmistakable flowers are arranged in a dense cluster, each having 4-6 tiny yellow petals (1.5-2 mm (0.1 in)) which are much shorter than the leaf-like sepals and five stamens. *S. procumbens* grows in tundra herb slopes and early snow patches in Greenland, Iceland and arctic regions of Fennoscandia and Asia, as well as in montane grassland from the British Isles (up to 1,300 m (4,300 ft)) to central and southern Europe (to 3,200 m (10,500 ft)).

Mountain plants in this genus include *S. purpurea*, a silvery haired species with red-purple flowers growing up to 5,300 m (17,400 ft) in the mountains from Kashmir to Bhutan, and the yellow-flowered *S. cuneata*, found at altitudes in excess of 3,000 m (8,900 ft) in the mountains of central Asia, especially Kashmir. *S. parviflora* thrives in the mountains of western and central Asia, extending eastwards to southern Yugoslavia.

**Rosaceae; 8 species**

### SMELOWSKIA

A small genus named after the eighteenth-century Russian botanist T. Smelowsky, which has a marked arctic-alpine distribution across eastern Asia and western North America. The best known species is *S. calycina*, an attractive plant with globular white, cream or lavender clusters of four-petalled flowers arising from a rosette of grey-green leaves. It is confined to the Brooks Range region of Alaska and the adjacent Siberian coast, where it grows in exposed sites on gravelly ground.

**Cruciferae; 6 species**

### STELLARIA

A cosmopolitan genus of annual or perennial herbs commonly known as stitchworts, chickweeds and starworts. The flowers have five sepals, five or fewer (occasionally absent) white or greenish, deeply bifid petals and up to 10 stamens. The flowers usually have nectaries.

In the Arctic most stitchworts are creeping or tufted perennial plants with white flowers. Several species have a more or less circumpolar distribution, including *Stellaria ciliatosepala*, although it is absent from most of Europe, *S. crassipes*, a high arctic species with solitary flowers, and *S. humifusa*, a particularly common plant along the arctic and subarctic coastline.

Long-stalked stitchwort *S. longipes* has bluish green foliage and upright flowering stems each bearing many flowers. It grows on mossy heaths throughout arctic Asia and America, including Greenland, although its European distribution does not extend west of Spitzbergen. *S. calycantha*, which usually has solitary flowers, is common in arctic and subarctic Europe.

**Caryophyllaceae; 120 species**

### TOFIELDIA

A genus of tufted rhizomatous perennial herbs native to northern temperate and arctic regions and also occurring in South America. The small flowers are arranged in terminal heads and have six spreading or erect petaloid perianth segments, six stamens and three free carpels with short, persistent styles.

The Scottish asphodel *Tofieldia pusilla* has dense rosettes of sword-shaped leaves and leafless flowering stems which may reach 20 cm (8 in) but are usually shorter. Between 5 and 10 white or greenish flowers are clustered near the tip. Despite its name the Scottish asphodel is a circumpolar species, particularly favouring bogs and other wet places.

The only other arctic member of the genus is the northern asphodel *T. coccinea*, which has purple flowers and is found in Siberia, North America and Greenland. False asphodel *T. glutinosa*, with white flowers in a dense interrupted spike, is a plant of wet meadows across Canada, extending to California, Idaho and Wyoming and occurring up to the tree line in the Rocky Mountains. Another species of high altitudes is Tofield's asphodel *T. calyculata*, which has elongated spikes of yellow (rarely reddish) flowers and occurs locally in the Pyrenees, Alps, Apennines and in Scandinavia.

**Liliaceae; 17 species**

*Stellaria humifusa*

# CHAPTER THREE

# BOREAL FORESTS

Boreal forests cover some 10 per cent of the Earth's total land surface. They form an almost unbroken ring around the northern hemisphere between latitudes 45°N and 70°N, between the frozen plains of the Arctic tundra to the north and the rich temperate forests to the south. There is no equivalent belt in the southern hemisphere only because no land exists at these latitudes.

The dominant plants are conifers, which are among the most ancient and primitive tree species in the world and uniquely adapted to the harsh climatic conditions prevalent in such high latitudes. Conifers are evergreen trees, with needlelike leaves that are shed a few at a time, and consequently cast a deep shade throughout the year. In addition, the low level of biological activity in cold climates mean that breakdown of the leaf litter is very slow, resulting in low nutrient levels, leached, acid soils and the build up of a thick layer of undecomposed needles on the forest floor which deters germination of seeds.

The plants of the forest floor are therefore restricted to those species which can tolerate low light levels all year round and can also cope with a short growing season and subzero winter temperatures, although deep drifts of snow provide some protection in the winter. Lichens and mosses are the most characteristic plants, but a few flowering plants can survive in the heart of the boreal forests. These are predominantly evergreen perennial herbs and small shrubs, including many members of the Ericaceae. Many plants opt to reproduce vegetatively since insect pollinators are rather thin on the ground, while the majority of those that do flower produce white or near-white blooms which stand out against the dark background in order to attract insects. Plants lacking the green pigment chlorophyll are also found (e.g. Monotropaceae). These plants (known as saprophytes) cannot make their own food through photosynthesis, but instead take in nutrients from the leaf litter. To do this the plant roots grow in intimate association with soil fungi which break down the organic matter of the leaf litter into a form that can be absorbed by the plant. Other plants with chlorophyll (notably members of the wintergreen family: Pyrolaceae) also commonly gain some of their food saprophytically in this way.

Facing page: Indian paintbrush, cow parsley and
Nootka lupin.

*Calypso bulbosa*

## ACHLYS

A tiny genus found only in western North America and Japan. Vanilla leaf *Achlys triphylla*, sometimes also known as deer-foot is easily recognized by its slender paired stems one of which bears a single leaf with three broad, fan-shaped leaflets with blunt teeth at the tips, and the other a narrow spike of small white flowers. These flowers have neither sepals nor petals, consisting solely of 6-13 conspicuous white stamens. *Achlys triphylla* grows in patches in the understorey of the humid coniferous forests of the Pacific northwest region of North America, south to northern California.

**Berberidaceae; 2 species**

## ACTAEA

This small genus of perennial herbs, commonly known as baneberries, is confined to northern temperate and boreal regions. The leaves are large and divided, the flowers small and white and the clusters of attractive berries may be glossy black, red, pink or white. These fruits are poisonous to humans, possibly affecting the heart, although some birds can gorge themselves without apparent ill effect.

*Actaea arguta* grows to almost 1 m (3.3 ft) in height in moist coniferous woodland throughout western North America, from Alaska to California and New Mexico. The flowers are arranged in dense racemes at the ends of the branches or in the leaf axils, the creamy white petals and sepals dropping soon after the flower opens, leaving masses of long white stamens. Local names for *A. arguta* include snakeberry and snakeroot, as the antispasmodic properties of the rootstock were once considered valuable in the treatment of rattlesnake bites. Both this species and *A. erythrocarpa* produce red berries.

The very similar red baneberry *A. rubra* of eastern North America may not be a distinct species from *A.*

*arguta*. White baneberry *A. pachypoda*, sometimes called doll's-eyes because its shiny white berries resemble the china eyes of Victorian dolls, is native to the forests of the eastern half of North America. The black-berried *A. spicata* is a foetid Eurasian baneberry of limestone woods. It was formerly known as herb Christopher, the root being used to treat skin diseases and asthma, although black snakeroot and bugbane are other common names.

**Ranunculaceae; 8 species**

## AMERORCHIS

Considered by some to belong to the much larger genus *Orchis*, the round-leaved orchid *Amerorchis rotundifolia* is typically a plant of northern damp woodlands in the boreal and low arctic zone of North America, from central Alaska across Canada and into Greenland. Each flowering spike bears a single round leaf at ground level and between 5 and 10 exquisite rose-coloured flowers, each with a prominent whitish lip spotted with red or purple spots, hence its other common name of fly-specked orchid. It is often found growing with another orchid *Cypripedium passerinum*.

**Orchidaceae; a single species**

## ANDROMEDA

Confined to northern temperate and boreal regions, there is some argument as to whether this genus contains one or two species. Marsh andromeda or bog rosemary *Andromeda polifolia* is a dwarf evergreen shrub with an almost circumpolar range, while the somewhat taller *A. glaucophylla*, which is confined to North America, may in fact merit only subspecific status.

*A. polifolia* has narrow, dark green leaves with inrolled margins, silvery hairy beneath, and terminal clusters of drooping, pink, urn-shaped flowers which fade to white with age. The flowers are pollinated by bumblebees and butterflies which are attracted to nectar secreted at the base of the ovary. Marsh andromeda prefers wet, acid habitats and is as much at home on moorland as in the dark forests of the Eurasian taiga. It is also found in the Arctic and in montane regions as far south as the Alps and Carpathians. The leaves and twigs of this ericaceous plant were formerly used for tanning leather in the USSR and it is a typical foodplant of the rosy marsh moth *Eugraphe subrosea*.

**Ericaceae; 1 or 2 species**

## ARUNCUS

A genus of one species which because of the plant's very variable form, has often been regarded as several different species and listed variously as *Aruncus sylvestris*, *A. vulgaris* and *A. dioicus*. The generic name comes from the Greek *aryngos* ('a goat's beard'), which probably refers to the long clusters of flowers and has given the plant its common name. The genus is closely related to *Spiraea* and is widely cultivated.

Goatsbeard is a tall perennial, growing to a height of over 2 m (6.6 ft), with spreading pinnate leaves topped by tall sprays of tiny whitish, unisexual flowers, the sexes occurring on separate plants. The flowers, which are about 4 mm (0.25 in) in diameter, and have five sepals and five petals; the male flowers have numerous stamens and the female, three pistils. *Aruncus dioicus* occurs in moist, shady conditions, especially montane coniferous forests in North America, eastern Asia, including Korea and Japan, and other scattered localities in Asia and Europe, including the Pyrenees.

**Rosaceae; a single species**

Muskeg, Alaska, USA.

## CALLUNA

The single species in this genus, *Calluna vulgaris*, is found across Europe, from Iceland to Turkey, and Asia Minor and is naturalized in eastern North America. It is a typical plant of the shrub layer in coniferous woodlands from the northern boreal forests to the pines of the Mediterranean. Where forest cover has been removed *Calluna vulgaris* dominates large expanses of the secondary communities of heaths and moors, which are maintained as such by grazing and periodic burning.

*Calluna vulgaris*, commonly known as ling, heather or Scottish heather, is an evergreen shrub which may reach 1 m (3.3 ft) in height in forests, although it is usually much shorter in open habitats. The leaves are minute, clasping the stem in four rows, while the pale pinkish purple flowers are arranged in short leafy spikes. In the southern part of its range the flowers are pollinated by bees and other insects, although further north they are wind pollinated.

In Scotland honey derived predominantly from *Calluna* 'fields' is a major constituent of the liqueur Drambuie. In some places ling was once used to flavour ale and a yellow dye produced from its bark was formerly used for colouring wool. *C. vulgaris* also provides food for sheep and grouse and material for brooms, thatching and basket work. Robert Burns was supposed to have drunk a 'moorland tea' based on heather tops mixed with the dried leaves of bilberry, blackberry, speedwell, thyme and wild strawberry.

Ling is also a favourite foodplant of the larvae of many northern moths, including the oak eggar *Lasiocampa quercus*, the pale eggar *Trichiura crataegi*, the fox moth *Macrothylacina rubi*, the emperor moth *Saturnia pavonia*, the ling pug *Eupithecia goossensiata*, the common heath *Ematurga atomaria*, the true lover's knot *Lycophotia porphyrea* and the heath rustic *Xestia agathina*.

**Ericaceae; a single species**

## CALYPSO

The single member of the genus, the calypso orchid *Calypso bulbosa*, is a circumboreal terrestrial orchid, almost completely confined to damp mossy places in the deep shade of coniferous forests. The genus is appropriately named after the beautiful Greek nymph Kalypso of Homer's *Odyssey*, who charmed Ulysses into staying on her secluded island for seven years on his return from Troy.

These small orchids rarely exceed 20 cm (8 in) in height, producing a solitary elliptical stalked leaf and a single exquisite flower, which is bright pink with a purple-spotted, slipper-like lip, from which the plant derives its other common name of fairy slipper. The vanilla-scented flowers are pollinated by bees and appear soon after the snow melts in the boreal forests of northern Scandinavia, northern Eurasia to North America.

**Orchidaceae; a single species**

## CHAMAEDAPHNE

The single species of this genus, leatherleaf *Chamaedaphne calyculata*, has a circumboreal distribution, growing mainly in wet coniferous forests and bogs. The generic name is derived from a combination of the Greek words *chamai* ('on the ground') and *daphne* ('laurel'). Leatherleaf is a dwarf evergreen shrub, reaching a maximum height of around 50 cm (20 in) and, like many ericaceous plants, has drooping urn-shaped flowers, which are white and form a one-sided leafy spike. The elliptical leaves were formerly used like tea by the North American Indians.

**Ericaceae; a single species**

## CHIMAPHILA

A small genus found in Eurasia and northern and tropical regions of America. The generic name is derived from the Greek *cheima* ('winter'), and *philos* ('to love'), no doubt in reference to the plant's evergreen habit.

Umbellate wintergreen *Chimaphila umbellata* is a dwarf rhizomatous shrub with vertical flowering stems up to 30 cm (12 in) tall and distinguished from all other wintergreens by its densely leafy stems. It has toothed leathery leaves and terminal umbels of 3-7 nodding pinkish flowers, and is more or less restricted to coniferous woodlands in northern Eurasia and North America.

Umbellate wintergreen is the commonest of all wintergreens in the Rocky Mountains, where it is variously known as prince's pine, pipsissewa or waxflower. The local name of pipsissewa is thought to originate from the Cree Indian word *pipisisikweu* ('it breaks it into small pieces'): a decoction of the boiled stems and leaves was formerly used to break up kidney stones or gallstones, as well as for bladder problems and the treatment of rheumatism.

*C. menziesii*, known locally as little pipsissewa, is a less common species of coniferous forests from British Columbia to southern California, while spotted wintergreen *C. maculata*, named for its mottled green and white leaves, is a plant of dry woodlands in the eastern half of North America.

**Pyrolaceae; 4 or 5 species**

## CIRCAEA

Commonly known as enchanter's nightshades, these perennial herbs are characteristic of northern temperate and arctic regions. The genus is named

*Calluna vulgaris*

*Cypripedium reginae*

where the young leaves were traditionally used as a pot herb and in salads. A less common species is white clintonia *C. umbellulata*, which has many erect white flowers and blackish berries, while *C. andrewsiana* has terminal clusters of rose-pink flowers.

**Liliaceae; 5 species**

### CORALLORHIZA

A genus of saprophytic orchids lacking chlorophyll, widely distributed across the northern temperate and boreal zones. Instead of obtaining their energy by photosynthesis, a fungus associated with the rhizomes helps these plants to absorb nutrients from the decomposing litter of the forest floor. Their common name is coralroots, a literal translation of the generic name which describes the much-divided rhizomes.

Coralroots have long been known for their powerful medicinal properties, although their scarcity and therefore high price prevent their being more commonly used. A decoction of the powdered root is of value in the treatment of pleurisy, typhus fever and other inflammatory diseases since it promotes perspiration without any excitatory side effects. It has also been used as a sedative.

Three species are especially typical of boreal forests: early or pale coralroot *Corallorhiza trifida*, striped coralroot *C. striata* and spotted coralroot *C. maculata*, the smallest and least conspicuous of which is *C. trifida*. This species has pale yellowish, nearly leafless stems, each of which bears a few flowers the same colour as the stems, but with a whitish lip. The plant has a circumboreal distribution across North America, Greenland and Eurasia, and also occurs in some tundra regions. In North America its range extends to the forests of New Mexico, and it also occurs sporadically in dune slacks and montane areas across much of Europe, south to the Pyrenees, the southern Apennines and northern Greece.

*C. maculata* has darker stems, frequently tinted purplish or reddish brown, and flowers easily identified by their purple-spotted, white lips. This is a much larger plant, sometimes reaching 80 cm (32 in) in height. It is the commonest coralroot in North America, occurring from Guatemala to Canada. *C. striata* is similar but has larger buff-coloured flowers with distinctive purple stripes. It occurs in deep shade in North American coniferous forests from Mexico to Canada.

Other North American species include Wister's coralroot *C. wisteriana* which flowers from March to May before any of the other species, and late or autumn coralroot *C. odontorhiza* which is the last to flower, its tiny 5 mm (0.25 in) flowers still blooming in October.

**Orchidaceae; 12 species**

### CORNUS

A wide-ranging genus of northern temperate and boreal regions, especially in North America and Asia with a few South American and African representatives. These plants are commonly known as dogwoods, the name deriving from the skewers, or 'dogs' that were formerly made from the wood. *Cornus canadensis* and *C. suecica* are herbs, other species being shrubs or trees.

Canadian dwarf dogwood *C. canadensis*, also known as bunchberry or ground dogwood, is common in the birch and spruce forests of Alaska, Canada and Greenland, extending south to the coniferous forests of California and Virginia. It is a rhizomatous herbaceous perennial with erect, four-angled flowering stems up to 20 cm (8 in) tall, bearing several pairs of opposite leaves and a flat-topped cluster of tiny, dark purple flowers at the tip. Each cluster is surrounded by four white or pinkish oval bracts which gives the appearance of a single large flower. In the autumn the flowers give rise to a dense cluster of bright red fruits, hence the name bunchberry, which are much favoured by white-tailed deer and

after the Greek enchantress Circe, who possessed magical powers and a vast knowledge of poisonous plants, with which she was reputedly able to turn men into swine.

Despite its specific name, the dwarf or alpine enchanter's nightshade *Circaea alpina* is in fact typical of the boreal forests of northern Eurasia and North America, although it is also found further south in the mountains of Central Europe, California and New Mexico. Dwarf enchanter's nightshade is distinguished by its several pairs of heart-shaped leaves and terminal racemes of tiny white or pinkish flowers, each of which has only two petals and is less than 3 mm (0.1 in) in diameter.

Other shade-loving members of this genus are more at home in temperate woodlands, including common enchanter's nightshade *C. lutetiana*, a Eurasian and North African plant, and *C. quadrisulcata* which occurs in damp shady woods in eastern North America.

**Onagraceae; 7 species**

### CLINTONIA

A small genus of bulbous plants, with four species in

North America and a single eastern Asian representative *Clintonia udensis* in the Himalayas. The plants are generally known as woodlilies, and the flowers are typically funnel-shaped, white, pink or carmine and arranged in terminal long-stalked umbels (rarely solitary). The generic name honours De Witt Clinton, a prominent naturalist and a former Governor of New York.

Queencup or bride's bonnet *Clintonia uniflora* occurs in moist coniferous woods from Alaska to northern California, and is especially common in the Rockies. It has bright green basal leaves which shelter a stem topped by a single (rarely two) white flower(s) about 3 cm (1.2 in) across. Another common name for this plant is beadlily, a reference to its globular blue fruits which, despite being mildly poisonous, are a favourite food of the ruffed grouse. Vegetative reproduction by the spreading, underground stems produces extensive patches of queencups on the forest floor.

The bluebead lily *C. borealis* has 3-6 drooping, yellow-green, bell-shaped flowers which give rise to clusters of beautiful blue berries. It is found in the coniferous forests of the southern Appalachians, ruffed grouse.

A very similar species is dwarf cornel *C. suecica*, a circumboreal plant of acid soils in coniferous forests and open moors which also grows in dry or rocky places in the Arctic, as well as in Holland and Japan. The red, globular, fleshy fruits of both species are collected by the Eskimos and various Indian tribes for winter consumption. They have an excellent reputation as a tonic for the appetite, so much so that in Scotland dwarf cornel is known as *lus-a-chraois* (plant of gluttony).

**Cornaceae; about 45 species**

### CYPRIPEDIUM

A genus of terrestrial orchids widespread across the temperate and warm regions of the northern hemisphere, usually in woodland habitats. The flowers of all species have the characteristic inflated bulbous lip associated with a complex pollination mechanism, which has given them the name lady's slipper orchids or moccasin flowers. The generic name is derived from the Latin for Venus' slipper.

*Cypripedium calceolus* is one of the most distinctive plants in this genus, with its curiously twisted reddish brown or greenish sepals above the pale yellow lip. It grows in damp, base-rich woodland, especially the coniferous forests of North America where it is found from Alaska and the Yukon south into the Rockies, but it also occurs in coniferous and deciduous woodland in northern Asia and Europe and in montane habitats further south. Although *Cypripedium calceolus* was once widespread in limestone woodlands in northern England, persistent over-collection has reduced the British range this beautiful orchid of to a single woodland in Yorkshire, where it is strictly protected. Studies of this species have revealed that the plants must mature for some 16 years before flowering.

Several other species are found in the boreal forests of the world, notably northern lady's slipper *C. passerinum*, a fragrant, pale-flowered orchid typical of boggy woods in Alaska and northwest Canada. The smaller circumboreal pink lady's slipper *C. guttatum* occurs in birch, coniferous and mixed woodland in the extreme northern regions of America, across much of Siberia, western and central USSR and Japan. Its solitary flowers have bold brown or

*Cornus canadensis*

reddish purple markings on both lip and sepals.

Pink lady's slipper *C. acaule*, one of North America's largest native orchids, is typical of the pine forests of the east ranging from Canada southwards to South Carolina, Georgia and Alabama; showy lady's slipper *C. reginae* and small white lady's slipper *C. candidum* both prefer swamps and damp woods on limestone over a similar geographic range. *C. macranthos* has pink flowers and grows in the pine and birch woods and clearings of central USSR, Siberia and further east into northern China and Korea.

**Orchidaceae; about 35 species**

### EMPETRUM

A tiny genus of dwarf, evergreen, sprawling or low-growing shrubs with a wide distribution throughout the cool temperate regions of both hemispheres. *Empetrum rubrum*, locally known as diddle-dee, is found in open habitats on some subantarctic islands, notably the Falkland Islands and Tristan da Cunha, as well as in the southern Andes.

The northern temperate, boreal and arctic species is crowberry *E. nigrum*, (also called crakeberry or

*Cornus canadensis*

curlew berry), a spreading, mat-forming evergreen shrub up to 70 cm (28 in) tall. In the subspecies *E. nigrum* ssp. *nigrum* the inconspicuous flowers are usually unisexual (either male or female), although found on the same plant, but those of *E. nigrum* ssp. *hermaphroditum* are hermaphrodite. The black globular fruits are edible, each containing several stone-like seeds, and are used to make jellies and preserves as well as providing a significant part of the winter diet of many birds.

Crowberry is a common understorey shrub in boreal forests and is also frequent in subarctic heaths and mires in North America, Greenland and Eurasia. It is found as far south as the Pyrenees, Alps and central Apennines, where it grows in montane moorlands and the drier parts of blanket bogs. The foliage is eaten by the caterpillars of various moths including the Scotch burnet *Zygaena exulans*, the weaver's wave *Idaea contiguaria*, the northern dart *Xestia alpicola* and the broad-bordered white underwing *Anarta melanopa*.

**Empetraceae; 2 species**

### GOODYERA

A cosmopolitan genus of terrestrial or semiepiphytic orchids, commonly known as jewel orchids because of their highly patterned leaves. The small, white, dingy pink or pale green flowers are arranged in terminal spikes above rosettes of tesselated leaves.

One species is particularly associated with boreal forests. Creeping lady's-tresses *Goodyera repens* has a long creeping rhizome and branching runner which give rise to rosettes of dark green basal leaves, netted with light-coloured veins. From each rosette arises a slender slightly twisted and markedly one-sided spike of 12-25 tiny, fragrant, creamy white flowers.

Creeping lady's-tresses occurs mainly in shady coniferous and mixed woodland, where it prefers mossy conditions in which the rhizomes and runners can thread their way easily through the humus. It has a more or less circumboreal distribution, in Eurasia extending from the Pyrenees and Himalayas into the taiga, the British Isles and Japan. The American representative of this species belongs to the subspecies *G. repens ophioides*, which is known locally as the lesser rattlesnake or net-leaved plantain.

*Goodyera repens*

Other forest plants in this genus are rattlesnake plantain *G. pubescens*, chequered rattlesnake plantain *G. tesselata* and green-leaved rattlesnake plantain *G. oblongifolia*, all of which are native to eastern North America. The 'rattlesnake' in the common name refers to the mottled leaves which resemble snakeskin. This similarity led to their use as a snakebite remedy in early herbal medicine and has also resulted in the over-collection of some species as ornamental plants.

**Orchidaceae; 40 species**

### LEDUM

A small genus confined to colder regions of the northern hemisphere, particularly wet boreal forests, tundra marshes and sphagnum moss bogs. Labrador tea *Ledum groenlandicum* is a dwarf evergreen shrub which may nevertheless attain heights of over 1 m (3.3 ft) in more sheltered localities such as the evergreen forests of the taiga. The leaves have thick cuticles and are dark above and woolly beneath, while the large white flowers grow in flattened terminal umbels. Labrador tea grows throughout arctic and boreal North America, extending, of course, into Labrador, and on to Greenland.

*L. palustre* has narrower leaves than *L. groenlandicum* and for this reason is sometimes known as narrow-leaved Labrador tea (also marsh tea or marsh rosemary). Its fragrant white flowers are arranged in dense, almost hemispherical clusters. This species has a circumboreal distribution but is also found in more southerly montane regions and, like Labrador tea, is common in the arctic tundra. Some authors regard *L. groenlandicum* as a subspecies of *L. palustre*.

It is thought that the leaves of *L. palustre* may have narcotic properties; in Germany they are used to make beer more intoxicating and are also used by the North American Indians to make tea. The leaves of the related *L. groenlandicum* were used when tealeaves were unavailable during the American War of Independence. Similar infusions are used today in the homeopathic treatment of coughs and chest and throat infections, whilst a strong decoction is reputed to kill lice. The larvae of the rosy marsh moth *Eugraphe subrosea* feed on the leaves.

**Ericaceae; 3 or 4 species**

### LINNAEA

This genus contains the single species twinflower *Linnaea borealis* an evergreen, prostrate or trailing subshrub which has a circumboreal distribution. Of all the plant and animal species classified by the great eighteenth-century Swedish taxonomist Carl Linnaeus, it was this delicate forest flower that he chose to be named after him.

Twinflower is usually a mat-forming plant, the upright flower stalks rarely exceeding 10 cm (4 in) in height. It has slender stems and small, almost circular or elliptical evergreen leaves, sometimes with a few shallow teeth. The nodding, pink, trumpet-shaped flowers are sometimes delicately striped with red and almost always occur in pairs, hence the plant's common name.

Several subspecies grow in the deep shade of the boreal forests of Eurasia and North America, extending locally south to the Alps and the eastern Carpathians in the Old World and into California, Arizona and New Mexico in the New World. In the British Isles twinflower is found in the native pine woods of eastern and central Scotland where it is becoming increasingly rare.

**Caprifoliaceae; a single species**

### LISTERA

A small genus of terrestrial orchids found throughout northern temperate and boreal regions. They are commonly known as twayblades because of the pair of flattened, round or heart-shaped leaves occurring either at the base or nearer to the midpoint of each flowering stem. The flowers are arranged in a lax

*Listera ovata*

inflorescence, each having more or less equal perianth segments and a much longer, deeply bifid lip. There are no spurs but nectar is secreted in the central furrow of the lip, attracting a wide variety of pollinating insects.

The inconspicuous lesser twayblade *Listera cordata* is particularly associated with boreal forests. The creeping rhizomes give rise to lax spikes of 4-12 tiny reddish green or purplish flowers with narrow, forked lips. They flower from late May to September and are typically pollinated by minute ichneumon wasps. Lesser twayblade occurs in the damp boreal forests of both Eurasia and North America as well as on open peaty moors and heathland south of the boreal zone. It is also found to heights of around 2,000 m (6,600 ft) in montane forest and tundra habitats including the Pyrenees, Alps and Apennines.

Other species are twayblade *L. ovata*, found from Europe to Siberia in forests, meadows and alpine habitats; broad-leaved twayblade *L. convallarioides*, from the moist woods of the western mountain ranges of the United States and Canada, and *L. smallii*, another North American species, commonly called Small's twayblade, which is reputed to flower only in the deep shade cast by rhododendrons.

**Orchidaceae; 25 species**

## LYSICHITON

This genus of robust, perennial stemless herbs contains only two species, one of which occurs in western North America, and the other on the opposite side of the Bering Straits in the Kamchatka peninsula. The American species, yellow skunk-cabbage *Lysichiton americanus* is a rhizomatous plant of marshy areas with minute hermaphrodite flowers aggregated into a yellow spike up to 25 cm (10 in) tall (known as the spadix), protected by a conspicuous yellow or cream bract (the spathe), which is open on one side. The leaves, which usually develop after the flowers, may be over 1 m (3.3 ft) long and up to 40 cm (16 in) wide. Yellow skunk-cabbage flowers soon after the snow melts from April onwards, and is found in the boreal forests of Alaska and in coniferous forests south to California.

The name skunk cabbage refers to the strong foetid odour of the flowers which attracts flies as pollinators. The sap was once used locally to treat ringworm, while the North American Indians used to bake the short, fleshy underground stem to supplement their winter diet and prepared a flour from the starch. All parts of the plant are said to be a favourite food of the black bear. The Kamchatka skunk-cabbage *L. kamtschatcensis* (*L. camtschatcense*) is very similar, and despite the smaller white spathe it may in fact belong to the same species as *L. americanus*.

**Araceae; 2 species**

## MAIANTHEMUM

A tiny genus of low-growing perennial herbs distributed across the northern temperate and boreal regions, whose members are commonly known as May lilies. The generic name also refers to the time of flowering and is derived from the two Greek words *maios* ('May'), and *anthemon* ('flower').

A typical species is maylily *Maianthemum bifolium*, which has creeping rhizomes and erect slender stems with a pair of broad heart-shaped leaves and a dense inflorescence of 15-20 tiny white, star-like flowers. The genus is unusual in that each flower has only two petal-like sepals, two petals and four stamens, in contrast to the usual 3-3-6 arrangement found in other members of the lily family. The flowers are visited by insects but self-pollination also occurs; the fruits are scarlet berries, each about 6 mm (0.2 in) in diameter.

*M. bifolium* is a plant of shady woodland throughout Eurasia including northern Spain and the Apennines. In the European boreal zone it is particularly associated with the wetter Norway spruce forests. Although colonies of up to 5,000 plants have been recorded in some British localities, May lily is declining in the British Isles due to the destruction of its woodland habitat.

*M. dilatatum*, known locally as false lily of the valley or deerberry, is a very similar species found in moist, shady forests from Alaska to the north Coast Ranges of California as well as in eastern Asia, including Japan. It is particularly common in the coniferous 'rainforests' of the northern Pacific coast, while Canada mayflower *M. canadense* is a plant of upland forests in Canada and the eastern United States.

**Liliaceae; 3 species**

## MONESES

The generic name is derived from the Greek *monos* ('single') and *hesis* ('delight'), which refers to the exquisite solitary flowers. The sole species of this genus is the circumboreal *Moneses uniflora*. It occurs in shady mossy forests, especially those of the coniferous boreal zone, but also occurs in coniferous woods to 2,100 m (6,900 ft) in montane regions further south. The erect flowering stems arise from rosettes of rounded, finely toothed basal leaves, each stem bearing a terminal, drooping flower about 2 cm (0.8 in) in diameter. The flowers are fragrant and have five creamy white petals surrounding a prominent green ovary.

Commonly known in North America as wood nymph or waxflower, *Moneses uniflora* is found from Alaska to Newfoundland, the Rocky Mountains and New Mexico. Its Old World name is one-flowered wintergreen, and here its range includes the whole of northern Europe and Asia from Iceland to northern Japan, and the Pyrenees, Corsica, Italy and Bulgaria. In Scotland, where it is confined to ancient pine woods, it is a very rare plant today due to the unfavourable effects of forestry operations.

**Pyrolaceae; a single species**

## MONOTROPA

Both species of this genus are found throughout northern temperate and boreal regions. They are fleshy saprophytic herbs, lacking chlorophyll and therefore unable to photosynthesize. Instead the roots function in symbiosis with a soil fungus, as a result of which the plant is able to absorb its food from the leaf litter. These species are therefore ideally suited to life in the deep shade of the boreal forests.

Yellow bird's-nest *Monotropa hypopitys* has waxy stems up to 30 cm (12 in) tall covered with many ovate, overlapping leaf scales. The whole plant, including the flowers, is yellowish, pinkish or ivory white. It grows in damp coniferous forests, beech woods and dune slacks throughout Europe (although rare in the south), extends into temperate and boreal Asia, including Japan and the Himalayas, and is also found in North America from the Panhandle

*Lysichiton sp.*

Left: *Empetrum nigrum*
Right:*Vaccinium uliginosum*

Below: *Vaccinium uliginosum*
Below right:*Vaccinium vitis-idaea*

*Vaccinium myrtillus*

'rainforests' of Alaska to Mexico. In North America this species is commonly known as false beechdrops or pinesap.

*M. uniflora* differs in having waxy white stems which blacken with age and are curved to accommodate the single white or pinkish, bell-like flower which hangs from the tip. This distinctive shape is no doubt responsible for its common name of Indian pipe. *M. uniflora* is found from the Alaskan and Canadian boreal forests to northwestern California as well as in the Himalayas and Japan.

**Monotropaceae; 2 species**

### MONTIA

A widespread genus of both hemispheres with one species particularly common in boreal forests. Minert's lettuce, or winter purslane *Montia perfoliata* is a fleshy annual with several hairless erect stems at the tip of each is a small, branched cluster of minute white five-petalled flowers. The most striking feature of winter purslane, however, is the pair of broad fleshy leaves which are fused into a shallow cup beneath the inflorescence.

*M. perfoliata* is native to Pacific North America, being particularly abundant in the coniferous 'rainforests' of Alaska and British Columbia, but has also been introduced to the British Isles where it thrives in a wide variety of habitats. The succulent leaves are edible, as indicated by its local name of Indian lettuce.

**Portulacaceae; 15 species**

### ORTHILIA

This genus contains a single, circumboreal species – serrated wintergreen *Orthilia secunda* – which is distinguished by its pale green, toothed leaves and one-sided inflorescence of about 10 nodding, greenish white flowers, each about 5 mm (0.2 in) in diameter. Although widespread in all boreal forests, it is also found in open moorland and on damp rock ledges. Its Eurasian distribution extends from Iceland to Japan, including Scotland and more southerly mountain

regions such as the Pyrenees and Sicily. In North America it occurs throughout the Alaska-Newfoundland boreal zone, south to New Jersey and California. Here this plant is appropriately known as side-bells, whilst in Europe it is commonly known as Yevering bells.

**Pyrolaceae; a single species**

### PTEROSPORA

The sole species of this genus, *Pterospora andromedea*, is found only in North America, where it grows in dryish coniferous forests with a deep layer of decaying plant material. Its range extends throughout the boreal zone from Alaska to Labrador, as well as at high altitudes in the Rocky Mountains. It is especially common in the deep humus of ponderosa pine forests.

Locally known as pinedrops, this species is a saphrophyte, its roots forming coarse, irregular masses that are intimately associated with a fungus which is able to break down the surrounding litter, so making nutrients available to the plant. *Pterospora andromedea* has unbranched, sticky purplish brown stems which may reach a height of over 1 m (3.3 ft). The plant lacks chlorophyll and the leaves are reduced to tiny scales on the stem. Loose terminal clusters of tiny, drooping, white or pale yellowish brown, egg-shaped flowers are produced late in the season.

The generic name is derived from the Greek words for 'winged seeds', referring to the net-like wing at one end of each minute seed which aids its dispersal on the breeze to a new site. *Pterospora andromedea* is a rare plant, medicinally of value in the treatment of fevers such as those induced by pleurisy and typhus. It is also known as Albany beech drops and giant bird's-nest.

**Monotropaceae; a single species**

### PYROLA

A largely northern hemisphere genus of perennial herbs with creeping underground rhizomes, commonly known as wintergreens because of their

evergreen foliage. Some species are found as far south as Sumatra and temperate South America. All wintergreens are partial saprophytes, supplementing the energy obtained by photosynthesis by having fungal associations which allow them to extract nutrients from the soil.

Several species thrive in the boreal forests, including intermediate wintergreen *Pyrola media* and round-leaved wintergreen *P. rotundifolia*, both Eurasian species; and common wintergreen *P. minor*, large-flowered or arctic wintergreen *P. grandiflora*, yellow wintergreen *P. chlorantha* and bog wintergreen *P. asarifolia*, all of which have a more or less circumboreal distribution.

All the boreal wintergreens produce basal rosettes of shiny leathery leaves, from which arise slender inflorescences consisting of several (5-25) drooping flowers, each with five petals, although the colour and shape varies with the species. *P. grandiflora*, for example, has greenish white spreading petals; the flowers of *P. chlorantha* are yellowish-green and bell-shaped, and those of *P. asarifolia*, also known as pink pyrola, are pink or reddish-purple. *P. media* and *P. minor* have pinkish white, globular flowers whereas *P. rotundifolia* has pure white, bell-shaped blooms, distinguished above all by their long, protruding, much curved styles. The tiny seeds of all species are dispersed by wind.

Round-leaved wintergreen is of value medicinally as a gargle or eye-wash, for inflammation of the bladder and to treat skin diseases. The aromatic leaves are popular in America as a salad vegetable and for making tea, while the spicy berries which remain in the spring are used in pies.

**Pyrolaceae; 35 species**

### TIARELLA

A small genus of slender erect perennial herbs essentially confined to North America but with a single eastern Asian representative. The genus is named after the Greek word *tiara*, a type of ancient Persian head-dress, which refers to the distinctive shape of the fruits.

Foamflower *Tiarella unifoliata*, also known as coolwort or false mitrewort, has tiny white five-petalled flowers, with reddish or yellowish anthers, which hang in loose clusters atop leafy stems. It is found from Alaska to central California and is particularly characteristic of wet habitats in the northwestern coniferous forests. False mitrewort *T. cordifolia* is a similar species from rich woods in eastern North America from Canada to North Carolina, westwards into Tennessee.

**Saxifragaceae; 3 to 7 species**

### TRIENTALIS

A tiny northern hemisphere genus of small perennial herbs containing just two species: *Trientalis latifolia*, of the western forests and prairies of North America, and *T. europaea*, a circumboreal plant. Some authorities recognize a third species – *T. arctica* - a white-flowered plant of wetlands in western North America, whilst a fourth – *T. borealis* (*T. americana*) – is a taxon of the eastern half of the continent. Both are in all probability subspecies of *T. europaea*. The generic name is derived from the Latin for 'one-third of a foot', referring to the average height of these plants.

Chickweed wintergreen *T. europaea*, known as starflower in North America, is a slender erect perennial, 10-25 cm (4-10 in) tall with a whorl of 4-7 stiff, bright-green lanceolate leaves emerging from the same point. Each white solitary flower has 5-9 petals and is about 2 cm (0.8 in) in diameter. Its habitats range from the ancient Caledonian pine woods of Scotland to the Asian taiga and boreal forests of North America; it also grows in secondary moor and heath communities and at heights of up to 2,000 m (6,600 ft) in the northern Alps. Western starflower *T. latifolia* has smaller pink flowers and is known locally as Indian potato, although there are some doubts as to its edibility.

**Primulaceae; 2 species**

### VACCINIUM

A large almost cosmopolitan genus of deciduous and evergreen shrubs and small trees of arctic and northern temperate regions and of high altitudes further south. Cowberry *Vaccinium vitis-idaea* (also called lingberry or foxberry) and arctic blueberry or bog bilberry *V. uliginosum*, are characteristic understorey shrubs of the extensive boreal forests and are also among the most common shrubs north of the Arctic Circle, dominating large areas of dwarf heath tundra in Eurasia and North America.

The deciduous arctic blueberry produces tiny rose-flushed, bell-like flowers and large blue-black berries which are eaten by both forest and tundra animals and man. Cowberry, on the other hand, has evergreen foliage and whitish flowers. The globular fruits are glossy and red when ripe and, although acid, are edible. Cranberry *V. oxycoccus* also has a wide range, occurring in boreal forests, bogs and wet heaths in Eurasia, Japan, North America and Greenland. It has pink flowers and red- or brown-spotted edible fruits which make a good sauce, traditionally eaten with turkey.

Another species, bilberry or whortleberry *V. myrtillus*, is a frequent understorey shrub in the Eurasian boreal forests, especially those dominated by Norway spruce. It is also widespread in deciduous woodlands and lowland heaths, although in the extreme southern part of its range it is confined to montane habitats. The flowers are greenish, sometimes tinged with pink, and the skin of the sweet, reddish fruits is alleged to improve night vision.

The blueberry *V. ovalifolium* is a North American species, particularly common in the lodgepole pine forests of the Rocky Mountains, but with a range extending from Alaska to Oregon. The sweet blue-black berries were much sought after by the North

American Indians and continue to be a favourite food of many mammals and birds, including both black and grizzly bears.

*Vaccinium* bushes provide food for the caterpillars of moths such as the small lappet *Phyllodesma ilicifolia*, the northern spinach moth *Eulithis populata*, the Scotch burnet *Zygaena exulans*, the pale eggar moth *Trichiura crataegi*, the oak eggar *Lasiocampa quercus*, the bilberry pug *Chloroclystris debiliata*, the little emerald *Jodis lactearia*, and two butterfly species: the green hairstreak *Callophrys rubi* and the small pearl-bordered fritillary *Clossiana selene*.

**Ericaceae; about 450 species**

### XEROPHYLLUM

This small genus of herbaceous plants is confined to North America. The generic name is derived from the combination of the Greek words *xeros* ('dry') and *phyllon* ('leaf') in reference to the plants' dry, wiry basal leaves.

Beargrass or turkey beard *Xerophyllum tenax* occurs in the less shady areas of the coniferous forests of the Pacific Northwest, south to central California. It produces a dense clump of long, narrow basal leaves from which arise stout stalks up to 2 m (6.6 ft) tall. These are topped by a club-shaped inflorescence of hundreds of tiny creamy white flowers, each with three petal-like sepals and three petals. Each individual plant blooms only once every 5-7 years. Another local name for this plant is Indian basket grass, since the dried and bleached leaves were formerly used by North American Indians to weave garments and watertight baskets.

The second species, *X. asphodeloides*, is found in the eastern United States from coastal New Jersey through the Appalachians to Georgia and into Tennessee, where it grows in dry sandy pine woods (the pine barrens) and mountain woods, but always on very acid soils.

**Liliaceae; 2 species**

*Xerophyllum tenax*

# CHAPTER FOUR

# TEMPERATE FORESTS

The temperate forests of the world vary considerably in composition, diversity and structure, but all experience the seasons changing and consist predominantly of plants adapted to the seasonal variations in precipitation and temperature that occur throughout the year. Most temperate forests are found in the northern hemisphere, occupying a zone between the broad band of boreal forests to the north and separated from the tropical forests to the south by a belt of grasslands and arid lands.

The main regions of the New World which support temperate forests are eastern and southeastern North America and southern Brazil, Argentina and Uruguay. In the Old World these habitats include the temperate rainforests of southeastern Australia and parts of New Zealand, the rich Manchurian and Japanese forests of eastern Asia and the extensive deciduous woodlands across much of Europe. Small areas are also found in East Africa, from Ethiopia to Kenya and Tanzania, as well as in the southern Andes and Tierra del Fuego.

Temperate forests are three dimensional structures dominated by deciduous trees and shrubs, i.e. those which lose their leaves in response to adverse conditions such as low temperatures and lack of water. These seasonal variations also affect flowering plants growing on the forest floor. During the winter the bare branches allow light to penetrate down to the forest floor, and when temperatures begin to rise in the spring and insect pollinators emerge from hibernation, the rich and diverse herb community bursts into flower before the trees can muster the energy to produce new leaves. In the summer when the trees are in full leaf and cast a deep shade, few herbs produce flowers other than a few saprophytic and parasitic species able to grow in the absence of light.

Flowering herbs with underground storage organs such as bulbs, corms and rhizomes are common in the world's temperate forests because they can draw on stored food reserves to produce flowers as soon as favourable conditions return. Members of the Liliaceae are particularly abundant.

Facing page: *Galanthus nivalis*

*Adoxa moschatellina*

## ADOXA

The sole species in this genus is Moschatel *Adoxa moschatellina*. It is a pale green perennial herb only 5-10 cm (2-4 in) tall with long-stalked, three-lobed basal leaves and erect, four-angled flowering stems bearing an opposite pair of stalkless three-lobed leaves and a tiny, terminal inflorescence. The globular flowering head is only about 6 mm (0.2 in) across and consists of five flowers: four facing outwards at right angles to one another and one facing upwards. This 'points-of-the-compass' arrangement is responsible for the plant's other common name of townhall clock.

The uppermost flower has four pale green petals and four yellow anthers whilst the lateral flowers possess five of each. In both cases the stamens are divided to the base, each bearing half an anther. The whole plant emits a musk-like fragrance towards dusk, which may be responsible for attracting small insects to the flowers, but self-pollination is also possible. The seeds are reputedly dispersed by snails.

Moschatel is a typical plant of old woods, hedgerows and mountain rocks in northern temperate regions, ranging across both Eurasia and North America. The whole plant is easily overlooked, this being reflected in the generic name which is a combination of the Greek words *a* and *doxa*, literally meaning 'lacking in glory'.

**Adoxaceae; a single species**

## ANEMONE

A large almost cosmopolitan genus of perennial herbs, especially diverse in northern temperate regions. Anemone flowers are usually solitary and terminal, with the 5-14 petaloid perianth segments and numerous stamens arranged in spirals.

Several species are particularly associated with woodlands, including wood anemone *Anemone nemorosa*, a common plant of temperate Eurasia. This perennial herb has three-lobed leaves and solitary nodding flowers up to 4 cm (1.6 in) across, each usually having six or seven white or pink-tinged

*Anemone coronaria*

*Anemone nemorosa*

petal-like perianth segments and numerous yellow stamens. Although the flowers do not produce nectar, they are visited for pollen by bees, flies and beetles. Wood anemones are among the first woodland flowers to appear in the spring.

In Greek mythology wood anemones are supposed to have appeared where the tears of Venus fell to the ground as she wandered through the forest weeping for the death of Adonis. They often carpet large areas of the forest floor and are capable of growing in a wide range of conditions, from calcareous to thin nutrient-poor soils, and even tolerate waterlogging. The larvae of the twin-spot carpet moth *Perizoma didymata* and the dot moth *Melanchra persicariae* feed on the foliage.

Yellow wood anemone *A. ranunculoides* is a woodland herb of central Europe and western Asia, identified by its deeply lobed leaves and small (1-2 cm (0.4-0.8 in)) bright yellow flowers, each with 5-8 oval perianth segments which are downy beneath. Southern Europe's blue wood anemone *A. apennina* is distinguished by its 9-15 narrow blue petals; *A. trifolia*, confined to southern Europe, is similar to the wood anemone but has white or blue anthers, while the northern Asian *A. altaica* has white flowers which are blue-veined on the inside.

In North America a familiar species of open woods in the west is blue anemone *A. oregana*, which has solitary blue-violet flowers and often forms large colonies, spreading by means of underground rhizomes. This species is sometimes found growing with the white flowered western wood anemone *A. lyallii*. *A. quinquefolia*, also known locally as wood anemone, is another white-flowered North American species, whose leaves are usually divided into five sharply toothed segments. It favours open woodlands from Quebec to North Carolina where it flowers between April and June.

Other plants in this genus are more typical of lowland grassland habitats. These include Canada anemone *A. canadensis*; Carolina anemone *A. caroliniana* which has pale blue flowers; long-headed thimbleweed *A. cylindrica* which grows in the prairies

of North America; and *A. sylvestris*, distinguished by its white flowers with yellow anthers and found in the Eurasian steppes. Mediterranean grassland species include the crown or poppy anemone *A. coronaria* which has solitary, bright red, blue, violet or white flowers up to 6 cm (2.4 in) in diameter, and *A. hortensis*, with up to 15 narrow violet perianth segments and blue anthers.

**Ranunculaceae; 120 species**

### ANEMONELLA
This genus contains just one species - rue anemone *Anemonella thalictroides* - which is native to the forests of the eastern half of the United States. It is a delicate plant, attaining a maximum height of 20 cm (8 in), with three-lobed leaves and white or pinkish flowers with 5-10 petal-like sepals; true petals are absent. Rue anemone is a typical member of the

spring flora in open deciduous forests, flowering between April and June.

**Ranunculaceae; a single species**

### ARALIA
This genus of perennial herbs is distributed across temperate regions of North America and eastern Asia, extending south into Malaysia. The rhizomes and roots of many species have medicinal properties and are much used in the treatment of pulmonary infections as well as in cases of rheumatism and syphilis and in urinary diseases.

Wild sarsaparilla *Aralia nudicaulis* is a typical representative of this genus with its loose hemispherical clusters of tiny greenish white flowers, each with five reflexed petals and five longer green stamens. The long-stalked leaves each have three pinnate branches and are arranged over the flowers

*Anemone occidentalis*

*Arisaema triphyllum*

rather like an umbrella. The flowers are followed by purplish black berries. Wild sarsaparilla is an inhabitant of upland woods from British Columbia to Newfoundland and south into the eastern and central United States.

Other American species are *A. spinosa*, a spiny shrub often called the Devil's walking-stick, bristly sarsaparilla *A. hispida*, another large spiny plant, and the spineless American spikenard *A. racemosa*. In eastern Asia a common species of upland forests is *A. cachemirica*, a large perennial herb with globular umbels of yellowish green flowers, found from Afghanistan to Tibet above 2,000 m (6,600 ft).

Chinese angelica *A. chinensis*, the leaves of which are eaten as a vegetable, is common in the Shennongjia region of China. *A. spinosa* yields a tonic, the rhizomes of *A. racemosa* are the source of a purgative and can induce sweating and *A. cordata* is used as a vegetable in Japan.

### Araliaceae; over 36 species

#### ARISAEMA

A large genus of perennial herbs distributed across tropical and eastern Asia, western North America and East Africa. The leaves may be divided into three (trifoliate), five (digitate), or seven to eleven more or less equal leaflets, radiating outwards from the tip of the leaf stalk. The inflorescence comprises a leaf-like, often brightly coloured, spathe which encircles a central spike or spadix on which numerous minute flowers are arranged. Male and female flowers are found on separate plants, the female spikes producing cylindrical clusters of red berries.

East Asian forest species include *Arisaema*

*costatum*, which is confined to Nepal, and has dark purple spathes, decorated with longitudinal white stripes, curved over the spadix and terminating in a narrow tail; *A. griffithii*, found from central Nepal to Bhutan, has a very broad, curled spathe distinguished by its purplish, ear-like flaps netted with dark green; and *A. tortuosum*, a species which occurs from southwest China to Kashmir and is identified by its green spathes from which protrude tapering, up-curved spadices with long purple tips. The cobra plant *A. nepenthoides* is one of the most distinctive Asian species, its mottled green, red and brown spathes resembling a cobra about to strike. It is found in forests and shrubberies between 2,000 and 3,300 m (6,600-10,800 ft) from southwest China to central Nepal.

Other Asian species include Amur Jack-in-the-pulpit *A. amurensis*, a herb of Ussuriland in the extreme southeast of the USSR; *A. fimbriatum*, which grows in Malaysia and is distinguished by its feathered spadix; *A. candidissimum*, which has white spathes with green and pink veins and scented flowers and is native to Yunnan; and the striking *A. sikokianum*, a Japanese species with whitish, club-shaped spadices and purple and green striped spathes. Five species are also native to east Africa, including *A. mildbraedii*, which has green and white spathes up to 23 cm (9 in) long and is common in wet montane forests between 1,400 and 2,500 m (4,600-8,200 ft).

The genus is no less diverse in North America, two of the best known species being green dragon *A. dracontium* and Jack-in-the-pulpit *A. triphyllum* (*A. atrorubens*), which is also known as Indian turnip. Both species favour wet woodlands with rich soils,

from southern Ontario and Quebec, through the Appalachians to Florida, Louisiana and Texas. Green dragon gets its name from the 'dragon's tongue' which protrudes from the greenish spathe, while Jack-in-the-pulpit is the perfect description for the short fat spadix beneath the curved, mottled green and purple spathe.

The tuber of *A. triphyllum* contains needle-like crystals of calcium oxalate which not only give it a peppery flavour but can cause severe irritation of the inside of the mouth and throat if eaten raw, and may also cause violent gastroenteritis, sometimes ending in death. If properly cooked, however, these tubers are valuable as a source of starch and were formerly much used by the American Indians, hence the name Indian turnip. As a powerful expectorant the powdered roots have been used to some effect in the treatment of croup, whooping cough, asthma, laryngitis and bronchitis.

### Araceae; 150 species

#### ARUM

A small genus of perennial herbs distributed from Afghanistan and Kashmir across Europe to the Mediterranean region, North Africa and the Canary Islands. The long heart-shaped leaves have a prominent network of veins and the spathe is usually green and leaf-like. The terminal spadix bears minute unisexual flowers, female below and male above, in which perianth segments are absent. The spadix generates high temperatures and gives off a disagreeable odour to attract flies. The berries are scarlet and fleshy, each containing between one and six seeds.

One of the best known species in western, central and southern Europe is *Arum maculatum*, variously known as cuckoo-pint, arum lily or lords-and-ladies. The black-spotted leaves appear in the spring before the pale yellowish green spathe and purple spadix. The flowers are pollinated by small flies, particularly midges. *A. maculatum* is a common inhabitant of woods and shady hedgerows as it is extremely tolerant of low light levels. Its range extends to the Ukraine and North Africa. The tubers have a high starch content and, although acrid and toxic when raw, when cooked are the source of Portland arrowroot and Portland sago. The juice was used to provoke abortion and to ward off snakebite.

A similar species is Italian lords-and-ladies *A. italicum* of southern and western Europe and North Africa, which is distinguished from *A. maculatum* by its larger spathes and orange-yellow spadices. The leaves are well developed before the onset of winter but the flowers appear rather later than in *A. maculatum*. Other woodland species are *A. orientale*, which thrives in shady habitats in eastern Europe and the Balkan peninsula, and *A. elongatum* from the southern Ukraine.

### Araceae; 15 species

#### ASARUM

A genus of perennial herbs of northern temperate regions, with dark brown, resin-scented flowers usually pollinated by flies. In some species, however, the flowers have evolved fungus-like appendages to encourage fungus-gnats to visit the plant, both to pollinate the flowers and to lay their eggs, although once hatched the larvae are unable to eat the plant tissue.

Asarabacca *Asarum europeaum*, also known as hazelwort or wild nard, is a perennial evergreen herb of shady woodlands. It has a creeping rhizome from which pairs of thick heart-shaped leaves arise at intervals, and solitary, bell-shaped, terminal flowers produced on long stalks in the leaf axils. Each flower has a brownish, three-lobed perianth, about 15 mm (0.6 in) long, containing 12 stamens. Asarabacca was formerly much grown as a medicinal plant: it was often administered as an emetic after alcoholic excess and was also a constituent of some snuffs. For this reason it is frequently encountered outside its native range of northern and central Eurasia. Manchurian wild ginger *A. heterotropoides* is native to the Changbai Mountains in northeast China.

Long-tailed wild ginger *A. caudatum* is a plant of moist shady woods in western North America from British Columbia to central California. It has brown-purple or yellowish, cup-shaped flowers up to 12.5 cm (5 in) across and the aromatic stems and rhizomes were used by early settlers as a substitute for tropical ginger. Other species of western North America are Hartweg's wild ginger *A. hartwegii* which grows in Oregon and California, and Lemmon's wild ginger *A. lemmonii* from California's Sierra Nevada.

Wild ginger *A. canadense* has drooping, dark reddish brown or greenish flowers about 4 cm (1.6 in) across and is distributed from Canada into the eastern United States on rich soils in woodlands. The rhizomes have a strong ginger-like odour and again can be used as a substitute for the real thing if boiled with sugar. They have also been used medicinally as a stimulant in cases of chronic chest complaints and spasms of the bowels and stomach. *A. arifolium*, which has more triangular leaves and greenish purple flowers, is found in the southern United States.

**Aristolochiaceae; about 70 species**

### ATROPA

A small genus with a distribution ranging from western Europe across Asia to the Himalayas. The generic name is derived from the Greek *Atropos* the Inflexible, one of the three Fates who is said to have cut off the threads of human lives with her shears.

The best known species is undoubtedly belladonna or deadly nightshade *Atropa belladonna*, a perennial bushy plant with bell-shaped, greenish or violet-brown flowers about 3 cm (1.2 in) long. It grows in damp, shady woods in Eurasia and the Mediterranean region. All parts of this plant are poisonous, especially the roots, but even the sweet shiny black berries are deadly and are often eaten by children with fatal results. A peculiar symptom of sufferers from belladonna poisoning is the complete loss of voice, while victims have also been seen to bend forward frequently from the waist and move their hands continually. The pupils of the eyes also become very

*Atropa belladonna*

dilated, which led to its former use by young Italian women to make their eyes brighter and larger, as well as having a more practical function in ophthalmic medicine.

Deadly nightshade is alleged to have been responsible for the poisoning of the troops of Marcus Antonius during the Parthian Wars, as well as being administered to an army of invading Danes by the Scottish soldiers of Macbeth, who then murdered the unfortunate victims in their sleep. Some ancient legends assert that the plants belong to and are tended by the Devil; yet others relate that at certain times belladonna is able to take the form of a beautiful enchantress, upon whose visage it is dangerous to gaze.

The deadly constituents of *Atropa belladonna* are the alkaloids atropine and hyoscyamine. Despite its virulence, the plant is of considerable medicinal value if used prudently, both roots and leaves having narcotic, diuretic, sedative and antispasmodic properties. In addition scarcely any eye operation can be performed without the aid of atropine to dilate the pupil. Applied locally, belladonna reduces irritability and pain and may be used as a lotion or liniment in cases of rheumatism, sciatica and gout. Small doses alleviate heart palpitations and its powerful antispasmodic properties are invaluable in the treatment of colic and spasmodic asthma. In large doses belladonna has been used with effect to treat children with whooping cough or croup.

Other species of Atropa include *A. baetica*, a green or yellow-flowered plant of shady calcareous rocks and screes in southern Spain and North Africa, and *A. acuminata* which has drooping pale purple flowers and is native to forests and shrubberies in the foothills of the Himalayas, from Pakistan to Himachal Pradesh. Like belladonna, both species are poisonous and used in medicine.

**Solanaceae; 4 species**

### CEPHALANTHERA

A small genus of orchids commonly known as helleborines (see also *Epipactis*), distributed across temperate regions of Eurasia, usually in deciduous

*Arum maculatum*

*Cephalanthera rubra*

arranged on a slightly zigzagged stem and are cross-pollinated by small bees. Red helleborines can exist for long periods in a purely vegetative state underground, which accounts for their ability to appear and disappear from a locality apparently at random. *C. rubra* also favours open woodlands on calcareous soils, usually dominated by beech or pine. It is essentially a European species, extending into the Near East, but is becoming rather rare in many lowland areas and is protected by law in the British Isles.

**Orchidaceae; 12 species**

### CIMIFUGA

A small genus widespread across northern temperate regions. Several species occur in eastern North America, the best known being black cohosh *Cimifuga racemosa*. This robust herbaceous plant grows in the rich woods that extend from the Canadian border along the line of the Appalachians south to Georgia. It grows to a height of over 2 m (6.6 ft) and has large sharply toothed, biternately compound (twice divided into threes) leaves. The white flowers are arranged in several slender spikes on a leafy stalk. Each has 4-5 sepals, which protect the flower in bud but usually fall as it opens, and numerous stamens; there are no petals.

*C. racemosa* is also known as bugbane because of its unpleasant odour which is reputed to keep insects at bay. The rhizome and roots contain an amorphous resinous substance called cimifugin or macrotin and a crystalline, bitter-tasting chemical known as racemosin. A root preparation was formerly widely used in American herbal medicine to treat such varied disorders as consumption, whooping cough, rheumatism and St Vitus's dance. It is also considered to be an antidote to the bite of the rattlesnake, from which this plant derives yet more common names,

*Cephalanthera damasonium*

woodland habitats. Plants in this genus typically have leafy stems and a few large, suberect white or pink flowers arranged in lax spikes. The perianth segments converge at their tips so that the flower never opens fully.

The generic name is derived from the combination of the two Greek words *kephale* ('head'), and *anthera* ('stamen'), which refer to the shape of the single stamen. Because there is only one stamen, *Cephalanthera* is regarded as one of the most primitive orchid genera, a fact reinforced by the ability of these plants to reproduce vegetatively by means of root buds which develop into aerial stems. This is a very effective technique in deep shade, where flowering is minimal.

The white helleborine *Cephalanthera damasonium* (*C. grandiflora*) is a fairly common plant of woods and shady places on calcareous soils, especially in beech forests. It occurs throughout much of Europe except the far north, extending into North Africa and

southern USSR, the Caucasus and Asia Minor. There are 3-13 creamy white, scentless flowers which open only briefly and are frequently self-pollinated.

The sword-leaved helleborine *C. longifolia* is distinguished by its narrow erect leaves arranged like a fan around the flowering spike, which carries about 10 pure white flowers. Cross-pollination is carried out by small bees. Like the white helleborine, this species favours calcareous woodlands and is distributed across much of Europe, North Africa, western Asia to Kashmir, Siberia and Japan. Other white-flowered species are the hooded helleborine *C. cucullata*, which is confined to montane forests and scrub in Crete, and the eastern hooded helleborine *C. epipactoides*, which favours open coniferous woods in the northern Aegean islands and Turkey.

Red helleborine *C. rubra* differs in having bright pink, occasionally lilac-tinged flowers which open much wider than those of other members of the genus. Up to 15 of these handsome flowers are

*Clematis vitalba*

such as black snakeroot and rattleroot.

Another American species is the mountain bugbane *C. americana*, which is a smaller plant lacking the unpleasant odour of black cohosh and occurring from Pennsylvania through the Appalachians to Georgia. *C. foetida*, a species with yellowish flowers found from southeast Europe to Siberia, is considered to be of high medicinal value in China and was also used to deter bugs.

**Ranunculaceae; 15 species**

### CLEMATIS

A large genus of woody lianes, shrubs and perennial herbs of temperate regions in both hemispheres extending into the tropical mountains of Africa. The generic name is derived from the Greek *klema* ('vine branch').

Plants in this genus have leaves arranged in opposite pairs which are usually compound and often end in tendrils. The radially symmetrical flowers are distinguished by the absence of petals, their place being taken by a petaloid calyx, while the fruits consist of achenes with persistent long, feathery styles.

The best known European and North African species is old man's beard or traveller's joy *Clematis vitalba*, a perennial woody climber with stems up to 30 m (98 ft) long, pinnate leaves and fragrant, greenish white flowers in axillary and terminal clusters. Nectar is secreted from the stamen filaments and the flowers are visited by bees and flies for both pollen and nectar. Traveller's joy is a common sight in temperate woodlands, hedgerows and thickets, usually on calcareous soils. The leaves are sometimes used as a tobacco substitute and the young shoots are edible.

*C. vitalba* is an important foodplant for the larvae of many moths, including the small emerald *Hemistola chrysoprasaria*, the sub-angled wave *Scopula nigropunctata*, the small waved umber *Horisme vitalbata*, the fern moth *H. tersata*, the double-striped

*Clematis hirsutissima*

pug *Gymnoscelis rufifasciata*, tne pretty chalk carpet *Melanthia procellata* and Haworth's pug *Eupithecia haworthiata*.

In Asia, the Himalayan region boasts around 25 species of *Clematis*, including such typical forest species as *C. barbellata*, with large, brown-purple, bell-shaped flowers; *C. grata*, with clusters of fragrant creamy white flowers; *C. tibetana*, distinguished by its nodding yellow flowers spotted with brown; and *C. buchaniana*, with leafy, branched clusters of creamy yellow, sweet-scented flowers. *C. hexapetala* is a white-flowered species of the Asian steppes.

Western North American species include Columbia virgin's bower *C. columbiana*, a semiclimbing plant with large, solitary, lavender-blue flowers, and vase flower *C. hirsutissima*, also known as sugar bowls, an erect hairy herb distinguished by its terminal, solitary, nodding dull-purple flowers. The climber white clematis or pipestems *C. ligusticifolia* has great masses of tiny white flowers. Its stems and leaves were formerly chewed by the American Indians as a remedy for colds and sore throats, while the crushed roots were said to revive a tired horse if placed in its nostrils.

On the eastern side of North America grows dwarf clematis *C. baldwinii*, also known by the misleading name of pink hyacinth, which has solitary, nodding bell-shaped lavender-blue flowers and the very similar leather flower *C. crispa*. Virgin's bower *C. virginiana*, a white-flowered climbing plant, is one of the most common eastern species; the male and female flowers are found on separate plants.

*Codonopsis clematidea*

*Convallaria majalis*

Other woody climbers are *C. flammula* which has pure white flowers, and *C. viticella*, with larger, fragrant, reddish-purple flowers, both of which are native to southern Europe and western Asia, while *C. montana*, an inhabitant of central and western China and the Himalayas, has numerous long-stalked, white or pink flowers. Rocky Mountain clematis *C. pseudoalpina* and matted purple virgin's bower *C. tenuiloba* are both found in southwestern North America. Among the tropical species are *C. brachiata* and *C. simiensis*, both of which are widespread lianes of the montane forests of East Africa.

**Ranunculaceae; about 230 species**

### CODONOPSIS

This genus is typical of the forests and uplands of central and eastern Asia, its range extending to Malaysia. The species resemble *Campanula* in general appearance but are usually strong smelling, have tubers and are often climbing plants.

Typical forest species include *Codonopsis convolvulacea*, a distinctive climbing perennial herb with shiny oval leaves whose large (4-5 cm/1.6-2 in across) blue, bell-shaped flowers have a reddish ring within, and *C. thalictrifolia*, an erect herbaceous perennial which has smaller solitary, pale blue, funnel-like flowers and tiny rounded or heart-shaped leaves. Other twining plants are *C. affinis*, which has branched clusters of tubular purple-tipped purplish or green flowers, each about 2 cm (0.8 in) wide; *C. viridis*, which is distinguished by its narrow, greenish yellow flowers blotched with purple within; and *C. rotundifolia*, which has broadly bell-shaped, greenish white flowers, veined with purple.

*C. ovata* is a Himalayan species with pale blue flowers; the robust *C. clematidea* is native to western Asia and has white, blue-tinged flowers; and *C. meleagris*, which grows in Yunnan Province in southwest China, has highly decorative flowers which are cream or bluish veined with brown on the outside, and purple or violet with green bases on the inside. Another spectacular species is the Ussuri bellflower *C. ussuriensis* of Japan and Manchuria, which has green, purple-tipped flowers and edible tubers. The tubers of *C. tangshen* are used in western China as a ginseng substitute, as are those of Asian bell *C. pilulosa*, from the Shennongjia forests of China, in which the roots are up to 2 m (6.6 ft) long.

**Campanulaceae; about 30 species**

### CONVALLARIA

A tiny genus of perennial herbs of northern temperate regions. The best known representative is lily-of-the-valley *Convallaria majalis*. This unmistakable plant has elliptical grey-green leaves and short spikes of 6-12 fragrant, nodding, white bells, each less than 1 cm (0.4 in) long. It is found across most of Europe and northeast Asia and is naturalized in North America. Lily-of-the-valley is widely cultivated for ornament, perfume and as a medicinal plant.

*Convallaria majalis* contains two glycosides of medicinal value: convallamarin, which acts upon the heart in the same way as digitalin and also has diuretic properties, and convallarin, which has a purgative action. This plant is valued as a cardiac tonic because it is less powerful than digitalin and large and frequent doses have no apparent ill effects. A decoction of the flowers is reputed to aid removal of obstructions from the urinary tract, whilst in some parts of Germany wine is made from the flowers mixed with raisins. The flowers are also used in the preparation of perfumes and in certain snuffs.

**Liliaceae; 3 species**

### CORYDALIS

This large genus of hairless, usually grey-green herbs is typical of the northern temperate zone, with a centre of distribution in the Sinohimalayan region, but there is also one species in the tropical African mountains. The flowers are tubular with the upper

*Cyclamen balearicum*

petal hooded and spurred serving as a storage organ for nectar produced by the staminal nectary. The tubers of some species can be used as a vegetable and the foliage is often eaten by the caterpillars of the clouded apollo butterfly *Parnassius mnemosyne*.

Several very similar species are characteristic herbs of the ground flora in European temperate woodlands, especially beech forests, including *Corydalis solida* and *C. bulbosa*, both of which have terminal oblong inflorescences of dull purple flowers up to 30 mm (12 in) long, with long slender spurs which are pollinated by long-tongued bees. *C. claviculata* is an annual climbing plant with pinnate leaves ending in branched tendrils, and inflorescences arising opposite the leaves and composed of tiny (5-6 mm/0.2 in) short-spurred, cream flowers.

Almost 50 species of *Corydalis* occur in the Himalayas, many in forested areas, including *C. cashmeriana*, a delicate perennial with sky-blue flowers; *C. rutifolia*, with pink or purple flowers; *C. chaerophylla*, with branched clusters of golden-yellow flowers; and *C. juncea*, with yellow flowers distinguished by the purple tips to the petals. Both *C. lutea* and *C. saxicola* (*C. thalictrifolia*) also have yellow flowers.

In North America, golden smoke *C. aurea*, also known as scrambled eggs, is a yellow-flowered species common in shady habitats over much of the western half of the continent; while Case's fitweed *C. caseana* is a tall plant with pinkish white flowers in clusters of up to 200 which grows in shady moist places in the southwestern mountains. Like many species of *Corydalis*, both plants contain alkaloids which are poisonous to livestock, particularly sheep.

Pale corydalis *C. sempervirens* has pouch-like pink and yellow flowers with long curved spurs and occurs in rocky forest clearings across Canada, through the Appalachians to northern Georgia, while yellow harlequin *C. flavula* is a much smaller eastern species with pure yellow, short-spurred flowers.

**Papaveraceae; about 300 species**

### CYCLAMEN

A genus of perennial herbs with swollen, long-lived corms distributed from the Mediterranean to Iran. The roots emerge from the base of the corm in

*Cyclamen persicum*, from the top in *C. hederifolium* and from all over in the other species. The rather fleshy leaves are simple, cordate, long-stalked, often blotched or marbled on the upper surface and purple beneath. The flowers are solitary and nodding at the tips of long, erect, leafless stems which are usually spirally coiled in fruit. The calyx is bell shaped and deeply five lobed and the corolla consists of a short tube with five large reflexed lobes. The sticky seeds are believed to be dispersed by ants.

The generic name is derived from the Greek *cyclos* ('a circle'), which may refer either to the ring of reflexed corolla lobes or to the spirals performed by the fruit stalks. All species occur in woods and thickets or on shaded rocky hillsides, usually on limestone.

Sowbread *C. hederifolium* (*C. neapolitanum*) is a southern European and southwest Asian species that blooms from August to November, the flowers appearing before the leaves. The pink (rarely white) flowers have lobes about 2 cm (0.8 in) long, each with a dark purple blotch at the base. The large rootstocks of this species formerly provided food for wild boar, hence its common name, although the juice is reputed to be poisonous to fish. The rootstocks are intensely acrid and are used medicinally as a purgative, but it has been suggested that small, flat cakes baked from sowbread have potent aphrodisiac properties. A paste called 'ointment of arthainta' was made from the fresh rootstocks and used to expel intestinal worms; when dried, powdered and taken as a snuff, the plant was reputed to cure baldness.

Common cyclamen *C. purpurascens* (*C. europaeum*) has sweet-scented rose-carmine flowers which appear at the same time as the leaves, between June and October. It is found from southeastern France to the western Carpathians and central Yugoslavia, also extending into western Asia. Other species produce flowers in the spring, again at the same time as the leaves, including *C. repandrum* of the central and eastern Mediterranean, which has fragrant rose-coloured (rarely white) flowers, and *C. persicum*, with large, white or pink flowers, the lobes of which vary from 2.5-4.5 cm (1-1.8 in) long. *C. persicum* is the ancestor of the majority of cyclamens which find their way into florists' shops. Despite its name it does not occur in Iran, but is found in southeast Europe, Greece and the Aegean region and Tunisia. Instead of coiling up in fruit like most cyclamens, the flower stalks of *C. persicum* extend and fall to the ground.

Greek cyclamen *C. graecum* is a pink-flowered plant from Greece, the Aegean and western Asia which flowers from September to December; *C. creticum* is native to Crete and has small white flowers opening from March to May; *C. coum* is a southeast European plant with small magenta flowers marked with conspicuous pale-centred violet blotches which appear from January to April; and *C. balearicum* is found only in southern France and the Balearic Islands and has small white, pink-veined flowers which bloom between February and April.

**Primulaceae; 17 species**

### DENTARIA

A small genus of woodland herbs distributed across eastern North America and Eurasia. The rhizome is subterranean, the toothed leaves are distinctively pinnate or palmate and the large four-petalled flowers vary from white to purple. These plants are sometimes known as toothworts, because of the tooth-like projections on the rhizome.

Coralroot *Dentaria bulbifera* is distinguished by brownish violet bulbils in the axils of the upper leaves, violet-tipped sepals and lilac or pale pink flowers. Insects rarely visit these flowers, seeds are only produced infrequently and the species relies on the bulbils to reproduce itself. Coralroot is a widespread herb of calcareous woodlands, especially beech forests, in Europe but is rare in the Mediterranean region.

Other European species are *D. heptaphylla* and *D. pentaphyllos*, both of which have white, pink or purple flowers and occur in damp shady habitats in western and central Europe, especially in montane woodlands; drooping bittercress *D. enneaphyllos* is a yellow-flowered species of the Alps, Carpathians and mountains of the northern Balkan peninsula; and *D. quinquefolia*, which has deep purple flowers, is an eastern European plant which extends into western Asia.

In eastern North America related species are cut-leaved toothwort *D. laciniata*, which has white or pink flowers in a terminal cluster above a whorl of three deeply divided stem leaves and grows in moist lowland woods from the Canadian border south to Florida, and two-leaved toothwort *D. diphylla*, which is distinguished by its opposite pair of stem-leaves and edible rhizomes.

**Cruciferae; about 20 species**

### DICENTRA

A small genus of Asian and North American herbs with much-divided leaves and pendulous four-petalled flowers. At the base of each of the two outer petals are large spurs or pouches which contain nectar to attract bee pollinators. The generic name is derived from the Greek for 'two-spurred'. Many species contain narcotic alkaloids such as corydalin and are valued for their medicinal properties. Preparations of these plants have been found useful in treating such diverse disorders as syphilis, skin inflammation and menstrual complaints.

Wild bleeding heart *Dicentra eximia*, which has several deep pink or red heart-shaped flowers hanging from a leafless stem, is found in rocky woods in the Appalachians from New York to Georgia, West Virginia and Tennessee. Dutchman's breeches *D. cucullaria* is distinguished by its clusters of fragrant, white, pantaloon-shaped flowers, the outer two petals of each flower having enormous inflated spurs that together form a 'V'. This species is typical of the rich woods of eastern North America. One of the most popular medicinal plants of the genus is squirrel corn *D. canadensis*, so called because its numerous yellow root tubers resemble maize kernels. It is found in much the same habitats as Dutchman's breeches, but has whitish heart-shaped flowers.

In western North America these eastern species are replaced by plants such as western bleeding heart *D. formosa*, identified by its pink heart-shaped flowers and blue-green fern-like leaves, and steer's head *D. uniflora*, a tiny plant with solitary, terminal, pink or white, bilaterally symmetrical flowers resembling a steer's skull with horns. Both species are typical of montane forests in the southwest, although *D. formosa* also extends to British Columbia.

Bleeding heart *D. spectabilis* is probably the best known and most showy member of this genus, with large rosy red or white flowers up to 2.5 cm (1 in) long. It is native to the temperate forests of China, Korea and Manchuria but is commonly cultivated for ornament in Europe and North America, where it is sometimes found in the wild as a garden escape. *D. macrocapnos* is a slender climbing plant of central Asia distinguished by its yellow, urn-shaped flowers, tipped with purple.

**Fumariaceae; 19 species**

### DISPORUM

A small genus of perennial herbs with creeping rootstocks distributed across eastern Asia, Indomalaysia and western North America, usually in forest habitats. *Disporum cantoniense*, a southeast Asian species which extends into the Himalayas, is an erect plant with many broadly lanceolate leaves and both terminal and axillary umbels of a few drooping funnel-shaped flowers. These may be white, greenish or purple and up to 2 cm (0.8 in) long, developing into black fleshy berries if fertilized.

The genus is more diverse in North America and includes such species as nodding mandarin *D. maculatum*, which is found in moist woods in the eastern half of the United States and is especially common in the southern Appalachians. The cream or yellow purple-spotted flowers hang singly or in pairs from the ends of the stems, directly opposite the last leaf. The fruits are distinctive red hairy berries. Yellow mandarin *D. lanuginosum* is distributed from New York to Georgia and has yellow unspotted

*Epipactis helleborine*

*Epipactis gigantea*

flowers and smooth red fruit.

In western North America the most common species is wartberry fairybell *D. trachycarpum*, another plant of deciduous woodlands which ranges from British Columbia through the Rocky Mountains to Arizona and New Mexico. Its creamy white flowers give rise to velvety yellow berries which later turn red. These fruits have a sweet taste and were formerly eaten raw by Blackfoot Indians, although today their

main consumers are grouse and rodents. Two other western species are Smith's fairybell *D. smithii* and Hooker's fairybell *D. hookeri*.

**Liliaceae; 10 species**

### EPIPACTIS

A small genus of largely terrestrial orchids, commonly known as helleborines and distributed from northern temperate regions into tropical Africa, Thailand and

Mexico. These herbaceous orchids have dull reddish brown or greenish flowers which are cross-pollinated by insects or possibly self-pollinated.

The northern temperate species include such typical forest species as the broad-leaved helleborine *Epipactis helleborine*, which has spikes of 15-50 drooping greenish to dull-purple flowers thought to be pollinated by wasps. It grows in woods and other shady places on a wide range of soils throughout most of Europe, North Africa and temperate Asia, including the Himalayas, ranging as far east as Japan. It has also been introduced to North America. Violet helleborine *E. purpurata* is rather similar but one-sided spikes of many pale green slightly fragrant, often violet-tinged flowers. It favours beech woods on base-rich soils and its range covers northwest and central Eurasia as far east as western Siberia.

Narrow-lipped helleborine *E. leptochila*, also known as green-leaved helleborine, has pale green or whitish flowers sometimes mottled with red and is found only in deep shade, usually in beech woods on calcareous soils but also in ash woods with hazel. It occurs only in northwest and central Europe. Pendulous-flowered helleborine, *E. phyllanthes* has pale yellowish green flowers and also prefers beech woods in western Europe.

The dark red helleborine *E. atrorubens* is one of the most attractive members of this genus, having spikes of 8-18 faintly fragrant, reddish purple flowers

*Epipogium aphyllum*

which are pollinated by bees and wasps. It favours limestone rocks and screes, often in woodland, in Europe, the Caucasus and northern Iran. *E. muelleri* has pale pink or greenish flowers and is confined to western and central Europe where it grows in calcareous open woods, while *E. microphylla* has whitish green with a rosy tinged flowers and occurs in similar habitats in south and central Europe, extending into Asia.

*E. royleana* is fairly common in damp woods and grasslands between Pakistan and Tibet in the Himalayans, each greenish flower having a red or yellow lip. The stream orchid *E. gigantea*, also known as giant helleborine or chatterbox, is a robust plant up to 90 cm (3 ft) tall, distinguished by greenish brown flowers with salmon-pink lips. It grows in wet conditions in a great variety of habitats from deserts to mountains in western North America, from British Columbia to Mexico. A Eurasian wetland species is the marsh helleborine *E. palustris* which has lax one-sided spikes of white or rose-pink flowers.

**Orchidaceae; 24 species**

### *EPIPOGIUM*

A genus of leafless saprophytic orchids without roots but with branched rhizomes which, in association with soil fungi, are able to absorb nutrients directly from the soil. The two species *E. roseum*, an inhabitant of the Old World tropics, and ghost orchid or spurred coralroot *E. aphyllum*, which grows only in the deep shade of oak or beech forests, although its range covers northern and central Europe, the Pyrenees, northern Greece and Krym (Crimea), the Caucasus, Siberia and the Himalayas.

*E. aphyllum* has whitish translucent stems, sometimes tinged with pink, bearing 1-4 nodding flowers, the perianth segments of which are often yellowish or reddish with a white, violet-spotted lip. The flowers are usually cross-pollinated by bumblebees and other insects. Ghost orchids are notably erratic plants, sometimes apparently disappearing from a locality for tens of years before flowering again. They are protected by law in Britain.

**Orchidaceae; 2 species**

### *ERANTHIS*

A small genus of tuberous, perennial herbs of temperate Eurasia, commonly known as winter

*Epipactis purpurata*

aconites because of their early flowering. Most species contain toxic alkaloids and produce a burning sensation in the mouth.

*Eranthis hyemalis* is native to southern Europe but because of its popularity as a garden plant it is widely naturalized in northern Europe and North America. The bright yellow flowers develop before the basal leaves, although each solitary bloom is subtended by a ruff of three deeply divided stem leaves. The flowers usually have six petal-like outer perianth segments, a similar number of inner perianth segments which are reduced to nectaries and about 30 stamens. They are pollinated by hive bees and flies. *E. cilicica* is a similar species native to western Asia, which has copper-coloured leaves and larger golden flowers.

**Ranunculaceae; 6-7 species**

### GALANTHUS

A small genus of bulbous herbs of great horticultural significance distributed from Europe to Iran but with a distinct centre of distribution in the Mediterranean region. These plants are commonly known as snowdrops, as their drooping flowers are often seen when the snow is still on the ground. The generic name is derived from the Greek and literally translates as 'milkflower'.

The bulbs grow in compact masses, each sending up a stem which bears a single terminal flower. The flowers are solitary, white and nodding. The outer three perianth segments are much longer than the

*Galanthus nivalis*

*Hedera helix*

inner segments, each of the latter having a green patch near the tip and sometimes also at the base. The flowers remain open a long time and are pollinated by bees.

The best known species is snowdrop *Galanthus nivalis*, also called fair-maid-of-February since its attractive flowers are among the first to bloom in the spring. It occurs in deciduous woodlands from north-central France and White Russia to the Pyrenees, Sicily and southern Greece, and into Asia Minor and the Caucasus. Snowdrops are widely cultivated as garden plants and have become naturalised to the north of their native European range.

Other species include *G. plicatus*, found in woodlands and scrub in the eastern Mediterranean and western Asia; *G. ikariae*, which occurs from Greece to the Caucasus; and the giant snowdrop *G. elwesii*, a southeast European woodland species whose range also extends into western Asia. This latter species is currently suffering from severe over-exploitation of its wild populations: it has been estimated that some 20 million bulbs are removed from the wild and exported from Turkey every year.

**Liliaceae (Amaryllidaceae); about 12 species**

*HEDERA*

A genus containing four or five species, commonly called ivies, which are spread across Europe, the Mediterranean region and into Asia. These plants are woody lianes with distinct juvenile and mature stages, usually with three-lobed leaves and rooting stems when young, but producing elliptical leaves and rootless flowering shoots later on.

Ivy *Hedera helix* is found throughout almost the entire range of the genus. It is a woody liane whose 30 m (98 ft) stems may be either climbing or creeping. The terminal, spherical umbels of flowers are not produced until the autumn and are pollinated by flies and wasps. The flowers are only 3-4 mm (0.1-0.2 in) across, and have five toothed sepals and five yellowish

green petals, developing later into black globose fruit which ripen over the winter and are an important source of food for nestling birds in the spring.

Ivy wood is used as a substitute for box (*Buxus sempervirens*), the young twigs are a source of dye and an infusion of bruised leaves was formerly used to relieve the symptoms of alcoholic excess. For this reason the plant was dedicated to Bacchus, who is often depicted wearing a wreath of ivy leaves. Throughout the ages ivy has been regarded as the symbol of fidelity; in an old Greek custom the priest would present newlyweds with a wreath of this plant. An ivy leaf is the badge of the Gordons.

Ivy is also an important food plant for the caterpillars of several butterflies, including the holly blue butterfly *Celastrina argiolus* and moths such as the yellow-barred brindle *Acasis viretata*, the swallow-tailed moth *Ourapteryx sambucaria*, the willow beauty *Peribatoides rhomboidaria* and the old lady *Mormo maura*.

Other plants in this genus are Persian ivy *H. colchica*, a large-leaved species of western Asia, from the Caucasus to Iran; *H. nepalensis*, found from Afghanistan to southwest China and Burma; Canary Island or Madeira ivy *H. canariensis* (*H. maderensis*); and Japanese ivy *H. rhombea*, which is native to Japan and Ryukyu Island.

**Araliaceae; 4-5 species**

*HELLEBORUS*

A genus of perennial herbs distributed across Europe, the Mediterranean region and western Asia, with two disjunct species in Tibet and China. Commonly known as hellebores, these plants have very distinctive flowers, the parts of which are arranged in spirals. The outermost whorl of perianth segments consists of five greenish or petaloid persistent sepals, while the inner whorl contains 5-12 shorter, green, tubular nectaries. The generic name is derived from a combination of Greek *elein* ('to injure'), and *bora*

('food'), referring to their poisonous nature.

All hellebores contain the highly toxic glycosides helleborin and helleborcin. *Helleborus niger*, known variously as black hellebore, melampode or Christmas rose, is one of the most poisonous species. According to Pliny, around 1400 BC it was used by Melampus, a soothsayer and physician, as a purgative in mania. In the sixteenth century it was believed that an animal which had eaten something poisonous or was troubled by a cough could be cured by leaving a piece of black hellebore root in a hole in its ear for 24 hours. In herbal medicine black hellebore is violently narcotic and was formerly much used in the treatment of dropsy, nervous disorders and hysteria, although great care must be taken with its administration.

Many hellebores favour woodland habitats and most prefer calcareous soils. Two common European species are bear's-foot or stinking hellebore *Helleborus foetidus*, and green hellebore *H. viridis*. The flowers of *H. viridis* have yellowish green, spreading sepals, whilst those of *H. foetidus* are bell-shaped and bordered with reddish purple. Both flower in March and April and are pollinated by early bees and other insects. The flowers of *H. niger*, which is native to central and southern Europe and western Asia, have spreading cream, white or pinkish sepals and appear in the middle of winter, hence its common name of Christmas rose.

Other species include *H. lividus*, which is confined to the Balearic Islands, Corsica and Sardinia; *H. cyclophyllus* from woods and thickets in the Balkan peninsula; *H. odorus*, which is found only in the eastern Mediterranean region; and *H. multifidus* which is confined to Yugoslavia and Albania. Two species of eastern central Europe are *H. dumetorum* and *H. purpurascens*, the latter having distinctive violet-purple flowers. Lenten rose *H. orientalis* is found in Greece and Asia Minor, its flowers ranging from greenish white through all shades of pink to black.

**Ranunculaceae; 20 species**

*Helleborus foetidus*

## HEMEROCALLIS

A genus of rhizomatous perennial herbs native to temperate Eurasia, from central Europe to the Far East and especially characteristic of the forests of China and Japan. Commonly known as day lilies or spider lilies, they have long linear leaves and large colourful, funnel-shaped flowers arranged in branched inflorescences. Many species are cultivated as garden plants.

A native of China, the orange or tawny day lily *Hemerocallis fulva* may exceed 1 m (3.3 ft) in height and is distinguished by its 8-10 cm (3-4 in) pink or yellow-orange scentless flowers, the perianth segments of which are covered with a network of veins and have wavy margins. As with most plants in this genus, the magnificent flowers last only one day; however, when dried, they are used as a food flavouring in China and Japan. The young flower buds are reputed to taste like green beans when cooked and served with butter.

Yellow or lemon day lily *H. flava* (*H. liloasphodelus*) grows to a height of around 80 cm (31 in) and has fragrant lemon-yellow flowers 6-8 cm (2.4-3 in) wide. It grows in shady habitats from eastern Siberia to Japan and most parts of the plant are edible. The east Asian *H. minor* which is also found in the Chinese steppes is a miniature day lily with clear yellow flowers, the backs of which are flushed with copper. The fragrant buds of *H. middendorffi* are eaten as a vegetable in Japan.

**Liliaceae; about 15 species**

## HEPATICA

A small genus of woodland herbs distributed across all northern temperate regions. The exact origin of the generic name is uncertain, possibly being derived from *epatikos* ('affecting the liver') or *epar* ('the liver'), since the leaves resemble that organ.

The leathery, dark green leaves are either kidney or heart shaped with 3-5 broad, angular lobes. The flowers are subtended by a whorl of three more or less entire stem leaves which resemble sepals. Both leaves and flowers have mild medicinal properties, being used to treat disorders of the liver, indigestion,

*Humulus lupulus*

*Hepatica nobilis*

bleeding of the lungs and diseases of the chest in general. An infusion of the dried herb is employed in skin diseases as well as for freckles and sunburn.

The best known and most widespread Eurasian species is probably *Hepatica nobilis*, in which the leaves are purplish beneath and mottled above and the flowers are up to 2.5 cm (1 in) across, while the similar *H. transsilvanica*, confined to montane woods in Romania, has flowers up to 4 cm (1.6 in) in diameter. New World representatives include *H. americana* which has round-lobed basal leaves and flowers up to 2.5 cm (1 in) wide and grows in dry rocky woods in eastern North America from Canada to northern Florida, and *H. acutiloba*, which is distinguished by its more pointed leaf lobes.

**Ranunculaceae; 10 species**

## HUMULUS

A genus containing just two species of climbing perennial herbs. Japanese hop *Humulus japonicus*, is native to the temperate deciduous woodlands of Manchuria and Japan. Hop *H. lupulus* is probably native to Europe and western Asia but is now cultivated throughout the world's temperate regions, including North America.

The cone-like leafy female inflorescences of *H. lupulus* are used in brewing beer. Male and female flowers are found on separate plants. In cultivation female inflorescences with undeveloped seeds are preferred, so male plants are generally excluded from hop plantations where possible. In some parts of the world hops are trained to grow up wires for easy harvesting, as in southeast England.

Hops were first used in brewing in the fourteenth

the trees are fully in leaf, often carpeting the forest floor with a sea of blue.

Bluebells are rather limited in their distribution, occurring as a native plant only in western Europe, from central Spain to the Netherlands, although the species is locally naturalized as a garden escape in central Europe. The sticky juice extracted from bluebell bulbs was formerly used as a substitute for starch in the stiffening of collars and ruffs, was also employed as a glue for book binding and for fixing feathers on arrows, and was mentioned by Tennyson as a cure for snakebite.

A very similar species is the Spanish bluebell *H. hispanica*, in which the flowers are more or less erect rather than nodding, although it is best distinguished from *H. non-scripta* by its blue, rather than cream, anthers. As its common name suggests this plant is native to Spain, Portugal and North Africa, where it also occurs in shady habitats but is again naturalized in other parts of southern and western Europe. Italian squill *H. italica* is a similar species with lilac flowers which occurs only in southeast France, northwest Italy and southwest Portugal.

**Liliaceae; 3-4 species**

### KREYSIGIA

The sole member of this genus is *Kreysigia multiflora*, an inhabitant of southeast Australia. It has unbranched sinuous stems up to 45 cm (18 in) long bearing alternate heart-shaped leaves with prominent parallel veins. The long-stalked flowers are produced in the spring. They arise from the axils of the leaves and are usually solitary, although two or three together are not uncommon. Each flower has six spreading pale pink or purple perianth segments which ripen into globular capsules. *K. multiflora* is a typical inhabitant of the brush gullies along the coast of Queensland and northern New South Wales.

**Liliaceae; a single species**

### LAMIASTRUM

The sole member of this genus is yellow archangel

century in the Netherlands, their chief functions being to improve the flavour and lengthen the life of beer. Fresh hops are strongly aromatic due largely to the presence of a volatile oil containing humulene and two crystalline bitter principles: humulone and lupulinic acid. They also contain tannic acid which 'cleans' the beer of vegetable matter.

The twining stems of hops are long (to 6 m/197 ft), flexible and prickly. They contain a tough fibre which was formerly used in Sweden to manufacture cloth and have also been used to make a type of paper known as bine. A fine brown dye can be prepared from the leaves and flowerheads. The hop was first mentioned by Pliny as a Roman garden plant, the young shoots being eaten like asparagus. The English name is derived from the Anglo-Saxon word *hoppan* 'to climb'.

*H. lupulus* is an important foodplant for the larvae of several butterflies, including the red admiral *Vanessa atalanta* and the comma *Polygonia c-album*, and the following moths: the currant pug *Eupithecia assimilata*, the pale tussock *Calliteara pudibunda*, the dark spectacle *Abrostola trigemina*, the knot grass *Acronicta rumicus* and the clouded drab *Orthosia incerta*.

**Cannabidaceae; 2 species**

### HYACINTHOIDES

A genus of bulbous herbs, formerly classified as *Endymion*, native to western Europe and North Africa. The best known species of the bluebell *Hyacinthoides non-scripta* with its spikes of 4-16 nodding bells which are usually violet-blue but may be pinkish or even white. Bluebells start to bloom in April, before

*Lamiastrum galeobdolon*

*Lamiastrum galeobdolon* (*Galeobdolon luteum*), a perennial herb found in the temperate forests of Eurasia. The flowers are arranged in dense whorls in the axils of the leaf-like bracts. Each 2 cm (0.8 in) long flower has a two-lipped corolla which is yellow with brownish markings within a five-toothed tubular calyx. The flowers appear in May and June and are pollinated by bees. Yellow archangel is a characteristic member of the ground flora in woods on heavy soils, especially those in which coppicing has taken place. It is common throughout most of Europe extending into Iran, but is rare in the Mediterranean region and the extreme north. The foliage is sometimes eaten as greens in Europe.

**Labiatae; a single species**

### LATHRAEA

A small genus of perennial parasitic forest herbs commonly known as toothworts and confined to temperate Eurasia. Toothworts have pale, branched, creeping rhizomes with rootlets which are swollen where they are attached to the roots of the host plant. The rhizome is also covered with whitish fleshy scales, in the axils of which the flowers are produced. Each flower consists of a bell-shaped, four-lobed calyx and a two-lipped corolla, with a crescent-shaped nectary at the base of the ovary.

The most widespread species is toothwort *Lathraea squamaria*, which occurs throughout most of Europe and western Asia as far as the Himalayas. It has erect whitish stems between 8-30 cm (3-12 in) tall, around which are arranged white or dull-purple flowers which are pollinated by bumblebees. Toothwort is usually parasitic on the roots of various woody plants, especially beech, hazel, elm and alder, although in some places in southern France it is apparently saprophytic.

Purple toothwort *L. clandestina*, which is confined to southern and western Europe, differs in having almost completely subterranean stems, with only the deep violet flowers, which may be 5 cm (2 in) long, protruding above the soil surface. This species usually parasitizes the roots of willows, poplars and alders and as a consequence is often found in riverine woods. *L. rhodopea* is a yellowish brown plant which is parasitic on the roots of various trees and is found only in the woodlands of southern Bulgaria and northeast Greece.

**Scrophulaceae; 7 species**

### LEUCOJUM

A small genus distributed from Europe to Morocco and Iran. The various species are often known as snowflakes and are typically inhabitants of damp woods on acid soils. The plants are characterized by their loose umbels of 1-7 bell-shaped, white or pink, nodding flowers. In some species the perianth segments are green tipped, so that the flowers are not dissimilar to those of snowdrops in general appearance (see *Galanthus*).

*Melittis melissophyllum*

Spring snowflake *Leucojum vernum* is a plant of damp shady habitats in the hills of central Europe. It flowers from February to April, is pollinated by bees, butterflies and moths and the seeds are dispersed by ants. The more widespread summer snowflake *L. aestivum*, sometimes called Loddon lily, of Europe, Asia Minor and northern Iran, is more frequently found in wet willow thickets by streams. It flowers from April to May and is also pollinated by bees, although the seeds contain air-filled tissues and are dispersed by water.

Most of the other species in this genus have very restricted distributions, such as *L. nicaeense*, found only in southeast France, and *L. longifolium*, which is confined to Corsica. *L. autumnale*, with very narrow leaves and pale pink flowers, usually two per stem, that appear in the autumn, is native to western Iberia, Sardinia and Sicily.

**Liliaceae (Amaryllidaceae); 9 species**

### MEDEOLA

The only species in this genus is *Medeola virginiana*, a perennial herb of moist woodlands in eastern North America. It is known as Indian cucumber-root because of its white brittle rhizomes which taste and smell rather like cucumber and were formerly used by the American Indians as a fresh vegetable. The plant also has diuretic properties.

This tall, somewhat woolly plant has leaves arranged in two whorls, the uppermost ring of three leaves being smaller than the lower whorl of 6-10 leaves which occupies the midpoint on the stem. Several nodding yellowish green flowers emerge from the centre of the upper whorl, each having six recurved, petaloid perianth segments. The fruit are dark blue-purple berries. Indian cucumber-root is found from eastern Canada to Florida, Alabama and Louisiana.

**Liliaceae; a single species**

### MELITTIS

The sole member of this genus – bastard balm *Melittis melissophyllum* – is a typical inhabitant of deciduous forests in Europe. It is a strong-smelling perennial herb with stems up to 0.5 m (20 in) in height bearing opposite pairs of stalked oval leaves with blunt-toothed margins. The axillary flowers are highly conspicuous, up to 4 cm (1.6 in) long, the pink-purple, white or cream corolla tube greatly exceeding the calyx. The flowers are pollinated by bumblebees and hawkmoths. Bastard balm grows only in shady places in western, central and southern Europe, extending into the Ukraine.

**Labiatae; a single species**

### NECTAROSCORDUM

Just two species belong to this Eurasian genus of bulbous perennial herbs, both of which smell strongly of garlic and are typical of damp shady woods. The basal leaves are linear and strongly keeled while the flowers are arranged in a terminal umbel.

The best known species is *Nectaroscordum siculum*, in which the umbel is composed of long-stalked, drooping flowers that become erect as the fruits mature. The flowers are broadly bell-shaped and consist of two whorls, each of three leathery perianth segments, the inner ones being longer and broader than the outer. Two subspecies have been recognized: *N. siculum* ssp. *siculum*, with greenish red flowers, which is confined to the western Mediterranean region, and *N. siculum* ssp. *bulgaricum*, with dull greenish white flowers tinged with pale pink on the outside, which is native to southeast Europe, extending into western Asia.

**Liliaceae; 2 species**

### NEOTTIA

A small genus of leafless saprophytic orchids confined to temperate regions of Eurasia, mostly in woodland. The generic name *Neottia* ('nest') refers to the tangled

*Neottia nidus-avis*

ball of roots, which resemble a bird's nest; these have also given the bird's nest orchid *Neottia nidus-avis* its common name and specific name. The roots grow in association with fungi and enable the plant to obtain nutrients directly from the soil.

Plants in this genus produce numerous flowers arranged in a spike, each flower having a two-lobed lip and more or less equal perianth segments which converge slightly to form a helmet. Although the flowers do not have a spur, nectar is produced from a slight concavity near the base of the lip. Small flies have been seen visiting the flowers but it is probable that most plants are self-pollinated. A curious feature

of this genus is that the plants are capable of flowering and setting seed in a completely subterranean environment.

Bird's nest orchid *Neottia nidus-avis* is a widespread inhabitant of beech and pine woods on calcareous soils. Its range extends throughout Europe to North Africa, where it is rare, Caucasus, central and northern Asia. This plant has no green leaves but the few stunted scales at the base of the stem do produce chlorophyll and the plant obtains a small amount of energy from photosynthesis. The flowers are greenish or yellowish white.

**Orchidaceae; 9 species**

## OBOLARIA

The sole member of this genus is pennywort *Obolaria virginica* a low (15 cm/6 in) fleshy plant with dull white or purplish flowers arranged in groups of three in the axils of purplish leaves at the tip of the stem. Each flower is about 1.3 cm (0.5 in) long and has four petals and two sepals. Pennywort is a perennial herb typical of the moist deciduous forests and thickets of eastern North America, its range extending from New Jersey to Florida, Texas and West Virginia. The generic name is derived from the Greek *obolos* ('a small coin'), and refers to the paired rounded leaves.

**Gentianaceae; a single species**

## PANAX

A small genus of North American and eastern Asian temperate woodlands. The generic name comes from the Greek *panakos* ('a panacea'), in reference to the miraculous qualities ascribed to these plants by the Chinese, who consider them capable of curing all ills. In China the forked roots are known as *Jin-Chien* ('like a man'), because they resemble the human form, from which is derived the common name of ginseng. The American Indian name of *garantoquen* has the same meaning.

The best known species is the eastern Asian *Panax ginseng*, the roots of which have been used for centuries in Chinese and Tibetan medicine, especially as a cure for tuberculosis and to slow the aging process. For this reason ginseng is often called the 'root of life' and is gaining popularity in the western world. *P. ginseng* is a perennial herb with a long slender stem terminating in three or four leaflets beneath a small pink or white umbel of five-petalled flowers. *P. ginseng* is now extremely rare in the wild due to the over collection of its roots, each of which

*Paris quadrifolia*

*Paris quadrifolia*

may fetch up to £10,000 ($18,000); it is protected by law in the USSR and China.

Japanese ginseng *P. pseudo-ginseng* is another eastern Asian species, the roots of which are used in cancer treatments in China. Its stems are topped with a whorl of 4-6 digitate leaves and a solitary umbel of greenish yellow flowers.

*P. quinquefolium* is a native of cool moist woodlands in the eastern half of North America as well as the forests of eastern Asia. Its whorls of three compound leaves are topped by solitary umbels of small greenish white or yellowish green flowers, each about 2 mm (0.1 in) wide. Again the root is highly prized by the Chinese as a heart stimulant and alleged aphrodisiac and is valued for its tonic properties in North America, where over-collecting has rendered it a threatened species in many states. Dwarf ginseng *P. trifolium* is a smaller pinkish-flowered version of *P. quinquefolium*, found in much the same habitats and geographical area of North America. The tubers can be eaten raw or boiled.

### Araliaceae; 6 species

### *PARIS*

A small genus of perennial rhizomatous herbs distributed across the northern temperate regions of the Old World. The tall erect stems are crowned with an unmistakable whorl of 4-8 pointed oval leaves. The solitary flowers arise from the centre of the whorl and have 4-6 narrow green sepals, 4-6 linear yellowish green petals and 6-10 stamens. The fruit is a poisonous berry-like capsule. The generic name is derived from *par*, referring to the regularity of the leaves.

Herb Paris *Paris quadrifolia* is probably the best known member of this genus, usually having four leaves, four sepals, four petals and eight stamens. The flowers are visited by flies, but if cross-pollination fails the stamens grow on to the stigmas to ensure that seeds are produced. Herb Paris grows in woods and other shady habitats throughout most of Europe, extending eastwards into the Caucasus and Siberia; it is rare in the Mediterranean region.

Herb Paris was formerly a very popular medicinal plant, although its use is now limited to homeopathy. It contains a powerful glycoside, paradin, which is narcotic and can be fatal in large doses. More prudent use of this drug, however, has been found to be beneficial in the treatment of bronchitis, spasmodic coughs, rheumatism, heart palpitations and cramp. Various parts of the plant have been employed with some success as an antidote against mercurial and arsenic poisoning, as an aphrodisiac and as a cure for madness, while the juice of the berries cures eye inflammations.

*P. polyphylla* is a similar species of the western Asian forests from Pakistan to southwest China, but is distinguished by its thread-like sepals which may be up to 10 cm (4 in) in length. The petals may be either yellow or purple and the globular fruits contain scarlet seeds.

### Liliaceae; 5 species

### *PHRYMA*

A tiny genus found in eastern North America and from India to Japan. There is some confusion as to whether or not the Old and New World plants should be treated as separate species or not, but here we shall deal with a single taxon *Phryma leptostachya*. This plant, which is commonly called lopseed because of its downward-hanging fruits, is also sometimes classified in a separate family, the Phrymaceae, of which it is the only representative.

Growing to a height of almost 1 m (3.3 ft), lopseed has coarsely toothed leaves below and a slender elongated spike of small white or pinkish flowers at the apex. Both leaves and flowers are arranged in opposite pairs. Each two-lipped flower is about 6 mm (0.2 in) long, the lower lip much longer than the upper, and has four stamens. Lopseed flowers in late summer and typically grows in moist woods and thickets. The dry fruits remain enclosed within the calyx and hang down against the stem.

### Verbenaceae; 1-2 species

### *POLYGONATUM*

A genus of perennial woodland herbs distributed across the northern temperate regions of the world, especially southwest China. The plants are distinguished by their semierect leafy stems which bear nodding flowers in the axils. The flowers range from tubular to bell-shaped, the flower parts arranged in threes, and the fruits are berries. Many species are called Solomon's seals (see also *Smilacina*), probably because of the distinctive scars formed on the rhizome when the stems are removed, although the name may possible refer to their medical prowess in the healing of open wounds and bones.

Many species of Solomon's seal were formerly much used in medicine, the root containing convallarin (see *Convallaria*) is said to be beneficial in cases of pulmonary consumption and bleeding of the lungs and is also used to treat inflammation of the stomach and bowels, piles and chronic dysentery. The bruised roots were once popular as a cure for black eyes and a decoction of the root in wine was drunk to aid the knitting of broken bones. The young shoots of *Polygonatum multiflorum* may be boiled

*Polygonatum odoratum*

and eaten as a vegetable and the flowers and roots were a popular constituent of snuff.

The most widespread species is Solomon's seal *P. multiflorum*, which is found from Europe across temperate Asia to Japan. It has round arching stems up to 80 cm (31 in) long with alternate elliptical leaves and axillary racemes of 2-5 flowers. Each greenish white flower is 9-15 mm (0.4-0.6 in) long, narrowly bell-shaped but contracted in the middle. They are either visited by bees or self-pollinated. Solomon's seal thrives in calcareous woodlands, particularly on limestone. The foliage of *P. multiflorum* is eaten by the larvae of the Solomon's seal sawfly *Phymatocera aterrima*.

Whorled Solomon's seal *P. verticillatum*, which is distinguished by its angled stems with leaves arranged in whorls, is found in montane woods over most of Europe except the extreme south, extending to the Caucasus, Asia Minor and the Himalayas. It is protected by law in Britain. Angular Solomon's seal *P. odoratum* is similar to *P. multiflorum* but has four-angled stems and scented cylindrical flowers which are not contracted in the middle. It is found in limestone woods across most of temperate Eurasia.

*P. hookeri* grows in southern Asia, especially southwest China, and is distinguished by its minute size (2-5 cm/0.8-2 in tall) and almost erect mauve or pinkish flowers. *P. cirrhifolium* is another easily identifiable species which, although superficially similar to *P. verticillatum*, has coiled tendril-like tips to the leaves and white flowers tinged with purple or green. Both species prefer forested habitats, as do *P. latifolium*, a robust species of eastern Europe and western Asia, and *P. orientale*, which occurs in montane forests in the Caucasus and Anatolia.

Smooth Solomon's seal *P. biflorum* is a native of the forests of eastern North America, as are hairy Solomon's seal *P. pubescens* and great Solomon's seal *P. canaliculatum*, the latter being one of the largest members of the genus at over 2 m (6.6 ft) tall. American Indians and early settlers formerly used the starchy rhizomes as food.

**Liliaceae; 53 species**

### *PRENANTHES*

A small genus of perennial herbs distributed across northern temperate regions, extending south into the African mountains. The much-branched stems bear lobed, stem clasping leaves and numerous violet or purple composite flowerheads with ray-florets only (disc-florets are absent).

Purple lettuce *Prenanthes purpurea* is a widespread Eurasian species which favours beech woods and other shady habitats, especially in the mountains. It has blue-green lyre-shaped leaves and long-stalked pink-purple flowerheads, each with 3-6 ray-florets arranged in open slightly drooping clusters. The larvae of the central and southern European lettuce shark moth *Cucullia lactucae* feed on the leaves. Further east in the forests and meadows of the Himalayan region between Afghanistan and central Nepal, grows *P. brunoniana*. This species has dissected leaves and lax terminal clusters of blue, purple or white flowerheads, each with 3-5 ray-florets.

North American species include white lettuce or rattlesnake root *P. alba*, which has pinkish drooping flowerheads arranged in clusters along the stem, each with 8-12 ray-florets. It grows in rich woods and thickets across southeast Canada and from New England through the Appalachians to upland Georgia. A bitter tonic was once made from the roots which was effective in treating dysentery, while the common name suggests that the plant was formerly employed in cases of snakebite. Other eastern North American

*Polygonatum multiflorum*

species are gall-of-the-earth *P. trifoliata*, tall white lettuce *P. altissima*, smooth white lettuce *P. racemosa* and lion's foot *P. serpentaria*.

**Compositae; 25 species**

## SANGUINARIA

The sole member of this genus bloodroot or red puccoon *Sanguinaria canadensis*, is native to the rich woodlands of eastern North America, from Canada to Florida and Texas. The generic name is derived from the Latin *sanguinarius* ('bleeding') which, like the common name, refers to the orange-red juice produced by the rhizomes.

Bloodroot is a perennial spring-flowering plant, each rhizome producing but a single blue-green 5-9 lobed leaf and a flowering stem about 15 cm (6 in) tall. When this palmately divided, scalloped leaf first appears it is wrapped around the terminal flower bud, but later increases in size. The solitary white waxy flower has 8-20 petals, with alternate petals slightly narrower, golden stamens and two sepals which fall as soon as the flower opens. These flowers open only in full sunlight and close at night, although they are relatively short lived. The seeds develop inside a narrow oblong pod, pointed at both ends and about

*Prenanthes autumnalis*

2.5 cm (1 in) long.

The juice produced by the rhizomes of *Sanguinaria canadensis* contains the alkaloids sanguinarine, chelerythine and protopine, the latter an opium alkaloid. The rhizomes also contain red resins and a high level of starch. Although many of these chemicals are powerful poisons, bloodroot was formerly widely used in medicine as an emetic and cathartic expectorant. Despite its nauseating flavour it is of value in treating such diverse complaints as asthma, bronchitis, pulmonary consumption, heart disease, nervous irritation, dysentery, ulcers and ringworm. The juice was formerly employed by the American Indians as a decorative skin dye and an insect repellent and has also been used with some success by French and American dyers.

**Papaveraceae; a single species**

## SARCODES

Another North American genus with a single species – the snow plant *Sarcodes sanguinea*, which grows only in coniferous forests in the southwestern United States from southern Oregon to southern California. This saprophytic forest herb first appears in April as the snow begins to disappear, hence its common name. It is extremely conspicuous among the snow as all aerial parts of the plant are brilliant scarlet. The stout fleshy stems, 20-60 cm (8-24 in) in height, bear overlapping scales in the lower part and five-lobed bell-shaped flowers above, each of which is situated beneath a slender arching bract.

*Sarcodes sanguinea* has no chlorophyll and is

*Sarcodes sanguinea*

therefore unable to obtain energy from the sun by photosynthesis. Instead it is saprophytic, the roots absorbing nutrients directly from decaying material in the soil.

**Monotropaceae; a single species**

### SHORTIA

A genus of perennial evergreen herbs containing a single North American species and five representatives in eastern Asia. Oconee bells *Shortia galacifolia,* the only American representative, was named in honour of the nineteenth century Kentucky botanist Dr Charles Wilkins Short. This extremely rare plant was first discovered in 1788 but was not seen again for almost a century, and although it shows no sign of spreading in its natural habitat along stream margins in the moist woodlands of the Appalachians (in North and South Carolina and

Georgia), it grows quite happily in gardens.

Oconee bells reaches a maximum height of 20 cm (8 in). Its shiny evergreen leaves are rounded, with distinctive scalloped margins, and the solitary, white, funnel-shaped flowers are produced terminally on erect, leafless stalks. Each flower is about 2.5 cm (1 in) wide and has irregularly toothed lobes. Fringed bell *S. soldanelloides* is a typical Asian species.

**Diapensiaceae; a single species**

### SMILACINA

A genus of perennial rhizomatous herbs with leafy stems distributed across northern temperate regions, essentially in eastern Asia, the Himalayas and North America. Plants in this genus are commonly known as Solomon's seal (see also *Polygonatum*). The alternate stalkless leaves clasp the stem and the small white flowers are borne in a terminal spike or branched

inflorescence. Each flower has three petals, three petal-like sepals and six stamens and is generally shaped like a small star. The berries are often bright ruby red when mature.

False Solomon's seal *Smilacina racemosa,* is a common North American species which has arching stems, pyramidal clusters of numerous small white flowers and translucent red berries. It grows in woods and clearings in eastern North America from Canada to Virginia, Georgia and Missouri and in moist forests in the mountains of the west. Another widespread North American species is star-flowered Solomon's seal *S. stellata,* also known as star flower, which has larger, distinctly star-shaped flowers and berries which eventually turn blackish red, while three-leaved Solomon's seal *S. trifolia* is native to boggy habitats from New Jersey to Canada.

Two Asian species are *S. purpurea,* with pendulous narrow clusters of purple (or rarely white) flowers, and *S. oleracea,* which is distinguished by its broad spreading inflorescences of pure white or pinkish purple flowers. Both species are widely distributed in the Himalayas and southwest China, where the young plants of *S. purpurea* are sometimes boiled and eaten as vegetables.

**Liliaceae; about 30 species**

### TAMUS

A genus of climbing perennial herbs distributed across Macaronesia, southern Europe, North Africa and western Asia. Some authorities regard all species as subspecies or variants of black bryony *Tamus communis.* The plants have large cylindrical to ovoid tubers which, despite their acrid taste, may be eaten boiled. The slender twining stems have alternate leaves and narrow axillary inflorescences of inconspicuous unisexual flowers, bell-shaped, with male and female flowers growing on different plants. Both sexes have six stamens but these are rudimentary in the female flowers. The brightly coloured berries are poisonous, as are most parts of the plant.

Black bryony *Tamus communis* has heart-shaped, dark green, shiny leaves distinctively patterned with 3-9 curved and branched veins. The greenish yellow flowers are 3-6 mm (0.1-0.2 in) in diameter and the 10-12 mm (0.4-0.5 in) berries are red or yellow. Black bryony is a common inhabitant of woods and hedgerows in southern and western Europe and Macaronesia, where its weak stems twine around trees and shrubs alike. Although the root is deadly if eaten, it has been used to effect on unbroken chilblains and to remove discoloration caused by bruises and black eyes.

**Dioscoreaceae; 4-5 species**

### TRILLIUM

A genus of rhizomatous perennial herbs, commonly known as wake robins, found from the Himalayas northwards into eastern Asia, including Japan, and across North America with a centre of distribution in the southern Appalachians. As their generic name suggests, both the leaves and floral parts of these plants are arranged in threes or multiples of three. The flowers are solitary and terminal, consisting of three green, persistent sepals and three larger variously coloured petals, and are commonly held above a whorl of three diamond-shaped leaves. The seeds are contained within colourful berries and are reputed to be dispersed by ants.

Most plants in the genus have medicinal properties. The local name for many North American species is birthroot, as the rhizomes were widely used among both Indians and early settlers to promote parturition, as well as having antiseptic, astringent and expectorant properties.

Purple trillium or stinking Benjamin *Trillium erectum* is a typical species of rich forests of eastern North America, from the southern Appalachians to the east coast of Canada. The nodding maroon or reddish brown flowers have an unpleasant odour

*Trillium grandiflorum*

*Trillium erectum*

97

*Viola biflora*

which attracts carrion flies that act as pollinators. According to the *Doctrine of Signatures* of early herbalists, plants were used in the treatment of ailments or organs they resembled, thus *T. erectum* was formerly used in cases of gangrene.

Other eastern species are Vasey's wake robin *T. vaseyi* of the southern Appalachians which is similar to stinking Benjamin but has pleasantly scented flowers; large-flowered or snow trillium *T. grandiflorum*, a frequently cultivated plant with large, waxy-white flowers, and several species in which the flowers appear closed, including red trillium *T. sessile*, also known as toadshade. Painted toadshade *T. undulatum* has pink-centred white flowers and is found in moist acid woods and swamps in the eastern half of North America. *T. persistens*, known only from Georgia, is listed as an endangered species by the United States Fish and Wildlife Service (1985).

Western wake robin *T. ovatum* grows in damp shady woods from British Columbia to California and Colorado, where it flowers as soon as the snow disappears. Each stem has three short-stalked leaves at the tip, within which nestles a single three-petalled flower up to 5 cm (2 in) across. The flowers are white when newly opened but acquire a pink flush with age. Other western species include Klamath trillium

*T. rivale*, of northwestern California and southwestern Oregon; giant wake robin *T. chloropetalum*, which occurs only west of the Cascade Mountains and the Sierra Nevada, and roundleaf trillium *T. petiolatum*.

**Liliaceae; 30 species**

### UVULARIA

A small genus of east North American woodland herbs, commonly known as bellworts. The generic name is derived from the resemblance of the drooping flowers to the uvula at the back of the throat; because of this similarity, early herbalists used the plants to treat throat diseases.

One of the most common species is sessile bellwort or wild oats *Uvularia sessilifolia*, which grows in woods and thickets from Canada to Georgia, Alabama, Missouri and North Dakota. The angled stems bear stalkless oblong leaves which are pale green above and white below. The terminal flowers, which grow either singly or in pairs, are creamy yellow, narrow, drooping bells, while the three-angled seed capsules resemble beechnuts.

Other species are perfoliate bellwort or strawbell *U. perfoliata*, in which the stem appears to pass through the middle of the leaves; large-flowered bellwort *U. grandiflora*, distinguished by its larger

bright yellow flowers; and Florida bellwort *U. floridana* and mountain bellwort *U. pudica*, both of which are very similar to *U. sessilifolia*.

**Liliaceae; 5 species**

### VIOLA

Although violets are found in many habitats, they are particularly diverse in the forests of the northern temperate region in North America and Eurasia. As a group they have alternate leaves and solitary (rarely two), bilaterally symmetrical flowers, the lower petal of which is spurred.

Many species have medicinal properties, especially sweet violet *Viola odorata*. Pliny describes a liniment of violet root and vinegar for gout and disorders of the spleen and states that a garland of violets will dispel the symptom of alcoholic excess. The ancient Britons used the flower as a cosmetic; an ancient poem recommends that violets be steeped in goat's milk to increase female beauty. The Romans made wine from the flowers of sweet violets and they were formerly used as a cure for insomnia. Violet leaves are used in cooling plasters and poultices, while the rhizomes and seeds are strongly emetic and purgative.

Today the chief use of violets is as a colouring agent and perfume, the latter being very expensive to extract in any quantity. The flowers are also crystallized as an attractive sweetmeat (in Devon and Parma) and have been used in salads. They are also the source of the medicinally employed Syrup of Violets, which forms a principal ingredient of Oriental sherbet and is reputed to have mild laxative properties. Syrup of Violets was also formerly employed in the treatment of such diverse ailments as ague, epilepsy, inflammation of the eyes, pleurisy and jaundice, among others.

In western Eurasia typical violets of deciduous woodlands include such widespread species as sweet violet *Viola odorata*, which has fragrant deep purple or white flowers; hairy violet *V. hirta* and the similar common dog-violet *V. riviniana*, both of which have scentless blue-violet flowers; and early dog-violet *V. reichenbachiana*, whose lilac flowers have dark purple spurs. *Viola mirabilis* has pale violet flowers and thrives in woodlands on base-rich soils, and *V. sieheana* has pale blue or white flowers and grows in southeastern Europe and western Asia.

Further east, forest violets include *V. wallichiana*, a Himalayan species with dark-centred yellow flowers which thrives on mossy rocks in forests to 3,000 m (9,800 ft), *V. indica*, a prominent Kashmir spring flower distinguished by its large fragrant, violet-blue flowers; *V. pilosa*, a central and southeast Asian species with lilac flowers; and *V. betonicifolia*, which is identified by its violet flowers and lance-shaped leaves with truncated bases, and is a denizen of central and southeast Asia and Australia.

The genus is no less diverse in the northern temperate regions of the New World, with such white-flowered species as sweet white violet *V. blanda*, whose fragrant flowers have purple-veined lower petals, and northern white violet *V. pallens* occurring in deciduous forests in the eastern half of North America. Other eastern violets are dog violet *V. conspersa*, which has bluish violet flowers, the lower petal with purple veins; long-spurred violet *V. rostrata*, with dark-centred pale blue flowers, common blue violet *V. papilionacea*, with blue, white or purple-veined flowers; and bird-foot violet *V. pendunca*, with large (to 4 cm/1.6 in wide) blue-violet flowers and orange anthers. Downy yellow violet *V. pubescens* is a hairy plant with yellow purple-veined flowers.

Canada violet *V. canadensis*, a fragrant white-flowered species, is found right across the northern half of the continent, while hooked-spur violet *V. adunca* has blue-violet flowers and grows in woodlands throughout North America. In the deciduous woodlands of western North America yellow-flowered violets are more characteristic, inducing *V. glabella* (commonly known as the stream, pioneer or smooth yellow violet), which grows in both coniferous and deciduous woods from Alaska through the Rockies to California's Sierra Nevada; yellow wood violet *V. lobata*, typical of dry, open forests in the southwestern mountain ranges; and redwood or evergreen violet *V. sempervirens*, which thrives in moist woods along the west coast.

Several violets also venture into the arctic region, including the two-flowered violet *V. biflora*, a scentless yellow-flowered species of Eurasian and Alaskan tundra and mountains further south; and the purple-flowered Labrador violet *V. labradorica* of heaths, herb slopes and snow patches in North America and southern Greenland, which is distinguished above all by its purple-bronze foliage.

The marsh violet *V. palustris* is found in arctic parts of North America, Greenland and Eurasia, also ranging as far south as the Azores, Morocco and the mountains of New England. It has kidney-shaped leaves and scentless pale violet blooms. In addition to the visible flowers, the marsh violet also bears smaller flowers which never open, hidden amongst the leaves. These produce large quantities of seed by self-pollination as an insurance policy against extremely short growing seasons and the absence of insect pollinators. This habit, known as cleistogamy, is common to many violets and other unrelated arctic plants.

European woodland violets, especially *V. odorata* and *V. riviniana*, are the sole foodplants of many butterfly larvae, including the pearl-bordered fritillary *Clossiana euphrosyne*, the small pearl-bordered fritillary *C. selene*, the violet or weaver's fritillary *C. dia*, the Queen of Spain fritillary *Issoria lathonia*, the high brown fritillary *Fabriciana adippe*, the dark green fritillary *Mesoacidalia aglaja* and the silver-washed fritillary *Argynnis paphia*.

**Violaceae; about 400 species.**

*Viola canina*

# CHAPTER FIVE

# GRASSLANDS

Natural grasslands occur on all five continents between latitudes 50° S and 60° N and cover about 20 per cent of the total land surface of the earth. They are found wherever average annual precipitation is insufficient to support tree growth but is not so low as to create desert conditions, and equally, where waterlogged conditions prevent forest development. Grasslands are thought to have evolved about 40 million years ago, when the earth's climate underwent drastic changes involving a considerable reduction in rainfall and the vast forests of the dinosaurs were gradually replaced by more open plant communities.

The principal tracts of natural grassland range from the tropical tree-studded African savannas and the seasonally flooded llanos of Venezuela to the temperate North American prairies, the Eurasian steppes, the Brazilian cerrados and the pampas of Argentina. Smaller areas of natural grassland exist in India and Australia, in the Southern Alps of New Zealand and the South African veld. Seminatural grasslands also occur in temperate regions where the deciduous forests have been cleared by man and are maintained by burning, grazing or cutting.

The dominant plants of grasslands are perennial grasses, of which there are some 10,000 species. Their main requirement for growth is abundant light but they can tolerate low rainfall, hot sun, fire, grazing and mowing and are a very successful group. These grasses are associated with highly diverse communities of forbs (herbs other than grasses), most of which are perennial, produce buds just above or below the soil surface for protection from grazing, burning or mowing, overwinter as basal rosettes or prostrate leafy shoots and usually produce insect-pollinated flowers. To a lesser degree, annuals and dwarf shrubs are also present.

The flowering period is limited and occurs during the wet season in tropical grasslands and in the spring or summer in temperate regions where rainfall is more or less evenly distributed throughout the year. In order to avoid competition for the available resources, especially light, grassland herbs adopt a variety of strategies. Some, especially bulbous species, flower before the main flush of growth; others are trailing plants, using the grasses as a support much as lianes twine around tropical forest trees; and others may have low-growing foliage but produce enormously long stalks that raise their flowers above the level of the grasses and attract passing insects. Many grassland herbs have yellow flowers which can be seen by most insects more clearly than flowers of other colours and therefore enhance their chances of pollination.

Facing page: *Pulsatilla vernalis*

## ACERAS

The sole member of this genus is the man orchid *Aceras anthropophorum*, which is found in Europe from Spain to southwest Turkey and Lebanon, and in North Africa. The generic name means 'without spur', a feature which distinguishes this plant from its close relatives in the genus Orchis. Hybrids between the two genera are extremely common, however, especially with the military orchid *Orchis militaris*, the monkey orchid *O. simia* and the lady orchid *O. purpurea*.

The man orchid is essentially a plant of calcareous grasslands, although it is sometimes found in rocky places or along woodland edges. It is a slender plant, usually between 10 and 30 cm (4-12 in) tall, although some northern Spanish specimens reach 40 cm (16 in) or more. The two tubers are oval and undivided and the five or six basal leaves are oblong in shape. Inflorescences are long and narrow, with up to 90 flowers per spike, each subtended by a short membraneous bract. Both sepals and petals are greenish yellow, streaked and edged with red, and all perianth segments are curved inwards to form a helmet.

The dull yellow lip has a very distinctive man-like shape, from which this orchid derives both its specific and common names. The middle lobe of the lip is split into two narrow segments forming the legs, and the slender lateral lobes form the arms. The head is represented by the helmet. In the absence of a true spur the nectar is stored in a shallow depression at the base of the flower. The whole plant is fragrant, having a faint odour of coumarin (like new-mown hay).

**Orchidaceae; a single species**

*Aceras anthropophorum*

## ANACAMPTIS

The only member of this genus is the pyramidal orchid *Anacamptis pyramidalis* which thrives in open grasslands on calcareous soils and occasionally in open woodlands and scrub. The flowers are distinguished from those of the closely related *Orchis* by their much longer and more slender spurs. *Anacamptis pyramidalis* is widespread and rather common in western, central and southern Europe from Spain to Turkey, extending into the USSR including the Caucasus, Scandinavia and the Baltic islands, and North Africa.

The pyramidal orchid is a slender plant with leafy stems ranging from 20-60 cm (8-24 in) in height, arising from two ovoid or globose tubers. The flowers are arranged in a dense spike (2-8 cm/0.8-3 in long) which is conical when the lower flowers open (and responsible for both the common and specific names of this plant) but becomes egg-shaped or cylindrical as the upper flowers open. The flowers vary from pale to dark pink, with long down-curved spurs. The dorsal sepal and the petals curve inwards to form a hood, the lateral sepals are spreading and the lip is three-lobed. Only butterflies and moths, with their long probosces, are able to pollinate the flowers attracted by the nectar within the spur.

**Orchidaceae; a single species**

## ANTHERICUM

An essentially African genus of perennial herbs with representatives extending into Europe. The plants have rhizomes or tubers (not bulbs), the above-ground part of which dies back in winter. The linear leaves taper sharply towards the tip and have a sheathing base, while the loose inflorescences are characterized by flowers which are positioned at right angles to the axis (rotate). The six more or less equal perianth segments are white, often with a median dark line.

In Africa the genus is widespread in grassland habitats, often flowering after the first rains. A typical species is *Anthericum cameronii* which has white flowers about 2 cm (0.8 in) across that emerge from the inflorescence axis in groups of 1-3 and grows in the highland grasslands of East and Central Africa between 1,000 and 2,200 m (3,300-7,200 ft). Other common and attractive representatives are *A. gregorianum*, a robust plant from the montane grasslands of East Africa, which has fleshy leaves and white flowers with a three-veined green median stripe on each segment, and the delicate *A. subpetiolatum*, which has unstriped flowers arranged in lax spikes, becoming congested towards the tip, and is equally at home in both grasslands and woodlands in eastern Africa from Ethiopia to Zimbabwe.

Of the three European species, one of the most common and widespread is St Bernard's lily *A. liliago*, which has simple, unbranched spikes of 6-10 flowers, each with perianth segments 16-22 mm (0.6-0.9 in) long, greatly exceeding the stamens. It grows in dry grasslands, open woods and on stony slopes from Belgium and Sweden to northern Portugal, southern Italy and Greece. *A. ramosum* differs in having branched pyramidal inflorescences with smaller flowers, the perianth segments ranging from 10-14 mm (0.4-0.6 in) in length. It grows in dry sunny grasslands and open scrub from northern France, southern Sweden and Latvia to the Pyrenees, central Italy, Turkey and Krym (Crimea), and is particularly associated with the steppe grasslands of central Europe. The third species, *A. baeticum*, is confined to the mountains of southern Spain, where it grows in wet meadows.

**Liliaceae; 50 species**

## ASPHODELUS

A small genus of annual or rhizomatous perennial herbs distributed from the Canary Islands through the Mediterranean region to the Himalayas. The

*Asphodelus albus*

linear leaves are all basal and the numerous white or pale pink flowers are arranged in dense inflorescences. Each flower has six perianth segments and six stamens and produces six seeds. The generic name is derived from a Greek word meaning 'sceptre' and the plants are commonly known as asphodels.

Asphodel *Asphodelus ramosus* is a typical perennial species of the Mediterranean, with flat, somewhat keeled leaves up to 40 cm (16 in) long and 3 cm (1.2 in) wide and solid much-branched flowering stems up to 1.5 m (5 ft) tall. The white perianth segments are 15-20 mm (0.6-0.8 in) long. In ancient times this plant was regarded as the preferred food of the dead and was often planted near tombs. The dried and boiled rhizomes yield a mucilaginous substance which in some countries is mixed with grain or potato to make asphodel bread. In Spain the rhizomes are fed to cattle, and they are used in to make a strong glue. Although not used in modern medicine, the Greeks and Romans recognized the value of these rhizomes as a remedy for spasms and in the treatment of menstrual problems.

Other widespread Mediterranean species are hollow-stemmed asphodel *A. fistulosus*, an annual or short-lived perennial with hollow leaves and 70 cm (28 in) flowering stems which may be simple or branched and bear flowers with perianth segments being 5-12 mm (0.2-0.5 in) long; and *A. aestivus*, a robust perennial with stems up to 2 m (6.6 ft) tall and perianth segments 10-14 mm (0.4-0.6 in), whose range extends from the Canary Islands to Iran. The rhizomes of hollow-stemmed asphodel are eaten by the Bedouin in North Africa and those of *A. aestivus* are a source of yellow dye for carpets in Egypt and a gum (tchirish) used by book binders in Turkey. *A. bento-rainhae* is similar to *A. ramosus*, but is confined to pastures and cultivated fields in central Portugal.

White asphodel *A. albus* has a more northerly range, extending from southern Europe into northwest France, Switzerland and Hungary, where it is a

*Anacamptis pyramidalis*

*Balsamorhiza sagittata*

*Asphodelus aestivus*

characteristic plant of montane meadows and pastures, woodlands and heathlands. The flat leaves are 15-60 cm (6-24 in) long and about 2 cm (0.8 in) wide and the flowering stem may exceed 1 m (3.3 ft) but is often shorter. The large flowers are arranged in a simple unbranched inflorescence and have narrowly elliptical perianth segments ranging from 15-30 mm (0.6-1.2 in) in length.

**Liliaceae; 18 species**

### BAPTISIA

A small genus of perennial herbs with blue, yellow, cream or white flowers, most species of which are characteristic of the prairies of eastern North America. The generic name is derived from the Greek *baptizein* ('to dye'), in reference to the blue dye resembling indigo which is obtained from many of the plants.

One of the best known species is wild indigo or rattleweed *Baptisia tinctoria*. It is a hairless bushy plant growing up to 90 cm (3 ft) tall with palmately compound leaves, each having three ovate to wedge-shaped leaflets. The yellow pea-like flowers are about 1.3 cm (0.5 in) long and are arranged in numerous elongated, terminal inflorescences, later producing short, rounded, blue-black pods. Wild indigo thrives in dry grasslands from southeastern Canada to Florida, Louisiana and Minnesota; it is particularly abundant following fire. The black woody root is yellowish internally and has purgative, emetic, stimulant, astringent and antiseptic properties.

Prairie false indigo *B. leucantha*, also known as wild white indigo, is a bushy perennial distinguished by its white or cream flowers, black, drooping, oblong seed pods and stems covered with a whitish bloom. It grows to a maximum height of 1.5 m (5 ft) in prairies and on disturbed ground from Ontario to Mississippi and Texas. Other species are large-bracted indigo *B. leucophaea*, with whitish flowers; *B. bracteata*, with softly hairy, yellow-white flower spikes; and blue false indigo *B. australis*, with blue

*Balsamorhiza sagittata*

flowers and sap which turns purple on exposure to air. Hair rattleweed *B. arachnifera* is known only from Georgia and is considered an endangered species by the United States Fish and Wildlife Service (1985).

**Leguminosae; 17 species**

### BOMBYCILAENA

A tiny genus of woolly yellow-flowered annuals distributed from the Mediterranean to Afghanistan and typical of dry, open steppe grasslands. Plants in this genus have alternate leaves, narrowed towards the tip, and two or three flowerheads aggregated in terminal or axillary clusters. The outer florets, with thread-like two-toothed corollas, are usually female, but the inner florets are hermaphrodite or male and have five-toothed broadly tubular corollas.

*Bombycilaena erecta* is a characteristic species of the Mediterranean and Pannonic steppes, ranging from southwest Europe to western Asia. It is a grey-white plant with stems up to 20 cm (8 in) tall and linear leaves with wavy margins. The roughly spherical clusters of flowerheads arising from the leaf axils are up to 1 cm (0.8 in) across and are usually overtopped by the subtending leaves. *B. discolor*, confined to the Mediterranean region, has whitish stems and leaves and brownish clusters of flowerheads which are not overtopped by the subtending leaves.

**Compositae; 3 species**

### BULBINE

A genus of rhizomatous or bulbous lilies with somewhat succulent linear leaves springing from the base of the plant, distributed through tropical and South Africa, especially the southwest corner of Cape Province, and in Australia. The flowers are usually yellow and the filaments of the anthers bear characteristic tufts of long yellow hairs.

*Bulbine abyssinica* is widespread in the grasslands of East Africa, from Sudan to Zimbabwe, generally above 1,200 m (3,900 ft). The more or less erect

leaves form a basal rosette and the sulphur-yellow flowers, about 8 mm (0.3 in) across, occur in short broad spikes. One of the most bizarre southern African species is *B. mesembryanthemoides*, a small succulent whose only above-ground foliage consists of two very soft and watery, pale green leaves 5-10 mm (0.2-0.4 in) across. The flower-stems are only 5-10 cm (2-4 in) tall and bear up to six widely spaced, bright yellow flowers with reflexed perianth segments. More robust species include *B. sedifolia*, with succulent banana-shaped leaves up to 13 cm (0.5 in) long, the shrubby *B. praemorsa* and cushion-like *B. frutescens*.

One of the two Australian species is *B. bulbosa*, a small erect perennial with narrow grooved leaves and yellow star-like flowers about 2 cm (0.8 in) across which are produced on a slender leafless stem about 30 cm (12 in) high. It occurs in grassland habitats on the plains and tablelands of Queensland, New South Wales, Victoria, South Australia and Tasmania, where it flowers in spring and summer.

**Liliaceae; about 30 species**

### CALOPOGON

A small genus of orchids, commonly called grass-pinks and confined to North America. The generic name derives from the Greek for 'beautiful beard' in reference to the crest of hairs on the flower lip.

The grass-pink *Calopogon pulchellus* has long grass-like leaves and fragrant spikes of 2-10 pink flowers which open in sequence from the base upwards. Each flower measures almost 4 cm (1.6 in) in diameter and has three sepals and three petals, all of which are bright pink, the uppermost yellow-bearded and held erect above the remaining five inward-curving segments. Grass-pink thrives in wet acid meadows throughout much of eastern North America from Nova Scotia and Newfoundland to Florida, Arkansas and Oklahoma.

The other members of this genus are the bearded

grass-pink *C. barbatus*, in which all the flowers open at the same time, found from North Carolina southwards; pale grass-pink *C. pallidus*, which has smaller pale pink or whitish flowers and occurs from Virginia to Florida and Louisiana; and *C. tuberosus*, which is a frequent plant of the pine barrens of New Jersey and swamps in North Carolina.

**Orchidaceae; 4 species**

*Calopogon tuberosus*

## CAMASSIA

A genus of bulbous lilies characteristic of neotropical grasslands. Five species occur in North America, mostly in the west, and there is a single South American representative.

Camas or quamash *Camassia quamash* has an unbranched stem up to 60 cm (2 ft) high which arises from a bulb about 2.5 cm (1 in) across and is surrounded by a basal rosette of grass-like leaves. The bright blue (rarely white) flowers have six free perianth segments and six stamens and are arranged in a showy spike. Camas is a characteristic plant of wet meadows in western North America, its range extending from British Columbia to California and Utah.

Quamash is the plant's Indian name. Its bulbs are starchy, nutritious and taste rather like potatoes when boiled. They can also be baked, roasted, dried or eaten raw and were formerly the main vegetable in the diet of the Indians of Northwest America, trappers and early settlers. Elk, deer and moose are said to graze the plant in early spring.

The only eastern member of the genus is wild hyacinth *C. scilloides* (*C. fraseri*), which thrives in moist meadows and open woods from Pennsylvania to South Carolina, Georgia, Alabama and Texas and is particularly characteristic of the Mississippi valley. It has underground bulbs and long flabby basal leaves with a distinct keel. The leafless flower stems are 15-60 cm (6-24 in) tall and bear elongated lax clusters of lavender-blue flowers subtended by long green bracts. Like quamash, the bulbs were used for food by Indians and early settlers.

Other species are Leichtlin's camas *C. leichtlinii*, which only grows west of the Cascade Mountains from southern British Columbia to the southern part of California's Sierra Nevada, and *C. howellii* and *C. cusickii*, both of which are confined to the western United States.

**Liliaceae; 6 species**

## COELOGLOSSUM

The sole member of this genus is the frog orchid *Coeloglossum viride*, which is widespread across northern temperate regions. It is most common in calcareous grasslands, although it may occasionally be encountered on more acid soils as well as in scrub and along woodland margins.

Frog orchids have two ovoid tubers with palmate lobes which give rise to stems between 10 and 35 cm (4-14 in) high. The pale green leaves are broadly lanceolate at the base of the stem, becoming narrower further up. The 5-25 flowers are arranged in a rather lax cylindrical spike and the ovaries are twisted, giving the inflorescence a somewhat untidy appearance. The greenish yellow petals and sepals, edged in red and tinged with purple, converge to form a rounded hood, and the yellowish brown strap-like lip is three-lobed at the tip, with the middle lobe shorter than the laterals. Northern plants usually have darker flowers than their southern counterparts and high altitude specimens are usually rather stunted. In all cases these small plants are often difficult to spot because they blend in well with their grassland surroundings.

**Orchidaceae; a single species**

## CROCUS

A large genus of herbaceous perennials with corms, distributed from the Mediterranean to western China, over half the species native to Europe. The leaves are all basal, flat or channelled above and strongly keeled below, appearing with or after the flowers. Each flower arises from a short subterranean stalk and is sheathed by a membranous bract which may be accompanied by a similar bracteole. The long, narrow corolla tube, which begins below ground, expands into six more or less equal petaloid perianth segments. The throat of the corolla tube is ringed with hairs and the ovary is situated below ground.

*Crocus purpureus*

*Crocus* flowers vary from yellow or orange to pink or purple; white-flowered albino plants occur sporadically in populations of almost all species. The flowers close in dull weather and are visited by bees, moths and butterflies for nectar produced by the ovary. The anthers discharge their pollen outwards so that the insects come into contact with the pollen while probing for nectar. Each species is characterized by either spring/summer or autumn/winter flowering.

Many crocuses are particularly associated with grassland habitats, but are often rather restricted in their distribution. Species confined to southwestern Europe, for example, include *Crocus carpetanus* (spring), whose solitary pale yellow or white throated lilac flowers grow only in the montane meadows of central and northwest Spain and northern Portugal, and *C. nudiflorus* (autumn), a meadow plant of southwestern France and Spain with deep purple flowers. *C. nevadensis* (spring) has cream, white or pale lilac flowers with yellowish throats and occurs in mountain meadows in southern and eastern Spain and North Africa.

At the eastern end of the Mediterranean typical grassland crocuses are *C. malyi* (spring), a white-flowered species confined to western Yugoslavia; *C. pelistericus* (late spring), whose deep purple flowers are found only in damp mountain meadows in southern Yugoslavia, particularly in melting snow patches; *C. hadriaticus* (autumn), with white or lilac-tinged, yellow-throated flowers, which is confined to western and southern Greece; and *C. banaticus* (autumn), a plant with lilac or purple flowers restricted to Romania, Yugoslavia and the western Ukraine.

The central Mediterranean area is home to *C. medius* (autumn), a grassland and woodland species with white-throated lilac or purple flowers which is known only from northwest Italy and southeast France; *C. longiflorus* (autumn), whose purple flowers have conspicuous yellow throats and are restricted to grasslands and woodland margins in southwest Italy,

*Crocus nudiflorus*

Sicily and Malta; and *C. imperati* (spring), a species confined to western Italy, whose handsome flowers have orange throats and perianth segments which are violet within and yellowish, striped with purple on the outside.

Crocuses are also characteristic plants of the Asian steppes, a typical species being *C. reticulatus* (spring), which has white or lilac flowers, striped with purple on the outside. *C. flavus* (spring), whose flowers range from pale yellow to deep orange, is a steppe species from the Balkan peninsula, southern Romania and western Asia, as is the lilac-flowered *C. pallasii* (autumn), whose range extends from southeast Europe through Turkey into western Asia.

The saffron crocus *C. sativus*, whose flowers have blue-violet or reddish lilac, widely spreading perianth segments, is probably native to southern Europe and western Asia, although its exact origin is unknown. It has been cultivated since at least 1600 BC for its orange-yellow or brick-red styles and stigmas, which are used as a bitter and aromatic spice (saffron) and in medicine; they are the richest known natural source of vitamin $B_2$. This is an expensive product, however, since it is said that more than 130,000 flowers are required to produce 1 kg (2.2 lbs) of saffron!

**Iridaceae; 80 species**

### DACTYLORHIZA

This genus of orchids is distributed across Alaska, Eurasia, the Mediterranean and Macaronesia. The generic name translates literally as 'hand-rooted', on account of the characteristic palmately lobed tubers, which not only store food but are also able to absorb water from the soil. For this latter reason most plants in this genus grow in damp grasslands and are commonly known as marsh orchids, although some species are more typical of drier habitats.

*Dactylorhiza* species very rapidly develop mature flowering plants from seed, the first true tubers being produced in the third or fourth year. The flowers possess free and more or less equal perianth segments, a three-lobed lip, are spurred and are subtended by leaf-like bracts (unlike the membranous bracts of the closely related genus *Orchis*). They are pollinated by bees and hybrids between the various species, and even between *Dactylorhiza* and other orchid genera, are extremely common.

A typical Eurasian species is the heath spotted

*Dactylorhiza insularis*

*Dactylorhiza incarnata*

orchid *Dactylorhiza maculata* which has flowers ranging from white through pale pink to mauve, but always with darker markings on the lip. Many subspecies have been recognized, most growing in wet acid grasslands, peaty heathlands and moorland bogs across most of Europe and into northwestern Asia. Other characteristic grassland species include the elder-flowered orchid *D. sambucina* and the common spotted orchid *D. fuchsii*, both Eurasian species, while the rose-purple orchid *D. aristata* is found in meadows in Alaska, the Aleutians and eastern Asia, including Japan.

The early marsh orchid *D. incarnata*, found throughout most of Europe, grows in meadows, fens, bogs and dune slacks, especially where the ground water is slightly alkaline. Many distinct subspecies have been identified, with flower colour varying from pure white through pale yellow, pink and purple to deep crimson. *D. pseudocordigera* is a similar species with purplish red flowers that occurs in fens and damp calcareous grassland in Norway and

Sweden, while the broad-leaved marsh orchid *D. majalis* has deep magenta to lilac flowers and grows in damp meadows and fens in western and central Europe, the Baltic region and the northern USSR.

Marsh orchids with more restricted distributions include the Madeiran orchid *D. foliosa*, a pink-flowered species confined to the mountains of Madeira; the Anatolian marsh orchid *D. cilicica*, found only in wet pastures and seepage zones in the mountains of eastern Turkey and Anatolia, and the Caucasian marsh orchid *D. cataonica*, found to 2,500 m (8,200 ft) in wet pastures in eastern Turkey and Armenia. The marsh orchid *D. elata*, whose flowering spikes may attain a height of more than 1 m (3.3 ft), has pale pink or reddish flowers and thrives in wet meadows and bogs in southwest Europe and north Africa. *D. hatagirea* is the only plant in this genus to extend into the Himalayan region, where it grows in damp montane grasslands between 2,800 and 4,000 m (9,200-13,100 ft).

**Orchidaceae; 30 species**

## DELPHINIUM

A northern temperate genus characterized by flowers with five sepals, one of which is spurred, and two or four petals, the upper pair with spurs entering the calyx spur and containing nectar. The generic name is derived from *delphin*, or dolphin, which the buds are said to resemble. Members of the genus are variously referred to as larkspurs or delphiniums and many species are found in grassland, often in the mountains.

The genus *Delphinium* is renowned for its medicinal properties, the active ingredient being the highly poisonous delphinine. A tincture is derived from the seeds and may be used for such diverse purposes as destroying lice and nits in the hair (it was thus employed by soldiers in the trenches during the First World War), and in the treatment of spasmodic asthma and dropsy. An infusion of the whole plant was formerly prescribed to treat colic.

Europe boasts a large number of very attractive delphiniums, many of which are typical of Mediterranean grasslands. *D. peregrinum*, which has bluish violet flowers, is an annual plant of the central and eastern Mediterranean, whose seeds when drunk with wine are reputed to cure the sting of the scorpion; another annual, *D. halterum*, has bright blue flowers and is typical of dry grasslands in the the western Mediterranean. Species with blue-purple flowers include the Spanish *D. obcordatum* and *D. verdunense* of southwestern Europe, while *D. staphisagria* is a very hairy annual or biennial plant with 1 m (3.3 ft) long spikes of dingy dark blue flowers. The steppe grasslands of Eurasia support such species as *D. schmalhausenii*, with deep bluish violet flowers, *D. puniceum*, with dark purple-violet flowers, and *D. rossicum*.

Many other Eurasian delphiniums are characteristic of mountain habitats. One of the most widespread is the violet-blue-flowered alpine larkspur *D. elatum*, various subspecies of which grow in montane grasslands between 1,200 and over 2,000 m (3,900-6,600 ft) in the Pyrenees, Alps and Carpathians, extending into the Eurasian Arctic. Other species have a more restricted range, such as mountain larkspur *D. montanum* which has pale blue flowers and is confined to the Pyrenees, and *D. dubium*, a smaller, dark blue-flowered plant found only in the southwestern Alps.

*Delphinium sp.*

Some 24 species of larkspur grow in the Himalayas, many at altitudes of over 4,500 m (14,800 ft), but characteristic grassland species are *D. denudatum*, which is the commonest low altitude species of the western Himalayas and has relatively small blue or violet flowers borne in a widely branched inflorescence with a few terminal spike-like clusters; *D. kamaonense*, with large deep blue flowers which is common on open grassy slopes in Nepal; and *D. scabriflorum*, with deep blue, densely hairy flowers.

Of the four species of *Delphinium* found in East Africa the commonest is *D. macrocentron*, a widespread plant whose range extends from the lowlands up to nearly 4,000 m (13,100 ft) above sea level, especially on Kilimanjaro and Mt Elgon. It produces magnificent spikes up to 2 m (6.6 ft) tall with flowers varying from dark blue to a deep green, although high altitude plants tend to be rather dwarfed.

The genus is also common in North America where typical species include Nelson's larkspur *D. nelsoni*, with blue-purple flowers, which grows at heights of over 3,000 m (9,800 ft) in the southern Rocky Mountains, and *D. bicolor*, a similar species from the northern and western Rockies. *D. glaucum*, with leaves up to 18 cm (7 in) in diameter and spikes almost 3 m (9.8 ft) in height, occurs in montane grasslands from the Californian Sierra Nevada to Alaska, while *D. polycladon* is a much smaller plant of the southwestern mountains of North America. In the United States the toxicity of various *Delphinium* species is a severe problem in the poisoning of livestock, especially in early spring, and is responsible for the greatest cattle loss on national forest range land.

The dwarf or arctic larkspur *D. brachycentrum* grows in tundra herb slopes and montane regions in northeast Siberia and the extreme northwest of Alaska, including the Brooks Range. It is among the smallest of all delphiniums, with bluish, violet or white flowers borne on stalks only a few centimetres high. Field larkspur *D. consolida* was once widespread in the cornfields of Europe, especially on sandy or chalky soils, but has declined in recent years as advances in agricultural technology and the increased use of herbicides have all but eliminated such attractive 'weeds'.

**Ranunculaceae; about 250 species**

*Dactylorhiza fuchsii*

*Filipendula vulgaris*

stem bearing a terminal cluster of rosy-purple flowers with yellow throats. It is a typical and fairly common plant of the central Rocky Mountains, usually occurring in damp grasslands between 1,000 and 3,600 m (3,300-11,800 ft). Further north in the mountain heaths and rocky slopes of Alaska and northeastern Siberia, grows the frigid shooting star *D. frigidum*, distinguished by its bright pink flowers with broad white throats and black stamens.

Other species include the robust *D. jeffreyi*, found from Alaska to the Sierra Nevada, and the white-flowered northwestern shooting star *D. dentatum*, which is easily identified by its coarsely toothed leaves and is an inhabitant of the northern and western Rockies. Sticky shooting star *D. redolens*, a typical plant of wet grasslands in the Californian ranges, occurring up to about 3,000 m (9,800 ft), is thickly clothed in a dense coat of sticky hairs. Few-flowered shooting star *D. pulchellum* has deep pink flowers with four or five lobes and is common in a variety of habitats, from coastal prairies to montane meadows. The roots and leaves of *D. hendersonii* were formerly roasted and eaten by Californian Indians.

**Primulaceae; 14 species**

### FILIPENDULA

A small genus of perennial rhizomatous herbs of northern temperate regions and typical of a variety of undisturbed grassland habitats, ranging from the

### DODECATHEON

A small almost exclusively North American genus, with a single species in eastern Siberia, commonly called shooting stars, birdbills, prairie pointers or American cowslips. Within North America the genus has a markedly western distribution, and several species ascend to the alpine zone. The flowers are nodding and brightly coloured with reflexed petals and fused downward-pointing, protruding stamens. The generic name is derived from an amalgamation of the Greek words *dodeka* ('twelve'), and *theoi* ('gods'), although the reasons for this are somewhat obscure.

Prairie pointers *Dodecatheon meadii* has rose, lilac or white flowers with yellow stamens and is typical of meadows, prairies and open woods in the United States from Pennsylvania to Georgia, eastern Texas and Wisconsin. It was a far more common species at the time when the European settlers first arrived, but has become scarce following the conversion of most of the extensive prairies of the North American plains to cereal fields.

*D. pauciflorum* is a perennial species with a rosette of oblong leaves from which rises a single flowering

*Dodecatheon conjurgens*

*Fritillaria meltogris*

Eurasian steppes to the American prairies and from calcareous meadows to wet pastures. Plants in this genus have pinnate leaves, usually with small leaflets between the larger ones, and branched inflorescences with numerous five- or six-petalled pale cream or pinkish flowers, sometimes purplish beneath, with 20-40 stamens.

One of the more widespread and variable species is meadowsweet *Filipendula ulmaria* which has leafy stems from 50-200 cm (20-78 in) tall, the basal leaves having up to five pairs of large leaflets, topped by somewhat irregular elongated inflorescences. The strongly scented, greenish white flowers have five (rarely six) petals and are usually less than 1 cm (0.4 in) across. Meadowsweet is essentially a temperate Eurasian plant with distinct subspecies occupying particular habitats: *F. ulmaria* ssp. *picbaueri*, for example, is a shorter plant of dryish steppes in central and eastern Europe and western Asia, while the more robust *F. ulmaria* ssp. *denudata* is a typical plant of wetland habitats in the same area.

Dropwort *F. vulgaris* (*F. hexapetala*) rarely exceeds 80 cm (32 in) in height and is characteristic of the dry grasslands of North Africa, Europe, Asia Minor and Siberia, usually on calcareous soils. The usually unbranched stems bear few leaves, these having 8-25 pairs of large leaflets, and terminal inflorescences wider than they are long. Each flower has six creamy white petals, purplish beneath. Queen-

of-the-prairie *F. rubra* has small fragrant, pinkish flowers with five petals and is found in the prairies and meadows of central and eastern North America.

The dried leaves of *F. ulmaria* contain coumarin and are used to give an aromatic bouquet to port, claret and mead (the common name meadowsweet is thought to be derived from 'meadsweet', rather than a description of the plant's habitat). The roots of *F. vulgaris* are rather bitter but were formerly eaten in continental Europe. The larvae of the emperor moth *Saturnia pavonia*, the powdered quaker *Orthosia gracilis*, the Hebrew character *O. gothica* and the brown-spot pinion *Argrochola litura* use meadowsweet as a foodplant.

**Rosaceae; 10 species**

### FRITILLARIA
A large genus of perennial bulbous herbs distributed from western Europe through the Mediterranean region to eastern Asia, as well as North America, especially the western region. The flowers are usually solitary and bell-shaped, the perianth segments often marked with alternate squares of light and dark. The generic name is derived from the Latin *fritillus*, meaning 'dice-box', which were formerly decorated with the same chequered pattern as *Fritillaria* flowers. In ancient times these plants were called leper-lilies, since the drooping flowers resemble the bells that lepers were once obliged to carry.

*Fritillaria pyrenaica*

*Fritillaria pudica*

*graeca* from the southern Balkan peninsula and the Aegean region; *F. messanensis* from the eastern Mediterranean to southern Italy and Sicily; and the three-bracted snakeshead *F. involucrata* from southeast France and northwest Italy.

In North America the Californian mountains provide a home to the scarlet fritillary *F. recurva*, a handsome plant with spikes of nodding, bright red flowers; the tiny *F. pinetorum*, with purplish mottled flowers which are widely bell-shaped and almost erect; and the similar spotted mountain bells *F. atropurpurea*, which is distinguished by its nodding purplish brown flowers, spotted with yellow and white. Other western North American species are mission bells *F. lanceolata*, also known as the checker lily; adobe lily *F. pluriflora*, yellow bell *F. pudica*; candy bells *F. striata*; black lily *F. camchatensis*, also known as the Kamchatka fritillary; chocolate lily *F. biflora;* and fragrant fritillary *F. liliacea*.

**Liliaceae; 99 species**

### GONIOLIMON

A small genus of perennial herbs with angular stems and leathery leaves arranged in a basal rosette, most members of which occur in steppes and dry grasslands in northwest Africa and in Eurasia from the USSR to Mongolia. The branched inflorescences are composed of numerous spikelets subtended by bracts, each of which consists of a few five-petalled flowers with sepals united to form a tubular calyx.

One of the more widespread species is *Goniolimon speciosum* which is distributed across northern and central Asia. The stems range from 10-50 cm (4-20 in) in height, the dense spherical flowerheads are 1-2 cm (0.4-0.8 in) across and the individual flowers have reddish purple petals. The rather similar *G. tataricum* is a shorter plant with smaller flowerheads

*Gymnadenia conopsea*

Many plants in this genus, today known as fritillaries, contain poisonous alkaloids. Imperialine, for example, which was isolated from the bulbs of the crown imperial lily of southern Eurasia *Fritillaria imperialis* in the nineteenth century, is a heart poison, and even honey from the yellow unchequered flowers of this magnificent plant is reputed to be emetic. Despite this, the plant is said to be cultivated as a food plant in the Middle East, the bulbs losing their toxic properties when cooked.

The crown imperial is one of three fritillaries native to the Himalayas, although it is rare in these mountains except in the Banihal pass which leads into the Kashmir valley. The remaining species – *F. roylei* and *F. cirrhosa* – both have yellowish green to brownish purple drooping, chequered flowers and grow at altitudes of up to 4,000 m (13,100 ft). The bulbs of both plants are used medicinally in China, where they are known as 'pei-mu', being ground up with orange juice and sugar as a treatment for chest ailments.

Several European species are characteristic of wet meadows, including the snakeshead fritillary *F. meleagris*, a widespread plant in the natural and seminatural grasslands of Europe, and *F. mealeagroides*, which is native to the southern USSR from the central Ukraine eastwards and a few localities in Bulgaria. The Tyrolean fritillary *F. tubiformis*, with purple and yellow chequered flowers, occurs in alpine meadows and pastures in the southwestern Alps; *F. macedonica*, with lilac and purple flowers, thrives in wet mountain grasslands in the northern Balkan peninsula; *F. gussichiae*, with red-tinged green flowers that lack the typical chequered pattern, is typical of shady habitats and subalpine pastures, also in the Balkan peninsula; and the Pyrenean fritillary *F. pyrenaica*, with dull purplish brown flowers chequered with yellow on the inside, grows in mountain meadows from southern central France to northwest Spain.

Other European fritillaries include woodland species such as *F. pontica* of the Balkan peninsula; *F.*

and a more easterly distribution, extending into Europe as far as southern Yugoslavia and being particularly characteristic of the steppes of western Kazakhstan.

Other grassland representatives of this genus are the white-flowered *G. collinum*, which extends into the Balkan peninsula from temperate Asia; *G. dalmaticum*, a reddish purple-flowered species confined to the Balkan peninsula; and *G. besseranum*, also with reddish purple flowers, from the western USSR, Romania and Bulgaria.

**Plumbaginaceae; 20 species**

### GYMNADENIA

A small genus of orchids distributed across the northern hemisphere, particularly in temperate Eurasia and northeastern North America. Plants in this genus differ from those of the closely related *Orchis* in having flowers with long slender spurs and three-lobed lips.

*Gymnadenia* species have tubers which are palmately lobed for about half their length, leafy stems and flowers arranged in a spike. The dorsal sepal and petals of each flower converge to form a helmet and the lip points downwards. Most species have fragrant flowers attractive to moths and butterflies, whose long probosces can reach the nectar stored in the spur, at the same time removing the pollinia, which are then rubbed off on to the stigma of the next flower visited. Because these insects also visit short-spurred flowers of other orchids, hybrids are sometimes formed, especially with *Dactylorhiza* species.

One of the most widespread species is the fragrant orchid *Gymnadenia conopsea*, which occurs from Spain, across Europe, the USSR and north China to Japan. Although typically a plant of calcareous grassland it is also found in high mountain pastures (to 2,500 m/8,200 ft), open woodland and moorland. One of Europe's best known orchid species, *G. conopsea* produces stems from 15-45 cm (6-18 in) tall with 4-8 linear-lanceolate keeled leaves the upper of which are small and bract-like. The cylindrical flower spike varies from 6-16 cm (2.4-6.3 in) in length and may have as many as 200 flowers crowded on to the stem. Each flower is subtended by a bract which is at least as long as the ovary. The flowers comply with the characteristics of the genus, the lateral sepals spreading widely and the lip having three more or less equal rounded lobes. The narrow, downward-pointing spur may be twice as long as the ovary. The flowers of *G. conopsea* are usually pink or reddish-lilac, although pure white spikes are not uncommon, and they are highly fragrant, often smelling rather like carnations.

Short-spurred fragrant orchid *G. odoratissima* is another Eurasian species, similar to *G. conopsea* but somewhat smaller. As the name suggests, the flowers have shorter spurs, about as long as the ovaries, a further distinction being the more or less diamond-shaped lip, in which the lateral lobes are much shorter than the middle lobe. The flowers vary from pale pink to white and have a particularly strong scent. *G. odoratissima* is restricted to mountainous regions, where it grows in grasslands, marshes and open woodlands, usually on calcareous soils. Its range extends from southern Sweden and western central Soviet Europe to northern Spain, northern Italy and central Yugoslavia.

**Orchidaceae; 10 species**

### HIPPOCREPIS

A small genus of annual or perennial herbs distributed across Europe, western Asia and the Mediterranean. Many species occur in grasslands, although others prefer calcareous rocks and dry stony places. The leaves are pinnate with a terminal unpaired leaflet, and the flowers are usually arranged in axillary heads. Each flower has a tubular or bell-shaped calyx with five more or less equal teeth, and yellow petals

characteristic of the pea family. The flowers are usually pollinated by bees. The seed-pods are compressed laterally and consist of a series of either oblong or crescent-shaped segments, in the latter case resembling a row of horseshoes which point alternately up and down.

Probably the best known and also one of the most widespread species is horseshoe vetch *Hippocrepis comosa*. This perennial herb, woody at the base, has leaves with 3-8 pairs of leaflets and flowering heads containing whorls of 5-12 flowers on stalks up to four times as long as the leaves. The pale yellow flowers are about 1 cm (0.4 in) long and the seed-pods, 3 cm (1.2 in) have horseshoe-shaped segments.

Horseshoe vetch is a typical herb of calcareous meadows and pastures and occurs throughout western, central and southern Europe as far north as southern England and northern Germany. It is sometimes used as a fodder plant in Europe. The larvae of the burnet moth *Zygaena transalpina*, the six-belted clearwing

moth *Bembecia scopigera*, Berger's clouded yellow butterfly *Colias australis*, the chalkhill blue butterfly *Lysandra coridon* and the Adonis blue butterfly *Lysandra bellargus* typically feed on the foliage.

Three annual species are widely distributed in dry grasslands and cultivated land in the Mediterranean region, including *H. unisiliquosa*, whose small yellow flowers are often solitary; *H. ciliata*, with 2-6-flowered heads, and *H. multisiliquosa*, with slightly larger flowers, again arranged in clusters of 2-6.

**Leguminosae; 21 species**

### IRIS

This large genus is more or less confined to northern temperate latitudes, with centres of distribution in the Mediterranean region, the central Asian steppes and North American prairies. Several species are also typical of higher altitudes, especially in the Himalayas and the mountains of southern Europe, as well as in the North American montane zone.

*Hippocrepis comosa*

*Iris foetidissima*

Commonly known as irises, the flowers are usually radially symmetrical, having three outer spreading, petal-like sepals known as falls, three inner erect petals known as standards, and three stamens. The plant is named after Iris, the Greek goddess of the rainbow, and since ancient times has been revered as a symbol of power and majesty. The sceptre is thought to have originated from the iris, the three parts of the flower standing for faith, wisdom and valour. The iris (*fleur-de-lis*) is also the emblem of France.

Perhaps the most widespread member of this genus in western North America is the Rocky Mountain iris *Iris missouriensis*, which has pale lilac sepals and petals veined with purple and occurs at heights of up to 3,400 m (11,200 ft). The rootstock of this plant contains irisin, a violent emetic, which was formerly ground up with animal bile by North American Indians and used to poison arrow-tips. *I. setosa* is another North American species, growing from coastal meadows to subalpine areas from Alaska to British Columbia.

The Eurasian irises are equally diverse and colourful. Typical lowland grassland species are *I. sibirica*, with violet-blue or white flowers, which occurs in the damp grasslands of western Asia, central and eastern Europe and Italy; *I. tenuifolia*, a fragrant lilac-flowered species of the sandy steppes of temperate Asia; and *I. ruthenica*, with white and violet flowers, which thrives in meadows and open woodlands in eastern Europe and central and eastern Asia. Other species are confined to the dry grasslands of the Mediterranean region, such as *I. planifolia*, a short-stemmed plant with blue to violet flowers; the yellow and violet-flowered Spanish iris *I. xiphium* of southwestern Europe; and *I. juncea*, with pure yellow flowers, which occurs in southwest Spain, Sicily and North Africa.

Many irises are typical of the montane grasslands

of Europe, including purple-flowered species such as the so-called English iris *I. xiphioides* (*I. latifolia*) of the Pyrenees and the mountains of northern Spain up to 2,200 m (7,200 ft); *I. reticulata* of the Caucasus and northwest Iran; *I. reichenbachii*, with violet-brown or greenish yellow flowers, which is found in the mountains of central Yugoslavia, southwest Romania and eastern Greece; and *I. marsica*, which is confined to calcareous rocky hillsides in the central Apennines up to 1,700 m (5,600 ft).

In the Himalayas typical species are the pale mauve *I. lactea*, found up to 3,300 m (10,800 ft); the large-flowered *I. clarkei* which grows in marshes and wet meadows between 3,000 and 4,000 m (9,800-13,100 ft) and is distinguished by its brilliant lilac flowers blotched with violet, and a yellow throat; and *I. goniocarpa*, a lilac-flowered iris of dry alpine slopes to 4,400 m (14,400 ft) from western Nepal to southwest China. Other Himalayan irises include *I. decora*, *I. hookerana* and *I. kemaonensis*.

**Iridaceae; about 300 species**

## *LEUCANTHEMUM*

A genus of perennial or rarely annual herbs distributed across Europe and northern Asia. The alternate leaves may be entire or pinnately lobed and the flowerheads are usually solitary. The outer florets are ligulate, female and white or pinkish, although in a few species they are yellow tubular or bell-shaped and either hermaphrodite or female. The inner florets are hermaphrodite and tubular or bell-shaped. The generic name is derived from a combination of the Greek words *leucos* ('white'), and *anthos* ('flower').

Perhaps the best known member of this genus is the ox-eye daisy *Leucanthemum vulgare* (*Chrysanthemum leucanthemum*), an extremely variable species which thrives in a wide range of open habitats from seminatural grasslands to roadsides and arable fields. Also known as the moon daisy, dog daisy or marguerite, it occurs naturally throughout Europe as far north as Lapland, extending into Siberia, and has also been introduced to North America and New Zealand. The whole plant has antispasmodic, diuretic and tonic properties and has been successfully employed in cases of whooping cough and bronchial catarrh. In Spain the roots are eaten in salads.

The ox-eye daisy is a perennial herb with erect simple or branching stems from 10-100 cm (4-40 in) tall. The dark green leaves are long-stalked and entire with toothed or notched margins below, but more

*Iris latifolia*

*Iris planifolia*

*Iris latifolia*

*Leucanthemum vulgare*

deeply lobed and stalkless above. The solitary flowerheads are 2.5 to 5 cm (1-2 in) across, with white ray-florets and yellow disc-florets. They are visited by a wide range of bees, flies, beetles, butterflies and moths. Another member of this genus particularly associated with grassland habitats is *L. chloroticum,* which is confined to meadows and pastures up to 1,800 m (5,900 ft) in western and central Yugoslavia.

**Compositae; about 25 species**

### LIATRIS
A genus of perennial herbs with underground corms, native to eastern North America. Most species are associated with open habitats, especially the prairie grasslands, and are commonly known as blazing stars. The flowerheads are composed of disc-florets only and are arranged in long terminal spikes. The protruding styles give the flowers a fluffy appearance, hence their other common name of gayfeathers.

Prairie blazing star *Liatris pycnostachya* is a typical species of damp prairies which grows up to 1.5 m (5 ft) in height and has coarse, hairy, very leafy stems topped by dense spikes of rose-purple stalkless flowerheads. The flowerheads are roughly cylindrical in shape and are subtended by spreading or recurved bracts with pointed, purplish tips. Rough blazing star *L. aspera* is another characteristic plains species with stiff stems covered with greyish hairs, rough linear leaves and terminal spikes of rounded lavender flowerheads. Each flowerhead is about 2 cm (0.8 in) across and is subtended by broad spreading bracts with pink translucent margins.

Dense blazing star *L. spicata* is a 2 m (6.6 ft) high species of low-lying, wet habitats, whose stems are topped with 30 cm (12 in) long spikes of close-set rose-purple flowerheads. Large blazing star *L. scariosa* has interrupted clusters of pink-lilac flowerheads and thrives in dry woods and clearings.

Both are typical species of eastern North America, while dotted gayfeather *L. punctata* has slender spikes of narrow, crowded flowerheads with pink-purple disc-florets and grows in the dry prairies of the central plains of Canada and North America, to the east of the Rocky Mountains.

The corms of *L. punctata* were formerly eaten by North American Indians, *L. spicata* is a diuretic and was once used locally to treat sore throats and gonorrhoea, while the roots of *L. squarrosa* and *L. scariosa* were employed as a cure for snakebite. The leaves of several plants in this genus are used to flavour tobacco and are reputed to deter clothes-moths.

**Compositae; 42 species**

### LINUM
A large genus of herbs or small shrubs with narrow stalkless leaves and flowers with five clawed petals which are longer than the entire sepals. The genus is distributed across temperate and subtropical regions, especially in the Mediterranean, and many species are particularly associated with grasslands. The flowers may be red, yellow, blue or white and the seeds have a mucilaginous coat which swells on wetting and has useful medicinal applications.

*Linum usitatissimum* has been cultivated for thousands of years and is the source of both linseed (the seeds) and flax (the fibres). Seeds and cloth woven from the fibres (linen) have been found in Egyptian tombs and both are mentioned on numerous occasions in the Bible. Linseed oil is used as a transparent varnish, as a home remedy for coughs, colds and irritations of the urinary tract, is sometimes given as a laxative and has been administered internally with great success in cases of pleurisy.

*L. usitatissimum* is a robust annual herb with solitary stems, pale blue flowers up to 3 cm (1.2 in) across and seed capsules about 1 cm (0.4 in) in

diameter. The origin of this plant is unknown but some researchers consider it to be derived from the very similar pale flax *L. bienne. L. usitatissimum* does not occur naturally in the wild, although where cultivated it may persist for a year or so, and occasionally occurs as a casual.

Pale flax *L. bienne* is either biennial or perennial with slender stems 30-60 cm (12-24 in) in height, numerous alternate linear leaves and pale blue flowers arranged in loose clusters together with leaf-like bracts. The five petals are 8-12 mm (0.3-0.5 in) long and have short claws, while the stigmas are club-shaped. This species is characteristic of dry grasslands in southern Europe, extending to Madeira and the Canary Islands, and up the Atlantic seaboard to Ireland, Wales and central France.

*L. flavum* is a yellow-flowered species from central and southeastern Europe and southwestern Asia; sticky flax *L. viscosum,* with attractive bright pink flowers up to 4 cm (1.6 in) across, is confined to southern Europe, especially in montane meadows; and *L. narbonense,* with large blue-violet flowers, is a typical representative of the Mediterranean flora. *L. suffruticosum,* a perennial species sometimes woody at the base, has large funnel-shaped white flowers with pink or purplish claws and is a typical species of southwestern Europe and North Africa. *L. volkensii* is a tropical East African species with stems to 90 cm (3 ft) and yellow flowers, sometimes with purple veins, which occurs in damp upland grasslands, and *L. grandiflorum* is a red-flowered plant native to North Africa.

Fairy flax *L. catharticum,* a tiny annual with stems reaching a maximum of 25 cm (10 in) and white flowers about 1 cm (0.4 in) in diameter, occurs in grasslands and on heaths, moors and dunes throughout Europe, extending into the Caucasus, Asia Minor and Iran; while perennial flax *L. perenne,* whose larger flowers (to 4 cm/1.6 in across) have sky-blue petals,

*Linum viscosum*

*Linum perenne*

*bertolonii*, the woodcock orchid *O. scolopax*, the false spider orchid *O. arachnitiformis*, the bumblebee orchid *O. bombyliflora* and the sawfly orchid *O. tenthredinifera*. The fly orchid *O. insectifera*, unusual in that the flowers are usually self-pollinated, extends further north than any other member of this genus, reaching central Sweden and parts of Norway, but is rare in the Mediterranean region and North Africa. The early spider orchid *O. sphegodes* and the late spider orchid *O. fuciflora* are both widespread in western, central and southern Europe. *O. fuciflora* and *O. sphegodes* are protected by law in Britain, where they are on the northernmost edge of their climatic range.

Other species have much more restricted distributions, including the eyed bee orchid *O. argolica*, a plant of Greece and Crete; crescent ophrys *O. lunulata*, almost entirely confined to Sicily; Rheinhold's bee orchid *O. reinholdii* from Rhodes, Corfu and Crete; the Cretan bee orchid *O. cretica*

is found in calcareous grasslands in western and central Europe and well-drained prairies and plains in North America. Narrow-leaved flax *L. angustifolium* is very similar to *L. bienne* but is a western North American plant, while Chihuahua flax *L. vernale* distinguished by its orange-yellow flowers with maroon flowers, is a typical species of calcareous desert habitats in New Mexico, western Texas and northern Mexico.

**Linaceae; about 200 species**

## OPHRYS

A distinctive orchid genus of western Eurasia and North Africa, the flowers of which are often insect-like in appearance. The generic name translates literally as 'eyebrow', which probably refers to the hairy nature of the rather fleshy spurless lip. This lip often carries a shiny area (the speculum) or other markings; above it are three spreading petal-like sepals which are longer than the petals themselves.

Many species bear a striking resemblance to insects, a fact reflected in their common names: fly, bee and sawfly orchids, to name but a few. The suggestion that male insects mistake the flowers for females of their own species and attempt to copulate with them was first made by Pouyanne, who called it pseudocopulation. This false mating results in pollination, since the pollinia stick to the insect and are then transferred to another flower. It seems that one species of insect is faithful to a single *Ophrys* species, which virtually eliminates the possibility of hybrids in the wild.

In the case of the mirror orchid *Ophrys speçulum*, for example, Pouyanne noted that the flowers are only visited by a wasp called *Campsocolia ciliata*. Despite the fact that the males have no probosces and thus need neither nectar nor food, it seems that they seek out mirror orchid flowers before the female wasps appear. It is thought that the combination of a powerful scent and the crude resemblance of the flower to the female wasp, both visually and tactually, serves to stimulate the male wasps to perform this pseudocopulation. The scent produced by *Ophrys* flowers has been found to resemble the pheromones (sexual attractants) secreted by the corresponding insect and is the main stimulus to pseudocopulation, although touch also plays an important part.

Over the geographical range of the genus there is considerable variation within species, leading to the classification of many subspecies and varieties, although it is thought that the genus is still evolving and several species are not yet stable. The greatest diversity of *Ophrys* species occurs in the Mediterranean region.

Some of the most typical grassland species of the Mediterranean region are the yellow bee orchid *O. lutea*, the brown bee orchid *O. fusca*, the horseshoe orchid *O. ferrum-equinum*, Bertoloni's bee orchid *O.*

*Ophrys apifera*

which as its name suggests, is known only from the Greek islands of Crete, Naxos and Karpathos; and the Cyprus bee orchid *O. kotschyi*, a rare species confined to Cyprus. The Kurdish bee orchid *O. kurdica*, which was only discovered in the early 1970s, is known only from a small area of southeast Anatolia, while *O. turcomanica* is restricted to hillsides in Kopet Dag and Turcomania in northeast Iran.

**Orchidaceae; about 30 species**

## *ORCHIS*

A genus of terrestrial orchids, most members of which occur in northern temperate Eurasia and North America, although a few species extend into the warmer zone in North Africa, southwest China and India. Many species are typical members of the grassland community but are able to thrive in a wide range of habitats, including woodlands and rocky places. Orchis was the son of a Satyr and a Nymph, killed by the Bacchanalians for his insult to a priestess of Bacchus. Following his death, on the prayers of his father, he turned into a flower bearing his name. Another possible origin of the generic name draws on the fact that *orchis* means testicle, as the twin tubers of this genus and of many other orchids do indeed resemble testicles.

*Orchis* species are characterized by the presence of two rounded or ovoid tubers, unlike the divided tubers of the closely related genus *Dactylorhiza*. The spurred flowers have free perianth segments, although all or some converge to form a hood in many species, with lips ranging from entire to three-lobed. The flower bracts are membranous, rather than leaf-like as in *Dactylorhiza*.

Pollination is carried out by a wide range of insects; including social and solitary bees, hoverflies and droneflies. Although the spur contains no nectar, visiting insects are fooled for long enough to remove the pollinia or transfer them to the stigma of another flower. Hybrids with other species of the genus are extremely common, while intergeneric hybrids also occur, particularly with *Serapias* and *Dactylorhiza*, but also with *Aceras*, *Anacamptis*, *Gymnadenia* and *Platanthera*.

Many plants in this genus are typical of the Mediterranean region, including perhaps the most attractive of all *Orchis* species; the pink butterfly orchid *O. papilionacea*. The plants vary from delicate individuals 15 cm (6 in) high to robust spikes up to 40 cm (16 in ) tall. The inflorescences consist of lax, more or less pyramidal clusters of 3-8 flowers, each with all perianth segments converging to form a loose deep red or purplish hood. The lip is entire with slightly jagged margins that curve forwards, and is usually pale pink. The pink butterfly orchid is found throughout the Mediterranean, extending eastwards into the Caucasus.

Other characteristic Mediterranean species are the long-spurred orchid *O. longicornu*, with a predominantly western distribution; the holy orchid *O. sancta*, which is confined to the eastern Mediterranean; the widespread but fairly local *O. lactea*; the four-spotted orchid *O. quadripunctata*, a local and uncommon species; the widespread wavy leaved monkey orchid *O. italica*; the lax-flowered orchid *O. laxiflora*, most frequent in the Mediterranean and extending as far north as the Channel Islands and Belgium; and *O. saccata*, another widespread but rather rare species. In *O. italica*, *O. lactea*, *O. sancta* and *O. longicornu* all the perianth segments combine to form a hood, but the remaining species having spreading lateral sepals.

In the seminatural, undisturbed grasslands of central and western Europe, species such as the green-winged orchid *O. morio*, the bug orchid *O. coriophora*, the burnt orchid *O. ustulata*, the toothed orchid *O. tridentata*, the monkey orchid *O. simia*, the military orchid *O. militaris*, the lady orchid *O. purpurea*, the early purple orchid *O. mascula*, the pale-flowered orchid *O. pallens* and the Provence orchid *O. provincialis* are more common. *O. mascula*, *O. pallens* and *O. provincialis* are characterized by flowers with spreading lateral sepals, while in the remainder all sepals and petals converge to form a hood. *O. militaris* and *O. simia* are protected by law in Britain, where they are on the edge of their climatic range.

Most members of this genus have tuberous roots full of a highly nutritious starch-like substance called bassorine, 28g (1oz) of which is said to be sufficient to sustain a man for a day. These roots have been used for many centuries in Turkey and Iran in the preparation of a wholesome drink called *sahlep*. *Sahlep* was formerly sold from stalls in the streets of London before coffee became popular. Species of particular importance in the preparation of *Sahlep* were *O. mascula*, *O. morio*, *O. militaris*, *O. ustulata*, *O. coriophora* and Anacamptis pyramidalis. It was alleged that witches used the tubers of *O. mascula* in their love potions, this species having a reputation as a powerful aphrodisiac.

**Orchidaceae; 35 species**

## *PAEONIA*

A genus of perennial herbs, usually with woody stems, which either die down in the winter or are evergreen. Members of this genus are commonly known as peonies and are widely distributed across Eurasia and western North America. They have erect tuberous stocks with fleshy roots and large, alternate, three-lobed leaves which may be further divided into narrow segments. The large, showy, often fragrant flowers range from 6-14 cm (2.4-5.5 in) across and have five free sepals, 5-10 yellow, white, pink or red petals and numerous stamens. Several species are typical of grassland habitats.

*Orchis simia*

The genus is supposedly named after the physician Paeos, who cured Pluto and other gods of wounds they received during the Trojan War with the aid of the roots of *Paeonia officinalis*. In ancient times it was thought that this plant, believed to be of divine origin, protected shepherds and their flocks at night, preserved the harvest from injury and diverted tempests. The seeds were formerly strung on necklaces to ward off evil spirits. The dried and powdered roots of *P. officinalis* are considered to be of great medicinal value in the treatment of convulsions and epilepsy and were once held to be effective in cases of lunacy. The roots of *P. albiflora*, a native of Siberia and northern Asia, are often boiled and eaten in broth by the local people, while the seeds are ground and added to tea.

*P. officinalis* is one of the more common peonias and thrives in both meadows and open woodlands in the mountains of southern Europe. It is a very variable plant and many subspecies have been described, but in general the lower leaves are divided into 17-30 segments and the flowers are 7-13 cm (2.8-5 in) in diameter; both the petals and the filaments of the stamens are bright red. *P. mascula* is another red-flowered southern European peony, extending as far

*Paeonia clusii*

north as France and Austria and into Asia Minor. It is distinguished from *P. officinalis* by its biternate leaves (sometimes divided into 9-16 segments) and 8-14 cm (3-5.5 in) flowers.

Narrow-leaved or magenta peony *P. tenuifolia* is a characteristic species of the central Asian and eastern European steppes. The lower leaves are commonly divided into more than 40 linear segments less than 5 mm (0.2 in) wide and the flowers are 6-8 cm (2.4-3 in) in diameter, with red petals and yellow stamens. *P. peregrina*, which occurs in montane grasslands in Italy, the Balkan peninsula and southern Romania, has lower leaves divided into 17-30 narrowly elliptical segments and red cup-shaped flowers 7-13 cm (2.8-5 in) across, the stamens having red filaments, while the northern Asian *P. anomala* has numerous leaf-segments, red flowers 7-9 cm (2.8-3.5 in) in diameter and yellow filaments. Both *P. rhodia*, endemic to Rhodes, and *P. clusii*, known only from Crete and Karpathos, have white flowers, while the tree peony *P. lutea* from western China has yellow flowers.

A typical North American species is the western peony *P. brownii* which grows in dry open habitats such as chaparral along the west coast from Washington to California and inland to Utah, Wyoming and Idaho. It has blue-green rather fleshy, divided leaves and roughly spherical flowers which are terminal and nodding. Each flower has five spoon-shaped sepals and five maroon or bronze petals with greenish margins. The northwestern Indians formerly made tea from the roots to cure lung diseases.

**Ranunculaceae; 33 species**

### PARNASSIA

A small genus of perennial herbs found over northern temperate and arctic regions with representatives in both Eurasia and North America. Members of this genus have simple leaves arranged in basal rosettes and solitary flowers located at the tips of the flowering stems. Each flower is radially symmetrical and has five petals, within which is a ring of five rudimentary stamens (staminodes) which produce no pollen but have nectar-secreting organs. The genus is named after Mount Parnassus, a snowcapped peak in Greece which is sacred to Apollo and the Muses.

One almost cosmopolitan species is *Parnassia palustris* which, like most members of this genus, is commonly called grass-of-Parnassus. It occurs in wet grassland, marshes, fens and on lake shores across most of Europe and temperate Asia, although it is rather rare in the south, as well as in the Atlas

*Parnassia palustris*

*Phyteuma hemisphaericum*

mountains in Morocco. Different races of this species are also found in North America. The white insect-pollinated flowers have rounded or oblong petals 7-12 mm (0.3-0.5 in) long which are marked with conspicuous veins. Two Asian species are *P. nubicola* and *P. cabulica*, both of which are common in the Himalayas up to 4,300 m (14,100 ft).

Fringed grass-of-Parnassus *P. fimbriata* is a North American species found by springs, along streambanks and in boggy areas in the Rocky Mountains, its range extending from Alaska to northern California and Colorado. It is easily identified by its 2 cm (0.8 in) wide white or cream flowers with conspicuously fringed petals and heart- or kidney-shaped basal leaves. Another Rocky Mountain species is *P. parviflora,* which has smaller unfringed flowers. *P. glauca* is a plant of eastern North America that has green-veined white flowers with yellow stamens and thrives in wet limestone grasslands and marshes.

**Saxifragaceae (Parnassiaceae); 15 species**

### PHYTEUMA

A genus of perennial herbs commonly known as rampions, distributed across the Mediterranean, Europe and temperate Asia, typically in grassland habitats although some are found in mountain regions. Rampions are unmistakable, with their small, stalkless flowers arranged in dense terminal spikes which can be spherical, oblong or cylindrical in shape. The corolla tube of each flower is deeply divided into four

*Phyteuma pyrenaicum*

*Polemonium boreale*

or five lobes which are fused into a narrow tube for most of their length, separating only at the base. The style passes through the corolla tube and emerges at the tip.

The blue-spiked rampion *Phyteuma betonicifolium* is confined to the Alps and Apennines, where it grows on siliceous soils in meadows, pastures and open woods between 1,000 and 2,600 m (3,300-8,500 ft). It is one of the larger rampions, reaching a maximum height of 70 cm (28 in) with oblong or cylindrical spikes of pale blue or violet flowers. Another alpine species is the globe-headed rampion *P. hemisphaericum* which has broadly globular sky-blue inflorescences. This plant has a wider distribution, however, occurring in the mountains of central Spain and the Pyrenees, as well as in the Apennines, where it prefers acid soils but can tolerate the climatic conditions of altitudes up to 3,000 m (9,800 ft).

Perhaps the most widespread of all the European rampion is another sky-blue species, the round-headed rampion *P. orbiculare*, which is very common in calcareous lowland grasslands in central and southern Europe, also extending into the mountains in the Jura, Vosges, Alps, Apennines, Pyrenees, Carpathians, and the Transylvanian and Dinaric Alps. The roots of this plant are edible and were formerly used in salads.

Other species include the dark rampion *P. ovatum* which has blackish purple flowers arranged in an ovoid spike. It is fairly common in meadows up to 2,400 m (7,900 ft) in the Pyrenees, Alps, Apennines and Dinaric Alps. *P. vagneri* has red purple flowers and is confined to the alpine pastures of the eastern and southern Carpathians; Pyrenean rampion *P. pyrenaicum* has cylindrical bluish inflorescences and is found only in the Pyrenees and the mountains of northern and central Spain; while the aptly named

black rampion *P. nigrum* is distinguished by its blackish purple ovoid flower spikes and occurs only in mountain meadows and woods from Belgium to eastern Austria.

Many rampions have extremely localized distributions, such as *P. gallicum* of the mountain pastures of southern central France; *P. tetramerum* from the eastern and southern Carpathians; *P. michelii* on acid soils in the southern Alps; *P. cordatum* on calcareous rocks in the Maritime Alps; *P. serratum* which is confined to the mountain rocks of Corsica; and *P. rupicola* which grows only on granite rocks in the eastern Pyrenees.

**Campanulaceae; 40 species**

### POLEMONIUM

A largely northern temperate genus of usually perennial herbs with a centre of distribution in North America, a few Eurasian representatives and a single Chilean species. Members of this genus are erect herbaceous perennials of meadows and moist habitats with alternate pinnate leaves and predominantly blue or violet flowers, each with five petals joined at the base to form a short tube, but with broad spreading lobes. The generic name is apparently derived from the Greek *polemos* ('war'), although the reason for this is not clear.

Jacob's ladder *Polemonium caeruleum* has dense terminal inflorescences of sky-blue flowers and grows in damp meadows and woods between 1,200 and 3,000 m (3,900-9,800 ft). Although mainly a plant of the boreal zone of North America, central northern Eurasia and western Siberia, it also occurs in the Pyrenees, central Alps, Dinaric Alps, Carpathians and the mountains of northern Europe, and is a native of limestone habitats in the north of England. *P. pulchellum* is a similar species of the Urals. Referring to *P. caeruleum*, Culpepper describes its use in the

treatment of such diverse complaints as malignant fevers and pestilential distempers, nervous complaints, headaches, trembling, palpitations of the heart, vapours, hysteric cases and epilepsies.

The genus also has several Arctic representatives, including *P. boreale*, a low-growing species of gravelly and sandy soils with a circumpolar distribution in arctic tundra, also occurring in montane regions further south. It is particularly common in the disturbed, nutrient-enriched ground around the entrances of lemming burrows. *P. acutiflorum* occurs in arctic and subarctic wetlands and riverbanks in both Eurasia and America. Both species have pale blue flowers.

Western North American species include the violet-flowered *P. pulcherrimum* of rocks and craggy habitats from southwest Canada to Arizona and Colorado up to 3,600 m (11,800 ft) and sky pilot *P. viscosum*, which has clear blue or purplish, broadly funnel-shaped flowers with orange anthers and is distinguished by its sticky foliage and unmistakable odour of skunk. *P. viscosum* is found only in the highest peaks of the Rockies at 2,700 to 3,700 m (8,900-12,100 ft) where it thrives in sheltered rock crevices.

Other common Rocky Mountain species are subalpine Jacob's ladder *P. delicatum* and *P. occidentale*, while *P. eximium*, another species with a strong musky odour, grows on dry rocky ridges high in the Californian mountains at 3,000-4,300 m (9,800-14,100 ft). Polemoniums lacking the characteristic bluish flowers are *P. carneum* of western North America, which has flesh-pink blooms; *P. brandegei*, a miniature yellow-flowered species of the Rocky Mountains; and *P. pauciflorum*, a Mexican plant with only a few drooping, tubular, deep yellow flowers.

**Polemoniaceae; 25 species.**

## PRUNELLA

A small genus of perennial herbs distributed across northern temperate regions, as well as northwest Africa and Australia. The plants are characterized by dense, terminal cylindrical inflorescences, with flowers arranged in whorls of six interspersed with orbicular bracts. Each flower has a two-lipped tubular or bell-shaped calyx and a corolla tube which exceeds the calyx, with a distinctly hooded upper lip and toothed lower lip. Members of this genus thrive in a variety of grasslands.

The most widespread species is probably selfheal *Prunella vulgaris,* which is very common in grasslands, woodland clearings and waste places, usually on neutral or calcareous soils, and occurs throughout Europe, temperate Asia, North Africa, North America and Australia. Its erect stems 5-30 cm (2-12 in) high and the opposite oval leaves are either entire or shallowly toothed. The bracts and calyces are usually tinged with purple and covered with long white hairs, and the corollas are violet, rarely pink or white. The flowers bloom in late summer and are pollinated mainly by bees. *P. vulgaris* is highly esteemed by herbalists for its astringent, styptic and tonic properties. An infusion of the herb is recommended for sore throats and ulcerated mouths, for internal bleeding and for piles.

Cut-leaved selfheal *P. laciniata* is distinguished by its pinnate or lobed leaves and larger creamy white, sometimes pinkish or pale blue-violet flowers. It thrives in dry calcareous grasslands in southern, western and central Europe, western Asia and North Africa. Large-flowered self-heal *P. grandiflora* is one of the more spectacular species of Eurasian meadows and steppes, the deep violet corollas up to 3 cm (1.2 in) long arranged in a shorter, roughly cuboid inflorescence. Another violet-flowered species, *P. hyssopifolia,* is confined to southwest Europe. It has narrow, stalkless leaves and prefers rocky limestone habitats in central and eastern Spain and southern France.

**Labiatae; 7 species**

## PULSATILLA

A genus of tufted perennial herbs with a stout rootstock, divided leaves and solitary flowers with six perianth segments covered with silky hairs on the outside; the perianth is composed of petaloid sepals and true petals are absent. A diagnostic feature of this essentially temperate Eurasian genus (a few species occur in North America) is that the styles elongate and become feathery in fruit, giving rise to masses of

*Pulsatilla vernalis*

plumes in place of the flowers. The genetic name is derived from *pulso* ('I beat'), supposedly referring to the plumed seeds being beaten about by the wind. These plants are commonly known as pasque flowers, probably because they start to bloom in April and coincide with Easter.

Most pasque flowers have a localized distribution, probably as a result of a combination of postglacial climatic change and their intolerance of bad drainage, ploughing and shade. Typical species of ancient well-drained grasslands in the lowlands include the common pasque flower *Pulsatilla vulgaris,* which has purple flowers and grows in England and western France north to Scandinavia; small pasque flower *P. pratensis,* a central and eastern European species whose flowers may be purple, red, pale violet, greenish yellow or white; and *P. patens,* with bluish violet flowers, which is most abundant in eastern Europe, although some subspecies extend through eastern Soviet Asia, the American prairies, Alaska and the Yukon. *P. turczaninovii* is a typical plant of the Chinese steppes.

Undisturbed mountain pasture is another favoured habitat of the pasque flower. Perhaps the best known species is the alpine pasque flower *P. alpina,* of which there are two subspecies; *P. alpina* ssp. *alpina* has purplish outer and white inner perianth segments and prefers calcareous soils, while *P. alpina* ssp. *apiifolia* has pale yellow perianth segments and grows on acid soils. Both subspecies are found throughout the mountains of central and southern Europe.

Other European montane species include the spring pasque flower *P. vernalis,* a delicate white-flowered plant with a pink or bluish flush, which is found from Scandinavia to southern Spain, northern Italy and Bulgaria; and white pasque flower *P. alba,* which is similar to the alpine pasque flower but has smaller flowers that are always white, and grows in the mountains of central France extending to central Italy and Yugoslavia.

There are also several dark-flowered species, difficult to distinguish at first glance, such as *P. halleri,* with dark violet blooms, which occurs in widely separated relict populations in mountain localities, including the Alps, western Carpathians and the Balkan peninsula. *P. montana* has bluish to dark violet flowers and occurs from southwest Switzerland to eastern Romania and Bulgaria, while a similar species, *P. rubra,* with brown, purple or blackish red flowers, is found in central and southern France, extending southwards into the mountains of Spain.

**Ranunculaceae; 30 species**

## RHINANTHUS

A genus of annual hemiparasitic herbs found throughout the northern hemisphere, with a centre of distribution in Europe. The generic name is derived from the combination of the Greek words for 'nose' and 'flower', in reference to the projecting beak of the upper part of the flower. All plants of the genus extract nutrients from the roots of the grasses among which they grow, thus impoverishing the grasslands.

Characteristics of *Rhinanthus* are opposite, stalkless, toothed leaves and flowers arranged in terminal spikes subtended by leaf-like bracts. The calyces are laterally compressed, oval or almost circular, with four short teeth. The yellow flowers are two-lipped, with the lower three-lobed lip shorter than the arched upper lip which is flattened laterally and bears two small teeth. The four stamens are located under the upper lip and nectar is secreted at the base of the ovary to attract pollinating bees. In fruit the calyces dry out and become inflated; the noise produced by the movement of the loose seeds within has given these plants their common name of yellow rattles.

Yellow rattlebox *Rhinanthus crista-galli* has erect stems 10-80 cm (4-32 in) tall and flowers arranged in one-sided spikes. It is found in fields, meadows and on moist slopes throughout North America, from

Alaska to Labrador, northwestern Oregon, Colorado and New York. This herb is said to be efficacious in the treatment of coughs and eye infections.

Greater yellow rattle *R. angustifolius (R. serotinus)* is a characteristic plant of meadows and cultivated ground in northern Eurasia, but is so rare in the British Isles as to warrant legal protection under the Wildlife and Countryside Act (1981). It has black-spotted stems up to 60 cm (24 in) tall and inflorescences of 8-18 yellow flowers with purple teeth longer than they are wide. *R. minor* is a more slender plant whose smaller yellow or brown flowers have violet teeth not longer than they are wide. It is a very variable species which occurs in grasslands throughout Europe, the Caucasus, western Siberia, southern Greenland and North America.

Other yellow rattles that thrive in grassland habitats are *R. aristatus,* which is confined to southern-central Europe from southeast France to southwest Yugoslavia; *R. rumelicus* from eastern-central Europe, the Balkan peninsula and western Asia; *R. wagneri,* known only from eastern-central Europe and the northern Balkans; *R. mediterraneus* which is restricted to the western and central Mediterranean region, and a whole host of species which are confined to one or other of the European mountain ranges.

**Scrophulariaceae; 45 species**

## SATYRIUM

A large terrestrial orchid genus from the tropical regions of the Old World, extending into more temperate zones in Arabia, South Africa and China. The genus undoubtedly gets its name from *Satyrion,* an ancient word for orchid, which itself is derived from a legend that these plants were a special food of the Satyrs, inciting them to excesses.

The genus is characterized by flowers with paired spurs equal to or up to twice as long as the ovary, although some species have four spurs, or none. Another feature is the broad, upward-pointing, hood-shaped lip. *Satyrium* species are typical of grassland habitats from swamps to semidesert conditions. Most are native to Africa.

The grasslands of tropical East Africa are home to *Satyrium sacculatum,* a magnificent species with flowering stems up to 120 cm (4 ft) tall, with 13-17 sheathing leaves. The dense cylindrical inflorescence bears numerous orange-yellow or reddish flowers, rarely white, each about 1.5 cm (0.6 in) across, with ciliate margins to the petals. The spurs are up to 1 cm (0.4 in) long, usually with a pair of shorter spurs in front.

Other East African species are *S. cheirophorum,* up to 70 cm (28 in) tall, with pale to bright pink flowers up to 2.5 cm (1 in) across, which occurs in upland grasslands 1,500-2,600 m (5,000-8,500 ft); *S. schimperi,* another upland grassland species extending to 2,900 m (9,500 ft), whose narrow cylindrical inflorescences bear greenish or yellowish flowers about 1 cm (0.4 in) across; and *S. crassicaule,* more typical of wet grasslands and swamps, which is distinguished by its many flowered, shortly cylindrical inflorescences of larger pink or mauve (rarely white) flowers.

*S. bicorne,* with scented greenish brown flowers and two opposite ovate leaves which lie flat on the ground, is a typical southern African species but is overshadowed by the spectacular *S. erectum,* also with broad paired basal leaves, but with large reddish flowers arranged in a loose spike. Two species found on open grassy slopes in the lower Himalayas are *S. nepalense,* with dense spikes of fragrant pink flowers, and the smaller but similar *S. ciliatum,* distinguished by its fringed sepals.

**Orchidaceae; 135 species**

## SERAPIAS

A small terrestrial orchid genus distributed from the Azores to the Mediterranean region, including the Austrian Tyrol, the lowlands of Switzerland, the

*Rhinanthus serotinus*

Levant and North Africa. Most species occur in grassland habitats. The name Serapias is thought to be derived from Osirapis, a Greek name for Apis the sacred bull of Memphis, which was thought to be an incarnation of the god Osiris.

*Serapias* species are characterized by ovoid or globose tubers and narrow, pointed leaves, with flowers arranged in a short spike. In these distinctive spurless flowers, all perianth segments converge to form a hood and the large downward-pointing lips are constricted in the middle to form a basal hypochile with two lateral lobes, and a pendant epichile which narrows towards the tip. Because of this conspicuous lip, these plants are commonly known as tongue

orchids. Tongue colour ranges from deep maroon in *Serapias cordigera* to red, salmon-pink or orange in *S. neglecta*, and to yellowish or pale pink in *S. lingua*. The helmet, or hood, is usually paler than the tongue and often has a greenish tinge.

Interspecific hybrids are common, with all possible combinations of pairs of parents having been recorded in the field. Hybrids with other genera often produce spectacular results, especially those with *Orchis*. Such intergeneric hybrids are not common, however.

Heart-flowered *S. cordigera* is characteristic of the western and central Mediterranean, extending to North Africa, Greece and southern Turkey, while scarce serapias *S. neglecta*, despite growing in large

colonies, is a rather rare orchid which occurs only in southern France, northern Italy, Corsica, Sardinia and southwest Yugoslavia, usually near the coast. Long-lipped serapias *S. vomeracea* is a circum-Mediterranean species and is the only member of the genus to be found as far north as Switzerland. In Israel it has been reported that bees spending the night within the flowers of long-lipped serapias emerge the following morning with body temperatures up to 3°C higher than that of the surrounding air.

The tongue orchid *S. lingua* is typical of the western and central Mediterranean, as is the small tongue orchid *S. parviflora*, although this species also occurs

*Serapias lingua*

*Trollius europaeus*

*Tulipa sylvestris*

from the eastern Mediterranean to the Canary Islands. *S. azorica* is confined to the Azores but is so similar to *S. cordigera* that it may in fact only be worthy of subspecific status.

**Orchidaceae; 10 species**

### SILAUM

A small Eurasian genus of hairless perennial herbs with 1-4-pinnate alternate leaves and flat-topped umbels of flowers. There are no sepals and the five petals are usually yellowish. A typical species is pepper saxifrage *Silaum silaus*. This variable species grows to a maximum height of about 1 m (3.3 ft) and has terminal and axillary umbels from 2-6 cm (0.8-2.4 in) in diameter, each with 4-15 rather unequal rays. It is a characteristic plant of old meadows and undisturbed grassy banks in western, central and eastern Europe, including Sweden and northern Spain, although it is absent from Portugal.

**Umbelliferae; 10 species**

### THYSANOTUS

A genus of perennial erect or rarely twining herbs almost completely confined to Australia with a centre of distribution in the southwest; two species extend into Indomalaya. The narrow leaves are restricted to the base of the stem and the blue or purple flowers are arranged either in umbels or in small clusters. The generic name is derived from *thysanus* ('a fringe'), in reference to the feathery margins of the petals.

A typical species is the fringed violet or common fringe lily *Thysanotus tuberosus*, which is abundant in grasslands all over Australia except the far north. It has a few linear basal leaves up to 15 cm (6 in) long and branched inflorescences, each branch terminating in an umbel of 1-4 flowers. The three delicate fringed petals are roughly oval in shape and a rich purple colour with a darker line down the centre of each.

**Liliaceae; 47 species**

### TROLLIUS

A genus of perennial herbs of northern temperate regions, commonly known as globeflowers. All parts of the flowers are spirally arranged, with 5-15 petaloid perianth segments, a similar number of small narrow honey-leaves and numerous stamens.

The most widespread species is European globeflower *Trollius europaeus*, in which the lemon yellow perianth segments are strongly incurved to enclose the honey-leaves and stamens, forming globe-like flowers up to 10 cm (4 in) across. It grows in damp grasslands throughout Europe, although only in mountain regions in the south, and in northern Asia. The leaves are eaten by the larvae of the golden plusia moth *Polychrysia moneta*.

The flowers of Asiatic globeflower *T. asiaticus*, which has bronze-tinged leaves, have orange-tinged petals less strongly incurved than in *T. europaeus*. *T. caucasicus* (*T. ranunculinus*) has fewer perianth segments per flower and grows in the Caucasus and Armenia. *T. acaulis* and *T. pumilus* are two Himalayan species typical of alpine slopes above 3,000 m (9,800 ft), the latter found up to 5,300 m (17,400 ft). Japanese globe-flower *T. japonicus* grows in Japan and at 1,800-2,100 m (5,900-6,900 ft) in the Changbai Mountains of northeast China.

In North America *T. laxus* is the most widespread species, distinguished by its greenish yellow or creamy white, bowl-shaped flowers. It occurs in wet habitats in the Rocky Mountains, from British Columbia to Colorado, and is also rare in moist meadows and swamps in the eastern United States, where it is listed as an endangered species.

**Ranunculaceae; 31 species**

### TULIPA

A genus of bulbous perennials commonly known as tulips, distributed across Eurasia and North Africa. The somewhat fleshy leaves are arranged alternately up the stem, decreasing in size towards the top. The flowers are terminal, usually solitary and consist of six free petaloid perianth segments which fall following fertilization. Many species grow in grassland habitats.

*Tulipa sylvestris* is one of the best known species, occurring naturally in meadows and grassy and rocky places in southern Europe and western Asia, as well as being widely naturalized in northern and central Europe. It has stems up to 45 cm (18 in) high which are topped by a single (rarely two) yellow flower, nodding in bud. The outer perianth segments are often streaked with green, pink or crimson and are smaller than the inner segments.

*T. gesnerana* is the name used to describe a complex group of species (including *T. schrenkii* and *T. urumoffi*) which may be the ancestors of the garden tulip. These plants were originally native to the steppe grasslands and cultivated ground of southwestern and south-central Asia, but no truly wild plants have yet been located because it is thought that altered forms were reintroduced to the area. The flowers range from pure yellow to scarlet or white. *T. biflora* has 1-3 white flowers, tinged with green and crimson and is native to Kazakhstan southeastern Soviet Europe and southern Yugoslavia. The solitary white flowers of *T. clusiana* are widespread from Iran to northern Pakistan, and *T. praecox*, with its solitary, orange, green-tinged flowers, is probably native to southwestern or south-central Asia.

Other species have more restricted distributions, including *T. goulimyi*, with bright orange to reddish brown flowers, which is confined to southern Greece; *T. saxatilis*, with up to four pinkish or lilac-purple flowers per stem, which is confined to the southern Aegean region; and *T. cretica*, known only from Crete, whose white flowers are tinged with pink or purple on the inside and greenish on the outside. *T. stellata*, a weed of Himalayan cornfields and dry slopes, either has white flowers with a broad red band on the outer side of the perianth segments, or yellow or red flowers.

**Liliaceae; 80 species**

### *VERATRUM*

A northern temperate genus of robust rhizomatous perennial herbs with leafy stems. The overlapping suberect leaves are alternate, broadly ovate or elliptical, with many parallel veins often giving them a pleated appearance. The numerous flowers are arranged in an inflorescence that may or may not be branched. They are usually hermaphrodite but sometimes male flowers are present. The six white, greenish, reddish brown or black perianth segments are spreading and the six stamens are inserted at the base of the perianth.

White false helleborine *Veratrum album*, has tall (to 1 m/3.3 ft), branched inflorescences of white, greenish or yellowish flowers 15-25 mm (0.6-1 in) across. It grows in damp grassland, mainly in the mountains, across much of Europe and temperate Asia but appears to be replaced by *V. misae*, a smaller plant with yellowish green flowers, in arctic Russia. *V. nigrum*, a characteristic plant of woodland margins and mountain meadows in central, southern and southeastern Europe, extending into western Asia, produces unbranched inflorescences (or branched only at the base) of smaller (9-15 mm/0.4-0.6 in) flowers with reddish brown or black perianth segments.

A typical North American species is false hellebore *V. viride* which grows to 1-2 m (3.3-6.6 ft) and has broad, branched inflorescences bearing numerous yellowish green flowers about 12 mm (0.5 in) across. Otherwise known as Indian poke, this species thrives in wet meadows from Alaska to Maine and south to North Carolina and Oregon, up to 2,700 m (8,900 ft) in the mountains. Californian corn-lily *V. californicum* differs in having slightly larger (to 2 cm/0.8 in across) white or pale green flowers and is found in wet meadows, swamps and creek bottoms from

Washington to California and into New Mexico.

Small-flowered veratrum *V. parviflorum* grows in drier woods from Virginia to Georgia, while Wood's false hellebore *V. woodii* has greenish purple or blackish flowers and grows in similar habitats from Ohio to Missouri and Oklahoma, as well as in Iowa. Sabadilla or cebadilla *V. officinale* is a Mexican species.

All plants in this genus contain powerful alkaloids and may be fatal if ingested. The exact chemical composition of the plants varies from species to species, the principal alkaloids being veratrine, pseudojervine, rubijervine, jervine, cevadine, protoveratrine and protoveratridine. All are highly poisonous and have emetic and sedative properties. Those obtained from *V. viride* prolong contractions of the heart and muscles, often with an accompanying slowing of the rate of respiration, and have been used in the treatment of pneumonia, peritonitis, arteriosclerosis and threatened apoplexy. The action of this drug may be severe, however, causing vomiting and rapid, irregular pulse in the later stages.

*V. album* is a far more toxic species and was once used in Europe to poison the tips of arrows and daggers. It was formerly used to treat mania, epilepsy and gout, and as a substitute for colchicum. It is almost never used internally because the severity of its actions, but has been employed with some effect in the form of an ointment or decoction in skin diseases such as scabies, or to kill lice. *V. officinale* has been used as a vermifuge, to destroy headlice, and to ease gout and rheumatism.

It is said that some Indian tribes would only accept a chief who had survived eating *V. viride*. Sheep that eat *V. californicum* during the early weeks of pregnancy give birth to lambs with deformed heads, while those that have eaten *V. album* produce lambs with a single central eye. The flowers of *V. californicum* are even poisonous to insects, causing serious losses among honeybees.

*Veratrum album*

# CHAPTER SIX

# ARID LANDS

Arid lands are characterized by low relative humidities, maximum temperatures in excess of 40°C (104°F) and constant winds caused by convectional warming of the air. The main feature, however, is that annual precipitation is less than 500 mm (20 in) and is normally exceeded by evaporation, leading to a water deficit.

Three main types of arid land can be distinguished. Mediterranean arid habitats, such as the garrigue and maquis around the Mediterranean Sea, the chaparral in California, South Africa's fynbos and the matorral in Chile are the result of a pronounced summer drought. Tropical semiarid regions, such as the caatinga of northeastern Brazil, the interior of Australia and the Tanzanian thorn scrub habitats, experience sporadic rain during the summer followed by winter drought. Semidesert and desert regions have scanty and infrequent rain throughout the year, with an annual precipitation of less than 250 mm (10 in) and levels of evaporation often in excess of precipitation.

The main desert and semidesert regions of the world can further be divided on the basis of winter temperatures. Those with cold winters include the Mojave in California and the Gobi desert of central Asia, while the Sahara in north Africa and the Sonoran in southwest North America are examples of warm-winter deserts. Where such warm-winter deserts are situated on the west side of the continents, for example, the Atacama on the Chilean coast and the Kalahari and the Namib on the Atlantic coast of Africa, the main source of water is condensation from the frequent fogs which sweep in from the sea.

Plants of arid lands display a remarkable tolerance to the lack of water and are often known as xerophytes. Adaptations to drought include long taproots to penetrate to deep-seated water sources, an extensive network of roots close to the surface to make maximum use of precipitation in the form of dew, thick cuticles and a reduced leaf area to cut down transpiration (the most extreme example being the spines of cacti) and cells that can store water for use during long periods of drought, resulting in succulent stems.

Annuals are common because seeds are well suited to surviving long periods of drought, germinating only when sufficient water is available for the plants to complete their life cycle. Perennial species with bulbs or tubers which can remain dormant during the dry season are also characteristic of arid lands, the parts of the plant above ground dying back in unfavourable conditions.

Facing page: *Xanthorrhoea sp.*

Right: dry slope vegetation, Tenerife.

Facing page: *Yucca brevifolia*

Above: *Opuntia ficus-indica*

Below: spring flowers, South Africa.

## ABRONIA

This genus is native to North America, especially the arid lands of the southwest. The ground roots of some species were formerly eaten by North American Indians.

Desert sand verbena *Abronia villosa* is a much-branched annual creeper with stout hairy stems up to 60 cm (24 in) long, which trail along the sand. The more or less erect flowering stems arise from the leaf axils and bear clusters of trumpet-shaped, five-lobed, rosy purple flowers, each about 1 cm (0.4 in) long and very fragrant. The tiny fruits have 3-5 papery wings to catch the wind for dispersal over long distances. *A. villosa* is common in open sandy deserts in southeast California, southern Nevada, western Arizona and the Sonoran, often carpeting huge areas after the winter rains.

Sweet sand verbena *A. elliptica* is distinguished by its fragrant heads of white flowers which give this plant its other name of snowball. It occurs from central Nevada to northern Arizona and northwestern New Mexico in sandy arid grassland among juniper and piñon. The very similar *A. fragrans* is found further north and west. Yellow sand verbena *A. latifolia* is a typical plant of the coastal dunes from British Columbia to southern California. Its hemispherical yellow flowerheads distinguish it from beach pancake *A. maritima*, with wine red flowers,

and beach sand verbena *A. umbellata*, with pink or white flowers, both of which are also denizens of the Pacific coast.

**Nyctaginaceae; 35 species**

## AGAVE

A large genus of short-stemmed shrubs or rhizomatous herbs native to the arid and semiarid regions of the New World, from the southern United States to tropical South America. The spectacular fast-growing inflorescences bear thousands of tubular erect flowers, each consisting of six petaloid perianth segments and six stamens. Agaves are known as century plants, because it was thought that flowering took place only after 100 years; in fact, the plant blooms 8-30 years after the appearance of the first leaves, although this varies according to the climate. The plants die after flowering.

Relics and graves in Mexico have revealed that the coarse fibres of *Agave* species were being used some 8,000 years ago to make nets and cords. Formerly of great importance in many aspects of life in the American southwest, various plants in this genus are used to produce tampico fibre, pulque (the fermented sap) and the distilled mescal or tequila. The buds were once eaten, the flowers once cooked in tortillas and the leaves were a source of soap, chemicals for stunning fish and a crude type of paper.

Agaves have been grown as ornamental plants since the first half of the sixteenth century in the south of Europe and have been naturalized in Spain, Portugal and southern Italy for about two centuries.

Sisal or hemp *Agave sisalana* is native to Mexico and central America, and is the most important species as a source of fibre. The coarse fibres are removed from the leaves by crushing and washing, then rendered pliable by drying, beating and crushing. The 2 m (6.6 ft) leaves have but a single vicious spine at the tip which often causes injuries during harvesting. For the first 8-15 years of the plant's life between 12 and 15 leaves can be removed (by hand) but after this time the flowering phase is reached. The liquid that oozes from the cut flowering stem is used to make the intoxicating Mexican liquor known as pulque. The fibres are used in the manufacture of twine, rope, nets, hammocks and carpets, although their use is declining now that synthetic alternatives are available.

Another Mexican species, henequen *A. fourcroydes*, is also an important source of fibre, but its leaves have spines along the margins, causing problems during harvesting. It is a longer lived plant which is cultivated in Mexico and Cuba, the fibres being used mainly for twine. The Salvador henequen *A. letonae* is grown in El Salvador for its finer fibre, often used in sacking. Both *A. funkiana* and *A. lecheguilla* produce fibres for brushes, while *A. vera-cruz* is a commercial source of fructose.

The American aloe or century plant *A. americana* is a very robust herb in which the stem is scarcely developed and the glaucous spear-shaped leaves, with their spiny margins, are 1-2 m (3.3-6.6 ft) long. Stolons, from which new plants develop, spring from the base of the plant. The magnificent pyramidal flowering spike may reach 10 m (33 ft) above the leaves but is more usually 4-7 m (13-23 ft) tall. The greenish yellow flowers, each less than 1 cm (0.4 in) long, are aggregated in dense clusters at the ends of the horizontal branches of the inflorescence. *A. americana* is native to eastern Mexico but is widely naturalized in the Mediterranean region and the Azores.

Typical century plants of the arid lands of the United States are the yellow-flowered *A. utahensis*, of the eastern Mojave Desert; desert agave *A. deserti*, of the Colorado Desert; and Parry's century plant *A. parryi*, native to the area between central Arizona, central Texas and northern Mexico. Further south, *A. couci* is confined to Venezuela; *A. shawii* occurs in Baja California; and *A. cundinamarcensis* is found only in the Cundinamarca region of Colombia. *A. arizonica*, which is known from only 12-14 sites in central Arizona, is listed as an endangered species by both the United States Fish and Wildlife Service (1985) and the IUCN Plant Red Data Book (1980).

**Agavaceae; more than 100 species**

## AIZOON

A widespread genus of annual herbs distributed across the Mediterranean region, Africa, southern Asia and Australia. The genus is characterized by alternate leaves and almost stalkless flowers in which the petals are absent. *Aizoon hispanicum* is a Mediterranean species with densely papillose leaves and solitary, yellowish flowers produced in the forks of the branches. It thrives in sandy and saline soils in arid steppe grasslands and along the coast.

*A. canariense* grows in both North and South Africa, and in southern Asia, where it appears after minimal rainfall in silty desert habitats. The branches, which bear fleshy, softly hairy leaves, radiate outwards along the ground to form neat stars up to 30 cm (12 in) wide. The petal-less greenish white flowers are about 3 mm (0.1 in) in diameter, the five calyx lobes spreading to form minute stars with yellow centres. The edible leaves of *A. canariense* may be used in salads and are a favourite food of the nomadic Tuareg and camels.

**Aizoaceae; 25 species**

*Agave sp.*

*Agave parryi*

## ANACAMPSEROS

A genus of xerophytic herbs with fleshy leaves, most of which are native to South Africa, but with a single Australian species. This plant, *Anacampseros australiana*, which is confined to the Flinders Range in South Australia, has a thick tuberous root, a rosette of bristly leaves and pink, radially symmetrical flowers.

Typical South African representatives are *A. alstonii*, a Namibian species which has leaves arranged in five straight rows and pure white flowers about 3 cm (1.2 in) across; *A. filamentosa*, a pink-flowered plant from Cape Province in which the leaves are covered with whitish threads; and the Transvaal species *A. lubbersii* which has tight rosettes of reddish leaves and white flowers. Other South African species are *A. lanceolata* and *A. telephiastrum*.

**Portulacaceae; 70 species**

## ANASTATICA

The sole member of this genus is the resurrection plant or rose of Jericho *Anastatica hierochuntica* which is found in arid regions from Morocco to southern Iran, especially on gravelly soils. This small annual flowers only after the winter rains, producing tiny white blooms only 3 mm (0.1 in) in diameter. As the seeds mature the leaves fall, the stems become woody and curl in on themselves and the whole plant forms a small ball to be blown around by the wind. Only after a thorough wetting will the stems uncurl and release the seeds, thus ensuring they have sufficient moisture to germinate.

In many areas *A. hierochuntica* is used as a charm for safe childbirth and is known locally as the Virgin's hand, since Mary was reputed to have clasped one of these plants in her hand during the birth of Christ.

**Cruciferae; a single species**

## ARIOCARPUS

A small genus of extremely slow-growing cacti native to southern Texas and Mexico. The small solitary plants are more or less spherical and have spirally arranged, triangular leaf-like tubercles. The large (up to 5 cm/2 in across) solitary, more or less funnel-shaped flowers are produced in the upper axils of young tubercles and vary from white to pink or yellow. Some species have been found to contain alkaloids, especially hordenine.

The Mexican species include *Ariocarpus retusus* which produces numerous pure white flowers and is often almost covered with sand, leaving only the tips of the tubercles above the surface; *A. trigonus*, with sharply triangular, upward-curving tubercles and lemon-yellow flowers; and *A. agavoides*, which has deep purplish pink flowers. *A. fissuratus* has calloused tubercles and pale pink flowers and is found in southwest Texas and northern Mexico.

Two Mexican species – *A. scapharostrus* from Nuevo León and *A. agavoides* from Tamaulipas – are listed in Appendix I of the Convention on International Trade in Endangered Species of Wild Fauna and Flora (CITES). *A. agavoides* is also listed as a vulnerable/endangered species in the IUCN Plant Red Data Book (1980).

**Cactaceae; 6 species**

## ASTROPHYTUM

A small cactus genus from northern and central Mexico. The plants are globose, becoming cylindrical with age, have prominent ribs and are either spineless or with straight or spiralling spines. The large flowers are yellow, often with a red throat, and in most species the ripe fruits burst open into a star shape.

*Astrophytum ornatum*, which may reach heights of over 1 m (3.3 ft), has eight strongly compressed ribs with wavy margins and clusters of 6-8 very stout spines. Its large yellow flowers are canary-yellow with a silky sheen. *A. myriostigma* differs in having five broadly triangular, spineless ribs which are

*Carnegiea gigantea*

densely white and woolly, while *A. asterias* is a grey-green, disc-like species with barely discernable ribs and flowers with a red throat. *A. capricorne* has long, tangled spines and carmine-throated deep yellow flowers.

**Cactaceae; 6 species**

### AZTEKIUM

This genus contains the single, rather uncommon species *Aztekium ritteri* which thrives on vertical slate rock faces in the Nuevo León district of Mexico. The generic name reflects the apparent resemblance of these cacti to Aztec sculpture.

*Aztekium ritteri* is a small very slow-growing, globose, grey-green cactus about 5 cm (2 in) wide and 3 cm (1.2 in) tall. When young it has short twisting spines which fall off as the plant matures. A cluster of pinkish white funnel-shaped flowers, each measuring about 8 mm (0.3 in) in diameter, is produced at the apex and the fruits are tiny bottle-shaped pink berries that remain embedded in the woolly apex of the cactus until they have decayed, so releasing the seeds. *A. ritteri* is listed in Appendix I of the Convention on International Trade in Endangered Species of Wild Fauna and Flora (CITES).

**Cactaceae; a single species**

### BAILEYA

A genus of yellow or orange flowered plants, commonly known as desert marigolds, confined to the arid lands of the southwestern United States and Mexico. Marigold is a contraction of Mary's Gold, in honour of the Virgin Mary.

*Baileya multiradiata* is a greyish woolly plant with branched stems only the lower halves of which have leaves. The terminal flowerheads are brilliant yellow, up to 5 cm (2 in) across and consist of tubular disc-florets surrounded by some 25-50 oblong ray-florets which often become papery and remain on the head even after the seeds have been shed. The plant flowers profusely throughout the summer, from April to October, and for this reason is much sought after as a garden plant, but its natural habitat is sandy or gravelly deserts.

Other species are *B. pauciradiata*, whose small

pale yellow flowerheads each have only 5-7 ray-florets, and *B. pleniradiata*, which has numerous ray-florets but is distinguished from *B. multiradiata* by having leaves further up the stems, and by flowering from March to May and from October to November.

**Compositae; 4 species**

### BRANDEGEA

The sole member of this genus – *Brandegea bigelovii* – is a rather local species native to southwestern North America, particularly the southern Mojave Desert. It is a twining vine-like plant with three- or five-lobed leaves, coiled tendrils and small star-shaped flowers. Unlike the fleshy gourds produced by most members of this family (for example, cucumbers and melons), the fruits are flattened, one-seeded and barely 1 cm (0.4 in) long.

**Cucurbitaceae; a single species**

### CARNEGIEA

A genus with one species, the saguaro, or giant cactus *Carnegiea gigantea* (*Cereus giganteus*) which, with its characteristic candelabra silhouette, is native to the deserts of the southwestern United States and Mexico. It is the largest of all cacti, reaching a height of 20 m (66 ft) and a thickness of some 60 cm (24 in). Mature individuals, which may be 200 years old, can weigh up to 12 tons.

The stout stems are supported by 12-30 blunt spine-covered ribs, as are the branches, of which there may be as many as 12 all growing more or less vertically. The phenomenal ability of the saguaro to store water in its stems allows it to flower every year regardless of rainfall. The widely funnel-shaped, white flowers, up to 12 cm (4.5 in) across, are produced in crown-like clusters at the tips of the branches. These vanilla-scented blooms usually only last for about six hours and are pollinated by birds during the day and by bats and moths at night.

The fleshy egg-shaped fruits, green on the outside and red inside, are edible and were once an important source of both food and drink for the desert-dwelling Indians. The pulp was eaten raw or preserved, the juice was fermented to make an intoxicating drink and the seeds were ground into a butter. The woody ribs of the column were used in the construction of

*Carnegiea gigantea*

133

*Cistanche phelypaea*

southwest Europe and North Africa, including the Sahara. The flowers of *C. salsa*, a plant of the steppes of southeast Soviet Europe, western Kazakhstan and central and southwest Asia, are pale yellow and violet. The young shoots of *C. phelypaea* are collected by the nomadic Tuareg and eaten like asparagus.

*C. tubulosa* is a tall (to 30 cm/12 in), yellow-flowered species of dry bushland and grassland in East Africa, where it is parasitic on shrubs and trees. It is also common in sandy habitats in Bahrain, where it flowers from December to February and is known as the desert hyacinth or desert tulip. Inland its main host plant is *Zygophyllum qatarense*, but it is also found in coastal dunes, parasitizing the roots of *Suaeda vermiculata* and *Arthrocnemum macrostachyum*.

**Orobanchaceae; 16 species**

### CITRULLUS

A tiny genus of climbing plants from tropical and southern Africa and Asia. Tendrils are usually present and the leaves are usually pinnately lobed. Each solitary unisexual flower, which varies from bright yellow to greenish yellow, has a five-lobed calyx and corolla, with three stamens.

Bitter apple *Citrullus colocynthis*, also known as bitter cucumber and vine of Sodom, is a perennial whose natural distribution extends across both arid and tropical regions of northern and eastern Africa and Asia. The poisonous fruits measure about 8 cm (3 in) in diameter and are globular, with pale yellow or green-mottled skins. They contain the alkaloid colocynthin, a powerful cathartic that has been known to cause death on occasion, despite which it was formerly used in medicine.

Bitter apple has been cultivated for its purgative fruits since the time of the Assyrians and is still grown today in the southern Mediterranean region, where it has become naturalized in several places. The broken fruits are reputed to be useful in keeping moths away from stored clothes.

shelters. The flowers and young stems have been used in the preparation of a cardiac stimulant and as a partial substitute for digitalin, although large doses may provoke hallucinations and mental confusion.

The saguaro is the state flower of Arizona, where it is protected by law. The individual cacti grow very slowly and are often killed or damaged by lightning during desert storms. The saguaro is sometimes referred to as 'the oak tree of the desert', since it is a focal point for animal life in these arid treeless lands. Gila woodpeckers make their nests in the thick stems, and these are then taken over by owls and other creatures when abandoned.

**Cactaceae; a single species**

### CEPHALOPENTANDRA

This genus contains the one species *Cephalopentandra ecirrhosa*, a perennial climbing plant native to the arid tropical regions of northeast Africa, particularly semidesert bushland on sandy soils. It has a hemispherical or elongated fleshy

tuber, which projects above ground, and two types of leaves: some are deeply divided with pointed lobes, while others have shallow rounded lobes. The yellow or cream flowers are unisexual and the fruits are reddish orange, many-seeded gourds.

**Cucurbitaceae; a single species**

### CISTANCHE

A small genus of perennial herbs without chlorophyll which are parasitic on the roots of other plants. They are distributed from the Mediterranean region and Ethiopia as far east as India and northwest China, often in arid habitats. The stout stems are clothed in numerous scale-like leaves and topped with dense spikes of colourful flowers. Each flower is subtended by two bracteoles and has a bell-shaped, five-lobed calyx and a two-lipped corolla.

Two species occur in Europe, both parasitic on woody plants of the Chenopodiaceae. *Cistanche phelypaea* has bright yellow flowers and is usually found in the arid grasslands and salt marshes of

*Cistanche phelypaea*

*C. lanatus* is an annual whose globular or ellipsoid fruits, 25 cm (10 in) across with dark green skins, are better known as water melons. It is native to South Africa but is widely cultivated in southern Europe and America for its refreshing red-fleshed fruits. The black seeds are used in soups in China and excess fruit is made into syrup in eastern Europe. The seeds were formerly used by Russian peasants in the treatment of dropsy, liver diseases and intestinal disorders; they are also known to have vermicidal properties.

**Cucurbitaceae; 3 species**

### CLIANTHUS

This genus of evergreen herbaceous perennials, commonly known as glory peas, has just two species: *Clianthus formosus* is native to the arid lands of Australia and *C. puniceus* is found in New Zealand. The generic name is derived from the combination of *cleo* ('glory') and *anthos* ('a flower'). The genus is characterized by pinnate leaves and large leaf-like stipules, while the conspicuous flowers, arranged in umbel-like clusters, arise on long stalks from the axils of the leaves.

The best known species is Sturt's desert pea or glory pea *C. formosus*. It is a low trailing plant with silver-haired foliage and dense inflorescences of deep red flowers, 8-10 cm (3-4 in) long and marked with black at the base of the standard. The flowers appear soon after the rains in October. The plant was first discovered by the explorer William Dampier (1652-1715), captain of HMS *Roebuck*, on the islands off the coast of northwestern Australia which later came to be known as Dampier's Archipelago. Only later was the plant also found growing across the whole arid interior of mainland Australia, especially in New South Wales, South Australia and in the north and west.

Parrot's bill *C. puniceus* is a soft woody plant with trailing branches and pendulous scarlet or pink flowers. It is confined to North Island, New Zealand and was formerly cultivated by the Maoris, although in recent years it has disappeared from many of its former localities and is in danger of becoming extinct. It is listed as an endangered species in the IUCN Plant Red Data Book (1980).

**Leguminosae; 2 species**

### COTYLEDON

A genus of succulent herbs and shrubs largely confined to the arid lands of southern Africa, although a single species ranges from East Africa to Arabia. The plants are usually compact with thick fleshy leaves and terminal inflorescences of drooping, tubular, yellow, orange or red flowers. The generic name is derived from the Greek *cotyle* ('a cup'), which refers to the concave leaves of many species.

The East African and Arabian species is *Cotyledon barbeyi*, an erect, many stemmed shrub with large, pendulous, red flowers. It is locally common in dry stony bushland, especially on small hills up to 2,400 m (7,900 ft).

One of the most common Namibian species is pig's-ears *C. orbiculata*, which grows up to 50 cm (20 in) high and has long grey-green leaves with reddish tips. The red pendant flowers are arranged in a loose cluster at the tip of a long leafless stalk. This flower stalk was formerly used like a flute in hunting; the noise produced resembles the call of a young klipspringer antelope, and therefore encourages the adult to investigate. Pig's-ears is toxic to grazing animals, causing severe stomach cramp and sometimes death, although the leaf juice is allegedly beneficial in the treatment of epilepsy.

Other southern African species include the rare *C. buchholziana*, with pinkish purple flowers; *C. cacaloides*, which has yellowish-red flowers; *C. jacobseniana*, distinguished by its reddish green blooms; and *C. teretifolia*, with white hairy leaves and long-stemmed inflorescences of drooping, bell-shaped, orange-red flowers. *C. schaeferana*, which grows in Namibia and parts of Cape Province, is one of the few species with erect flowers, these having greenish tubes with distinct red lines and pinkish lilac lobes. *C. wallichii* and *C. paniculata* are shrubby species of Cape Province.

**Crassulaceae; about 35 species**

### CYNOMORIUM

This tiny genus of perennial parasitic herbs is distributed from the Mediterranean to Mongolia. The plants lack chlorophyll, instead drawing their nourishment from other plants via the roots. Fleshy, reddish male, female and hermaphrodite flowers occur in a dense inflorescence, each flower having 1-5 narrow or oval perianth segments.

The most widespread species is desert thumb *Cynomorium coccineum*, distributed across the European Mediterranean region, North Africa and southwest Asia, although nowhere common. It parasitizes the roots of a variety of plants, particularly members of the Chenopodiaceae, usually in saline habitats. The whole plant is dark red to purplish black and reaches a maximum height of about 30 cm (12 in). The stem is clothed in triangular scale-leaves and the terminal inflorescence is club-shaped or cylindrical. Pollination is carried out by flies attracted by the foetid odour given off by the plant.

In many instances the spikes of *C. coccineum* are half buried in the sand, from which its common name is derived. The whole appearance is so unlike a flowering plant that in the Middle Ages it was classified as *Fungus melitensis*, the Maltese mushroom. The roots are used as a condiment by the Tuareg.

**Balanophoraceae (Cynomoriaceae); 2 species**

### DOROTHEANTHUS

A small genus of succulent annual herbs with large brightly coloured flowers, confined to southern Africa. The mature fruits are spongy and have five valves that open in wet conditions to distribute the seeds, closing again as dry conditions return.

The best known species (because of the ease with which it can be grown in cultivation) is undoubtedly the Livingstone daisy *Dorotheanthus bellidiformis*. It is a small branching plant, growing to about 12 cm (4.5 in) in height, with narrow fleshy basal leaves

*Cynomorium coccineum*

covered with glistening papillae. The mass of flowers completely dominates the foliage and can be all shades of white, pink, red, orange and yellow. Each many petalled flower is solitary, terminal, and 1-6 cm (0.4-2.4 in) in diameter.

*D. bellidiformis* grows in flat sandy habitats in Great Namaland and Cape Province, as does an even smaller species, *D. rourkei*, which attains a height of only 5 cm (2in). It has flat, green, papillose leaves and flowers of about 3.5 cm (1.4 in) in diameter which are reddish with a golden sheen.

**Aizoaceae; 14 species**

## ECHINOCACTUS

This was once a large genus but has recently been revised and reduced to only a few species, all of which occur only in the southwestern United States and Mexico. The plants are usually very large, solitary or freely branching from the base, ranging in general outline from disc-shaped to globose or columnar. The largest species reach diameters of 1 m (3.3 ft) and heights of 3 m (10 ft) and are commonly called barrel cacti. They have numerous ribs and very stout spines which are often brightly coloured. The flowers are produced in a ring near the apex and are usually yellow or pink.

Two Mexican species of *Echinocactus* are golden barrel *E. grusonii*, which has sharp yellow spines and is sometimes called mother-in-law's armchair, and *E. platyacanthus*, with brownish or greyish spines. Both are robust globose cacti that become columnar with age, reach heights of 1-2 m (3.3-6.6 ft) and have silky yellow flowers, those of *E. grusonii* opening only when exposed to full sunlight. Mexican giant barrel *E. ingens*, *E. grandis*, *E. palmeri* and *E. visnaga* are sometimes considered to be local forms of *E. platyacanthus*.

Two rather different species are the dark green, depressed globose *E. texensis* and the grey-green almost spherical *E. horizonthalonius*, both of which are found in Texas, New Mexico and Mexico. The spines are stout and ringed and the flowers are usually pinkish red, those of *E. horizonthalonius* having a sweet fragrance. Most plants in this genus have juicy red-fleshed fruit, which in *E. horizonthalonius* is edible.

**Cactaceae; about 16 species**

## EDITHCOLEA

The only species in this genus is *Edithcolea grandis*, a low succulent plant native to dry rocky habitats in east and northeast Africa. The plants have no leaves but consist of short, semierect, five-angled stems up to 30 cm (12 in) tal, covered with thorn-like yellowish or grey-green knobs. The conspicuous, solitary, terminal flowers are yellow with numerous reddish brown markings, each having five triangular-ovate lobes which are joined for half their length and a deep corolla tube lined with purple hairs.

*E. grandis* is now a rare species as a result of over-collection for its splendid flowers, despite the fact that it rarely thrives in cultivation. Some authorities recognize a second species *E. sordida*, recorded from the island of Socotra in the Indian Ocean, which has deep purple flowers.

**Asclepiadaceae; a single species**

## ESCHSCHOLZIA

A small genus of poppy-like perennial herbs with watery sap native to western North America, although several species have become naturalized in Europe. The fern-like leaves are often blue-green and the flower buds are characterized by their convergent sepals which form a hood, although these are shed when the four-petalled flower opens.

The most typical desert species is the Mexican gold poppy *Eschscholzia mexicana*, which has much-divided bluish leaves and solitary, orange-yellow, cup-shaped flowers up to 4 cm (1.6 in) wide and borne on long stalks. As with all species in this genus,

the flowers close at night and on cloudy days, each petal rolling longitudinally around a few stamens. When open their spicy fragrance attracts beetles which pollinate the flowers. Mexican gold poppy is characteristic of open gravelly desert slopes from southeastern California to Texas and northern Mexico, flowering after the winter rains from March to May. In Arizona it is used as an indicator of the presence of copper in the soil.

The very similar California poppy *E. californica* has deep yellow or orange (rarely cream) flowers with fan-shaped petals and many stamens. It is the state flower of California, where it blooms from February to September in open grassy habitats. The colourless latex contains a mild narcotic and is used by the American Indians as a cure for toothache.

Other characteristic species of arid lands are *E. parishii* from the southern Mojave Desert to the Colorado Desert, where it blooms in March and April; the smaller flowered *E. minutiflora*, also of the Californian deserts, and the tufted *E. glyptosperma*, which is largely confined to the Mojave.

**Papaveraceae; 8-10 species**

## ESPOSTOA

A tiny genus of columnar cacti up to 4 m (13 ft) tall, which branch from the base, have long spines and are sometimes densely woolly. They are native to Peru and Brazil, often in the arid lands which occur at altitudes of over 2,000 m (6,600 ft). The nocturnal flowers are scaly and hairy, and range from white to red.

*Espostoa melanostele*, from northern and central Peru, reaches a maximum height of about 2 m (6.6 ft), with stems being up to 15 cm (6 in) in diameter and thickly felted with white hairs. Numerous spines are present, amber-yellow when young, turning black with age. The white flowers are about 5 cm (2 in) across and the pear-shaped fruits may be white, yellow or reddish. *E. lanata* is a much larger candelabra-type cactus, with strawberry-like carmine-red fruits. It is native to northern Peru.

**Cactaceae; about 4 species**

## FAGONIA

This genus is widely distributed across the arid lands of both hemispheres, the majority of species ranging from the Mediterranean region to southwest Asia, northwest India and southwest Africa in the Old World, but with six representatives in southwest North America. Plants in this genus are herbs, often with spinose stipules and flowers with five deciduous sepals and five clawed petals, although in some species the petals are absent.

The Mediterranean species is *Fagonia cretica*, a hairless perennial of dry stony habitats with sprawling

*Eschscholzia californica*

*Fagonia sp.*

branched stems and opposite trifoliate leaves. The solitary magenta flowers, which are produced in the axils of the leaves, are about 1 cm (0.4 in) in diameter.

In arid southwest Asia the genus is more diverse, including species such as *F. bruguieri* and *F. indica*, both with mauvish pink flowers about 6 mm (0.2 in) across, but distinguished by their leaves; those of *F. bruguieri* are trifoliate, those of *F. indica* oblong or oval-lanceolate. *F. ovalifolia* is a very similar species. In this area *Fagonia* species never attain large proportions since they are a favourite food of camels and the spiny tailed lizard.

*F. californica* is a New World species with intricately branched stems, trifoliate leaves and purplish flowers about 1 cm (0.4 in) in diameter. It is a common plant of rocky habitats in the Colorado Desert and the southern Mojave.

**Zygophyllaceae; 30 species**

### FENESTRARIA
A genus of two species confined to South Africa, particularly in the southern Namib Desert and in Cape Province at the mouth of the Orange River. The generic name literally means 'a collection of windows'; the stems are buried beneath the sand to avoid the extreme heat and insolation of the desert and only the tips of the erect cylindrical leaves emerge, each having a lens-like 'window' to admit light for photosynthesis. Both species are clump-forming succulents. *Fenestraria rhopalophylla* has white or pinkish flowers with many narrow petals and yellow centres, while *F. aurantiaca* has yellowish flowers.

**Aizoaceae; 2 species**

### FEROCACTUS
This cactus genus is native to southwestern North America. The generic name is derived from the Latin *ferox* ('fierce'), because of the vicious spines of many species. The stems of the candy barrel cactus *Ferocactus wislizenii*, which occurs from southern Arizona to western Texas and northern Mexico, are candied as sweetmeats.

These cacti are large plants, either solitary or forming large colonies, ranging from globular to columnar in general outline, and generally having hooked spines. They are often known as barrel or hedgehog cacti. The broadly funnel-shaped flowers are produced in profusion near the apex, the colour varying through shades of red to yellow. Among the

*Ferocactus acanthodes*

*Ferocactus acanthodes*

solitary globose species are *F. hamatacanthus*, whose glossy yellow flowers often have red throats, and devil's-tongue *F. latispinus*, a central Mexican species with white, pink, red or purple flowers.

  *F. emoryi* is a massive columnar species from Arizona and the Sonoran Desert which reaches a height of 1.5 m (5 ft), while the yellow-flowered *F. acanthodes*, native to the arid lands of California, southern Nevada, Arizona and Baja California, is even larger, mature individuals often topping 3 m (10 ft). One of the more spectacular colonial representatives is the Mexican *F. robustus*, a yellow-flowered cactus in which the huge (5 m/16.5 ft across and over 1 m/3.3 ft high) colonies may consist of hundreds of individual 'heads', each only 20 cm (8 in) in diameter. Other Mexican species are the yellow-flowered *F. flavovirens*; *F. fordii*, which has rose-pink flowers; the rare *F. schwarzii*, known only from Rancha del Padre, Sinaloa; and the red-flowered *F. gatesii*.

**Cactaceae; 23 species**

### FERRARIA

A small genus of perennial herbs with bizarre flowers and a disagreeable odour, largely confined to South Africa, although there is a single species in tropical Africa. *Ferraria divaricata* grows up to 45 cm (18 in) high and has branched stems and blue-green iris-like leaves. Its flowers are 5.5 cm (2.2 in) across, yellow or greenish with triangular purple-brown markings on the perianth segments, the margins of which are 'crisped'. *F. uncinata* is a shorter plant with curved leaves, its smaller mustard-yellow flowers having bluish markings and tightly 'crisped' margins. *F. divaricata* is found on sands and shales in Great Namaland, the Kalahari Desert and the Great Karoo, while *F. uncinata* is more or less confined to Great Namaland.

**Iridaceae; 10 species**

### FRITHIA

This genus is found only in the arid Transvaal Mountains near Pretoria in South Africa. The sole species is *Frithia pulchra*, a stemless succulent herb whose greyish green club-shaped leaves have apical 'windows' through which sunlight shines on to the photosynthetic tissues within (see *Fenestraria*). The conspicuous flowers have numerous carmine-purple petals and white centres.

**Aizoaceae; a single species**

### KINGIA

The sole member of this genus is *Kingia australis*, a native of the arid grasslands of western Australia, and very similar to the Australian grass-trees (see *Xanthorrhoea*). Commonly known as black gin, these robust plants can grow up to 2 m (6.6 ft) high and are topped with long, grass-like, toothed leaves which radiate in all directions. Numerous aerial roots are concealed at the bases of these leaves. The white flowers are carried in spherical terminal inflorescences on thick stems about 30 cm (12 in) long and the fruits are densely clothed with white hairs. Individual plants may reach a considerable age; the oldest known specimen is thought to have sprouted from seed about 650 years ago.

**Xanthorrhoeaceae; a single species**

### KOELPINIA

A small genus of annual herbs with solitary often branched stems, narrow leaves and 1-3 terminal flowerheads per branch, each consisting of whitish yellow ray-florets only. The distinctive seeds are linear-cylindrical and strongly incurved, with long hooked projections along the back and at the apex. The best known member of this genus is *Koelpinia linearis*, a plant typical of semidesert habitats from southeastern Spain (Almería), southeastern Soviet Europe and western Kazakhstan to central Asia and North Africa. Its inconspicuous yellow flowers are produced after the winter rains in February.

**Compositae; 5 species**

### LAPEIROUSIA

This genus of attractive perennial herbs with corms is widely distributed across Africa south of the Sahara, but is particularly diverse on the southwest coast. Here, some 15 species grow in arid habitats in Great Namaland, most of which are less than 15 cm (6 in) tall but are noted for their large, brightly coloured flowers.

*Lapeirousia silenoides* is one of the more spectacular species, having a single basal leaf and numerous bracts arranged up the stem, from which arise magenta to cerise flowers with creamy yellow markings, each with a slender whitish perianth tube up to 5 cm (2 in) long and spreading lobes. *L. arenaria* has cream to pinkish flowers with a red spot at the base of the three lower perianth segments, a feature which is also noticeable in the white flowers of *L. divaricata* and the cream or yellowish blooms of *L. fabricii*. *L. anceps* and *L. comymbosa* have deep violet or purple flowers and *L. laxa* has red flowers with dark blotches on the three lower lobes.

**Iridaceae; 30 species**

### LEPTORHYNCHOS

An exclusively Australian genus of herbs or undershrubs with alternate entire leaves and long-stalked flowerheads consisting solely of yellow tubular disc-florets. The generic name is derived from a combination of *leptos* ('slender'), and *rhynchos* ('beak'), in reference to the beaked seeds. Possibly the best known species is the delicate perennial herb scaly buttons *Leptorhynchos squamatus*, a slightly woolly plant with almost hemispherical yellow flowerheads. It grows in dry sandy country in Queensland, New South Wales, Victoria and South Australia.

**Compositae; 9 species**

### LITHOPS

A genus of hairless succulent herbs confined to southern Africa and commonly known as living stones or pebble plants. The plants produce annual growths of one or more pebble-like bodies consisting of a pair of mottled grey-green or brownish fleshy leaves on top of a dual column. The leaf tips are flattened and often contain transparent 'windows' (see *Fenestraria*), allowing the plant to photosynthesize even when partially buried in the desert soil.

The solitary, many petalled, daisy-like flowers emerge from between the leaves and are either white or yellow. After flowering the plants cease to grow and a new shoot develops which draws moisture from the old leaves, these eventually withering away. Living stones thrive in very dry desert regions where they blend in well with their surroundings.

White-flowered species include *Lithops elisae* from Cape Province, and *L. salicola* from Orange Free State, both of which have greyish white bodies. *L. optica*, *L. opalina* and *L. julii* are all white-flowered species from Namibia, while *L. bella* and *L. pseudotruncatella*, from the same geographical area, have bright yellow flowers. Two yellow-flowered species from Cape Province are *L. dorothae* and *L. comptonii*.

**Aizoaceae; 37 species**

### LOPHOPHORA

Just two species belong to this genus, *L. lewinii* and *L. williamsii* (although some authorities recognize but a single, very variable species – *L. williamsii*, and others add a third: *L. ziegleri*). The young cacti are solitary, later offsetting to form colonies, each individual depressed globose (button-like) in shape, up to 7 cm (2.8 in) high and 8 cm (3 in) wide. They are spineless, greyish or blue-green with 5-13 broad spiralling ribs divided by horizontal furrows into low tubercles. The flowers are produced at the apex, are about 2.5 cm (1 in) in diameter and have many pale pink, carmine, white or yellowish petals. These plants are found in southern Texas, southern New Mexico and northern Mexico, particularly on limestone soils in desert habitats.

Commonly known as mescal buttons, dumpling cacti or peyote, these cacti contain some 30 alkaloids, four of the most important being anhalonine, mescaline, anhalonidine and lophophorine, which confer a bitter and disagreeable taste on the buttons. The ingestion of four or five dried buttons produces brilliantly coloured hallucinations and a feeling of weightlessness, with physical effects including muscular relaxation, nausea, vomiting and loss of time sense. The value of mescal buttons in medicine is uncertain, but they have been used to treat hysteria, asthma, gout, neuralgia and rheumatism.

On the other hand, petote has been used for thousands of years by the Kiowa Indians for producing exaltation during religious ceremonies or rituals, and by Yaqui Indian sorcerers for enlightenment. In the United States a federal permit is required to possess any part of a peyote plant, but despite this it has almost been eliminated in Texas; it is still very common in parts of Mexico, however.

**Cactaceae; 2 species**

### MAMMILLARIA

The largest genus of cacti apart from *Opuntia*. *Mammillaria* species are typical of arid regions and are found from the southwestern United States to Colombia and Venezuela and Cuba, Haiti and the Bahamas, with a centre of distribution in Mexico. The generic name refers to the nipple-like projections on the stems.

*Mammillaria* are small to medium-sized cacti with globose to shortly columnar stems which may be upright or decumbent, solitary or colonial. The flowers are produced in profusion in a ring around the apex and are usually pink or red, more rarely white or yellowish. In most species the flowers are regular, but in a few they are irregular. The small red fruits are edible and are known as *chilitos*.

Some of the more distinctive species are *Mammillaria candida*, with clumps of almost spherical stems about 8 cm (3 in) in diameter, densely covered with white spines and topped by dull rose-red flowers, from the San Luis Potosí region of Mexico; and *M. beneckei*, a south Mexican species with a ring of large pale yellow flowers atop a dark green or reddish, white-spined stem up to 35 cm (14 in) wide.

*M. longimanna* is a central Mexican cactus with finger-like pale green tubercles up to 7 cm (2.8 in) long and funnel-shaped bright yellow flowers, while *M. senilis*, which occurs at altitudes of 2,500-3,000 m (8,200-9,800 ft) in northern Mexico, produces mounds of globose to cylindrical stems completely covered in fine white spines and has orange-red to violet, obliquely funnel-shaped flowers.

Other Mexican species include the old-lady cactus *M. plumosa*, which has peach-coloured flowers and stems covered with soft, feathery, white spines; *M. carmenae*, whose globose stems are covered with rosettes of soft yellow-white spines and ringed with white, pink-flushed flowers; and *M. pectinifera*, with globose stems and spines arranged in flattened comb-like patterns, but completely dominated by a ring of large, bell-shaped, yellowish or pink flowers.

*M. tetrancista* has pink-purple flowers and grows in Arizona, Utah, Nevada and Baja California; the fishhook cactus *M. macrocarpa* has many hooked spines and lavender flowers and grows in dry gravelly places in deserts and arid grassland from southeastern California to western Texas and northern Mexico;

*Mesembryanthemum sp.*

*Mesembryanthemum sp.*

and the foxtail cactus *M. alversonii* of Californian arid lands has magenta flowers and clusters of short, cylindrical, brown-spined stems resembling foxes' brushes.

**Cactaceae; 168 species**

### MESEMBRYANTHEMUM

A genus of herbs with fleshy leaves distributed across the arid lands of the Mediterranean region, Arabia, South Africa, southern Australia, California and the Atlantic Islands. The leaves may be flat or almost cylindrical, alternate or opposite, and the flowers have numerous petals.

*Mesembryanthemum nodiflorum* is a spreading, branched annual with fleshy cylindrical leaves and curious crystalline shining papillae on the upper stems, resembling hoar frost. The similar ice plant *M. crystallinum* is distinguished by its flattened oval leaves and dense covering of crystalline papillae. Both species have solitary yellowish or white flowers and thrive on maritime sands, rocky cliffs and salt marshes around the shores of the Mediterranean Sea, extending to Portugal.

*M. crystallinum* was formerly cultivated in the Canary Islands for the extraction of soda. It has also been introduced to North America, where it thrives in dry coastal and desert habitats in California and Baja California. *M. forskahlei* is a small succulent Arabian species, also with leaves and stems covered with glistening papillae, while the flowers are composed of many fragile, white, pink-tipped filaments surrounding a cluster of yellow stamens. This rather uncommon plant flowers from January to April in sandy desert habitats.

**Aizoaceae; 70 species**

### MOLTKIOPSIS

The only member of this genus is *Moltkiopsis ciliata*, a perennial xerophytic herb of arid lands in North Africa, extending to Iran. The plants reach a height of about 15 cm (6 in) and often form small clumps on dune slopes. The curved stems bear oval, grey-green, hairy leaves with slender spines on the margins. The

tubular flowers, which are various shades of pink and blue, are about 1 cm (0.4 in) long and appear from March to May.

**Boraginaceae; a single species**

### MONOPTILON

A tiny genus of the sandy and stony deserts of southwestern North America. The Mojave desert star *Monoptilon bellioides* is an unmistakable annual which grows flat on the ground with branches radiating out in all directions, the whole plant 2.5-25 cm (1-10 in) in diameter. The flowerheads are about 2 cm (0.8 in) across and are produced at the ends of the branches, facing upwards with white or pinkish ray-florets surrounding the tubular yellow disc-florets. *M. bellioides* flowers from January to May and again in September, depending on rainfall.

**Compositae; 2 species**

### OBREGONIA

*Obregonia denegrii* is the sole member of this genus. The plants resemble artichokes, having tuberous roots from 12-20 cm (4.5-8 in) in diameter topped by hemispherical rosettes of thick, flat, leaf-like tubercles, strongly keeled beneath. Spines are present only in young plants. The 2 cm (0.8 in) white or pinkish funnel-shaped flowers are produced at the woolly apex and the white berry-like seeds initially remain concealed in the wool but become club-shaped and protrude when ripe.

*O. denegrii* is known only from the arid valleys of Tamaulipas in Mexico, on dry limestone hills at about 800 m (2,600 ft). It is listed as a vulnerable/endangered species in the IUCN Plant Red Data Book (1980) and in Appendix I of CITES (the Convention on International Trade in Endangered Species of Wild Fauna and Flora).

**Cactaceae; a single species**

### OPUNTIA

The largest genus of cacti, with a distribution extending from Massachusetts and British Columbia to the Galápagos Islands and the Straits of Magellan,

*Moltkiopsis ciliata*

although most species occur in Mexico, Peru and Chile. Members of this genus are found in arid habitats from sea level to over 4,500 m (14,800 ft). Many species have been introduced to other parts of the world, particularly South Africa, Australia and the Mediterranean region.

*Opuntia* species are usually freely branching shrubs or trees with jointed stems consisting of cylindrical or flattened segments. Some species have narrow needle-like leaves instead of spines. The flowers are produced singly from the tips of the branches or at the margins of the stem joints, and are usually yellow or reddish, rarely white. The species with cylindrical segments are known as chollas, while those with flattened stem joints are usually called prickly pears.

One of the more distinctive species is the tree-like *Opuntia brasiliensis*, native to southern Brazil, Paraguay, Bolivia and northern Argentina, which has a cylindrical trunk and whorled crown of flattened or rounded branches. Mature plants may reach a height of 4 m (13 ft), at which stage they produce small yellow flowers on the edges of the leaf-like side-shoots. Other tree-like species are *O. moniliformis*, with orange-yellow flowers, from

*Opuntia bigelovii*

*Opuntia phaeacantha*

Hispaniola and the Island of Desecheo; *O. subulata*, with reddish flowers, from southern Peru; and the 10 m (33 ft) *O. auberi*, with rose-red flowers, from central and southern Mexico.

Other species produce bush-like shrubby plants, such as *O. miquelii* of the Atacama Desert in Chile, which has branching, cylindrical shoots, stout downward-pointing spines and pinkish flowers, and *O. tunicata*, a profusely spiny shrub with greenish yellow flowers which thrives in desert habitats in Mexico, Ecuador, Peru and northern Chile. The teddybear cholla or jumping cholla *O. bigelovii* is a robust species up to 1 m (3.3 ft) high with a short trunk and a crown of spreading, very spiny branches which bear purple flowers at their tips. It grows in the Colorado and Mojave Deserts (Nevada, Arizona and California), as well as in Baja California and the Sonoran Desert.

Yet other species have a cushion-like habit, including the yellow-flowered Chilean *O. dimorpha*, in which the compact cushions made up of globular-ovoid joints are up to 20 cm (8 in) high and 30 cm (12 in) wide; *O. floccosa*, an orange-flowered species of high altitudes (4,000-4,500 m/13,100-14,800 ft in the Peruvian and Bolivian Andes) with cushions up to 2 m (6.6 ft) across, covered with long white woolly hairs; and *O. articulata*, of western Argentina, distinguished by its short grey-green sections with paper-like flattened spines and pinkish flowers.

Perhaps the best known type of *Opuntia* is that with flattened, disc-like joints and fleshy fruits. Many species of this type occur in Mexico, including *O.*

*stenopetala*, with fiery red flowers and scarlet fruits; rabbit-ears or bunny-ears *O. microdasys*, with pale yellow flowers and globose deep red fruits; and the larger *O. scheerii*, with 10 cm (4 in) wide bluish green shoots, pale yellow flowers and red fleshy fruits. In the arid lands of the southwestern United States typical species are *O. rhodantha*, with robust spines and large purplish-red flowers; *O. macrocentra*, which lacks spines and has cup-shaped, yellow-orange flowers; and *O. phaeacantha*, a prostrate plant with pale yellow or pink flowers and pear-shaped spiny fruits.

The Mojave prickly pear *O. mojavensis*, which has pale yellow to orange flowers and conspicuous red-purple fruits, is found in the eastern Mojave Desert, while beaver-tail *O. basilaris*, which thrives in the arid lands of California, Arizona and Utah, is a spineless species with lavender or purplish stem joints and rose-coloured flowers.

Indian or Barbary fig *O. ficus-indica* is another member of this genus with flattened stem joints. It is native to tropical America but is cultivated for its edible fruit and as a hedge plant in the Mediterranean region, where it is widely naturalized. It has pale yellow flowers and red or yellow ovoid spiny fruits up to 9 cm (3.5 in) long. In homeopathy a tincture is made from the flowers and woody parts to treat spleen disorders and diarrhoea. The cochineal insect cactus *O. cochinellifera* is native to Mexico but is cultivated for cochineal in the West Indies and elsewhere.

The tiger pear *O. aurantica* is perhaps the most

widespread species in the world. Although native to the West Indies it was introduced to South Africa and eastern Australia and rapidly became the dominant plant of the plains, to the detriment of the grazing lands. Today it is largely controlled by moth larvae, introduced from the plant's native habitat – one of man's most successful experiments in biological control.

**Cactaceae; about 300 species**

### *PALAFOXIA*

A small genus typical of the arid lands of the southwestern United States and Mexico. *Palafoxia sphacelata* is a slender, erect, sparsely leaved plant with a few flowerheads at the ends of the upper branches. The flowerheads may be up to 4 cm (1.6 in) across and consist of dusky pink disc-florets and distinctive ray-florets, each of which widens towards the tip and divides into three narrow lobes. It flowers from May to October and is a typical species of the sandy plains, deserts and dunes of the American Southwest, from Kansas to New Mexico, Texas and Mexico.

Spanish needles *P. arida* is an annual distinguished by its lack of ray-florets, each flowerhead composed solely of pale lavender disc-florets. Its common name is derived from the four slender pointed scales which top the fruits. *P. arida* is a common plant of sandy flats and washes of the arid regions of California, Utah and Arizona.

**Compositae; 12 species**

## PELECYPHORA

This cactus genus contains just two species *Pelecyphora strobiliformis* and *P. aselliformis* both native to the deserts of Mexico. They are globose or shortly cylindrical cacti with fleshy rootstocks that form clumps by budding off new plants. The bell-shaped or funnel-like flowers are carmine-violet and are produced near the apex.

*P. strobiliformis* grows in the Tamaulipas region of Mexico. The individual plants are up to 6 cm (2.4 in) across and are completely covered with scale-like, overlapping, grey-green tubercles, each broadly triangular, fairly thin and leaf-like. The large showy flowers are bright reddish violet and are about 4 cm (1.6 in) in diameter. *P. aselliformis* is a larger species, the globose stems reaching 10 cm (4 in) in diameter and becoming club-shaped with age. It differs from its relative in having hatchet-shaped tubercles raised above the surface by up to 5 mm (0.2 in), and in its smaller flowers. This species is rare in the San Luis Potosí area of Mexico and is listed in Appendix I of the Convention on International Trade in Endangered Species of Wild Fauna and Flora (CITES).

**Cactaceae; 2 species**

## PSATHYROTES

A small genus of the arid lands of the American Southwest. The best known species is probably *Psathyrotes ramosissima* which is commonly known as desert velvet because of its grey woolly hairy leaves. It is usually an annual and is distinguished by its compact cushion-like form and strong odour of turpentine. The numerous leaves are thick and coarsely toothed, and the tiny terminal flowerheads (6 mm/0.2 in across) are composed entirely of yellow or purplish tubular disc-florets.

Desert velvet is a common plant of dry compacted soils on flats and ledges in the Californian Deserts, extending to Utah, Arizona and northwestern Mexico. Although usually blooming from March to June, its flowers are sometimes seen in the winter months. *P. ramosissima* is also known as turtleback, because of its rounded outline and the intricate pattern formed by the rounded overlapping leaves.

**Compositae; 5 species**

## PTERODISCUS

A genus of tropical and southern Africa, most members of which occur in arid habitats and have thick fleshy stems and attractive tubular flowers with five corolla lobes narrowing into a tube. The Tanzanian species *Pterodiscus angustifolia* has many purplish green succulent branches arising from the fleshy base to a height of around 25 cm (10 in). The narrow deep green leaves are also succulent, with wavy margins and a toothed apex. The scented funnel-shaped flowers are deep yellow, with purplish

*Carnegiea gigantea, Ocotillo sp.* and *Opuntia sp.*

markings in the corolla tube.

Another East African species *P. ruspolii*, a plant of open semidesert scrub and grassland in dry, sandy or rocky habitats, differs in having non-succulent leaves and bright orange-yellow flowers, sometimes with a red or purple central spot. *P. auranticus* is a succulent yellow-flowered species of Namibia and Angola, while the trailing *P. procumbens* of South Africa has red or purple flowers. Cape Province representatives include *P. luridus*, whose yellowish flowers are covered with tiny red dots, and *P. speciosus*, a succulent plant with purplish pink flowers.

**Pedaliaceae; 18 species**

### *RAFINESQUIA*

A tiny genus containing just two species confined to the arid lands of the southwestern United States. The genus is named after C. S. Rafinesque, an early American naturalist. Desert chicory or plumeseed *Rafinesquia neomexicana* is an annual with grey-green branched stems bearing pinnate leaves and beautiful fragrant flowers with ray-florets only, pure-white above and purplish beneath. The seeds are topped with feathery hairs to catch the wind for dispersal. Desert chicory is found in sandy or gravelly places in the deserts of southeastern California, southern Utah and Mexico. *R. californica* is a similar species with smaller flowers, found on coastal slopes as well as in desert habitats.

**Compositae; 2 species**

### *SANSEVIERIA*

A genus of perennial herbs with short rhizomes and tough thick leaves native to dry tropical and southern Africa, Madagascar, Arabia and southern Asia. Many plants in this genus are succulent and some are epiphytic.

*Sansevieria intermedia* has stiff, cylindrical, slightly mottled leaves arranged in a spiral, from the centre of which arises a spike of white and dirty reddish flowers; the perianth segments are fused into tubes with six spreading lobes. It is locally common in dry rocky bushland in East Africa, especially in the Rift Valley. Another East African species, *S. suffruticosa*, is a branched bush-like plant, each branch consisting of 7-18 long cylindrical leaves and a 40 cm (16 in) inflorescence of some 25 greenish white flowers.

The genus is very variable, with new species being discovered all the time. Some of the more distinctive African representatives are *S. cylindrica*, a white-flowered species with cylindrical leaves from southern tropical Africa, particularly Natal; *S. grandis*, an epiphyte from Somalia with broad flattened leaves with reddish margins; and *S. thyrsiflora*, a creeping flat-leaved plant with scented white flowers which grows in southeast Africa.

African or bowstring hemp *S. guineensis* is a native of tropical Africa; *S. angolensis* occurs in tropical western Africa; and *S. roxburghiana* is found in India. The leaves of all three species contain fibres for making paper, ropes, fishing nets, sails and other marine equipment. *S. zeylanica*, which has distinctive yellow stripes on the margins of the leaves, is native to Sri Lanka but is widely grown for ornament.

**Agavaceae; 50 species**

### *SCHWANTESIA*

This small genus of dwarf succulents is more or less confined to southwest Africa. They are compact plants distinguished by their unequal pairs of leaves and solitary flowers. *Schwantesia ruedebuschii* is a rare species of Namibia which forms clumps up to 10 cm (4 in) high. It has boat-shaped white-mottled leaves, which expand towards the tip and are covered with thick blue teeth, and attractive pale yellow flowers. The more common *S. acutipetala* is distinguished by its smooth, narrow, blue-green leaves which taper sharply towards the tip and sometimes have reddish margins. It also has yellow flowers and is native to Great Namaland and Cape Province.

**Aizoaceae; 11 species**

### *SCLEROCEPHALUS*

The sole member of this genus is *Sclerocephalus arabicus*, a xerophytic annual herb distributed across the arid regions of the northern hemisphere Old World from Macaronesia to Iran. It is only 3-4 cm (1.2-1.6 in) tall, but the stems radiate out from a central root to form a flattened cushion up to 10 cm (4 in) wide. The stems bear cylindrical, fleshy, grey-green leaves and minute flowers are arranged in spiny rounded heads about 8 mm (0.3 in) across. *S. arabicus* can grow in the driest of conditions and flowers from February to May.

**Caryophyllaceae; a single species**

### *STANLEYA*

A small genus native to western North America, most species of which grow in arid habitats and have yellow flowers; however white desert plume *Stanleya albescens*, which occurs from Arizona and Colorado to Mexico, is distinguished from the other species by its white flowers. Many have the ability to absorb and accumulate selenium from the soil and are thus toxic to livestock.

Perhaps the best known species is desert plume *S. pinnata* (also called golden prince's plume) a conspicuous inhabitant of the arid lands of Oregon, California and Texas. It is a tall plant, reaching a height well in excess of 1 m (3.3 ft), and has stout blue-green stems with divided leaves topped by slender elongated spikes of yellow flowers. Each flower has four yellow sepals and four sulphur-yellow petals up to 15 mm (0.6 in) long, which are densely hairy on the inner surface. The 7 cm (2.8 in) seed-pods are narrow and curve downwards. *S. elata*

*Xanthorrhoea sp.*

is another yellow-flowered species, although the petals lack hairs and the leaves are undivided; it grows in the Death Valley region.

## Cruciferae; 6 species

### STAPELIA

A genus of almost leafless succulent plants with clumps of fleshy stems and usually four-angled branches, native to southern Africa with one species in tropical East Africa. The attractive flowers are star-shaped with five broad fleshy lobes, and are often luridly marked. They produce a foetid odour that attracts flies which pollinate the blooms as they lay their eggs. For this reason members of this genus are commonly known as carrion flowers.

The only East African species, occurring in Kenya, Tanzania and Rwanda, is *Stapelia semota*, an uncommon short-stemmed succulent. The leaves are very reduced, represented only by fleshy spine-like processes, and the flowers are usually chocolate-coloured, about 5 cm (2 in) across, with narrow lobes. A variety with greenish yellow flowers formerly occurred in Nairobi but is now thought to be extinct as a wild plant.

The numerous species from South Africa include *S. clavicorona* from Transvaal, with deeply furrowed stems, the angles of which are armed with teeth, and pale yellow flowers marked with purplish lines and having ciliate margins, and the spectacular Zulu-giant or giant toad-plant *S. gigantea* from Natal, Transvaal and Zululand, with pale yellow flowers up to 14 cm (5.5 in) across which are decorated with many wavy crimson lines. Three more species from Transvaal are *S. kwebensis* which has small, chocolate-reddish, fleshy flowers with many transverse wrinkles; *S. leendertziae* which has bell-shaped dark purple flowers with recurved lobes; and *S. nobilis*, a much-branched plant with pale green stems and flowers that are yellow above with reddish transverse lines, and purple below.

Typical species of Cape Province are *S. asterias*, with pale green, downy, four-angled stems and flowers with long dark brown lobes and reddish cilia; *S. comparabilis*, with robust very succulent stems and hairy brownish purple flowers up to 10 cm (4 in) across with yellowish transverse markings; *S. erectiflora*, with tiny, long-stalked purplish flowers densely covered with white hairs; and the magnificent *S. grandiflora*, whose flat deeply lobed flowers can be 16 cm (6.5 in) in diameter and are purplish brown with white marginal hairs. Other species from Cape Province are shaggy toad-plant *S. hirsuta*, *S. pillansii* and *S. virescens*.

## Asclepiadaceae; about 50 species

### TRIBULUS

This genus of annual or perennial herbs is distributed across the tropical and warm regions of the Old World, but is especially characteristic of the arid lands of Africa. The hermaphrodite flowers consist of five deciduous sepals, five short-lived petals and 10 stamens.

*Tribulus terrestris* is a hairy sprawling annual of dry open habitats. It has branched stems, opposite pinnate leaves and yellow flowers from 5-9 mm (0.4-0.9 in) in diameter. The distinctive fruits, consisting of a five-part spiny, star-shaped capsule, are dispersed in the coats of animals and also puncture their feet. Among the Akumba people of East Africa, a former test of manhood was to walk across a threshing floor covered with the spiked fruits of this plant without showing pain.

With common names as varied as devil's thorn, Maltese cross (from the shape of the seeds), puncture vine (from the ability of the seeds to pierce bicycle tyres!) or burra gookeroo, *T. terrestris* is native to the arid lands of the Old World, from southern Europe to eastern USSR and India, but is particularly widespread in Africa. It has become widely naturalized, however, and is regarded as a bad weed in California. After 50

years of attempting to control this plant with herbicides, in 1961 the Californian Department of Agriculture introduced two weevil species from India, which feed selectively on *T. terrestris* and control its spread.

The ability of *T. terrestris* to absorb and accumulate selenium and nitrates from the soil renders it very toxic to stock, the symptoms manifesting themselves as 'bighead'. The seeds are used to treat male impotence, gonorrhoea and incontinence, although they are also thought to act as an aphrodisiac.

*T. cistoides* is a less common East African species, where it favours warm, arid habitats with sandy soils. It is a creeping perennial with yellow or cream-coloured flowers up to 2.5 cm (1 in) across. Another African species, *T. zeyheri*, is a hairy, annual or biennial distinguished by its much larger lemon yellow flowers (to 5 cm/2 in across). It thrives on sandy beaches and dry plains in eastern and southern regions of the continent.

## Zygophyllaceae; 25 species

### TRICHOCAULON

A small genus of succulent plants from the arid lands of South Africa and Madagascar, characterized by thick fleshy stems, often globose or cylindrical in shape, covered with a dense layer of tubercles. The flowers are usually rather small and emerge from between the tubercles near the apex of the plant.

*Trichocaulon cactiforme* is a South African species with greyish green, oval-cylindrical stems and pale yellow, red-spotted, star-like flowers emerging in a cluster at the tip. *T. pillansii*, from Cape Province, has freely branching many angled stems, with yellowish bell-shaped flowers. *T. flavum* is a cylindrical South African plant with grey-green stems and pale green or yellowish, scarcely lobed flowers.

Several species occur only in Namibia, including *T. keetmanschoopense*, whose grey or purplish globose stems are about 15 cm (6 in) long and bear numerous small yellowish flowers with red-brown spots; *T. meloforme*, with round or oval grey-green stems and purple-spotted flowers, yellow above and dark red beneath; and *T. pedicillatum*, which grows in the Namib Desert and has small dark reddish brown flowers covered with minute papillae.

**Asclepiadaceae; about 15 species**

## WHITEHEADIA

This genus contains the single species *Whiteheadia bifolia* a bizarre perennial bulbous herb from Great Namaland (southern Namibia) and South Africa. It has a distinctive pair of flattened ovate leaves which lie flat along the ground and can grow up to 30 cm (12 in) long and 20 cm (8 in) wide, although the flowering spike reaches a height of only 10 cm (4 in). The greenish cup-shaped flowers are arranged in a dense spike but are concealed by conspicuous pale green, drooping bracts. *W. bifolia* thrives in arid country, although it normally grows in the shade of rock outcrops.

**Liliaceae; a single species**

## XANTHORRHOEA

A small Australian genus of tall elegant perennials with spreading foliage and cream-coloured or white flowers, consisting of two whorls of three segments each, arranged in dense elongated inflorescences. The species are usually known as yaccas or grass-trees, although they do also have the local name of 'blackboys'; since most grow in arid bushlands and are frequently charred by fire (without lasting damage to the plant itself). They are slow-growing, long-lived, tree-like plants with thick stems topped by a shock of narrow grass-like leaves. Resins produced at the bases of the old leaves were formerly used to fix spearheads to shafts, but are now used as a varnish. The wood is sometimes used for making bowls and other utensils.

*Xanthorrhoea preissii* is a southwest Australian species characterized by trunks up to 5 m (16.5 ft) tall and leaves up to 1 m (3.3 ft) long. Individuals of this species are known to live for more than 350 years, often not producing flowers until they are about 200 years old, although it is thought that flowering may be stimulated by fire. *X. australis* is a smaller species, reaching a maximum height of about 2 m (6.6 ft), although its flower spikes can be 4 m (13 ft) long. *X. pumilio* is found in Queensland and is unusual in having leaves only 3 cm (1.2 in) long.

**Xanthorrhoeaceae; 15 species**

## YUCCA

Sometimes referred to as the 'giant lilies' of North America, plants in this genus are usually tree-like, with thickened stems bearing rosettes of stiff leaves and huge inflorescences. The genus is distributed across the warmer parts of the continent. The leaves are usually pungent and the white bell-shaped flowers have six free perianth segments, are stalked and pendulous. The fruits are either capsules or fleshy and berry-like.

The pollination of yuccas is highly specialized. The flowers open only at night and are visited by moths of the genus *Pronuba* (*Tegeticula*), the female having specially adapted mouthparts to collect pollen. After gathering a pollen ball she flies to another

*Yucca schidigera*

*Yucca aloifolia*

flower, deposits her eggs in the ovary, then climbs to the top of the ovary and spreads her load of pollen over the stigma, thus ensuring pollination. The developing ovules are sufficient in number both to feed the larvae and to produce some viable seed.

Many species of *Yucca* are of some economic importance. The tough fibres in the leaves are used in the production of rope and paper, the fleshy flowers and some fruits are edible, and the rhizomes of some species contain saponin which can be used as a hair tonic, detergent, fish poison and foaming agent for drinks.

Perhaps the best known species is the tree-like Joshua tree *Yucca brevifolia*, which is widely distributed in the southern United States and across much of northern Mexico, often forming 'forests'. It has stiff overlapping leaves about 35 cm (14 in) in length and the 5 cm (2 in) white flowers bloom from March to May. Blue yucca or datil *Y. baccata* is a much smaller plant which is common in the arid lands of California, Nevada, Utah, Colorado, Arizona, New Mexico, Texas and Mexico. It has bluish green leaves, red-tinged flowers and large fleshy fruits that were formerly eaten by American Indians.

Mojave yucca *Y. schidigera* has yellowish green, spine-tipped leaves borne on trunks up to 1 m (3.3 ft) high, and dense clusters of creamy, purple-tinged, almost spherical flowers. It thrives in arid habitats from southern California to Baja California, southern Nevada and northwestern Arizona, but is particularly common in the Mojave Desert, where it often grows alongside *Y. brevifolia*. Our Lord's candle *Y. whipplei* is a species of southern California and northern Baja California, where it thrives on stony slopes in chaparral. Its spectacular flowers are produced only once and then the plant dies.

More eastern species include the plains yucca *Y. angustifolia*, which occurs from the Rocky Mountains east across the prairies of the central United States;

bear-grass or Adam's needle *Y. filamentosa*, a stout plant of sandy beaches, dunes and old fields from New Jersey south along the coastal strip to Florida and Alabama; Spanish bayonet *Y. aloifolia*, which grows from North Carolina to Florida and Alabama; and soapweed *Y. glauca*, a typical western plains species whose distribution extends to Iowa and Missouri. *Y. filamentosa* is naturalized in southeast France and northwest Italy, while Roman candle or Spanish dagger *Y. gloriosa*, from the southeastern United States, is naturalized on sand dunes and waste ground in northern and central Italy.

*Y. faxoniana* is a tree-like species from northern Mexico and Texas, with thick stems up to 4 m (13 ft) in height, rarely branching. The strap-like leaves are about 1 m (3.3 ft) long and the inflorescence is pyramidal. Other Mexican species include *Y. rigida*, with bluish green leaves up to 3 m (10 ft) long, and the showy *Y. schottii* from the Animas Mountains. Spineless yucca *Y. elephanitipes* is a native of Mexico and Guatemala. It has 1 m (3.3 ft) long, sword-shaped leaves and is often cultivated as a hedge plant. When mature the plant produces lozenge-shaped inflorescences up to 90 cm (3 ft) long, bearing yellowish white pendulous flowers that can be boiled and used as a salad.

**Agavaceae; 30 species**

### ZYGOPHYLLUM

A large genus of herbs or shrubs with opposite fleshy leaves, widely distributed across the arid regions of the Old World from the Mediterranean to central Asia, and in South Africa and Australia. The hermaphrodite flowers have four or five deciduous sepals and a similar number of clawed petals. Many species contain alkaloids. The flower buds of some species are used as a substitute for capers.

Bean caper *Zygophyllum fabago* is a tall perennial herb or shrub which grows in dry habitats in the

eastern Mediterranean region and central Asia, especially in the sand and gravel deserts of China. Each leaf has one pair of fleshy leaflets, in the axil of which one or two flowers are produced. The upper half petals are bicoloured with cream and the lower half orange. The pendulous, bean-like seed-pods are cylindrical and at least three times as long as they are wide. *Z. ovigerum* is a similar species with shorter broader fruits, which thrives in the saline soils of southeastern Soviet Europe and western Kazakhstan, extending into the steppes of western and central Asia.

*Z. macropterum* has orange flowers and winged fruits and grows in saline habitats in western and central Asia, while the woolly hairy, shrubby *Z. album* has white flowers and thrives in western Asia, North Africa and on the shores of the Mediterranean. *Z. qatarense*, with creamy white flowers and pear-shaped fruits, is Bahrain's most common and dominant plant. The plants absorb salt from the soil and secrete it in crystalline form over the leaves and stems. In this way moisture is retained in the succulent parts and the plant is rendered unpalatable to browsing animals.

More than 40 species of *Zygophyllum* occur in southern Africa, including *Z. meyeri*, a shrub with yellow or white flowers and oblong fruits, and *Z. morgsana*, a taller plant with yellow flowers and unmistakable fruits with four prominent membrane-like wings. Both species are unpalatable to browsing animals and thrive in dry sandy and rocky habitats in Cape Province and Great Namaland.

Other species are *Z. fontanesii* of dunes and coastal rocks in the Canary Islands, which has corky, probably sea-dispersed fruits; *Z. auranticum*, a yellow-flowered species from southern Australia; and the low-growing Namibian species *Z. clavatum*, distinguished by its minute yellowish flowers.

**Zygophyllaceae; 80 species**

*Tribulus zeyheri*

# CHAPTER SEVEN

# TROPICAL FORESTS

Tropical forests are the most complex and species-rich ecosystems in the world, despite occupying only about 6 per cent of the earth's land surface. They are confined mainly within a belt between 15° north and 15° south of the equator, particularly from the Guinea coast to the Congo Basin in central Africa and throughout much of southeast Asia and Central and South America, although small areas occur in northwest Australia and eastern Madagascar. The most extensive tropical forests occur in the Amazon Basin.

Although an immense diversity of plant life exists in the tropical forest habitat, more than 90 per cent of species are tall trees and shrubs which form a multilayered closed canopy. Terrestrial herbs are rather rare because of the deep shade in the heart of the forest, but a few families are well represented in these conditions, including the Araceae, Begoniaceae, Rubiaceae and Zingiberaceae, as are saprophytic and parasitic species, such as members of the Rafflesiaceae. Many herbaceous plants have carved out a niche higher in the canopy by growing epiphytically on the forest trees, especially orchids and bromeliads, and woody climbers (lianes) are also common.

With between 1,500 and 2,500 mm (60-100 in) of annual rainfall and a dry season that never lasts for more than three months, water is available for plant growth throughout the year. Temperature and relative humidity are also constantly high, so most tropical forest plants grow continuously and many bloom all year round. Epiphytic species often have spongy aerial roots that can absorb moisture from the atmosphere, as well as leaves arranged in cup-shaped rosettes which serve to trap water and plant debris from the canopy and provide the plant with essential nutrients.

Many researchers believe that flowering plants evolved in the tropical forests since the greatest concentration of so-called 'primitive' angiosperm groups are found in these ecosystems. The Latin American tropical forests are far more diverse than those of Africa, while the equivalent habitats in southeast Asia are even richer.

Facing page: tropical undergrowth, Costa Rica.

Epiphytes, Braullio Carillo forest, Costa Rica

## ABRUS

A pantropical genus of which *Abrus precatorius* is undoubtedly the best known species. This woody, rather hairy climber, which occurs throughout the tropics on dry soils, is known by a variety of common names, including crab's-eyes, coral pea, Indian liquorice, Paternoster bean and rosary pea. It has pinnate leaves and axillary clusters of typically pea-like, pink or lavender flowers. The twisted oblong or rectangular pods are about 4 cm (1.6 in) long and contain 3-5 shiny red seeds, each with a prominent black spot.

These seeds contain the toxic substance abrin and are highly poisonous. If the seed-coat is crushed, one seed is sufficient to cause death, although they are apparently less toxic if swallowed without chewing. The seeds have a long history as agents of criminal poisoning in India. Because of their attractive colour they are sometimes strung for rosaries and jewellery and are used for the eyes of figurines.

Since one seed of *A. precatorius* weighs about one carat, the seeds (called rati) have been used in India since ancient times for weighing gold (the Ganda system). It is said that the weight of the famous Koh-i-noor diamond was ascertained in this way. The roots and stems have been used as a substitute for

*Allamanda cathartica*

liquorice and contain alkaloids used in India in the preparation of a contraceptive and abortifacient.

**Leguminosae; 17 species**

## ALLAMANDA

A small genus of mostly evergreen forest lianes, distributed across the tropical regions of the New World. All species produce hairy seeds, are toxic and exude a white juice (latex) from broken stems. The genus is named after the Dutch botanist *Allamand*.

Golden trumpet *Allamanda cathartica* is probably the best known species. Native to Brazil, Guyana and other regions of northern South America, it is nevertheless widely cultivated as an ornamental plant. A quick-growing climber, it reaches a height of about 6 m (20 ft) and has leathery pointed leaves arranged in whorls of three or four at the base of the stems, but in pairs higher up. The conspicuous, bright yellow, trumpet-shaped flowers may be 8 cm (3 in) in diameter and are produced in small groups at the ends of the stems. Each flower has a narrow corolla tube, twisted in the bud stage but flaring out into five broad overlapping lobes when open. Another widely cultivated species with large yellow flowers is *A. neriifolia*, while *A. violacea* has reddish violet blooms. Both are native to Brazil.

**Apocynaceae; 12 species**

## ALPINIA

A large genus found throughout the warm and tropical regions of Asia to the Pacific. Each flower has a bell-shaped calyx, from which emerges a prominent lip formed from two fused rudimentary stamens (staminodes), the three petals with arranged around the lip. There is only one fertile stamen. The aromatic rhizomes have a ginger-like scent. The genus is named after the famous seventeenth century Italian botanist Prospero Alpino.

Red ginger *Alpinia purpurata* is a southeast Asian species widely cultivated elsewhere as an ornamental, especially in the Caribbean. It has alternate, lanceolate leaves rather like those of the banana. The spike-like inflorescences are in evidence for most of the year and are composed of conspicuous, glossy, bright red, wax-like bracts which conceal the small white flowers.

Shell ginger *A. zerumbet* (*A. speciosa*), which is native to China and southern Japan, reaches a height of about 3 m (10 ft) and has alternate dark green leaves and pendulous inflorescences up to 30 cm (12 in) long. Each flower has a white bell-shaped calyx and the three-lobed 4 cm (1.6 in ) lip is yellow and spotted and striped with red. In the Caribbean, where

*Alpinia purpurata*

*Amorphophalus*

spadix, which grows 7.5 cm (2.9 in) per day, reaches an eventual height of some 2.5 m (8.3 ft) and the corms may weigh 50 kg (110lbs) (in *A. brooksii* the corms are alleged to weigh up to 70 kg (154lbs) while the inflorescence is said to top 4 m (13 ft)). Both species emit a terrible stench, to attract carrion flies and beetles, for which they are sometimes known as corpse flowers.

*A. bulbifer*, from northeast India, produces modest 25 cm (10 in) inflorescences which are white tinged with red and exude a fruity odour. Elephant-foot or elephant-yam *A. campanulatus* of the East Indies has enormous red and yellow inflorescences and purple-mottled, much-divided leaves. The young leaves of this species, also known as telingo potato, can be boiled and eaten, as can the huge corms, which often weigh in excess of 25 kg (55lbs) and contain large amounts of vitamin A and calcium. *A. variabilis* is an Indonesian species and *A. prainii* is native to Malaya; the corms of both species are edible.

**Araceae; 90 species**

### ANTHURIUM

A large genus of perennial terrestrial and epiphytic aroids which may be woody or herbaceous, erect or creeping, or climbing. Members of this genus are native to the tropical regions of the New World, especially Colombia. The bisexual flowers have four perianth segments, four stamens and a single ovary and are arranged on a spadix protected by a usually inconspicuous green or yellowish spathe, although this may be large, ovate-lanceolate and brightly coloured (red or purple) on occasion. The berries hang from the spadix by two threads when ripe.

Many species are widely cultivated for their heart-shaped leaves with distinctive venation. In the Colombian species *A. crystallinum* the network of veins in the upper surface of the leaves is traced in silver, while in *A. warocqueanum*, the leaves droop vertically from their petioles; the Costa Rican *A. bakeri* is also widely cultivated. The epiphytic *A. scherzerianum* from Central America and *A. andraeanum* from Colombia are cultivated for their waxy, heart-shaped, flaming red spathes and go by the common name of flamingo-lily, oil-cloth plant or painter's palette. In South America the dried leaves of some species are used to perfume tobacco.

Many epiphytic species are native to the montane and lowland rainforests of the Caribbean, including *A. hookeri*, from the West Indies and Guyana, which has deep blue spadices; *A. grandifolium* from Dominica, which is sometimes terrestrial and has thin green spathes and dark brown spadices up to 50 cm (20 in) long; and the widespread *A. palmatum* distinguished by its glossy eight-lobed leaves, whose bark was formerly mixed with scrapings from conch shells as a cure for yaws.

**Araceae; over 700 species**

this species is naturalized on some islands, the Carib Indians formerly prepared a tea from the rhizomes.

Galangal *A. officinarium* occurs naturally in eastern and southeast Asia and is cultivated in China and Thailand for its rootstocks, which resemble ginger and may reach lengths of up to 1 m (3.3 ft). These were used in Europe as a spice for over 1,000 years, having probably been introduced by Arabian or Greek physicians, but are now used only in the USSR and India. The powder is valued as snuff for catarrh, the volatile oil is used in perfumery in India and the many medicinal uses of the root include the treatment of flatulence, vomiting and seasickness.

The similar Siamese ginger or greater galangal *A. galanga*, which is native to tropical southeast Asia, also produces an essential oil, while the rhizome is used as a condiment and its flowers are eaten in Java. The word galangal is derived from the Arabic *Khalanjan*, which may be a perversion of a Chinese word meaning 'mild ginger'.

**Zingiberaceae; 250 species**

### AMORPHOPHALLUS

A genus of stemless herbaceous perennials of the Old World tropics in which the leaves are produced after flowering. Many species have edible corms, although the toxic alkaloids must first be removed by boiling. Some species are used as emergency foods in the Pacific Islands, Indonesia and other Asian countries.

A typical species is the leopard palm *Amorphophallus rivieri* of southeast Asia, which produces an inflorescence sometimes more than 1 m (3.3 ft) tall. The dark violet spathe is funnel-shaped and the spadix bears naked female flowers near the base and male flowers consisting solely of stamens immediately above. The upper zone of the spadix is sterile, dark purple and emits a foetid odour which attracts carrion flies. While laying their eggs on the spadix the flies inadvertently pollinate the plant. After the inflorescence has died back the plant produces a single large leaf with a divided blade almost 1 m (3.3 ft) across hence its alternative common name of devil's tongue. The corms are peeled, boiled and eaten in China.

*A. titanum* is a Sumatran species sometimes considered to be the largest herbaceous plant in the world, although *A. brooksii*, also native to Sumatra, may rival this claim. *A. titanum* has leaves almost 5 m (16.5 ft) in height and 2 m (6.6 ft) across, while the

*Anthurium andraeanum*

*Bauhinia petersiana*

## BAUHINIA

A large pantropical genus of forest lianes, although a few species are shrubs or trees. The genus was named by Carl Linnaeus in honour of two Swiss botanists, the brothers John and Caspar Bauhin (1541-1613 and 1560-1724 respectively). Members of this genus have distinctive, two-lobed leaves resembling camels' footprints. Although a member of the pea family, the large flowers have five almost equal petals. Many species are pollinated by bats or birds as well as insects.

Bauhinia lianes climb through the tropical forest by one of two means. Either they attach themselves by spirally coiled tendrils, or they have flattened stems, known as monkey staircases that bend backwards and forwards, snake-like, as they climb as in the snake climber *B. anguina*, an Indian species.

A typical climbing species is camel's-foot *B. vahlii*, a huge evergreen climber from the tropical forests of southern Asia and India. Its stems measure more than 1 m (3.3 ft) in diameter and the leaves and shoots are clothed with rusty brown hairs. The large (to 46 cm/ 18 in), dark green leaves have heart-shaped bases and are cleft to about one-third of their length into two lobes with rounded tips. The cream flowers are about 5 cm (2 in) across and are arranged in flat-topped terminal clusters; the petals are obovate and have silky hairs on the undersides. The woody pods contain flattish, shiny, dark brown, edible seeds about 2.5 cm (1 in) long. The foliage of *B. vahlii* is used for fodder, the leaves for plates and wrappings and the bark yields a fibre used for making ropes.

**Leguminosae; 250 species**

## BOUGAINVILLEA

A small genus of lianes and small trees from the tropical regions of Central and South America, most of which have spines to help them cling as they

*Bougainvillea sp.*

155

climb. The genus is named after Louis Antoine de Bougainville (1729-1811), a French navigator who circumnavigated the world between 1766 and 1769, claiming the Society Islands (including Tahiti) for the French. Members of this genus are sometimes called paper flowers and are widely cultivated for ornament.

The rather insignificant, five-lobed, tubular flowers of *Bougainvillea* species are surrounded by persistent brightly coloured bracts, arranged in groups of three, and themselves resembling flowers. These make the flowers more conspicuous and attract hummingbird pollinators. After fertilization the bracts turn green and dry out, later acting as parachutes for the mature fruits.

The best known representative is probably *Bougainvillea spectabilis*, one of the world's most popular tropical ornamental plants. It grows wild in eastern Brazil, particularly the Amazon region, but is widely cultivated in the gardens of the Mediterranean region. The bracts are pink in the natural state, but a great range of colours exists in the cultivated forms. Tropical Brazil is also home to the similar *B. glabra* which has small yellow-edged flowers in groups of three, although these are almost completely concealed by the lilac, pink or purple membranous bracts.

**Nyctaginaceae; 14 species**

### BRASSAVOLA

A small orchid genus whose species are native to tropical America but sometimes cultivated as ornamentals. They are epiphytic or rock-inhabiting and have slender stems supporting a solitary leaf, rarely two. The large showy flowers are arranged in a loose lateral or terminal cluster, each having long, narrow and very similar sepals and petals and a broad clawed lip, often with fringed margins.

One of the most widespread species is *Brassavola nodosa*, whose pale green flowers with their white, purple-spotted lips are found at low elevations from Mexico through Central America to Panama and Venezuela. Although usually epiphytic on trees or rocks, this plant is not averse to growing on cacti and is often seen on the roots of mangroves along the coast. A very similar but much rarer species is *B. acaulis*, an epiphyte of damp shady forests from Guatemala to Panama.

The heavily scented flowers of *B. cucullata* are

*Bougainvillea sp.*

among the most spectacular of this genus. The ivory or white petals and sepals are about 12 cm (4.5 in) long while the broad white lip with serrated margins may be up to 10 cm (4 in) across. This widespread but rather uncommon species is epiphytic on trees in humid tropical forests up to 1,800 m (5,900 ft) in Mexico, Guatemala, El Salvador, Honduras, the West Indies and northern South America.

**Orchidaceae; 15 species**

### BULBOPHYLLUM

A huge genus of tropical epiphytic orchids, most of which grow in the eastern hemisphere in Africa, Asia and Australia. These orchids have creeping rhizomes with stout pseudobulbs at intervals, from which arise one or two leaves and spike-like inflorescences of numerous flowers, although some species produce solitary blooms. The petals are much smaller than the sepals and the lip may be simple or three-lobed. The flowers can be any colour except pure blue. Some species have fragrant, fly-pollinated flowers, such as *Bulbophyllum macranthum*, a clove-scented orchid from Malaysia, while others emit foul odours to attract flesh flies.

Two New World species are *B. aristatum*, a rather uncommon epiphyte of humid forests up to 1,500 m (5,000 ft) from Mexico through Central America to Panama, and the rat's-tail orchid *B. pachyrhachis*, which occurs over a similar range, but extends to the West Indies, and favours low altitude humid forests and thickets. *B. aristatum* has small, dark red or purplish flowers, commonly marked with white stripes, whilst *B. pachyrhachis* has pendulous inflorescences which are much swollen whilst in bloom and may act as water-storage organs. The flowers are usually greenish yellow, spotted with purple.

In the Old World typical species are *B. affine*, a

*Bulbophyllum longistelidium*

creeping orchid with yellowish green flowers, conspicuously streaked with brown, which is native to the lowland tropical forests of northern India and Nepal, and *B. vaginatum*, a fairly common but highly distinctive southeast Asian orchid with ivory-coloured flowers arranged in dense, star-like terminal heads consisting of about 15 small blooms, each with two greatly elongated sepals. The rarer *B. medusae*, native to Borneo, Sumatra and Malaya, has a similar inflorescence, the elongated perianth lobes of each flower producing the Medusa-like effect from which this plant obviously derives its specific name. *B. minutissimum* is an Australian representative.

**Orchidaceae; 1,200 species**

### CATHARANTHUS

Seven of the eight species of this tropical genus are confined to Madagascar. The generic name is derived from the Greek *katharos* ('pure'), and *anthos* ('flower'). The best known species is undoubtedly *Catharanthus roseus* (*Vinca rosea*, *Lochneria rosea*) which is variously called rosy or Madagascar periwinkle, old maid or Cayenne jasmine. Although originally native to Madagascar this sprawling annual or perennial herb is now widely cultivated for its attractive reddish, pink or white flowers with darker centres; it has also become naturalized throughout the tropical regions, especially the Caribbean, Africa and western India.

More importantly, rosy periwinkle contains some 67 named alkaloids. In 1923 considerable interest was raised by claims that this species contained chemicals with the ability to cure diabetes. During the intensive screening that followed it was discovered that rosy periwinkle contains a number of powerful alkaloids with the power to retard the progress of leukaemia. The most important of these are vincristine and vinblastine, which since 1960 have increased the chances of successfully treating Hodgkin's disease by 400 per cent, have given lymphocytic leukaemia

*Cattleya amethystoglossa*

patients a 91 per cent chance of recovery and have proved effective in fighting several types of cancer. The annual sales of these alkaloids now exceeds £11 million ($20 million).

Other members of the genus are also used in medicine, although on a much smaller homeopathic scale. For example, the Madagascan *C. lanceus* and *C. trichophyllus* are both used locally to treat such diverse disorders as toothache, neuralgia and congestion of the breasts as well as having vermicidal, diuretic, emetic and haemostatic properties.

In the Caribbean, where members of this genus are not native, the leaves of *C. roseus* have nevertheless long been used by the Caribs to prepare a tea for diabetes, while *C. albus*, which has white flowers with a greenish centre, is used in the treatment of high blood pressure and certain types of leukaemia and may provide a possible cure for cancer. *C. coriaceus* with reddish violet flowers is confined to Madagascar and listed as an endangered species in the IUCN Plant Red Data Book (1980).

**Apocynaceae; 8 species**

*Costus geothyrsus*

### CATTLEYA

A genus of orchids found only in the tropical regions of Central and South America and named after William Cattley, an English botanist and gardener. The plants are epiphytic or rock-inhabiting and have leathery, succulent leaves and few-flowered terminal inflorescences of large showy flowers; the predominant colour is brilliant mauve-pink or rose-purple. The petals are much broader than the sepals and the lip ranges from simple to deeply three-lobed. It is known that some species of *Cattleya* are pollinated by bees which visit the flowers only in the 15 minutes preceeding dawn. *Cattleya trianae* is depicted on Colombian stamps.

*C. granulosa*, a rare species of the tropical forests of Guatemala and Brazil has flowering stems bearing 5-8 glossy, strongly scented flowers up to 12 cm (4.5 in) across. The five perianth segments (petals and sepals) are olive-green, decorated with dark red spots, while the outer lobes of the three-lobed lip are whitish on the margins and pink or yellowish within. The pink, white and yellow middle lobe is fan-shaped with fringed margins and numerous small outgrowths in the centre, from which the specific name is derived.

*C. aurantica* is a fairly common epiphyte in the tropical forests of Mexico, Guatemala, El Salvador and Honduras, which also takes advantage of shade trees in coffee plantations. The flowers range from orange-red to yellow, the petals and sepals has spotted or streaked with brown, while the lip bears maroon or blackish markings. *C. deckeri* which favours tall forest trees that emerge into the sunlight, is distributed from Mexico through Central America into the West Indies and probably northern South America. The similar but rather uncommon *C. skinneri* has large rose-coloured or purplish flowers and a similar geographic range, while *C. pachecoi,* with lemon-yellow or whitish flowers, is confined to Guatemala.

Other Cattleyas include *C. mossiae* from the tropical forests of Venezuela; the yellow-flowered *C. citrina* from Mexico; the Brazilian rainforest epiphyte *C. intermedia;* and *C. bowringiana*, an impressive Central American terrestrial orchid which produces up to 47 flowers per spike. This latter species nearly became extinct in the wild due to over-collection for use in ornamental hybrids, but is now beginning to recover following stringent protection measures.

**Orchidaceae; 30 species**

### COLOCASIA

A small aroid genus from tropical Asia. The best known species is probably cocoyam, dasheen or taro *Colocasia esculenta*, whose starch-rich potato-like corms provide one of the most widely used foods of all tropical plants. This herbaceous plant is native to Burma and Assam but is also frequently cultivated elsewhere, particularly in Polynesia and the West Indies. The often striped or spotted, heart-shaped leaves, supposedly resembling elephants' ears, are about 30-40 cm (12-16 in) long, supported by stalks of up to 1 m (3.3 ft). Flowers, with yellowish white spathes and club-shaped spadices, are rarely produced.

In the West Indies the young furled leaves are used to make a popular soup called Calalou (callaloo), the national dish of Trinidad, while the boiled corms, which may weigh up to 4 kg (8.8lb) apiece, form an important part of the West Indian diet. This is also the case for the people of the Pacific Islands and southeast Asia, where *C. esculenta* has been cultivated for more than 2,000 years. In India a liniment is prepared from the root of *C. macrorhiza* which is used in local medicine to cure intermittent fevers.

**Araceae; 6 species**

### COSTUS

A genus of perennial rhizomatous herbs and shrubs which is distributed across the tropical regions of America, Africa and from Asia to Australia. In Greek the generic name means a spicy pepper-like root, and in Latin it refers to an Indian shrub whose roots are used in the preparation of an aromatic ointment. The flowers are distinguished by the presence of a staminodal labellum, i.e. sterile stamens that have become fused together to form a conspicuous 'lip'. *Costus spicatus* is a central American species widely used in native medicine.

Crape ginger *C. speciosus*, native to India and Burma, is now widely cultivated in tropical gardens. It has strongly aromatic roots, erect semiwoody stems and lanceolate, silky haired leaves up to 20 cm (8 in) long arranged in spirals. The flowers are about 4 cm (1.6 in) across and are arranged in dense egg-shaped or oval spikes about 10 x 5 cm (4 x 2 in). Each flower is subtended by a conspicuous red bract and has a whitish corolla tube from which emerges the showy white funnel-shaped 'lip'.

Spiral ginger or ginger-lily *C. afer* is native to Senegal and Lagos. It is distinguished by its smaller leaves, which narrow at the tip into a long 'tail', and flowers which have white lips yellow at the base with

*Dendrobium ostrinoglossum*

irregularly toothed margins. In the stepladder plant *C. malortieanus*, a Costa Rican species, the inflorescences are short cones, each flower having a pink corolla tube and brown-striped lip. The African *C. spectabilis* is a bizarre plant which differs from all other members of the genus in having rosettes of four or six large fleshy leaves that lie flat on the ground and from the centre of which emerge a few stalkless bright orange or yellow flowers.

**Zingiberaceae (Costaceae); about 90 species**

### CRYPTOCEREUS

A tiny genus of epiphytic cacti with nocturnal flowers. There are just two species: *Cryptocereus anthonyanus* is native to the Chiapas region of Mexico, while *C. imitans* is confined to Costa Rica. (Some authorities place *C. imitans* in the genus *Weberocereus*.)

The genus is characterised by climbing stems with aerial roots that produce dense clusters of branches at intervals. The stems are flattened and deeply notched on either side to give an alternate pinnate effect and the large, faintly scented flowers bloom only at night. *C. anthonyanus* has climbing stems about 1 m (3.3 ft) long and up to 15 cm (6 in) wide, with glossy green branches. The long, narrow outer perianth segments of the flowers are brick-red and recurved, while the shorter inner segments are cream or yellow and more or less erect. *C. imitans* is similar, but has white flowers.

**Cactaceae; 2 species**

### DENDROBIUM

A huge genus of epiphytic orchids with stem-like pseudobulbs, lateral sepals dilated at the base to form a sac or spur, and extrafloral nectaries. Dendrobiums are found across the warm and tropical regions of Asia (including Japan), Australia and New Zealand, from Sri Lanka to the Pacific Islands of Samoa and Tonga. Those growing in tropical forests are mainly evergreen, but elsewhere they are usually deciduous, producing flowers from thin, leafless, pseudobulb stems.

The generic name is derived from the combination of the Greek words *dendron* ('tree'), and *bioein* ('to live'), in reference to the epiphytic habit of many species. The stems of some species are used for basketwork and in northern Australia the aborigines use a gum produced by the plants to fix their body paints.

More than 50 species are native to Australia, including the evergreen *Dendrobium phalaenopsis*

from Queensland and the islands of Timor and New Guinea. It has slender cylindrical pseudobulbs up to 70 cm (28 in) long from which arise oblong, dark green leaves and a curved flower stem bearing up to 15 flowers. Each flower is about 8 cm (3 in) across and has three pink or cherry-red sepals, two lateral petals twice as broad as the sepals and usually of a darker hue, and a dark purple lip with three lobes. The tongue orchid *D. linguiforme* has fleshy tongue-like leaves about 2 cm (0.8 in) long and inflorescences of 4-20 fragrant flowers with slender, snow-white sepals and petals. The ironbark orchid *D. aemulum* has swollen, erect stems each with a terminal pair of oval leaves; the flower stem, which arises from the leaf axils, carries an inflorescence of 3-20 fragrant white flowers with red-streaked lips.

Other Australian species are the pencil orchid *D. beckleri*, a distinctive plant of the Queensland rainforests with narrow, cylindrical, fluted leaves and numerous solitary whitish, green-tinged flowers with purple-striped lips; and the rather similar cucumber orchid *D. cucumerinum*, whose blunt

cylindrical leaves covered with tubercles bear a striking resemblance to cucumbers. *D. bifalce* is a lowland rainforest species with yellowish, red-spotted flowers, while the cream-flowered *D. adae* is found only in the highland forests of North Queensland. The antelope orchid *D. canaliculatum*, and the evergreen Cooktown orchid *D. bigibbum*, the state flower of Queensland, are two northern Australian species which are widely cultivated in Europe.

Most dendrobiums are found in the warm and temperate regions of Asia, with some 26 species in the tropical forests of the Himalayas. *D. amoenum* has paired, violet-scented flowers which emerge from the nodes of pendulous, leafless pseudobulbs; the sepals and petals are white with violet tips, while the lip has a yellow band across the middle and a purple spot near the tip. *D. densiflorum* differs in having dense, pendulous clusters of yellow flowers with orange funnel-shaped lips, while *D. fimbriatum* has brilliant yellow flowers, about 7 cm (2.8 in) across, and short, fringed lips with a large reddish brown patch in the centre.

*Dendrobium ruppianum*

Southeast Asian species include *D. anosmum*, which produces beautiful pink flowers from leafless stem-like pseudobulbs; pigeon orchid *D. crumenatum*, the most common epiphytic flowering plant in Singapore, with pendulous masses of fragrant white flowers; and *D. aphyllum*, which produces pale pink, yellow-lipped flowers in twos and threes from the nodes of the pseudobulb after the leaves have fallen. *D. pauciflorum*, an Indian epiphyte of the riverine jungles of West Bengal and Sikkim, has 1-5 small, golden-yellow flowers edged with purple or red. It is listed as an endangered/extinct species in the IUCN Plant Red Data Book (1980): only a single individual has been found (1970) since the nineteenth century and attempts at cultivation have proved unsuccessful.

**Orchidaceae; about 900 species**

### DENDROPHTHOE

A genus of parasitic or semiparasitic shrubs widely distributed across the tropical regions of the Old World. The generic name is derived from the combination of *dendron* ('tree'), and *phthoe* ('destroy'), which neatly sums up the parasitic habit.

The Australian *Dendrophthoe vitellina* is a typical species. It has thick oval, alternate leaves and large

*Epidendrum ibaguense*

*Epidendrum sp.*

flowers arranged in short, dense, axillary clusters. Each flower has a yellow tube, five elongated, recurved, bright red corolla lobes, long yellow anthers protruding from the tube. The fruits are small sticky berries which are spread by birds in a manner akin to mistletoe. Commonly known as long-flower mistletoe this species parasitizes many different host plants in the coastal forests of Queensland and New South Wales.

**Loranthaceae; 30 species**

### ECCREMOCACTUS

A tiny genus of epiphytic cacti with pendant shoots found only in the dense tropical forests of Costa Rica and Ecuador, usually at low altitudes. The jointed branches are flat and stout with notched margins and the funnel-shaped nocturnal flowers are open only slightly. The best known species (considered by some authorities to be the only member of this genus) is *Eccremocactus bradei*. It has light green branches

*Epidendrum ciliare*

up to 30 cm (12 in) long which are erect when young but later become pendulous. The somewhat asymmetric pinkish white or cream flowers are 5-7 cm (2-2.8 in) long.

**Cactaceae; 3 species**

## EPIDENDRUM

A large, very variable, tropical American genus of epiphytic, rock-inhabiting or more rarely terrestrial orchids which range in size from very small to over 3 m (10 ft) tall or long. The largest genus of neotropical orchids, *Epidendrum* spp range from North Carolina to western Louisiana, through Mexico, Central America and the West Indies to Argentina.

The flowers vary from minute to large and showy and are usually white (*Epidendrum nocturnum*), yellow and green (*E. ciliare*), but are sometimes more colourful: *E. ibaguense* has brilliant magenta, purple, scarlet and crimson flowers. The petals are generally much narrower than the sepals and the lips are simple or three-lobed. The generic name is derived from a combination of the Greek words *epi* ('upon'), and *dendron* ('tree'), in reference to the epiphytic habit of many species.

A typical epiphytic species of tropical forests is *E. abbreviatum*, a small Central American species with greenish white flowers, each petal having a central purple stripe and the lip several longitudinal purplish streaks. *E. anceps*, which has greenish brown, dull red or tawny flowers, occurs in damp forests to 2,000 m (6,600 ft) in Florida, Mexico, Central America, the West Indies and northern South America, while *E. boothii*, which grows in dense tropical forests from Mexico to Panama and Cuba, has fragrant greenish white or yellowish flowers.

Other epiphytic tropical forest representatives are *E. bractescens*, an uncommon orchid of Mexico, British Honduras, Guatemala, Honduras and the Bahamas; *E. chondylobulbon*, found only in Mexico and Guatemala; the widespread cockleshell orchid *E. cochleatum*, whose distribution ranges from Mexico to Panama, throughout the West Indies and into northern South America; and *E. imatophyllum*, which often grows in the nests of ants in trees of swampy forests throughout Central America to Brazil and Peru. *E. mutelianum*, a yellow-flowered species confined to Guadeloupe, is described as a vulnerable species in the IUCN Plant Red Data Book (1980).

Epidendrums often found in terrestrial habitats are *E. laucheanum* of Central America and Colombia; the widespread, common and very variable *E. paniculatum* of wet tropical forests from Mexico through Central America to northern South America; *E. virgatum*, a common orchid of the montane forests of Mexico, Guatemala and Honduras; and *E. teretifolium*, another widespread species found from Mexico to Venezuela and the West Indies.

**Orchidaceae; about 500 species**

## EPIPHYLLUM

A genus of freely branching epiphytic cacti from the tropical forests of Central America, extending to northern South America and Mexico. Epiphyllums either have erect or pendant branches, or are climbing plants with aerial roots. The flattened, spineless branches have notched or deeply serrated margins. Although the large, long-tubed flowers bloom at night they often stay open the following day; they are usually white or cream, perfumed and have extrafloral nectaries.

*Epiphyllum anguliger* has bright green fleshy branches with pronounced midribs and wide-toothed margins, the lobes of which protrude more or less at right angles. This Mexican species has sweet-smelling flowers up to 15 cm (6 in) long, with an 8 cm (3 in) tube, flesh coloured outer perianth segments and pure white inner segments. *E. chrysocardium*, also native to Mexico, has fern-like branches with narrow lobes up to 15 cm (6 in) long, each ending in a canoe-shaped point, and flowers with dull mauve outer

*Gloriosa superba*

perianth segments and creamy white inner segments; the plant's specific name means 'heart of gold' in reference to its golden-yellow stamens.

*E. cartagense* is a Costa Rican species whose white flowers have a reddish tube, while *E. caudatum*, known only from the Oaxaca region of Mexico, has smaller white flowers. *E. crenatum*, a species of Honduras and Guatemala, has stiff glaucous branches with deep notches in the margins and diurnal cream flowers, while the huge white flowers (to 24 cm/9.5 in across) of *E. guatemalense* are found only in Guatemala. A species with even larger white flowers is *E. grandilobum*, a native of Guatemala.

One of the rarest members of this genus is another Costa Rican species, *E. lepidocarpum*, found only in the Cartago area, while perhaps the most widespread is *E. phyllanthus* which grows in many parts of central and South America, including Costa Rica, Colombia, Ecuador, Brazil, Peru, Bolivia, Panama, Guyana, Trinidad and Tobago. *E. oxypetalum* is a widely

cultivated species with edible flowers which start to open about 9 pm, are fully open within 90 minutes and are withered by dawn.

**Cactaceae; 16 species**

## GLORIOSA

It is thought that there is just one variable species, *Gloriosa superba*, in this genus, although other authorities recognize as many as six separate species, including *G. rothschildiana* and *G. simplex*. The genus is confined to tropical forests in Africa and Asia and the plants are commonly known as glory-lilies or flame-lilies because of their large, brightly coloured flowers. The generic name is derived from the Latin *gloriosus* ('full of glory'). The tubers are poisonous and contain alkaloids such as colchicine; in India they are taken to commit suicide.

*Gloriosa superba* is a herbaceous climbing or creeping perennial which may reach 5 m (16.5 ft) in height and ascends by means of spirally coiled tendrils

*Guzmania minor*

at the tips of the leaves. It has a V-shaped tuberous rootstock from which arise branched stems with leaves in pairs or whorls of three. The magnificent nodding flowers are produced in the axils of the upper leaves and are about 7.5 cm (2.9 in) across. Each flower has six sharply recurved, upward-pointing perianth segments with wavy or crisped margins. They are usually yellow at the base and crimson at the tip, although pure yellow or red flowers are sometimes found. The six stamens also radiate outwards and the style is sharply twisted to one side so that self-pollination is possible in the absence of insects.

**Liliaceae; a single species**

### GUZMANIA

A large bromeliad genus of terrestrial or epiphytic plants with rosettes of robust leaves. Guzmanias are confined to Central and tropical South America and the Antilles, with a single species in the United States. Epiphytic species have broad basal leaves that fit closely together to form a pitcher where water collects. These leaves are able to absorb water and dissolved nutrients. The yellow or white flowers are usually arranged in rod- or cone-shaped inflorescences, surrounded by whorls of conspicuous red bracts. The genus is named after the Spanish apothecary and botanist A. Guzman.

A typical species is the epiphyte *Guzmania ligulata*, native to the Antilles, which has leaves up to 45 cm (18 in) long, green above and red-lined below. The inflorescence reaches a height of 40-50 cm (16-20 in) and emerges from the centre of the leaf rosette. The scarlet outer bracts are arranged in a spiral around the yellowish inner bracts, which are often almost transparent. The flowers are produced in the axils of the inner bracts. Each flower has six milky white perianth segments, the outer three erect and fused into a tube for half their length, the inner three connected only at their tips, forming a bell-shaped structure with vertical slits. As with all bromeliads,

the scarlet bracts only acquire their colour as the plant comes into flower.

Other species include *G. plumieri*, a terrestrial plant of montane habitats in Dominica, which has dark red bracts and yellow flowers, the colours more pronounced with altitude; and the epiphytic *G. dussii*, typical of montane forests in the Antilles, which has rosettes of light green leaves about 1.5 m (5 ft) across and inflorescences topped by erect, pink-streaked bracts and golden-yellow flowers.

**Bromeliaceae; 128 species**

### HELICONIA

A large genus of perennial herbs which is sometimes placed in the Musaceae or Strelitzaceae. Its distribution covers tropical America and the southwest Pacific; some 40 species are found in the Caribbean. *Heliconia* species are inhabitants of tropical forests, where they are particularly associated with clearings. The genus is named after Mount Helicon, the abode of the Greek muses in Euboea.

These plants are similar to bananas in general appearance and are commonly called wild plantains.

*Guzmania remyi*

*Heliconia rostrata*

*Guzmania hilde*

They are large herbs with rhizomes from which arise false stems formed from the rolled leaf sheaths. The two-ranked paddle-shaped leaves are topped by rigid inflorescences dominated by brightly coloured boat-shaped bracts, also arranged alternately in two ranks giving rise to the local name of lobster-claw. Each bract houses a compact branched cluster of flowers typically with three sepals, three petals, five fertile stamens and a sixth, sterile petal-like stamen. The flowers produce an abundance of nectar at the base of the petals which oozes into the bract and is diluted by any collected rainwater, attracting hummingbirds for pollination.

Bastard plantain or balisier *Heliconia bihai*, also known as parrot's claws, is native to the forests of tropical America and may reach 3.7 m (12 ft) in height. The inflorescences are about 60 cm (24 in) long and 30 cm (12 in) wide and have a series of scarlet and yellow bracts concealing inconspicuous, whitish flowers which produce edible fruits. *H. caribaea* is a West Indian species with 2 m (6.6 ft) leaves which are commonly used by the Caribs for thatching, lining baskets and covering foodstuffs. The compact inflorescences have red bracts, white flowers and blue seed capsules and may be held as much as 3 m (10 ft) above the ground.

*H. wagneriana* is a Panamanian species reaching a height of 2.5 m (8.2 ft), deep pink bracts, with tinged with yellow or orange towards the margins; while parrot's plantain *H. psittacorum*, from Guyana and Brazil, rarely exceeds 1 m (3.3 ft) in height and has fiery orange-red bracts concealing greenish yellow flowers. Beaked heliconia *H. rostrata* is a 3 m (10 ft) Peruvian species with pendulous inflorescences on dull reddish stalks. Each spike consists of as many as 12 brilliant red beak-like bracts, fading to yellow and green around the edges, from which emerge the sulphur-yellow flowers.

**Heliconiaceae; about 100 species**

### HOYA

A large genus of evergreen climbing or epiphytic shrubs distributed across China, southeast Asia, Australia and the Pacific. Hoyas are commonly known as waxflowers, the glossy blooms having five fleshy, horn-like processes which spread out to form a star.

Most species have succulent opposite leaves and axillary umbels of flowers, and many are popular house plants because of their long-lived fragrant flowers.

*Hoya fusca* is an epiphyte found in forests in southern China and the southern foothills of the Himalayas with axillary umbels of tubular cream, yellow or pale orange flowers, while the Burmese *H. lanceolata* produces long, drooping branches with fleshy, stalkless leaves and tubular white flowers

*Heliconia dominica*

with pink centres. The species with the largest flowers is *H. sussuela* (*H. imperialis*), a native of Borneo and Malaysia, which has umbels of up to 14 brownish purple flowers, each about 7 cm (2.8 in) in diameter.

The shrubby *H. bella* from India and much of southeast Asia has white flowers with contrasting purple, rose or violet centres, *H. carnosa*, a climber with pendulous umbels of fragrant translucent white or pinkish flowers with red centres is distributed from southern China to eastern Australia; and *H. australis*, a robust climber from New South Wales and Queensland is distinguished by its white-spotted leaves and pale pink flowers with reddish centres that have a scent reminiscent of honeysuckle. The lilac-flowered *H. purpureofusca* and *H. coriacea*, with creamy yellow flowers, are both forest climbers from Java. Typical Indonesian species are *H. coronaria*, with large pale yellow flowers spotted with red, and *H. moteskei*, which produces pinkish white flowers with maroon centres

**Asclepiadaceae; about 90 species**

### MARCGRAVIA

A tropical American genus of climbing epiphytes with two types of foliage: the climbing shoots have small, rounded, reddish or yellowish, stalkless leaves that are pressed against the surface up which the shoot is climbing, while the mature pendulous shoots have stalked, oval, leathery green leaves. The flowers are bisexual with four persistent sepals and five petals fused together to form a cap which falls off when the flower opens. Sterile flowers are also present, their bracts modified into nectar-secreting pitchers which attract pollinating birds such as hummingbirds, bananaquits and todies or lizards or bees, depending on the species of *Marcgravia*.

The genus is named after George Marcgraaf, a seventeenth-century writer on Brazilian natural history. Representative species are *Marcgravia umbellata*, a widespread tropical American climber, *M. rectiflora*, a West Indian liane with stems to 10 m (33 ft) and pendulous nectaries, and *M. myriostigma* from Brazil, which is apparently pollinated by bats.

**Marcgraviaceae; 45 species**

black or purplish tubes and throats. *M. foetida* is a common forest-edge species with large white, cream or yellow-orange flowers which grows in both tropical and East Africa, while *M. rostrata* has deep yellow flowers and spiny, pinkish orange fruits. Another species of the Old World tropics, *M. mixta*, has bright red fruits which are said to resemble bullocks' hearts.

### Cucurbitaceae; 45 species

### *MUCUNA*

A large genus of lianes distributed across both Old and New World tropical and subtropical regions. The fruit are covered with fine stiff hairs which penetrate the skin and cause irritation. Some species are pollinated by bats.

*Mucuna pruriens* is a slender climber of tropical Asian forests with alternate, lanceolate, long-stalked leaves and large white and purple flowers arranged in groups of two or three. The hairy pods are brown, thick and leathery, about 10 cm (4 in) long and contain 4-6 seeds. The stiff hairs from the pods are mixed with syrup, honey or molasses for use as an antihelmintic medicine. The hairs pierce the bodies of intestinal worms which then writhe free of the gut walls to be removed by a strong cathartic. The roundworm *Ascaris lumbricoides* and the pinworm *Oxyuris vermicularis* are destroyed by this treatment, but tape worms are not affected. Although usually considered to be a safe remedy there is some risk of enteritis. The seeds are said to be an aphrodisiac and a decoction of roots or seeds was formerly used to treat cholera in some parts of India.

*M. gigantea* is a large, woody liane of East African forest margins which reaches lengths of about 15 m (50 ft). The flowers, which are produced mostly on the lower part of the plant, are pale creamy green, white or pale lilac. *M. astropurpurea* is essentially an Indian species, its range extending from the Himalayas to Sri Lanka. It has spectacular drooping clusters of blue-purple flowers which give rise to intricately sculptured, oval seed pods up to 25 cm (10 in) long. *M. bennettii* is a large species of New Guinea's tropical forests, which produces magnificent oblong clusters of scarlet flowers. *M. rostrata* has orange flowers and is native to tropical America, while *M. imbricata* is a purple-flowered Indian species.

### Leguminosae; 100 species

### *MUSA*

A tropical Asian genus of giant perennial forest herbs which grow to a height of about 9m, (29.5 ft), the trunks consisting of the sheathing bases of the leaf stalks. The leaves may be up to 5 m (16.5 ft) long and 1 m (3.3 ft) broad when mature. They are undivided when young but are later torn into strips by the wind along the lines of the lateral veins.

Great flowering spikes rise from the centre of the crown of leaves, with male flowers in the upper half and bisexual flowers below. The bisexual flowers have an inferior ovary topped by a two-lipped 5 cm (2 in) long tube containing five stamens and a single style. These flowers contain large quantities of nectar and are pollinated by bats, birds, butterflies and moths.

The fruits are bananas, rich in carbohydrates. As they mature the inflorescence becomes pendulous under their weight. Wild bananas which develop from pollinated flowers contain three rows of pea-sized black seeds but cultivated bananas develop from unpollinated flowers and are seedless. The edible banana *M. paradisiaca* ssp. *sapientum* is thought to have originated from crosses between two Indomalayan species: *M. acuminata* and *M. balbisiana*.

Another useful crop species is *M. textilis*, found from India to the Philippines and Borneo. The fruit are not edible but the stem fibres are the source of abacá fibre or manila hemp, used for making ropes, mats, blankets and manila paper. Cultivated ornamental species include *M. superba* from China,

*Hoya bella*

### *MOMORDICA*

A genus of annual or perennial scrambling or trailing plants with fleshy rootstocks and white or yellow flowers, native to tropical regions of the Old World. Tendrils, formed from modified shoots, aid the plants as they climb, the leaves are palmate and the unisexual flowers occur on the same plant. The fruits are usually thick-skinned gourds with brightly coloured flesh and flattened seeds.

One of the best known species is balsam pear *Momordica charantia*, an annual herb which climbs to about 2 m (6.6 ft) with the aid of undivided tendrils. The leaves are circular or kidney-shaped, with 5-7 lobes, and the flowers are five-lobed and orange-yellow. The inferior ovary of the female flower develops into a rather knobbly oblong fruit which droops from a slender stalk. It is green when young but turns bright orange as it matures, the edible, blood-red flesh containing numerous grey-brown flattened seeds. Balsam pear was originally native to the Asian tropics but has since been spread

by man throughout the tropical regions of the New World.

*M. charantia* has many medicinal uses. It has been employed as a treatment for high blood pressure, colds and fevers, to check the growth of cancerous tumours, as a vermifuge for children, as a means of birth control and as an abortifacient. In its native Asia the young fruits of balsam pear are added to curries and salads or pickled.

The closely related balsam apple *M. balsamina* is also common in the tropics and is distinguished by its broad, ovoid fruits with ridged skins. Its circular three- or five-lobed leaves are used in the preparation of a tea and as a tonic. The pulped fruit (without the seeds) can be used as a poultice, and when added to almond oil it can be applied as a liniment to burns, chapped hands and for other skin inflammations.

Many species grow in East Africa, although only a few thrive in the tropical forest. *M. friesorum* is a climbing or trailing perennial of upland rainforest, distinguished by its large yellowish flowers with

*Musa sp.*

the 4 m (13 ft) high *M. basjoo* from southern Japan (also a source of fibre), *M. coccinea* and *M. beccarii*, all of which have flowers subtended by colourful bracts. *M. ingens*, a native of New Guinea, is the largest herb known to science.

**Musaceae; 35 species**

### NEPENTHES

A genus of carnivorous 'pitcher' plants which is confined to the Old World, from Assam through Malaysia and southeast Asia to northern Queensland in Australia and the island of New Caledonia. Madagascar, the westernmost outpost of the genus, boasts two species. It has been suggested that the generic name is derived from the combination of two Greek words meaning 'not' and 'grief', from the magic potion known as Nepenthe, mentioned by Greek and Roman poets, which was said to cause forgetfulness of sorrows and misfortune. The stems of some species are used locally as twine, while pouring the contents of a pitcher over the head of the patient is reputed to be a cure for incontinence.

The plants are typically climbers of damp humid tropical forests from sea level to over 2,500 m (8,200 ft), and reach maximum heights of about 15 m (50 ft); and non-climbing species are also found in drier, more open habitats. The unisexual flowers are small (about 3 mm/0.1 in across) green, reddish or bronze-tinted and are borne in clusters, males on one plant and females on another. Tendrils emanating from the tips of the long flat leaves assist the climbing species. The pitchers develop from the ends of these tendrils, although lack of light or low humidity may preclude pitcher formation.

The typical pitcher is more or less cylindrical, somewhat bulbous in the lower half with a rounded base. The mouth is rimmed by a hard glossy collar, corrugated with parallel ribs, each terminating within the pitcher in a sharp downward-pointing tooth. Between the teeth lie the nectar-secreting glands. The pitcher is also topped by a brightly coloured lid, liberally sprinkled with nectar glands on its under-surface, both colour and nectar serving to attract

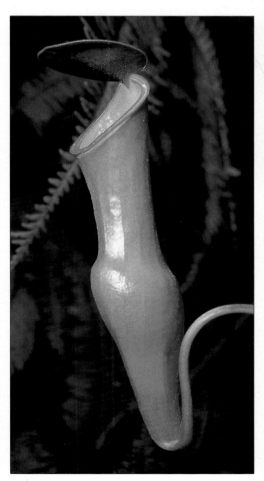

*Nepenthes pervillei*

*Nepenthes sp.*

insects. The lid also forms a protective canopy over the pitcher, important in areas of high rainfall to prevent the pitcher from filling with water.

Immediately beneath the rim the inner surface of the pitcher is waxy, but below this lies the digestive zone: a smooth surface pitted with numerous microscopic glands which both secrete enzymes and absorb the products of digestion. A small quantity of digestive fluid is always present in the base of the pitcher. Both terrestrial and winged insects are attracted to the pitcher. Although they can feed in relative safety on the lid and rim, sooner or later exploratory foraging will result in the insect venturing into the waxy zone, where small flakes of loose wax clog their feet and break away, tumbling the victim into the pitcher, where it soon drowns.

The victim's struggles stimulate the glands to produce acid and enzymes which start the digestive process immediately. Experiments have shown that midge-like flies are digested within a few hours, while the chitinous husk of a medium-sized fly will

be all that remains after two days. Bacteria, although present in all but newly opened pitchers, are thought to play only a minor part in this rapid and efficient digestive process.

In the wild it is not unusual to find the remains of centipedes, scorpions, small mammals and reptiles in the pitchers, although insects, especially ants, make up the bulk of the catch. Spiders, on the other hand, are able to scale the waxy walls with ease, and several species adopt the pitchers as hunting grounds. Mosquito and other fly larvae, crustaceans and protozoans are all able to use the aquatic environment to their advantage and are apparently unaffected by the digestive enzymes.

Monkey cup *Nepenthes mirabilis* is one of the most widespread species, with a range covering southern China, Malaya, Indo-China, Sumatra, the Philippines, Borneo, Celebes, Moluccas, New Guinea and Queensland. It is a very variable plant, although the leaf margins are always toothed. The lower pitchers are about 5-10 cm (2-4 in) long, cylindrical

*Paphiopedilum barbatum*

and swollen at the base, while the upper pitchers are long and funnel-shaped. These pitchers are generally light green, but may be tinted with red.

Typical tropical forest species are *N. bicalcarata*, a tall climbing plant confined to the swampy forests of Borneo; Raffles' pitcher plant *N. rafflesiana*, found on the edge of tropical forests in Borneo, Sumatra and Malaysia; *N. rajah* which produces the largest pitchers of the genus (to 35 cm/14 in long) and is also native to Borneo; *N. ventricosa* of the Philippines; and *N. maxima* of Borneo, Celebes and New Guinea.

**Nepenthaceae; about 70 species**

### PAPHIOPEDILUM

A genus of epiphytic or terrestrial orchids native to tropical Asian forests from India across the Malayan archipelago and the Spice Islands to New Guinea. The species are tufted plants with strap-shaped to ovate leaves and white, yellow, green, brown, violet, deep crimson or purple flowers borne on erect stems. The flowers are usually warty and have hairy margins.

The generic name is a combination of *Paphos* (the birthplace of the goddess Venus) and *pedilon* ('slipper'), in reference to the prominent slipper-shaped lip of the exquisite flowers.

*Paphiopedilum sukhakulii* is a typical terrestrial species of the montane forests of Thailand. The specific name of this plant, which went undiscovered until 1964, honours the Thai orchid collector Sukhakul. It has a compact rosette of narrow oval leaves up to 25 cm (10 in) long, from which arises a dark brown flower stalk about 25 cm (10 in) tall. The solitary terminal flower is 10-12 cm (4-4.5 in) in diameter and characterised by two downward-pointing, fused lateral sepals scarcely visible behind the large lip. The third vertical sepal is white or yellowish green and decorated with numerous longitudinal green stripes. The pale green petals, striped with dark green and dotted with red, spread out horizontally and the narrow slipper-like lip is purplish brown near the aperture becoming greenish towards the 'toe'.

*Paphiopedilum sp.*

*Passiflora sp.*

thorns, the five stamens the wounds and the three styles, broadened at the tip into club-shaped stigmas, are said to represent the nails (one transfixing each hand and one the feet of the crucified Christ). The ten perianth segments represent the ten faithful apostles (that is, without Judas and Peter), while the lobed leaves and tendrils symbolize the hands and scourges of Christ's persecutors.

Many species yield edible fruits or are cultivated as ornamentals for their beautiful flowers and strong fragrance. The fruits of the South American species reminded the Conquistadores of pomegranates, called *granadas* in Spanish, so they named them *granadillas*. Those with edible fruits include the giant or common granadilla *Passiflora quadrangularis*, native to Jamaica and South America, whose fruits are up to 25 cm (10 in) long and weigh over 4 kg (8.8 lbs); the Brazilian *P. alata*, a red-flowered species with fruits the size of goose eggs, and the apple-fruited granadilla or sweet calabash *P. maliformis*, which grows in the West Indies.

The most commercial species is granadilla, passionfruit or maracuja *P. subpeltata* (*P. edulis*). Although a native of Brazil, this species is widely cultivated in plantations in other parts of South America, Australia and Hawaii for its egg-sized yellow or purplish fruits. These are about 7-8 cm (2.8-3 in) across, aromatic, gelatinous and said to resemble oranges in flavour. A single plant will produce about 100 fruits in a year. It is a perennial climbing plant with stems up to 15 m (50 ft) long and alternate, usually three-lobed, leaves. The solitary flowers range from 4-7 cm (1.6-2.8 in) in diameter and are white with purplish corona threads.

In addition, several species of passion-flower are used in homeopathic medicine. The juice of the leaves of the sweet calabash *P. maliformis* and *P. pallida* are used in Brazil to counteract intermittent fevers, while the bitter and astringent leaves of water lemon or yellow granadilla *P. laurifolia* are employed as an antihelmintic (the fruits of this species are

Other terrestrial species are ivory lady's slipper *P. bellatulum* (*P. concolor*), from Thailand, Burma and North Vietnam; *P. insigne* from northeast India; and *P. glaucophyllum* from Java. *P. callosum* and *P. villosum* are native to Indo-China, *P. venustum* is a Nepalese species with mottled leaves, and *P. lawrenceanum* grows in Borneo.

Rather rare species include *P. charlesworthii*, a Burmese plant which has suffered from the over-zealous attentions of collectors since the nineteenth century, and *P. fairrieanum*, formerly widespread over much of Assam but now lost from many of its former sites. *P. druryi* which is confined to Kerala State in southern India, is listed as an endangered/extinct species in the IUCN Plant Red Data Book (1980).

### Orchidaceae; 36 species

### *PASSIFLORA*

A large genus of climbing plants with axillary tendrils and entire or lobed leaves, distributed across the tropical and warm regions of America, with a few species in Asia, Australia and Madagascar, usually in forest habitats. The flowers have five petaloid sepals and five petals, giving the impression of a ten-petalled flower. The sepals and petals surround the corona, which is believed to be formed from the enlarged top of the flower stalk and has an inner and outer ring of fine filaments. The corona is thought to attract insect and bird pollinators. In the centre, rising above the corona, is a column composed of five stamens and a three-carpelled ovary with spreading styles. Nectar is secreted at the base of the column.

*Passifloras* are commonly known as passion flowers, because their floral design reminded the Catholic missionaries in South America of Christ's crucifixion. The corona symbolizes the crown of

*Passiflora vitifolia*

edible). The roots of *P. contrayerva* and *P. normalis* are reputed to contain an antidote to poison and those of *P. quadrangularis* contain a powerful poisonous narcotic which is antihelmintic in small quantities. The leaves of the white and purple-flowered *P. foetida* are used as a poultice for skin inflammations, and to treat sore throats, kidney disorders, hysteria and female complaints.

Blue passion flower *P. caerulea* is native to Brazil, Peru and Argentina. It is a vigorous climber with 5-7 lobed leaves and scented flowers up to 8 cm (3 in) in diameter, with white or pinkish perianth segments and a blue corona. It is widely cultivated as an ornamental plant in tropical and temperate zones alike, having been introduced to England in 1699. *P. suberosa* is a slender trailing vine with greenish flowers and fruits, native to the Americas, from Texas to Patagonia and the West Indies, while *P. racemosa* is a South American species with spectacular pendulous clusters of scarlet flowers. *P. herbertiana* is one of the eight species native to Australia; the subspecies *P. herbertiana insulae-howei* is confined to the lowland rainforests of Lord Howe Island and is listed as an endangered species in the IUCN Plant Red Data Book (1980).

**Passifloraceae; 370 species**

### RAFFLESIA

A small genus from western Malaysian tropical forests, named after the naturalist and collector Sir Thomas Stamford Raffles, who was also the founder of Singapore. All plants in this genus are parasitic on the roots of tropical lianes. Rather like fungi, the vegetative organs of *Rafflesia* are reduced to a network of fine threads which can only survive in the tissues of their host and are only able to enter the plant via a wound. No leaves are produced and chlorophyll is absent.

The flowers, however, are among the largest known. The cabbage-like buds may appear on the soil surface or up to 4 m (13 ft) above the ground. They take up to nine months to open to their full extent – 90 cm (3 ft) or more in diameter in the case of *Rafflesia arnoldii* – and then wither away in the space of a week. These unisexual solitary flowers have no petals, but have a fleshy petaloid calyx with 4-6 lobes. They emit a foetid smell like that of rotting meat which is thought to attract carrion flies and other insects as pollinators.

The best known species is *Rafflesia arnoldii*, which was discovered in 1818 by Dr Joseph Arnold and Sir Thomas Stamford Raffles. It is native to Sumatra and parasitic on *Tetrastigma* vines, and has scarlet white-spotted flowers weighing up to 7 kg (15.4lbs). It is now becoming very rare – possibly because of the scarcity of large forest herbivores, whose hooves are thought to be responsible for damaging the vines and thus allowing the germinating seeds to enter the host plant. *R. arnoldii* is listed as a vulnerable/endangered species in the IUCN Plant Red Data Book (1980). Two other species of *Rafflesia* have not been seen since the Second World War and may well be extinct.

**Rafflesiaceae; 13-14 species**

### SARCOCHILUS

A small genus of epiphytic orchids found in Polynesia and southeast Asia, although most species occur in Australia. The plants are characterized by flat leaves and stems often covered with the persistent sheathing bases of the leaves, with flowers arranged in axillary inflorescences. The generic name is derived from the combination of *sarx* ('fleshy'), and *cheilos* ('lip'), which describes the fleshy labellum of the flowers.

The orange-blossom orchid *Sarcochilus falcatus*, is a species of the dense coastal forests of Queensland and New South Wales, where it is equally at home growing on rocks or tree-branches. Each inflorescence has 3-10 white flowers with orange and red-streaked lips. The fragrant flowers of *S. olivaceus* are distinguished by their narrow, olive-green segments and whitish lip, again with red markings. This species thrives in more or less the same habitats and has the same geographical range as *S. falcatus*.

**Orchidaceae; 12 species**

### STROPHOCACTUS

A cactus genus containing a single species which is fairly common in the swampy tropical forests of Brazil, in the region of Manaus. *Strophocactus wittii* is an epiphytic high-climbing and freely branching plant. Its flattened, leaf-like, occasionally triangular stems cling closely to the support with the aid of aerial roots emerging from the midrib of the shoot. The stem margins are not notched, but instead bear rosettes of bristles and numerous short spines up to 12 mm (0.5 in) long. The large, night-blooming flowers have long slender tubes and are flesh-pink or reddish on the outside, pure white within; they reach a maximum length of about 25 cm (10 in). *S. wittii* is sometimes known as the strap cactus because of its flattened stems.

**Cactaceae; a single species**

### THUNBERGIA

A genus of climbing and erect herbs and shrubs with bracteoles enclosing the calyx and showy tubular white, yellow, red, purple or blue flowers. Representatives are found throughout the Old World tropics, particularly in Africa, and many are characteristic of tropical forest habitats. The genus is named after the Swedish botanist Carl Peter Thunberg (1743-1828).

The best known and most widely cultivated species is the sky vine *Thunbergia grandiflora*, also called the blue trumpet vine or Bengal clock vine, which is a native of northeast India. This liane has large oval

*Rafflesia arnoldii*

or heart-shaped, evergreen leaves about 20 cm (0.8 in) long, with toothed or lobed margins. The broadly funnel-shaped flowers, which may be white, pale or dark blue, are arranged in small clusters and are produced all year round. Each flower has two distinct lips, with two of the five corolla lobes directed upwards and three pointing down. *T. grandiflora* is usually pollinated by large female carpenter bees, which are directed towards the reproductive parts of the flower by means of dark longitudinal lines (honeyguides) at the entrance to the corolla.

The annual black-eyed Susan *T. alata*, is a climbing or trailing plant native to tropical East Africa and has cream, yellow or orange, black-centred flowers about 4 cm (1.6 in) across, while *T. erecta*, from tropical West Africa, is an erect shrub. Among the most vigorous climbers is the clock vine *T. fragrans*, an Asian species found from northern India to China and southeast Asia, which has scented white funnel-shaped flowers to 5 cm (2 in) across. *T. coccinea* is a scarlet-flowered climber of northern India and southwest China, while the Indian *T. mysorensis* has red and yellow flowers.

**Acanthaceae (Thunbergiaceae); 100 species**

### UTRICULARIA

A large cosmopolitan genus of carnivorous plants, commonly known as bladderworts, and especially common in tropical regions. Most bladderworts are aquatic, but some have evolved to live in wet soils. Yet others, particularly the large-flowered species of South America, are epiphytic on moss and rotting bark on rainforest trees, while some of the aquatic species are able to live in the small pools that collect in the leaf rosettes of other tropical forest epiphytes such as bromeliads.

A characteristic of all bladderworts, however, is that at no time in their life cycle do they have roots of any kind. The majority form long branching stems or stolons, from which leaves develop vertically in the terrestrial and epiphytic species. In aquatic bladderworts, however, the leaves are replaced by divided processes, which may function as leaves, although they may in fact be modified shoots. The common feature of all species is their tiny stalked and bladder-like traps which may arise from either stems or leaves, but are never found above the surface of the water or substratum. In many species these bladders are smaller than a pinhead, but are of ingenious construction and very effective in trapping microscopic prey.

Bladderwort traps are filled with water, even in terrestrial species (which can only thrive in wet soils), and range in size from 0.25 to 5 mm (0.01-0.2 in). They are normally transparent, may be round, oval or pear-shaped, and are laterally flattened. The base of the trap, or bladder, is attached to the plant by a narrow stalk. At the opposite end is an entrance covered by a hanging flap, around which grow numerous appendages, known as antennae, which are usually branched or wing-like. In a typical aquatic species the antennae form a funnel which serves to guide potential victims towards the entrance, as well as protecting the trigger mechanism from accidental contact with non-prey items.

The 'door' of the trap is hinged in the upper portion and sealed with mucilage where it rests against the lower part of the bladder. Its outer surface is slightly convex and covered with stalked glands which secrete both mucilage and sugar, possibly to attract small invertebrates. Near the bottom edge of the door are four pointed bristles, known as trigger hairs, which are directed outwards. The interior of the trap is lined with two types of glands, some forked and some with four 'arms'.

An unsprung trap has concave sides due to a partial vacuum within, which ensures that the door remains tightly sealed. The slightest touch of an aquatic animal on the trigger hairs at the base of the door is sufficient to break the tension and suck both

*Utricularia quelchii*

door and victim inside. Once the vacuum is released, the door returns to its former position and traps the victim inside, and the bladder becomes convex. It is thought that the four-armed glands are then responsible for extracting water from the trap, so that over a period of up to two hours most of the water is removed, the vacuum restored, and the trap ready to receive its next victim. The prey may remain alive for some time within the trap, although eventually it dies and is digested by enzymes secreted by the four-armed glands. The products of this digestive process are then absorbed by both types of glands.

The flowers vary considerably from species to species. Many bladderworts have dull, inconspicuous blooms; others, however, are large and colourful, especially those of terrestrial species in Australia, where the plants are known as fairy aprons, or in the South American epiphytes, where they resemble orchids. In general the flowers are spurred and two-lipped, resembling toadflaxes (*Linaria*), but they may be solitary or many to a stem, and the range of colours is quite incredible.

One of the better known aquatic species is greater bladderwort *Utricularia vulgaris*, which is widespread across North America, Eurasia and North Africa. It favours acid to neutral waters over 60 cm (2 ft) deep in shady conditions and forms dense masses from which rise 20 cm (8 in) flowering stems bearing 3-8 bright yellow flowers. Similar yellow-flowered species are *U. australis* (*U. neglecta*), an essentially Old World plant of both hemispheres; *U. minor* and *U. intermedia*, both confined to temperate regions of the northern hemisphere; and swollen bladderwort *U. inflata* of the southeastern United

*Utricularia vulgaris*

*Vanda sp.*

States. *U. purpurea* is an aquatic species of North and Central America distinguished by its purplish flowers

Epiphytic bladderworts of the South American rainforests include *U. alpina* which has white flowers up to 3.5 cm (1.4 in) in diameter and grows in the West Indies, Central and South America; *U. endresii* from Costa Rica, which has spectacular drooping pale lilac flowers with a yellow centre, each up to 5 cm (2 in) in diameter; the pale violet-flowered *U. reniformis*, found both as an epiphyte and in sphagnum bogs in the Brazilian rainforest; and another Brazilian species, *U. longifolia*, with 5 cm (2 in) wide bluish flowers with orange centres.

The terrestrial bladderworts are also primarily plants of tropical habitats, although a few occur in the cooler regions of North America and Australia. The most widespread species is undoubtedly *U. subulata*, which ranges over the whole of the New World, Portugal, tropical Africa, Madagascar, Thailand and Borneo. Its narrow, grass-like leaves only emerge from the ground for about 6 mm (0.2 in), while the slender reddish flowering stems, up to 7.5 cm (2.9 in) tall, each bear up to 7 bright yellow flowers with orange centres.

Other terrestrial species include small bladderwort *U. lateriflora* and fairy aprons *U. dichotoma*, both of which are violet-flowered and confined to Australia; redcoats *U. menziesii*, a Western Australian species with unusual scarlet flowers; *U. peltata*, of tropical regions in the southern hemisphere in both Old and New Worlds; horned bladderwort *U. cornuta*, a yellow-flowered North American species; and the South African *U. sandersoni*, which has delicate sprays of tiny, pale blue flowers.

**Lentibulariaceae; 180 species**

### VANDA

A genus of epiphytic evergreen orchids widespread in the tropical and subtropical forests of Asia, from the Himalayas to Malaysia. The strap-shaped or cylindrical leaves are usually arranged in two opposite rows and the erect or pendulous flower stems arise from the leaf axils. The fleshy flowers are large, spurred and arranged in clusters, with three-lobed lips, the middle lobe of which is fleshy.

*Vanda caerulea* is a northern Indian species with erect leafy stems about 1 m (3.3 ft) long and pale blue flowers up to 12 cm (4.5 in) across arranged in spikes of 7-20. Collection of this orchid is now prohibited since its overwhelming popularity in Europe in the nineteenth century devastated the wild populations in Assam. One of the most common Himalayan species is *V. cristata*, an epiphyte whose 3-5 cm (1.2-2 in) flowers have yellow-green oblong, spreading sepals and petals and a distinctive purple-blotched, buff-coloured lip.

The pink-flowered Kinta weed *V. hookerana* was once very common in the forests of the Kinta Valley in Malaya, but is now decimated by tin-mining and forest clearance; its range also extends to Borneo and Sumatra, where it favours swampy coastal forests. This orchid is also called the bone plant because the leaves were formerly used in the preparation of a hot poultice for aching joints. Together with *V. teres*, a Burmese species, *V. hookeriana* is widely used in the cultivation of ornamental hybrids, while their natural hybrid Vanda Miss Joaquim, with magnificent rose-pink flowers, is the national flower of Singapore.

**Orchidaceae; 35 species**

## VANILLA

A large genus of terrestrial orchids which is distributed across all tropical regions. The stems either bear leaves or adventitious roots and the lily-like green, white or pink flowers are large and arranged in spikes. The spreading sepals are similar to the petals and the lip is either simple or three-lobed. Several species of *Vanilla* are cultivated for their aromatic properties and are the only economic plants among the 30,000 members of the Orchidaceae.

*Vanilla planifolia* (*V. fragrans*) is the commercial source of vanilla and was used by the Aztecs to flavour cocoa. It is a climbing plant, native to the forests of Mexico, Central America and northern South America, which reaches a height of up to 10 m (33 ft), supporting itself by means of tendril-like adventitious roots. The stems bear succulent lanceolate leaves and the flowers are produced in axillary inflorescences. Each greenish yellow flower remains open for only a few hours in the morning and is pollinated by hummingbirds or large flying insects.

The long narrow capsules ripen gradually over a period of up to seven months, but if they are to be used for flavouring they must be collected while still greenish yellow and before splitting open. Only after a month-long process involving steaming or boiling, fermenting and drying is the aromatic compound vanillin produced, together with 35 other aromatic substances. *V. planifolia* has been known since the discovery of America and is now grown in many parts of the world as a commercial crop, despite the fact that vanillin was first synthesized artificially in 1874. Madagascar produces about two-thirds of the world's vanilla today, although natural pollinators are absent and the flowers are pollinated by hand.

Two other species, *V. pompona* (*V. grandiflora*) from Mexico, Central and northern South America, especially Venezuela, and *V. tahitensis* from Tahiti, are also cultivated but do not supply such a high quality product. Other New World species are *V. inodora*, *V. mexicana*, *V. phaeantha* and *V. pfaviana*, while *V. roscheri* is a liane from East Africa in which the leaves are reduced to brown membranous scales.

**Orchidaceae; 100 species**

## WEBEROCEREUS

A small genus of slender-stemmed epiphytic cacti from the dense tropical rainforests of Costa Rica and thickets in Panama. The climbing or arching shoots may be rounded, flattened or three- or four-angled, and the medium to large, night-blooming flowers are shortly funnel-shaped.

*Weberocereus biolleyi* has almost cylindrical spineless stems and aerial roots that hang down from the branches of forest trees in Costa Rica. The small nocturnal flowers are bell-shaped and fleshy, ranging in colour from yellowish green through pink to reddish brown. *W. trichophorus* is a climbing species, also from Costa Rica, with rounded green shoots about 1 cm (0.4 in) thick bearing strong yellow spines and black curly hairs. The funnel-shaped flowers are flesh-pink on the inside, purple without.

**Cactaceae; 3 species**

## XANTHOSOMA

A tropical American genus of large rainforest herbs with large arrow- or spear-shaped leaves on long petioles arising from edible tubers. The native distribution extends from Mexico through Central America to Brazil and eastwards to the West Indies.

Yautia *Xanthosoma sagittifolium* has been cultivated for centuries for its edible rootstocks rich in starch. The 1 m (3.3 ft) long leaves, glossy green above and bluish beneath, are borne on stems up to 2 m (6.6 ft) tall, although wild plants have smaller leaves. The spathe protects a spadix with female flowers at the base, although fruits are rare in cultivated plants. Yautia tubers, which weigh up to 2 kg (4.4lbs), contain crystals of calcium oxalate and must therefore be boiled before eating. They are grown mainly in

Vanilla sp.

Xanthosoma robustum

tropical regions of the New World, especially in Cuba. The young leaves are eaten like spinach. In Asia the burnt stems of this introduced plant are used to prepare poultices for the strained muscles of working elephants!

Other species are Indian kale or spoonflower *X. lindenii*, which grows wild in Colombia; *X. jacquinii*, native to the forests of Colombia, Venezuela, Mexico and the West Indies; and blue taro or blue ape *X. violaceum*, also cultivated for its tubers (and regarded by some as a variety of *X. sagittifolium*) and whose edible leaves have conspicuous violet petioles. *X. brasiliense* also has edible leaves.

**Araceae; about 45 species**

## ZYGOPETALON

A genus of epiphytic orchids native to tropical regions of the New World, particularly South America. The leaves are thick and lanceolate and the flower stems are erect, bearing yellow-green blooms with brown or purple markings. These conspicuous flowers may be either solitary or arranged in few-flowered spikes. The sepals and petals are similar and the lip is spreading and three-lobed. The generic name is derived from the Greek *zygon* ('yoke') which refers to the yoke-like swelling at the base of the lip.

*Zygopetalon grandiflorum* is a rare forest species in Mexico, Guatemala, British Honduras and Costa Rica. It has yellowish green sepals and petals, each with 5-7 broad reddish brown stripes, and a white lip longitudinally streaked with red and fringed on the lateral margins. *Z. mackaii* is an epiphytic species of the Brazilian rainforests, while *Z. intermedium*, which has handsome golden, bronze-striped flowers with very elongated trailing petals, is a terrestrial species in the same region.

**Orchidaceae; 35 species**

173

CHAPTER EIGHT

# FRESHWATER WETLANDS

Freshwater habitats or wetlands are widely distributed across the earth, although they cover less than 2 per cent of the total land area. The rich and diverse flowering plant communities vary with rock type and nutrient status but are primarily dependent on whether the wetland is seasonal or permanent and whether the water is flowing through the system or is stationary.

Freshwater habitats range from tiny mountain streams to great continental rivers such as the Nile and the Amazon, from the abyssal Lake Baikal to the tiny dewponds of western European agricultural landscapes, and from the sweeping expanses of tropical swamps and marshes to the rapidly disappearing peatlands, fens and bogs of the cooler parts of the globe.

Flowering plants that thrive in aquatic habitats are usually known as hydrophytes. Many species grow in water or waterlogged soils and have stem tissue called aerenchyma, which consists of large, thin-walled cells separated by air spaces and allows air entering via the pores (stomata) in stem and leaves to pass down to the roots. Completely submerged plants are able to absorb oxygen and carbon dioxide from the surrounding water, and some species are able to store these gases in hollow chambers (lacunae) within their stems. Aerenchyma is used by floating plants as an aid to buoyancy.

Some species with permanently submerged foliage produce flowers on long stalks which rise above the surface of the water and are pollinated by insects or the wind. Others have underwater flowers with pollen grains in buoyant capsules that rise to the surface, where they are released to drift down onto the stigmas. The seeds of freshwater plants are often dispersed by water, but the predominant means of reproduction for many species is vegetative, new plants developing rapidly from fragments of the parent.

Facing page: waterlily, Florida, USA.

Cypress swamp, Everglades, Florida, USA.

Above: *Sagittaria sagittifolia*

Right: *Victoria regia*

Above: Okavango Delta, Botswana.

## ACORUS

Just two species belong to this genus of both Old World and New World wetlands, and by far the better known is sweet flag *Acorus calamus*, so called because all parts of the plant are fragrant when bruised, giving off a vanilla-like aroma. An emergent species found along streamsides and riverbanks and growing in swamps and marshes, sweet flag reproduces vegetatively by means of underground rhizomes that have a sweet smell and taste. The sword-like leaves may grow to over 1 m (3.3 ft), while the tiny greenish yellow flowers are packed in diamond-shaped designs on a club-like spadix which emerges at an angle of about 45° to the stem. There is no spathe. The fruits are small, gelatinous berries.

Sweet flag occurs throughout northern temperate regions (although in the northern hemisphere it is native only to Asia and North America), as well as from India south to Sulawesi. The rhizomes have been used in medicine since the time of Hippocrates (460-377 BC), especially for the treatment of dysentery, toothache, anaemia and gout. Extracts of the rhizomes were also a component of 'oil of holy ointment', used for anointing altars and sacred vessels in the Old Testament (the 'sweet calamus' of Exodus XXX. 23), and the leaves were formerly spread on church floors. More recently, sweet flag rhizomes have been used for making candy in the United States, and are still an important flavouring in 'eaux-de-vie' in continental Europe.

*Acorus calamus* was introduced to the British Isles and much of northern Europe from southern Asia in the sixteenth century and is now well established over much of the area. In Britain, however, the flowers never produce viable fruit, the plant relying on vegetative reproduction. The generic name is derived from *Acoron*, the Greek name of the plant as used by Dioscorides, which in turn is said to be a derivation of Coreon (the pupil of the eye), since it was used in ancient times to cure diseases of the eye.

**Araceae; 2 species**

## ALDROVANDA

The sole species of this genus, *Aldrovanda vesiculosa*, is a rootless, floating aquatic plant of acid waters. It is distributed across central Europe, Africa, from India to Japan to northeast Australia. The solitary white or greenish flowers are produced in high summer and open just above the surface of the water.

Commonly known as the waterwheel plant, *A. vesiculosa* has a single short stem, rarely exceeding 15 cm (6 in), with leaves arranged in whorls, usually of eight. Each broad leaf terminates in 4-8 stiff pointed bristles and a bilobed trap containing trigger hairs and digestive glands. Although much smaller (2 mm/0.1 in long), the traps are not dissimilar to those of the Venus flytrap (see *Dionaea*). *Aldrovanda* traps are very sensitive to tactile disturbance, closing rapidly to ensnare microscopic aquatic invertebrates.

**Droseraceae; a single species**

## ALISMA

A small genus of northern temperate regions and Australia. The generic name is said to be derived from *alis*, the Celtic word for water, which presumably refers to its preference for a waterside habitat. *Alisma* species are commonly known as water plantains, although *Alisma plantago-aquatica* was called mad-dog weed because its roots enjoyed a reputation as a cure for hydrophobia. In America the roots are considered effective against rattlesnake bites, while in Japan they are used medicinally under the name of *Saji Omodaka*. The submerged fleshy portion of the stems and the root-like tubers of several species were formerly dried and eaten by American Indians.

Water plantains are emergent plants which thrive on the margins of lakes and rivers and even in roadside ditches. The roots are fibrous and the submerged base of the stem is swollen and fleshy. From this base arise broad, ribbed leaves on long

*Alisma lanceolatum*

triangular stalks that superficially resemble the leaves of plantains (*Plantago*), hence the common name. The flower stalk may be over 1 m (3.3 ft) in height and is much branched, producing more or less pyramidal inflorescences. The individual flowers have three oval spreading sepals, three rounded petals with fringed margins, ranging through shades of pink to white, and six pale green stamens.

Several water plantain species are native to North America, including *A. subcordatum*, found on the east coast from Quebec south to New York and west to Wisconsin, and common water plantain *A. plantago-aquatica*, which is widespread throughout the northern hemisphere, including most of North America. The ribbon-leaved water plantain *A. gramineum* is native to the northern United States, southern Canada, central and eastern Europe and the western USSR. It was first discovered in Britain in 1920, and is confined to a shallow, artificial pond in Worcestershire and is protected by law. Narrow-leaved water plantain *A. lanceolatum* is distributed across Europe, western Asia, North Africa and Macaronesia.

An interesting phenomenon has been noted regarding the timing of flower opening in Britain, and also in Holland, where three species of *Alisma* occur. Each flower only lasts for part of a single day. In *A. lanceolatum* the flowers open from 9-10 am and are already beginning to wither by midday, whereas in *A. plantago-aquatica* they do not open until 1-2 pm, and in *A. gramineum* they first unfurl in the early evening. This may be a mechanism by which the various species avoid hybridization.

**Alismataceae; 9 species**

## APIUM

A small genus of annual, biennial or perennial herbs of temperate regions which have pinnate or ternate leaves and umbels of white flowers. One of the better known species is wild celery *Apium graveolens*, an erect, strong-smelling biennial which grows in damp places by rivers and ditches across Europe, southwest

Asia, North Africa and Macaronesia. It is cultivated in two forms: var. *dulce*, or celery, and var. *rapaceum*, which is celeriac.

Other species that thrive in damp habitats include fool's watercress *A. nodiflorum*, whose shiny bright green leaves are sometimes mistaken for watercress and are eaten without any apparent ill-effects; in England's West Country, fool's watercress was once regularly served as an accompaniment to meat dishes. It grows in ditches and shallow ponds in western, central and southern Europe, temperate Asia and North Africa, and has been introduced to North America and Chile. Creeping marshwort *A. repens* is a similar species of European damp meadows and ditches, while lesser marshwort *A. inundatum* is a submerged or floating perennial of lakes, ponds and ditches which is confined to western Europe.

**Umbelliferae; 20 species**

### APONOGETON

A genus of aquatic herbs native to the Old World tropics and South Africa. The best known species is Cape pondweed *Aponogeton distachyos*, a perennial with floating leaves, long, spongy stems and edible tuberous rootstocks. Where their natural pond habitat dries out in summer the plants die back to the subterranean rhizomes until the onset of the winter rains. The inflorescence consists of two terminal rigid spikes, each with about ten white fragrant flowers.

Cape pondweed, also known as water hawthorn, has been introduced to freshwater habitats in many parts of the world, although it is native to the Cape region of South Africa and is a popular aquarium plant. A much rarer species in the wild is the Madagascar lace plant or lace-leaf *A. madagascariensis*, which has become extinct over much of its natural island range following extensive collection of its attractive foliage for aquaria. Lattice-leaf *A. fenestralis* is a similar species with both submerged and floating leaves, also popular as an aquarium plant.

The highly esteemed traditional South African dish called *waterblommetjiebredie*, is a stew of mutton and mature spikes of Cape pondweed flowers. The demand for these blooms is now so great that they are canned commercially and are even cultivated in artificial ponds.

**Aponogetonaceae; 44 species**

### ARETHUSA

The sole member of this genus – dragon's mouth *Arethusa bulbosa* – is native to eastern North America. Arethusa was one of the nereids (Greek nymphs of the Mediterranean, daughters of Nereus) beloved of the river god Alpheus, who begged Artemis to save her from him and was changed into a fountain bearing her name.

This orchid has a single, bright pink, scented flower, about 5 cm (2 in) long, borne at the tip of a smooth stem 12-25 cm (4.5-10 in) high. Each flower has a showy pink, dark-spotted lip, crested down the centre with three rows of yellowish hairs, two side petals arching over the lip and three erect sepals, all of which are a deep rose-pink. At the time of flowering no leaves are present, but these develop as the fruit matures.

Dragon's mouth thrives in bogs, swamps and wet meadows from Ontario and Newfoundland to Quebec, south through the Appalachians to North Carolina, and west to Minnesota. In the north of its range it does not flower until August, but further south the spectacular flowers often appear in May.

**Orchidaceae; a single species**

### BALDELLIA

This genus has just two species: lesser water plantain *Baldellia ranunculoides*, native to Europe and North Africa, and the smaller but very similar *B. alpestris*, which occurs only in the mountains of northwest

Spain and northern and central Portugal.

*B. ranunculoides* is a glabrous perennial herb 5-20 cm (2-8 in) high, with a vertical rosette of pointed, linear-lanceolate leaves that taper downwards into long petioles. The inflorescence consists of long-stalked hermaphrodite flowers usually arranged either in a single umbel or in whorls around the stem. Each flower has three white, pale pink or purplish petals, 7-10 mm (0.3-0.4 in) long. It thrives at the margins of fens, ponds and ditches, usually preferring calcareous peat, and occurs in southern, western and central Europe, north to southern Norway and east to Lithuania and Greece, as well as in similar habitats in North Africa.

**Alismataceae; 2 species**

### BERULA

A tiny genus of perennial aquatic herbs of northern temperate regions, and eastern and southern Africa. The best known species is narrow-leaved water parsnip *Berula erecta*, an erect or decumbent

stoloniferous plant of the ditches, canals, ponds, fens and marshes of Europe and western Asia. It may reach almost 1 m (3.3 ft) in height but is usually much smaller, and is distinguished by its blue-green pinnate leaves and small irregular umbels of white flowers. Narrow-leaved water parsnip is poisonous.

**Umbelliferae; 2 species**

### BUTOMUS

The sole member of this temperate Eurasian genus is the flowering rush *Butomus umbellatus*. An erect, hairless perennial up to 1.5 m (5 ft) in height, with linear, pointed, three-angled and twisted leaves. Slightly exceeding the leaves in height is a rounded stem topped by a magnificent umbel of rose-pink flowers. Each flower has three sepals and three larger petals, all of which are pink with darker veins, while the flower stalks, or pedicels, which may be up to 10 cm (4 in) long, are all of different lengths.

Flowering rush thrives in still or slow-moving water in ditches, ponds and canals and also at the

*Baldellia ranunculoides*

*Butomus umbellatus*

the plant's habit of flowering only once every two years. The rhizomes are a source of edible starch but the foliage and fruit are poisonous.

Also known as the wild calla lily, this plant is distinguished by its glossy, dark green, heart-shaped leaves and broadly oval white spathe surrounding a short, yellow spadix dotted with tiny hermaphrodite flowers. Its preferred habitats are cool swamps, wet woods and pond edges.

**Araceae; a single species**

### CALLITRICHE

A small, almost cosmopolitan genus of submerged, amphibious or terrestrial herbs characterized by their simple leaves and tiny unisexual flowers, although both male and female flowers occur on the same plant. Commonly known as starworts, they are very variable and hybrids frequently occur. Several species are very sensitive to pollution and have been used to indicate the presence of particular contaminants in freshwaters in southern Germany.

Many species are native to Europe, including some with rather restricted distributions such as *Callitriche truncata*, found only in southeastern Soviet Europe and southern and western Europe as far north as England; *C. lusitanica*, which is confined to Iberia, *C. platycarpa*, a very common species whose range is restricted to base-rich waters in northwestern and central Europe, and *C. hamulata*, which prefers acid waters in the same area.

More widespread species include *C. stagnalis*, common throughout Europe, the Canary Islands and North Africa, *C. hermaphroditica*, a species of northern and eastern Europe, USSR, Iceland and the

*Caltha palustris*

margins of rivers. It occurs over most of Europe, except for Scotland and some of the islands, throughout temperate Asia and is naturalized in North America. The rhizomes are powdered and made into bread in parts of the USSR.

**Butomaceae; a single species**

### BYBLIS

There are just two species in this genus: *Byblis gigantea* is a large plant from southwestern Australia, while *B. liniflora* is much smaller and occurs in northern Australia and New Guinea. The genus is named after Byblis, the beautiful daughter of Miletus (the son of Apollo). Presumably the glistening drops of mucilage that adorn the leaves and stems recall the tears shed by Byblis when her twin brother rejected her amorous advances, after which she turned into a fountain. In bright sunlight these drops act as prisms, splitting the light into all the colours of the spectrum, for which these species are commonly known as rainbow plants.

The plants are insectivorous, securing their prey by means of a sticky mucilaginous substance produced by numerous stalked glands on the leaves and stems. Stalkless glands are also present, these secreting digestive enzymes which break down the chitinous parts of the victim (usually an insect) into a fluid that

can be assimilated by the plant. Since the leaves are held almost vertically, the underside, or outer surface, is most densely covered with mucilage-secreting glands, together with the stems, flower stalks and sepals. The less conspicuous enzyme-secreting glands, however, occur on both sides of the leaf. The genus is unique among carnivorous plants in having digestive glands on the stems.

*B. liniflora* is an annual or short-lived perennial of wet soils, with thin, straggling stems, rarely exceeding 28 cm (11 in) in height. The leaves are thread-like and the lilac flowers rise on long slender stalks from the leaf axils. *B. gigantea*, which favours poor sandy soils, has a woody basal stem from which shoots appear at the onset of the winter rains. It may reach some 60 cm (24 in) in height, with yellowish green leaves up to 30 cm (12 in) long, and produces an abundance of large (2 cm/0.8 in) lilac-violet flowers with contrasting yellow stamens.

**Byblidaceae; 2 species**

### CALLA

The sole species of this genus, water arum *Calla palustris* – is an aquatic herb of northern temperate regions in northern, central and eastern Europe, northern Asia and North America. The generic name, used by Pliny, means 'uncertain', and may refer to

Faeroes; and *C. brutia*, found in western and southern Europe, North Africa and the Near East. Two native North American species are *C. terrestris* and *C. peploides*, both of which are also naturalized in France.

**Callitrichaceae; 17 species**

*CALTHA*

A small genus of perennial herbs with more or less heart-shaped leaves, distributed across temperate and subpolar regions, particularly in marshy habitats. Few-flowered inflorescences bear large colourful flowers, each composed of five or more petal-like sepals, true petals being absent. The generic name is derived from the Greek *calathos* ('goblet'), in reference to its cup-shaped flowers.

The most widespread species is the marsh marigold *Caltha palustris*, also known as king-cup in Europe and cowslip in the United States. It is a common plant of wet ditches, streams and wet meadows and flushes, the stems ranging from creeping and rooting to erect, and is found throughout the temperate northern hemisphere, excepting Greenland, but is rare in the Mediterranean region. Although generally considered to be poisonous, marsh marigold leaves were formerly used as pot-herbs by North American Indians, but require frequent changes of water during cooking to remove all traces of the toxic alkaloids. The buds were also pickled and used as a substitute for capers, while its juice was used to colour butter. Marsh marigolds are also among the flowers dedicated to the Virgin Mary and were formerly widely used in garlands to celebrate May Day festivities.

Other North American species include floating

*Caltha leptosepala*

marsh marigold *C. natans*, a small pink- or white-flowered plant with buoyant stems, distributed from Alaska to Minnesota, and elk's-lip *C. leptosepala*, so called because of the shape of the long leaves, which has large, solitary, white flowers, each with 8-12 sepals and numerous yellow stamens. This species ranges from southwest Canada to New Mexico, forming carpets in wet subalpine meadows and along streambanks in the Rocky Mountains to 3,000 m (9,800 ft) or more and at lower altitudes in more southerly regions.

*C. howellii* is another American species with solitary white flowers which thrives in marshy and boggy habitats in the Sierra Nevada and the North Coast Ranges between 1,400 and 3,200 m (4,000-10,500 ft), while twin-flowered marsh marigold *C. biflora*, with two flowers per stem, occurs in similar habitats from Alaska to California. *C. asarifolia* has yellow flowers and grows in coastal bogs from Oregon to Alaska, and *C. polysepala* is a robust yellow-flowered species of the Carpathian mountains in western Asia.

*C. arctica* is a typical high latitude species of the northern hemisphere which grows only in the arctic region of Siberia and western North America. In the subantarctic zone, *C. dionaeifolia* occurs on Tierra del Fuego and Hermite Island, and arrow-leaved marsh marigold *C. sagittata*, which has horizontal, fleshy, creeping rhizomes, slender leaves with heart-shaped bases and whitish green flowers up to 3 cm (1.2 in) across, is native to the Falkland Islands, where it grows in or alongside streams or in damp shingle near the sea. Two species are native to New Zealand: white caltha *C. obtusa*, which grows only on South Island, its fragrant flowers appearing soon after snow melt, and yellow caltha *C. novae-zelandiae*, whose flowers consist of pale yellow pointed sepals.

**Ranunculaceae; 10 species**

*CEPHALOTUS*

The sole member of this genus, and indeed of the family, is *Cephalotus follicularis*, a carnivorous species known as the West Australian pitcher plant or flycatcher plant. It is a perennial found only in the peaty swamps of a narrow coastal strip in southwestern Australia, between the Donelly River and Cheyne Beach to the east of Albany, where it was discovered by Robert Brown in 1801 and described by the Frenchman La Ballardière in 1806. Despite the presence of insect-trapping pitchers, this plant is not an obligate carnivore and is also able to maintain itself by photosynthesis.

The leaves are of two types: the oval bright green foliage leaves, capable of photosynthesis, and the pitchers. These latter develop between July and January on long stalk-like petioles which carry them clear of the rosette of foliage leaves to rest permanently on the ground when mature. In plants growing in shady conditions, the pitchers remain green, but those in bright sunlight turn a deep crimson-red.

The mature pitchers are normally from 3-5 cm (1.2-2 in) long, resemble bristly moccasins in general appearance, and have three pronounced vertical ridges down the front which are thought to guide terrestrial insects towards the mouth. The lids open when the pitchers are mature, revealing a wide mouth ringed with spiked ribs and curve into the pitcher and prevent trapped insects from escaping. The sides of the well are glossy, containing numerous enzyme-secreting glands in the upper portion. All but the oldest pitchers contain a watery 'enzyme soup', which serves to digest insects that lose their footing on the slippery walls of the pitcher. Ants are among the primary prey of *Cephalotus follicularis*, but flying insects attracted by nectar-producing glands on the outside of the pitcher are also common victims.

The flowers of the West Australian pitcher plant are petal-less and inconspicuous, about 3 mm (0.1 in) in diameter and have six greenish white sepals. They are borne in a cluster at the end of a tall, slender stalk which may rise some 60 cm (24 in) above the rest of the plant. This curious species has suffered greatly from over-collecting in recent years. Today it is listed on Appendix II of the Convention on International Trade in Endangered Species of Wild Fauna and Flora (CITES), which protects the wild population to a certain extent by restricting international trade.

**Cephalotaceae; a single species**

### CERATOPHYLLUM

A tiny genus of submerged aquatic herbs with a more or less cosmopolitan distribution. The plants are generally known as hornworts, because of the horn-like texture of the old translucent leaves. The leaves are arranged in whorls around long slender stems, with each leaf divided into several linear or thread-like filaments. The unisexual flowers are solitary in the axils of the leaves, with male and female flowers at different nodes. Pollination takes place underwater; the anthers break off and float up through the water, releasing the pollen to fertilize the female flowers *en route*.

Hornworts survive the winter by sinking to the bottom in the autumn, returning to the surface waters with the onset of spring. In some parts of the world their prolific growth can choke waterways, but has been controlled using Chinese grass-carp as a biological control. The foliage provides shelter for young fish, but also for bilharzia-carrying snails and malarial mosquito larvae.

Although only two species are described here, up to 30 are recognized by some authors. Rigid hornwort *Ceratophyllum demersum* has once or twice-forked leaves and fruits with two spines at the base, while the rarer soft hornwort *C. submersum* has leaves divided three or four times and fruits without spines. Both species thrive in still fresh or brackish water, in ponds and ditches throughout Europe, temperate Asia and North Africa, while rigid hornwort is also widespread in North America. Both hornworts are popular aquarium plants.

**Ceratophyllaceae; 2 species**

### CICUTA

A small genus of northern temperate regions, especially North America. Most species are highly poisonous, including the sole European species cowbane or water hemlock *Cicuta virosa*, the roots of which produce tetanic convulsions and are fatal to cattle, and the American cowbane *C. maculata*, said to be the most poisonous plant native to the United States, which has been responsible for several infant deaths.

*C. virosa*, is a tall hairless perennial with triangular leaves divided several times into narrow toothed leaflets. The convex umbels are 7-13 cm (2.8-5 in) in diameter and composed of many tiny (3 mm/0.1 in) white flowers which are pollinated by insects. It thrives in shallow water in ditches and marshes from north-central Europe, including the British Isles, through temperate Asia.

American cowbane *C. maculata* has magenta-streaked stems and small, dome-shaped, white-flowered umbels about 8 cm (3 in) wide. It grows in wet meadows, damp woodlands and freshwater swamps from Canada and southern Ontario to Nova Scotia, through New England to Florida and into Texas. Other American species, all of which are poisonous, are western water hemlock *C. douglasii*, found throughout the Rocky Mountains from Alaska to Alberta, to Arizona and New Mexico; *C. bulbifera*, a smaller plant of the northern Rockies; and *C. mackenzieana* of Alaska and western Canada.

**Umbelliferae; 8 species**

*Cephalotus follicularis*

## DAMASONIUM

A tiny genus found in southern Eurasia, western North America and southern Australia. The best known species is thrumwort or starfruit *Damasonium alisma*, an erect, hairless annual up to 20 cm (8 in) tall, with long-stalked, floating or submerged leaves. The hermaphrodite flowers, about 6 mm (0.2 in) in diameter, have white petals, each with a yellow spot at the base. The distinctive fruit has 6-10 long-beaked carpels arranged in a star-shaped cluster, hence the common name. Starfruit, which occurs in Europe, North Africa and Asia, is now rare over much of its European range, decreasing as its natural habitat of gravelly ditches and farm ponds gradually disappears. It is protected by law in Britain.

**Alismataceae; 5 species**

## DARLINGTONIA

The sole member of this genus of carnivorous herbs is the Californian pitcher plant or cobra lily *Darlingtonia californica*. It was discovered in 1841 near Mount Shaston in California by J. D. Brockenridge and later described and named by John Torrey in honour of his colleague Dr William Darlington. The distribution of this strange plant borders the Pacific Coast of the United States in southwest Oregon and northern California, generally occurring in peat bogs and around springs in the mountains.

Cobra lilies are so called because their tubular pitchers, which terminate in hood-like structures, resemble nothing so much as one of these venomous snakes rearing up to strike at its prey. The pitchers arise in an upright cluster from an underground rhizome, reaching 10-75 cm (4-30 in) in height. The tube is inflated at the tip to form a dome-like hood, beneath which is located an elliptical mouth. From the upper margin of the mouth hangs a forked, leafy structure known as the 'fishtail', which represents the apex of the leaf. The pitcher tube twists so that the mouth and fishtail point outwards, to enhance the possibility of attracting prey.

Insects and other small invertebrates are attracted to nectar secreted by glands on the hood, the rim of the mouth and the fishtail. When they have finished feeding, light shining through the window-like areolae in the roof of the dome confuses the victims into flying upwards instead of out through the mouth. The inside of the pitcher is smooth, offering virtually no foothold to the exhausted insects, and numerous downward-pointing hairs prevent their escape. No digestive enzymes are secreted, but a watery substance exuded by the pitcher walls collects in the bottom of the tube. Here bacteria accumulate which are able to break down the bodies of drowned insects, and the nutrient 'broth' so formed is gradually absorbed by the plant.

The flowers of the cobra lily are also rather spectacular: there are five pale green, tongue-shaped sepals which spread out over a nodding crimson flower rather resembling a fritillary (see *Fritillaria*). On account of the limited geographic range of *D. californica* and the threat from over-collection, this plant is listed in Appendix II of CITES (Convention on International Trade in Endangered Species of Wild Fauna and Flora).

**Sarraceniaceae; a single species**

## DECODON

The sole member of this genus, swamp loosestrife or water willow *Decodon verticillatus,* is confined to the eastern and southeastern United States, where it grows in swamps, bogs and on the margins of shallow ponds and lakes. This robust herb forms large thickets of many intertwined arching stems, each up to 2.4 m (8 ft) long. If a stem comes into contact with the water, it may develop a patch of spongy, air-filled tissue allowing it to float and eventually to produce roots and new arching stems. The bell-shaped, bright pink, five-petalled flowers are produced in the axils

*Drosera intermedia*

of the paired or whorled upper leaves. Although swamp loosestrife is confined to North America today, fossil evidence shows that, under different world climatic conditions, its range once extended to Eurasia.

**Lythraceae; a single species**

## DIONAEA

Like many of the carnivorous plant taxa, this genus contains but a single species the Venus's flytrap *Dionaea muscipula*. This incredible product of evolution grows only in moist sandy areas and pine forests on the coastal plain of North Carolina and northeast South Carolina in the southeastern United States – an area commonly known as the pine barrens. It was first recorded in the eighteenth century by Arthur Dobbs, then Governor of North Carolina. The generic name was conferred on the plant by the Swedish botanist Linnaeus, Dionaea being one of the Greek names for Venus.

The leaves, which are also capable of photosynthesis, are arranged in a rosette, the winged petioles supporting the bilobed trap for which these plants are famous. Spaced along the margins of the lobes are 15-20 spine-like teeth which interlock when the trap is sprung. On the central cushion of each lobe are a few trigger hairs, usually three, while the entire surface is covered with microscopic glands. Those in a band immediately below the spines produce nectar, while those on the remainder of the lobe have a digestive function, their red pigmentation imparting a pinkish flush to the inside of the trap (the nectar-secreting zone remains green).

Insects and other invertebrates are attracted to the plant by both the scent of the nectar and the reddish colour of the traps, although some, including spiders, may be incidental visitors. One touch of a trigger hair is insufficient to spring the trap: two or more contacts of the trigger hairs within about 20 seconds is necessary, since the trap remains closed for some 24 hours and could waste much of its working life if, for example, windblown debris was to operate the mechanism accidentally. Each trap is only able to

catch and digest three insects during its life, after which it becomes inactive or dies.

Another interesting feature is that the trap closes in two distinct stages. The first phase involves an interlinking of the teeth, enabling many smaller insects to escape and therefore avoiding the onset of the digestive processes except in cases worth the effort. The trap remains in this state for about 30 minutes, after which, if there has been a false alarm, it will gradually reopen, taking about 24 hours to complete the process.

If a sizeable victim has been caught, however, the second phase begins, in which the two lobes compress tightly and crush the victim. Acid enzymes are then secreted from the digestive glands, which are also responsible for the absorption of the products of digestion. All that remains are the chitinous husk and wings of the insect. The exact processes by which the trigger hairs so rapidly release the turgidity pressure that holds the two lobes apart are as yet not fully understood.

The Venus's flytrap produces clusters of white flowers at the top of a leafless stalk which grows from the leaf rosette in May and June. Each flower is about 2.5 cm (1 in) in diameter and has five sepals and petals. Because of the severe depletion of wild populations by over-collection for the houseplant trade, *D. muscipula* is classified as an endangered species in both North and South Carolina and is protected by law in North Carolina.

**Droseraceae; a single species**

## DROSERA

A more or less cosmopolitan genus of carnivorous perennial herbs, especially common in the southern hemisphere, in which the upper surface of the leaf-blade is thickly covered with reddish tentacles, each tipped with a glistening drop of mucilage. The common name of sundews translates literally from the Latin *ros solis*, their former name, while the generic name derives from *droseros*, a Greek word meaning 'dewy'.

Almost all sundews, although ranging widely

through both hemispheres in a variety of climatic conditions, are found in poor, usually acid soils such as those associated with peat bogs. Some of the Australian species, however, have adapted to much drier habitats. The dimensions of the various species are very variable, with leaves ranging from 1.5 mm (0.06 in) to around 60 cm (24 in) in length. The leaves may form rosettes at ground level or occur on the stems, their shape ranging from circular or linear in outline to much divided.

The longest tentacles are found around the edges of the leaves. These are directed outwards, usually in approximately the same plane as the leaf and, on tactile stimulation, are able to move inwards towards the centre, sometimes with amazing rapidity. Towards the middle of the leaf the tentacles diminish in size and become increasingly upright until, at the very centre, they are completely vertical.

Each tentacle comprises a gland-tipped stalk, the glands usually being reddish in colour and having three distinct functions. They secrete mucilage to trap and overcome their prey, they produce enzymes which, together with a weak acid contained in the mucilage, digest the bodies of their victims, and they are also able to absorb the resultant nutrient 'broth', although in this they are aided by tiny hairs scattered over the leaf surface and the stalks of the tentacles.

An insect inadvertently landing on a sundew leaf (it is still not known whether the plant actively attracts its victims, since no nectar-producing organs are present) will stick to these tentacles, and in its struggle will become firmly ensnared. If the victim is trapped towards the outer zone of the leaf, the tentacles are able to bend inwards, so carrying their prey to the centre where the glands are thickest and digestion and absorption most rapid. In many species the leaves themselves curl around a victim thus bringing more glands into contact with the body. This movement, however, may take many hours and does not start until the insect is overcome. It therefore plays no part in the actual trapping of the victim, as was once thought.

Sundew flowers may be solitary or many to a stem, ranging from 2.5 mm (0.1 in) in diameter in the smallest species to almost 5 cm (2 in) in the largest. The five petals may be any colour from white to purple, red, orange or yellow, depending on species, local variety or habitat. In South Africa, for example, *Drosera cistiflora*, one of the most beautiful of all sundews, found in western Cape Province, may have white, cream, pink or mauve flowers, or even a bright scarlet form.

The Australian forked sundew *D. binata*, found in Queensland, New South Wales, Victoria and South Australia, has papery white or pink flowers and distinctive leaves with two narrow lobes ascending from a long petiole, which themselves may divide into two several times. It is one of over 60 species found on this island continent, most of which occur in Western Australia. The pygmy sundews are unique to Australia, including *D. pygmaea*, which has leaves so small they are seldom larger than a single tentacle of *D. binata*.

Round-leaved sundew *D. rotundifolia* and great, or narrow-leaved, sundew *D. anglica* are circumboreal species (extending as far south as Japan, Florida and central Europe) of wet acid moors and peat bogs; oblong-leaved sundew *D. intermedia*, also known as the love-nest sundew, favours similar habitats in northern and western Europe, extending east into the USSR. The juice of round-leaved sundew has been used with some success in the treatment of whooping cough, corns and warts, while in America it has been advocated as a cure for old age!

Thread-leaved sundew *D. filiformis*, which has lavender-rose flowers and stringy leaves, occurs in the southeastern United States on wet, sandy areas near the coast. Other North American species include spatulate-leaved sundew *D. leucantha*, pink sundew *D. capillaris* and dwarf sundew *D. brevifolia*. Two

species of sundew are even found in the Himalayas, including *D. peltata*, with stalked, half-moon-shaped leaves borne alternately on an erect stem 10-30 cm (4-12 in) tall, which also occurs in India, China, Japan, southeast Asia, Malaysia and eastern Australia.

**Droseraceae; about 80 species**

### EGERIA

This tiny genus of two species of aquatic herbs is native to still or slow-moving waters in subtropical South America. The better known species is *Egeria densa*, which, because of its popularity as an aquarium plant, has been accidentally introduced into the wild in many parts of the world, including northwest and central Europe.

In both species all the foliage is completely submerged, but the flowers are pollinated above the surface by insects. The linear leaves are stalkless and arranged in whorls. Spikes bearing either male or female flowers are produced by the same plant; the male spike has 2-4 flowers while the female spike has a single flower. Each flower has three sepals and three petals, the white petals longer (up to 11 mm/0.4 in) and wider than the sepals.

**Hydrocharitaceae; 2 species**

### EICHHORNIA

A small genus of tropical and subtropical American aquatic plants which was named after the Prussian minister J. A. F. Eichhorn. The best known species is undoubtedly the water hyacinth *Eichhornia crassipes* (*E. speciosa*), a floating plant with leaves arranged in a rosette around a short stem which terminates in numerous comb-like roots. The leaf stalks are distinctly swollen, the tissue within containing air cells which increase the buoyancy of the plant, while the broad leaf blade is smooth, pale green and oval or kidney-shaped.

The large flowers of the water hyacinth are arranged in a compact spike. Each flower has six bluish purple or lavender perianth segments, united at the base, the upper segment having a conspicuous yellow spot at its base. The stamens, which have yellow-tinged anthers, project from the centre of the flower and curve upwards distinctively. The floating rosettes reproduce by means of runners which arise in the axils of the leaves, each producing a new rosette in a manner similar to that of the household spiderplant *Chlorophytum elatum*.

*E. crassipes*, a native of Brazil, was introduced to India at the end of the nineteenth century and to Africa in the middle of the twentieth century. In many countries its exceptional ability to reproduce itself vegetatively has resulted in the choking of many bodies of natural and artificial water, as well as increasing the incidence of bilharzia and malaria by providing shelter for their host creatures of snails and mosquito larvae. It is now one of the world's most menacing aquatic weeds, since herbicides seem to have little effect. Alternative methods of control include putting it to use as compost or pig food, for paper making and as a source of potash.

Water hyacinth has also been introduced to North America, where it has become a major pest of subtropical waterways in the southern United States. Research is currently exploring the possibility of using it to remove nutrients from over-enriched waters, as well as heavy metals and other toxins from polluted areas. *E. crassipes* has also been introduced to, and caused similar problems in, Portugal, Indonesia and Australia. Other species include the peacock hyacinth *E. azurea*, native of Brazil whose flowers have two different forms.

**Pontederiaceae; 7 species**

### ELATINE

Commonly known as waterworts, the aquatic or marsh herbs of this small genus are distributed throughout the tropical and temperate regions of the world. The simple leaves are opposite or whorled and

the flowers are hermaphrodite, each having three or four petals.

Six-stamened waterwort *Elatine hexandra* has short-stalked strap-shaped leaves arranged in whorls of four or opposite pairs around the stem, with tiny long-stalked flowers in the leaf axils. Each six-stamened flower has three greenish sepals, arranged alternately with three pale pink petals. It grows in ponds with acid waters and on wet mud in western and central Europe. Eight-stamened waterwort *E. hydropiper*, from northern and central Europe, the southeastern USSR, western Asia and North Africa, is very similar but the flowers are stalkless and have four sepals, four petals and eight stamens.

Other species are *E. ambigua* from southern and eastern Asia; *E. brochonii* from North Africa; *E. macropoda* from the western Mediterranean region; and *E. hungarica* from eastern Europe extending into western Asia. *E. alsinastrum* is a popular aquarium species from the Mediterranean and Eurasia, noted for its handsome whorled foliage.

**Elatinaceae; 12 species**

### EURYALE

The sole member of this genus, golden waterlily *Euryale ferox*, occurs in Asia from China to northern India, although fossil evidence shows that it was once also found in Europe. In China this handsome waterlily has been cultivated for its edible and medicinal seeds and rhizomes for around 3,000 years, the seeds being a source of arrowroot.

*E. ferox* is rather similar to the Amazonian waterlily (see *Victoria*), but the leaves are not turned up to form a rim, the flowers are smaller and all the anthers are fertile. The floating leaves are rounded or oval, from 30-120 cm (12-48 in) in diameter, green and corrugated above and red or purple with thick spiny veins, beneath. The leaf stalks are also prickly, 1-2 m (3.3-6.6 ft) long, and automatically lengthen and curl with changes in water level so that the leaves are always floating. The partially submerged flowers, which have many petals and stamens, are bright red within and shining green on the outside.

**Nymphaeaceae; a single species**

### GROENLANDIA

The sole member of this genus is opposite-leaved pondweed *Groenlandia densa*, which is native Europe, western Asia and North Africa. It aquatic herb with submerged leaves but emergent flowering spikes, each bearing up to four hermaphrodite wind-pollinated flowers. The leaves are all arranged in opposite pairs, or sometimes in whorls of three, a feature which distinguishes *Groenlandia* from its close relative *Potamogeton*, in which the leaves are alternate. Opposite-leaved pondweed thrives in streams, canals, ditches and ponds, wherever the water is clear and rich in nutrients, often over calcareous substrata.

**Potamogetonaceae; a single species**

### HAMMARBYA

The sole member of this northern temperate genus is the bog orchid *Hammarbya paludosa*. Although it is a local and uncommon orchid it occurs in northern, central and eastern Europe, USSR and northeast Asia and North America. The flowering spikes are 3-12 cm (1.2-4.5 in) tall, with numerous tiny, yellowish green flowers which are rotated through a full 180° so that the lip points upwards. The flowers are pollinated by tiny flies.

Bog orchids, as their name suggests, thrive in acid marshes and bogs, usually in conjunction with sphagnum mosses. They have an interesting method of vegetative reproduction which involves the development of small buds, called bulbils, at the tips of the leaves. When mature these bulbils drop into the surrounding sphagnum moss and are quickly infected by a fungus which enables the orchid to obtain food in the wet, oxygen-poor soil. Their

*Eichhornia crassipes*

*Hammarbya paludosa*

development into adult flowering plants takes only a few years and is relatively rapid in comparison with other orchids.

**Orchidaceae; a single species**

### *HELIAMPHORA*

A small genus of carnivorous plants confined to the Guyana Highlands in South America. Commonly known as sun pitchers, their pitchers are rather primitive in design, consisting of little more than a leaf rolled around and sealed to form a slender tube, the apex of the leaf remaining unjoined. The Venezuelan uplands in which they grow experience one of the highest rainfalls in the world, resulting in the formation of numerous streams and swamps which form an ideal habitat for the plants.

The pitchers vary according to species from 5-35 cm (2-14 in) in length and fill with rainwater soon after they mature. The upper parts of the pitcher are covered with nectar glands to attract prey, these becoming interspersed with long, downward-pointing hairs where the tube proper begins. Within the tube the surface becomes smooth and glossy, offering little foothold to insects, which fall into the liquid below. Unlike more advanced members of this family (see *Sarracenia*), sun pitchers have no enzyme-secreting glands and are completely reliant on bacteria living in the pitcher to break down the bodies of their prey. The nutrients so obtained dissolve readily in the water and are easily absorbed by the plant.

Sun pitcher flowers are nodding and several to a stem. Although there are no petals, each flower has

*Hottonia palustris*

between four and six petaloid sepals which are usually white, turning pink with age. The smallest sun pitcher, *Heliamphora minor,* which has pitchers on average only 7 cm (2.8 in) tall, is confined to Mt Auyan-Tepui; the slightly larger *H. nutans* is confined to Mount Roraima; while *H. heterodoxa*, in which the pitchers may be 25 cm (10 in) tall, occurs only on Mt Ptari-Tepui, where it was first discovered as recently as 1951.

**Sarraceniaceae; 5 species**

### HELONIAS
There is but a single member of this genus – swamp pink *Helonias bullata* – which is confined to the eastern United States of America. This handsome lily, which may reach almost 1 m (3.3 ft) in height, has more or less leafless stems terminating in dense, oval clusters (1 cm/0.4 in) of small up to 7.5 cm (2.9 in) long, fragrant, pink-purple flowers. Each flower has six pink perianth segments (3 sepals and 3 petals) and six protruding blue-tipped stamens.

*Helonias bullata* grows in swamps and bogs from New York to Virginia and the mountains of northwest Georgia, but is becoming increasingly rare as drainage takes its toll on the wetlands of the eastern United States.

**Liliaceae; a single species**

### HIPPURIS
The sole member of this genus is a perennial aquatic herb with a more or less cosmopolitan distribution, although distinct ecological races may occur. Mare's-tail *Hippuris vulgaris* has erect emergent stems up to around 1 m (3.3 ft) tall if partly submerged, but only reaching a maximum of 20 cm (8 in) in terrestrial forms. The narrow hard-tipped leaves are arranged around the stem in whorls of 6-12. The small, greenish, solitary flowers, most of which are hermaphrodite, are situated in the axils of the leaves and are pollinated by wind.

Mare's-tail grows in lakes, ponds and slow-moving streams, often in base-rich waters, throughout most of Europe, western and northern Asia, North Africa, North America and southernmost South America. The young leaves are eaten by Eskimos and a decoction was formerly considered efficacious in the treatment of intestinal ulcers, internal bleeding and minor inflammations of the skin. *Hippuris* is the Greek word for 'mare's tail'.

**Hippuridaceae; a single species**

### HOTTONIA
This genus of floating aquatic herbs is named after Hotton, an early Leyden professor of Botany. The distributions of the two species do not overlap, since *Hottonia palustris* occurs only in Europe and western Asia and *H. inflata* is essentially a North American plant. Both species often form great carpets on standing or slow-moving water, flowering prolifically for a season before disappearing without a trace for several years.

The water-violet *H. palustris* has finely divided submerged leaves arranged in whorls around the floating stem. The white or lilac-pink flowers about 2 cm (1.8 in) in diameter have a five-lobed calyx with a yellow eye and are arranged in whorls. They produce nectar and are pollinated by insects. Featherfoil *H. inflata* differs in having inflated hollow stalks bearing whorls of tiny, greenish white flowers, both terminally and at the nodes. Each 8 mm (0.3 in) wide flower, is inconspicuous compared with the larger green sepals.

**Primulaceae; 2 species**

### HYDROCHARIS
Another genus of exclusively aquatic herbs, both species of which are confined to the Old World. The best known species is frogbit *Hydrocharis morsus-ranae*, whose natural range covers most of temperate Eurasia and which has also become naturalized in

*Heliamphora nutans*

North America. Frogbit is a floating herb with stalked, rounded or kidney-shaped leaves and unisexual flowers. One to four male flowers are arranged in a stalked spike, but the female flower is solitary. Both types of flowers have three crinkly white petals, 10 mm (0.4 in) long and with a yellow spot at the base. Frogbit grows in ponds, ditches and slow-flowing rivers, usually in calcareous districts, but is generally decreasing as wetland drainage and water-based contaminants take their toll. This species is also popular in large freshwater aquaria.

**Hydrocharitaceae; 2 species**

### LIMOSELLA
This is a small, almost cosmopolitan genus of annual herbs, several of which are typical of the muddy margins of ponds, especially those drying up in the summer. For this reason they are commonly known as mudworts.

Mudworts are creeping plants with runners growing above or below ground, producing new rosettes at the nodes. *Limosella aquatica* is probably the best known and most widespread species, with a distribution ranging across most of Europe (except the Mediterranean), Egypt, arctic and temperate Asia, Japan, India, Greenland and North America from Labrador to Northwest Territory and the mountains of California and Colorado. It has small, bell-shaped, white or lavender flowers only 2-5 mm (0.1-0.2 in) wide on long stalks which arise from the centre of the rosettes of slender spoon-shaped leaves. *L. aquatica* is not a common species, especially in Europe, since its preferred habitat is declining as the drainage of small wetlands for agriculture is becoming increasingly common.

Other species of mudwort are *L. australis*, which grows in similar habitats, especially those subject to periodic flooding, in Wales, eastern North America from Labrador to Maryland, Africa and Australia; and *L. tenella*, which is confined to muddy lakeshores in northwest Greece (Timfi Oros).

**Scrophulariaceae; 11 species**

*Menyanthes trifoliata*

## LITTORELLA

A small genus of perennial aquatic herbs with three widely distributed species: one in Europe, excluding the Mediterranean region, one in North America and one in temperate south America. The latter, *Littorella australis,* occurs in southern Patagonia and Tierra del Fuego.

The European species is shoreweed *L. uniflora,* which often forms extensive mats in shallow water. It has slender, far-creeping stolons which produce roots and new rosettes at the nodes, and semicylindrical leaves. The unisexual wind-pollinated flowers are borne in short spikes, with male flowers in the upper part and female flowers below. Each is only a maximum of 6 mm (0.2 in) in diameter, the male flowers slightly larger than the female. Flowers are only produced when the water level drops and the plant is exposed, probably as a failsafe against adverse conditions.

Shoreweed grows in shallow water down to depths of about 4 m (13 ft), or just exposed on the sandy and gravelly shores of base-poor lakes and ponds. It is fairly common throughout western, central and northern Europe and is also found in the Azores.

**Plantaginaceae; 3 species**

## LURONIUM

The sole member of this genus, floating water plantain *Luronium natans,* is a slender aquatic herb confined to western and central Europe where it flourishes in lakes, tarns and canals with acid waters. The floating stems may be up to 50 cm (20 in) long and are rooted at the base. The lower, submerged leaves are reduced to flattened, translucent petioles, while the long-stalked floating leaves have oval or elliptical blades. The solitary hermaphrodite flowers are produced on long slender stems arising in the axils of the leaves, each of the three white petals having yellow spots at the base.

**Alismataceae; a single species**

## MENYANTHES

The only species in this genus is bogbean or buckbean *Menyanthes trifoliata,* which has a circumboreal distribution. The rhizome is used medicinally, as a hop substitute in the fermentation of beer and is also powdered for bread by the Eskimos and in northern Eurasia. Bogbean was formerly valued as a food for preventing scurvy and was also used as a herb tobacco. The generic name, bestowed on the plant by Linnaeus, is derived from two Greek words meaning 'month' and 'flower', possibly suggesting that the plant remains in flower for a month. However, over most of its range bogbean flowers between May and August.

*M. trifoliata* is an aquatic or bog plant with long-stalked, three-lobed leaves and spikes of star-like, pale pink or white flowers about 1.5 cm (0.6 in) in diameter with fringed petals. Both leaves and flowers are raised above the surface of the water. It is distributed across most of Europe, although rare in the Mediterranean region, as well as throughout northern and central Asia, northern Morocco, Greenland and North America. Bogbean is a food-plant of the caterpillars of the elephant hawkmoth *Deilephila elpenor.*

**Menyanthaceae; a single species**

## MYRIOPHYLLUM

A genus with a more or less cosmopolitan distribution, particularly diverse in Australia. Commonly known as water-milfoils, these are perennial aquatic herbs with leaves in whorls of 3-6, rather similar to the hornworts (see *Ceratophyllum*) but with pinnate rather than dichotomously branched leaves. Several species are used as oxygenating plants in aquaria.

Water-milfoils may be free floating or anchored to the substratum by means of rhizomes, but the leafy shoots are usually submerged. The inflorescence, however, is aerial and consists of a leafy spike

*Myriophyllum spicatum*

around which the flowers are arranged in axillary whorls. The wind-pollinated flowers may be hermaphrodite or unisexual, the upper flowers male, the lower female. Both types of flower are inconspicuous; the male blooms have four small, boat-shaped petals which are reduced or absent in the female.

Spiked water-milfoil *Myriophyllum spicatum,* in which the male flowers have dull red petals, is found in lakes, ponds and ditches in calcareous districts in Eurasia, North Africa and North America. Alternate-flowered water-milfoil *M. alterniflorum* has red-streaked, yellow-petalled male flowers and prefers base-poor or peaty waters throughout Europe, including central USSR, to southern Scandinavia and Finland, and also occurs in Iceland and Greenland, North America and the Azores.

Whorled water-milfoil *M. verticillatum* has greenish yellow male flowers and thrives in base-rich waters in Eurasia north to the Arctic Circle and south to North Africa, as well as in both North and South America. Parrot's feathers *M. aquaticum* is native to tropical America but is a popular aquarium plant and has become naturalized in southern England, southwest France, Africa and the United States. *M. heterophyllum* is native to eastern North America, and *M. verrucosum* is an Australian species with pinkish, hermaphrodite flowers.

**Haloragidaceae; about 40 species**

## NAJAS

This genus of submerged, aquatic, annual or perennial herbs has a more or less cosmopolitan distribution, although it is particularly abundant in temperate and warm regions. Some species are bad weeds of rice fields, but may be put to good use as a green fertilizer and are often valuable as fish food. *Najas* is the only genus in the family.

The narrow leaves are arranged in opposite pairs, or sometimes in whorls of three, and the flowers are unisexual and usually found on the same plant. Male flowers have a single stamen, while female flowers have no perianth and a single carpel. The slender naiad *Najas flexilis* is a brittle annual with stems up to 30 cm (12 in) long which is native to northern and central Europe, USSR and North America, where it grows in lakes. The holly-leaved naiad *N. marina* is a cosmopolitan species of slightly brackish waters, although absent from the colder temperate regions.

*N. gracillima* is an eastern North American species which is extensively naturalized as a weed of rice fields in northern Italy, while *N. graminea* is native to southern Asia, North and East Africa and Australasia but has become naturalized in rice fields

and ditches in northern Italy, Romania and Bulgaria. Little naiad *N. minor* is found in eastern Asian wetlands where it sometimes causes problems by choking irrigation ditches, but is a valuable fish food; in Hawaii the leaves are eaten as a salad vegetable. *N. tenuifolia* occupies a very specific niche, growing only in mudpools at temperatures of around 60°C (140°F) in Java.

**Najadaceae; 35 species**

## NARTHECIUM

A small genus of marshland herbs of northern temperate regions. Commonly known as bog asphodels, they have numerous, erect basal leaves and short inflorescences composed of flowers with six petaloid perianth segments which are more or less free to the base.

The various species tend to have rather restricted distributions. For example, Europe is home to three yellow-flowered species that occur nowhere else. The most common of these is *Narthecium ossifragum,* found in bogs and wet acid heaths in northern and western Europe, east to Sweden and south to northern Portugal. The inflorescences have 6-20 small flowers, yellow inside and greenish outside. These were formerly used as a substitute for saffron in the Shetland Islands and as a hair dye in Lancashire in the seventeenth century.

Other European species are *N. reverchonii,* confined to damp montane habitats on Corsica, and *N. scardicum,* a marshland plant confined to the mountains of the Balkan peninsula. California bog asphodel *N. californicum,* which has yellowish-orange flowers about 1.3 cm (0.5 in) across, grows in springs and bogs in northern California and southern Oregon, while the rarer *N. americanum* is a feature of the New Jersey pine barrens.

**Liliaceae; 7 species**

## NELUMBO

Just two species belong to this genus of perennial aquatic herbs: American lotus *Nelumbo lutea,* which is native to eastern North America, and sacred lotus *N. nucifera* which ranges from warm regions of Asia (from Japan to the Caspian Sea) to Australia. The generic name is derived from the Cingalese word for the lotus flower.

*N. lutea (N. pentapetala)* has bowl-shaped leaves 30-60 cm (12-24 in) wide, carried up to 90 cm (3 ft) above the water on long stalks attached in the middle. The pale yellow, fragrant flowers up to 25 cm (10 in) across have numerous petals and petal-like sepals. This species is found in ponds and slow-moving streams along the east coast of America, from southern

*Narthecium ossifragum*

Ontario to Florida and Texas. Its seeds and rhizomes are edible.

N. nucifera is a sacred plant in India, China and Tibet, where it is known as 'padma' and is devoted to Brahma, whose sacred colour is red. Its white or pink, many petalled flowers, 10-25 cm (4-10 in) in diameter are carried above the water on long stalks. They open in the morning and the petals have fallen by the evening. The floating leaves have a circular shiny blade up to 90 cm (3 ft) across to which the 1-2 m (3.3-6.6 ft) spiny leaf stalk is attached at the centre. This species has long been cultivated in eastern Asia for its starch-rich seeds which are large, floury and taste faintly of aniseed. The rhizomes, edible raw or cooked, are the source of Chinese arrowroot and many parts of the plant are used in local medicine. Sacred lotus is also known as the Egyptian bean, having been introduced to Egypt in about 500 BC, although it is no longer present in the Nile.

**Nelumbonaceae; 2 species**

### NUPHAR

A small genus of perennial waterlilies distributed across northern temperate and cold regions. They have oblong or broadly elliptical, floating or submerged leaves and yellow or purplish cup-shaped or globe-like flowers held above the water surface. Each flower has 4-6 yellowish green sepals and numerous yellow, spoon-shaped petals, usually shorter than the sepals.

Yellow waterlily Nuphar lutea has both leathery floating leaves and thin, translucent submerged leaves and yellow flowers 4-6 cm (1.6-2.4 in) in diameter which are pollinated by small flies and smell of alcohol, hence its local name of brandy bottle. It thrives in lowland lakes, ponds and streams throughout most of Europe, northern Asia and North Africa. Least yellow waterlily N. pumila has smaller,

less fragrant flowers and occurs in upland lakes in northern and central Europe and northern Asia east to Manchuria.

North American species include common spatterdock N. advena, from the United States, which has yellow-green flowers up to 10 cm (4 in) across and leaves usually raised above the water; and bullhead lily N. variegatum, also known as yellow pond lily, which has heart-shaped floating leaves and smaller cup-shaped flowers and is found across Canada and the eastern United States. Small pond lily N. microphyllum distributed from Canada to New Jersey, has leaves only 10 cm (4 in) long and flowers 2.5 cm (1 in) across, while arrow-leaf pond lily N. sagittifolium has leaves at least three times as long as wide and grows in still waters from Virginia to northeast South Carolina.

The Indian pond lily N. polysepala is another North American species, with heart-shaped leaves and flowers up to 10 cm (4 in) across, which may be floating or held just above the surface of the water. It grows in ponds and slow streams from Alaska to California and Colorado. The seeds were formerly ground up for flour and roasted like popcorn by the Klamath Indians, while the rhizomes of N. advena were eaten by other North American Indians.

**Nymphaeaceae; 20 species**

### NYMPHAEA

A cosmopolitan genus of perennial waterlilies, particularly common in the tropics. The generic name pays tribute to the Greek goddesses (nymphs) who dwelt in the world's wild places. According to Pliny these flowers arose from the body of a nymph who had died of unrequited love for Hercules. The rhizomes and seeds of some species are edible and many hybrids between the various species have been cultivated as ornamentals.

Both the large, brightly coloured flowers and the

rounded or heart-shaped leaves may be either floating or held above the surface. Each flower has four greenish sepals and numerous coloured petals, the outermost at least much longer than the sepals (a feature distinguishing this genus from the closely related Nuphar, in which the petals are shorter than the sepals). In some species the flowers open at night.

The white waterlily Nymphaea alba has more or less circular leaves 10-30 cm (4-12 in) across, dark green above and paler or reddish beneath. The flowers, which are open most of the day, are 5-20 cm (2-8 in) in diameter with 20-25 elliptical white or pink-tinged petals arranged around as many as 125 stamens. When newly opened the flowers give off a faint fragrance which attracts a few bees, flies and beetles, but in most cases they are probably self-pollinated. This is essentially a European species, found in lakes, ponds and slow-moving streams, usually at depths of 0.5-3 m (1.7-10 ft). N. candida is another white-flowered European species which occurs in northern, central and eastern Europe, extending west to northern Spain.

Asian waterlilies include the pygmy, or small white, waterlily N. tetragona (= N. pygmaea), small enough for aquarium use and distinguished by its relatively tiny white flowers only 4 cm (1.6 in) across, which have only about 10 petals and open in the afternoon. It is the smallest member of the genus, with oval leaves only 3-5 cm (1.2-2 in) in diameter. Its range covers most of Asia, from Siberia to Japan; North America, from Canada to Maine, Michigan and Minnesota; it is also native to northeast Europe.

In North America the best known and most widespread species is the fragrant waterlily N. odorata, which has floating leaves up to 30 cm (12 in) across and white or pink flowers which rarely exceed 10 cm (4 in) in diameter and have yellow stamens. The flowers usually open from early morning until noon and the rhizomes are a favourite food of

*Nymphaea alba*

*Nelumbo nucifera*

muskrats. This species is native to the eastern United States and Canada, but has also become naturalized in many quiet pools in the west.

The yellow waterlily *N. mexicana*, sometimes known as the sun-lotus or banana waterlily, has bright yellow flowers up to 12 cm (4.5 in) across which are raised about 10 cm (4 in) above the water surface and open from midday to late afternoon. The oval leaves, dark green with brown blotches above and reddish brown beneath, may also rise out of the water in crowded situations. *N. mexicana* was first discovered in Mexico but its natural range also extends to South Carolina and Florida. It is also widely cultivated in Kashmir and other Asian localities.

Several species occur in African fresh waters, including *N. caerulea* (= *N. capensis*), which has blue or mauve flowers up to 20 cm (8 in) across and is widespread in dams, shallow ponds and quiet backwaters of the major rivers over most of Africa but is rare in the south. *N. lotus* is a less common, white- or cream-flowered species which grows in Lake Victoria and Lake Jipe, among other localities (it is also found in hot springs in Romania and extends into warm regions of Asia). Both of these African waterlilies have been found in wreaths on Egyptian mummies dating back to 2000 BC, while *N. caerulea* was used as a narcotic in Ancient Egypt. Another African species, *N. maculata*, has smaller, purple-tinged, white flowers, leaves only about 10

cm (4 in) across and is characteristic of the Gambia, while *N. zanzibarensis* is a typical east African species.

Australia boasts five species of waterlily, the most impressive of which is *N. gigantea*. Its floating, heart-shaped leaves are about 12 cm (4.5 in) in diameter and the flowers are raised well clear of the water, the blue petals contrasting vividly with the bright yellow stamens.

The seeds of *N. lotus* were made into bread in India and the rhizomes were eaten in Africa, despite the fact that the rest of the plant contains the toxic alkaloid nupharin. The underground tubers of *N. alba* were formerly used as a vegetable in northern Europe.

**Nymphaeaceae; 35 species**

*Nymphaea alba*

## NYMPHOIDES

A more or less cosmopolitan genus of aquatic or semiaquatic perennial herbs superficially resembling the waterlily genus *Nymphaea*, although the clusters of small, five-petalled flowers, are quite different from the solitary, many petalled flowers of waterlilies. Some species of *Nymphoides* have edible tubers, while the seeds are used in medicine. On the whole they grow rapidly and are a potential weed menace in the tropics.

*Nymphoides aquatica* has long-stalked, floating, heart-shaped leaves, from which it acquires its common name of floating hearts. The small white flowers, up to 2 cm (0.8 in) across, are arranged in flat-topped clusters, and are found in ponds and

*Nymphoides peltata*

slow-moving streams on the coastal plain of eastern North America between southern New Jersey and Florida and inland to Texas. *N. cordata* has smaller leaves mottled with purple above and is distributed from Newfoundland to Florida, west into Louisiana and north to Ontario.

Fringed waterlily *N. peltata* is a temperate Eurasian species with stems up to 160 cm (5.2 ft) long from which arise kidney-shaped or rounded leaves and few-flowered axillary inflorescences. Each bright yellow flower is 3-4 cm (1.2-1.6 in) in diameter and has distinctive fringed petals. Fringed waterlilies occur in still and slow-flowing rivers across most of Europe and northern and central Asia. Water snowflake *N. indica* is a pantropical species with white or yellow flowers, while *N. cristata* is essentially a plant of eastern Asia.

**Menyanthaceae; 20 species**

### ORONTIUM

The only species in this genus, golden club *Orontium aquaticum*, is native to eastern North America. The rhizomes and seeds have a high starch content and are edible once boiled. It is a perennial aquatic herb with long-stalked, elliptical leaves which may be floating or extend above the surface of the water. The minute flowers are borne on a short (up to 5 cm/2 in), golden-yellow, club-like spadix (hence its common name), and the blue-green fruits are bladderlike and probably distributed by water. Golden club grows in shallow ponds, swamps and marshes from Massachusetts and central New York to Florida and Louisiana, mostly along the coastal plain, but also

*Pinguicula vulgaris*

extending inland to Kentucky and West Virginia.

**Araceae; a single species**

### OTTELIA

A genus of submerged aquatic plants, particularly diverse in tropical and warm regions of the Old World, with a single New World species. The long-stalked leaves have wide blades, are either submerged or partly emergent, and the insect-pollinated flowers are usually hermaphrodite, solitary and carried above the surface of the water. Each flower has three sepals and three much longer and wider petals.

*Ottelia alismoides* is a widespread species with white flowers each 2-3 cm (0.8-1.2 in) petal having a yellow patch at the base. It is native to southeast Asia, Australasia and northeast Africa, but is also naturalized in rice fields in northern Italy, and the leaves are eaten as a green vegetable in Malaysia. *O. ulvifolia* has conspicuous pale yellow flowers and is locally common in East African pools and swamps, while swamp lily *O. ovalifolia* is a white or pale yellow-flowered species common in freshwater ponds throughout Australia, except Tasmania.

**Hydrocharitaceae; 30 species**

### PELTANDRA

A tiny genus of aquatic plants native to North America. The name is derived from the combination of two Greek words: *pelte* ('small shield'), and *aner* (stamens) in reference to the distinctive, shield-shaped stamens.

Arrow arum *Peltandra virginica* is found in shallow ponds, slow-flowing rivers, marshes and swamps, often in large colonies along the east coast of the United States, from Florida and Texas to Canada. As its name suggests, it has long-stalked, arrow-shaped leaves which curl around a slender greenish spathe that protects the club-like spadix within. The flowers are unisexual: those in the upper regions of the spadix are male, while the female flowers at the base give rise to clusters of black berries. The starchy rhizomes, when roasted, were once an important part of the diet of North American Indians. A rarer species, *P. sagittifolia*, is very similar.

**Araceae; 3 species**

### PINGUICULA

This small genus of carnivorous perennial herbs, commonly known as butterworts, is confined mainly to the northern hemisphere, in arctic, temperate and tropical regions. They are particularly abundant in North America and the Mediterranean region, but three species cross the equator into South America. All butterworts prefer wet conditions, although they are found in both acid and alkaline wetlands. Many species appear to be able to exist by photosynthesis alone and are, therefore, not obligate carnivores, although most species actively trap insects and other invertebrates in the summer.

Butterwort leaves are usually pale yellowish green and greasy because of drops of mucilage secreted by the numerous stalked glands that cover the upper surface. The generic name derives from the Latin *pinguis* ('somewhat fat'), in reference to these greasy leaves. Other stalkless glands are responsible for digesting the prey and absorbing the nutrients so produced. The leaves do not have nectar-producing organs, but have a faint odour of fungus which may be attractive to insects. On average the victims are very small, including aphids, springtails, midges and ants, but are caught in great numbers. As soon as an insect alights on the leaf it is hindered by the sticky surface, and its movements to free itself stimulate the production of more mucilage, such that the victim is soon overwhelmed.

In most butterworts, the leaf margins themselves are capable of limited movement, rolling over the bodies of victims in the outer zone of the leaf, thus bringing more glands into contact with the insect and speeding the process of digestion and absorption.

*Pistia stratiotes*

Closer to its centre the leaf can recede beneath the prey, providing a hollow that allows the digestive enzymes to act more efficiently. Both actions ensure that the insect is dealt with rapidly before rain can wash the enzymes away, while the inrolled margin prevents the bodies from being swept off the leaf. humans from the mischief of witches and fairies. The juice of the leaves was formerly used to kill head lice and is still used today to soothe skin sores and chapped hands in humans, and inflamed udders in

Some butterwort flowers are violet-like in appearance, while others more closely resemble small gloxinias. They are solitary, bilaterally symmetrical and spurred, the colour varying from white through pink, lilac, purple, red or even yellow.

Perhaps the best known species is common butterwort *Pinguicula vulgaris*, which is widespread in Eurasia, Canada and the northern United States, especially in mountain areas. The leaves are broad, with upturned margins, and the flowers are a rich

purple. In Elizabethan times it was thought that this species protected cattle from the arrows of elves, and cattle. This substance was also commonly used to curdle milk in Scandinavia, the end product being a ropy substance (called Tätmiölk by the Lapps) which does not separate from the whey. On the other hand, the presence of common butterwort was thought to cause liver flukes in domestic animals, although this is now known to be attributable to grazing livestock on wet pastures, where both butterwort and the free-living phase of the parasites abound.

Large-flowered, or Irish butterwort *P. grandiflora*, is a common western European species which grows in similar conditions to common butterwort, although it favours limestone habitats, and its leaves are said to act as a laxative. Other Eurasian species are alpine butterwort *P. alpina*, a white-flowered montane plant descending to sea level only in Scandinavia; long-leaved butterwort *P. longifolia*, native to the mountains of southern Europe; *P. lusitanica* of bogs and wet heaths in western Europe and North Africa; and *P. hirtiflora* of wet rocks in the mountains of Italy and the Balkans.

Six species of butterwort grow in moist habitats in the southeastern United States, including yellow butterwort *P. lutea*, which is unusual in having deep yellow flowers up to 3 cm (1.2 in) in diameter; violet butterwort *P. caerulea*, whose pale violet flowers are veined with purple; dwarf butterwort *P. pumila* which has pale, lavender-coloured flowers; and primrose-leaved butterwort *P. primulifolia* which is usually found in running water. *P. caudata* is a robust Mexican species with large succulent leaves and carmine-pink flowers, while other Mexican butterworts include the smaller violet-flowered *P. mexicana* and *P. gypsicola*.

### Lentibulariaceae; 46 species

#### PISTIA

The sole member of this tropical and subtropical genus is water lettuce *Pistia stratiotes*, also known as river lettuce or tropical duckweed. It is an aggressive aquatic plant which rapidly covers vast expanses of open water, sometimes growing in such compact masses that it looks like solid ground. This species is a popular aquarium plant and has been known since the time of Pliny (AD 77).

Water lettuce is a small floating aquatic with rosettes of stalkless velvety leaves with parallel veins, densely clothed with short, depressed hairs that repel water. The lower sides of the leaves are swollen with spongy air-filled tissue that also assists the plant in keeping afloat. The inconspicuous unisexual flowers are borne on a short greenish white spadix, male at the apex and female below, and they appear in April. It is a species of still waters, typically occurring in ponds, lakes, ditches and swamps, and its rapid vegetative growth makes it a potential menace in tropical watercourses. Although essentially a tropical species, *P. stratiotes* extends into the southeastern United States where it particularly favours the Florida cypress swamps.

### Araceae; a single species

#### PONTEDERIA

This small genus of emergent aquatic plants is confined to the New World. They have stout creeping rhizomes and emergent leaves from which arises an erect aerial stem bearing a spike of numerous small, violet-blue flowers. Each flower has 6 petaloid perianth segments forming a two-lipped corolla, both lips being three-lobed.

The best known species is pickerel weed *Pontederia cordata* which has flowers about 8 mm (0.3 in) wide with blue anthers. It is native to North America but is occasionally planted in wild situations in western Europe and has become naturalized on lake margins and in irrigation ditches in northern Italy and southern Switzerland. In its natural habitat pickerel weed grows in freshwater marshes and on the margins of lakes, ponds and streams along the east coast of North America from Nova Scotia to Florida and as far west as Missouri and Oklahoma, where it flowers from June to November. It is also a weed of rice fields in South America.

Among the pollinators of pickerel weed is a bee (*Dufourea novae-angliae*) which visits no other plant, timing its emergence to coincide with the plant's flowering. The young leaf stalks, known locally as *wampee*, can be cooked like greens and the seeds may be eaten like nuts.

### Pontederiaceae; 5 species

#### POTAMOGETON

A cosmopolitan genus of perennial aquatic herbs with submerged or floating leaves, a few members of which are subterrestrial. Commonly known as pondweeds, all species of this, the largest genus of aquatic plants, are rooted in the substratum, having creeping rhizomes and more or less erect shoots with alternate leaves. The flowering spikes rise above the surface of the water and bear small and bisexual flowers. In most species pollination takes place in the air, but in a few it occurs underwater. Hybridization between the various species is common.

Pondweeds are found in a wide variety of freshwater habitats, in deep or shallow, stagnant or fast-flowing water, and in acid or base-rich conditions. A few species can tolerate brackish conditions, while others grow subterrestrially in sphagnum bogs or dried-out ponds; in the latter the floating leaves become aerial.

Most pondweeds have a wide distribution. *Potamogeton vaginatus*, for example, occurs in brackish waters in northwest Europe, northern Asia and North America, while fennel-leaved pondweed (called sego pondweed in the United States) *P. pectinatus* has thread-like leaves and branches and is an almost cosmopolitan species; in North America its prolific growth may cause problems by choking canals and irrigation ditches. American pondweed *P. epihydrus*, with elliptical floating leaves and ribbon-like submerged leaves, is very rare as a native plant in Britain, growing only in South Uist in the Outer Hebrides, but it is widely distributed in North America.

Shining pondweed *P. lucens* occurs in base-rich

*Pontederia cordata*

*Pistia stratiotes*

*Pontederia cordata*

Some species have broad floating leaves, some have finely divided submerged leaves, and some have both types of foliage. In all species the small white flowers are held just above the surface of the water on slender stalks. Both ivy-leaved crowfoot *Ranunculus hederaceus*, a sprawling annual or perennial with wide kidney-shaped leaves, and the similar round-leaved crowfoot *R. omiophyllus* have broad floating leaves, are native to western Europe and thrive in mud or shallow water.

*R. circinatus, R. fluitans* and *R. trichophyllus* have thread-like submerged leaves. These annual or perennial plants are found throughout most of Europe in shallow pools and clean rivers, although *R. fluitans* is confined to western and central Europe, and *R. circinatus* is also found in North America. Of the European species with both types of leaves, the most common are *R. baudotii*, a brackish water plant, *R. peltatus,* which thrives in ponds and ditches, and *R. aquatilis,* which favours shallow fresh waters and is also found across much of North America. *R. polyphyllus* is an interesting species of eastern Europe and western Asia. It is an aquatic buttercup with dissected submerged leaves arranged in whorls and small yellow flowers.

Of the yellow-flowered, usually emergent species, several are now very rare because of wetland drainage in Europe. One of the most threatened is adder's-tongue spearwort *R. ophioglossifolius*, a Eurasian and Mediterranean species which grows in wet mud by ponds. This species is the subject of probably the world's smallest nature reserve (in Gloucestershire, England) and is protected by law in Britain. Creeping spearwort *R. reptans*, which roots at the nodes and covers large patches of waterside mud, is another rather rare species of northern Europe, now more or less confined to lake margins in montane habitats, although it also grows in Greenland. It flowers only when its watery habitat recedes, probably as a fail-safe in case of drought, which is then endured by the seeds.

More common species include lesser spearwort *R. flammula*, which was formerly used in the Highlands of Scotland to raise blisters; a tincture is said to cure ulcers. Celery-leaved buttercup *R. sceleratus* is another common yellow-flowered species of pond edges and muddy ditches, but the tall sword-like leaves of greater spearwort *R. lingua* are now a rather rare sight in European wetlands, although its range extends into northern Asia.

The yellow water buttercup *R. flabellaris* is a North American aquatic species of quiet waters and muddy shores which extends across most of the continent

waters throughout Europe and western Asia, while bog pondweed *P. polygonifolius*, grows in shallow acid bog pools and ditches in Europe, northwest Africa and eastern North America. Perfoliate pondweed *P. perfoliatus*, in which the stem appears to pass through the middle of each leaf, is found throughout northern temperate regions and also in Australia.

Broad-leaved pondweed *P. natans*, identified by its heart-shaped floating leaves, is common throughout the northern hemisphere. Its starchy rootstock was formerly used as a source of food, whilst in East Anglia (England) the floating leaves were thought to give rise to young pikes, hence its local name of pickerel weed.

**Potamogetonaceae; about 90 species**

### RANUNCULUS

This large genus is native to temperate and boreal regions. Many species are submerged or floating aquatic herbs with white flowers, commonly called water crowfoots, while other yellow-flowered species are emergent plants which thrive at the margins of fresh waters.

Europe boasts a wide range of water crowfoots.

*Ranunculus hederaceus*

*Ranunculus aquatilis*

from Canada to Louisiana. The golden-yellow flowers are held above the water on stout hollow stems and both dissected submerged leaves and lobed floating leaves are usually present. The swamp buttercup *R. septentrionalis* has leaves divided into three-lobed segments and lax clusters of glossy yellow flowers on weak stems up to 90 cm (3 ft) high. It is typical of swamps and marshes in shady habitats in eastern North America. *R. trullifolius* is one of the most common buttercups in the Falkland Islands, where it grows in shallow pools, open mud and wet sands. It is a creeping plant with rosettes of small, fleshy, wedge-shaped leaves on long slender stalks and solitary yellow flowers about 1 cm (0.4 in) in diameter.

**Ranunculaceae; about 250 species**

## SAGITTARIA

This cosmopolitan genus of perennial aquatic herbs is especially diverse in the Americas. These plants are commonly and generically known as arrowheads because of the distinctive shape of the leaves (Latin *sagitta* = arrow). The rhizomes of some species are a rich source of starch, especially wapato *Sagittaria latifolia*, which was an important food for the North American Indians, and *S. chinensis*, which is used by the Chinese. Arrowhead juice may be used to make ink, but is more widely known for its diuretic properties and as a prevention for scurvy.

Arrowhead *S. sagittifolia*, also known as swan potato or water archer, is a robust perennial, 30-90 cm (12-36 in) in height with submerged, floating and aerial leaves. Those occurring beneath the water are linear and translucent, those at the surface are lanceolate to ovate and those leaves that emerge from the water have long stalks and arrow-shaped blades. Each plant produces both male and female flowers in whorls on the same spike, with the smaller female flowers mainly in the lower part of the inflorescence. Both sexes have three white petals up to 1.5 cm (0.6 in) long, each with a dark violet patch at the base. Arrowhead grows in shallow water in ponds, canals and slow-flowing rivers on muddy substrata and is a widespread species in Eurasia.

In North America, common species include grass-leaved arrowhead *S. graminea*, a plant with grass-like leaves which grows in shallow ponds and muddy habitats throughout eastern North America, the Great Plains and Texas, and wapato duck potato *S. latifolia* which has the typical arrow-shaped leaves and is found across most of the United States and into South America. *S. cuneata* is another widespread North American species. Canadian arrowhead *S. rigida* has white petals with pale yellowish bases. It occurs naturally from Quebec to Tennessee and Minnesota but has also been introduced to the River Exe in southwest Britain.

Less common North American species are the giant arrowhead *S. montevidensis*, also found in warm regions of South America, and the bunched arrowhead *S. fasciculata*, which occurs only in North and South Carolina and is considered an endangered species by the United States Fish and Wildlife Service (1985).

**Alismataceae; 20 species**

## SARRACENIA

A small genus of carnivorous plants native to eastern North America and commonly known as trumpet pitchers. Most of the species are found in damp habitats on the coastal plains of the southeastern States, but one subspecies of the Huntsman's cup *Sarracenia purpurea* grows as far north as arctic Canada. They are popular as house plants, not only because of their interesting form and showy flowers, but also for their value in the control of houseflies and even wasps.

Although pitcher form varies greatly among the species, the basic arrangement consists of leaves fashioned into long, upright, funnel-shaped tubes, terminating in a lid-like structure called the hood. Many species have red or purple venation in the upper part of the tube and hood, while in others this coloration may suffuse the whole pitcher.

Where the mouth of the upright trumpet-shaped pitcher is not interrupted by the hood, it has a rounded rim (the nectar roll), covered with a profusion of nectar-producing glands. In addition, the entire external surface of the pitcher is dotted with nectar glands, particularly towards the top of the tube. The inside of the pitcher has a waxy surface which offers little foothold for potential victims. The upper regions are also clothed with short downward-pointing hairs that deter trapped insects from escaping, while lower down the waxy surface gives way to enzyme-secreting glands. The fluid produced by these glands often accumulates in the base of the pitcher.

*Sarracenia* pitchers attract both flying and terrestrial insects, neither of which stand much chance of escape once within the trumpet. The enzyme solution in the base of the pitcher rapidly breaks down all but the hardest parts of its victims, aided by bacteria introduced to the mature pitcher on the bodies of the insects themselves. The nutrients are then assimilated by the plant, but the chitinous cuticles and wings remain, becoming compacted into the base of the tube by the weight of future victims.

The flowers are also exquisite: large, solitary and nodding, sometimes exceeding 7.5 cm (2.9 in) in diameter. Each bloom consists of five petal-like sepals, beneath which hang the true petals, surrounding a curious umbrella-shaped pistil. The flowers range from pale yellow through pink to deep crimson in colour, with sepals usually darker than petals, while the pistil varies from pale green to white.

Most species of trumpet pitcher have more or less upright pitchers, including the yellow trumpet *S. flava* which has yellow pitchers and flowers, and the green pitcher plant *S. oreophila*, an endangered species known only from northeastern Alabama in the Appalachians, which has yellowish green, fragrant flowers and rather shorter trumpets. This species is now listed on Appendix I of CITES (Convention on International Trade in Endangered Species of Wild Fauna and Flora), along with *S. jonesii* from North

*Sagittaria sagittifolia*

*Sarracenia purpurea*

## SCHEUCHZERIA

The sole member of this genus, and indeed of the family, is *Scheuchzeria palustris*, a perennial herb which grows in sphagnum bogs throughout the colder parts of the northern hemisphere. It has a creeping rhizome and linear leaves, and hermaphrodite wind-pollinated flowers borne on lax inflorescences. Each flower has six yellow-green perianth segments, 2-3 mm (0.1 in) in length, and six stamens. *Scheuchzeria palustris* is commonly known as Rannoch-rush, since in Britain it is found only on Rannoch Moor in Scotland, while its European distribution extends to the montane bogs of the Pyrenees, Alps and Carpathians. Rannoch-rush is now very rare over much of lowland Europe and its populations are still decreasing as a result of the drainage of undisturbed bog habitat for agriculture.

**Scheuchzeriaceae; a single species**

## STRATIOTES

This genus contains the single species, the water soldier *Stratiotes aloides*, also known as soldier's arrow or water aloe. It is confined to Europe and northwest Asia where it grows in still or slow-moving, base-rich waters. The generic name is derived from the Greek word for soldier, presumably in reference to the sword-like leaves. The plant once had a reputation as an unfailing cure for all wounds made by iron weapons.

The water soldier is a perennial aquatic plant with large crown-like rosettes of rigid, serrated, many veined leaves, 15-20 cm (6-8 in) long, rather resembling those of an aloe, hence the specific name *aloides*. The unisexual insect-pollinated flowers are produced on separate plants, both male and female flowers having three white petals, each up to 2.5 cm (1 in) long. At flowering time the rosettes float half-

and South Carolina, and the Alabama pitcher plant *S. alabamensis* ssp. *alabamensis*.

The white trumpet or crimson pitcher plant *S. leucophylla* has white, crimson-veined pitchers and ruby red flowers; the pale pitcher plant *S. alata*, which has creamy flowers, is the only species to occur in Texas; and the sweet trumpet *S. rubra* has bronze-flushed flowers with green pistils, is the smallest species with upright pitchers and is unusual in that it sometimes grows in deep shade.

Other trumpet pitchers have a somewhat different appearance, the pitchers lying more or less flat along the ground. The parrot pitcher *S. psittacina*, which usually grows on wet, sandy, frequently flooded plains, is the only carnivorous plant capable of trapping both terrestrial and aquatic invertebrates. Other species with horizontal pitchers are the hooded pitcher plant *S. minor* which has clear yellow flowers and is the most common of the Florida pitchers, and the huntsman's cup *S. purpurea*, a plant of very wet conditions with numerous subspecies.

**Sarraceniaceae; 8 species**

## SAURURUS

A genus of bog plants consisting of a single North American species and a single east Asian species. The generic name is derived from the combination of two Greek words, *sauros* ('lizard') and *oura* ('tail') in reference to the shape of the drooping flower cluster, which is also reflected in the common name of lizard's tail.

The most familiar species is *Saururus cernuus*, native to eastern North America from Ontario to Florida, Texas, Missouri and Kansas. It is a shallow water species of shady marshes and stream margins with heart-shaped alternate leaves and 15 cm (6 in) flowering spikes which droop at the tip. The tiny, fragrant, whitish flowers have neither sepals nor petals, but instead have showy stamens about 4 mm (0.2 in) in length.

**Saururaceae; 2 species**

*Stratiotes aloides*

submerged at the surface, but in the autumn they sink down to the lower levels to overwinter. The ability of the plants to rise and fall in this way is allegedly linked to the amount of calcium carbonate present on the veins and margins of the leaves.

As a general rule only female plants occur in the north of the water soldier's range, and only male plants in the extreme south, but both sexes occur in the area in between. Where only one sex is found, the water soldier is still able to propagate itself vegetatively by the production of new plants at the ends of runners.

### Hydrocharitaceae; a single species

#### SUBULARIA

A genus containing just two species: one in the mountains of tropical East Africa and one in the northern temperate zone. Both species are small annual or biennial aquatic herbs with fibrous roots and leaves confined to a basal rosette, each leaf triangular in cross section with a pointed tip. The short few-flowered inflorescence is often submerged and bears small white flowers, although sometimes the petals are absent.

The most widespread species is awlwort *Subularia aquatica*, one of the world's few annual aquatic plants, which has leaves 2-7 cm (0.8-2.8 in) long and flowers about 2.5 mm (0.1 in) in diameter, with petals longer than the sepals. These flowers are nectarless and rarely visited by insects, so they have evolved an automatic self-pollination mechanism. Awlwort is not a common plant, occurring only on the margins of base-poor lakes and pools in the mountains of western and northern Europe from Ireland to the USSR, including Siberia. It is also found in northern Greenland and North America.

### Cruciferae; 2 species

#### TRAPA

According to different authorities this genus either contains one very variable species or about 15 distinct ones. Here the water chestnut *Trapa natans* is considered the sole species, with an essentially Old World distribution covering central and southern Europe, Asia and Africa. It is perhaps most famous for its place in Chinese cuisine, the fruits being rich in starch and fats, and is sometimes cultivated. Long before the invention of the wok, however, water chestnuts were a major source of food for Neolithic man, since at this time the species was also widespread in continental northern Europe.

*T. natans* is an annual aquatic herb of still, nutrient-rich waters, which may be rooted in the substratum or free-floating. It has unbranched stems and submerged stalkless leaves as well as lax rosettes of long-stalked (to 17 cm/6.5 in) floating leaves with broadly triangular, toothed blades. The flowers occur in the axils of the floating leaves, have four white petals about 8 mm (0.3 in) long and keeled sepals that become fused to the ovary in fruit, forming 'horns'. The ripe fruits take the form of a nut measuring up to 3.5 x 5.5 cm (1.4 x 2.2 in), although size and the number of horns vary considerably in different parts of the world.

Some of the various 'species' are *T. quadrispinosa* in central and southern Asia, ling nut *T. bicornis* in eastern Asia and singhara nut *T. bispinosa* in tropical Asia. Local names for *T. natans* are water caltrops, saligot and Jesuit's nut.

### Trapaceae; a single species

#### VICTORIA

Only two species belong to this genus of tropical South American water lilies: the Amazon or royal water lily or water-platter *Victoria amazonica* (otherwise known as *V. regia*) and the Santa Cruz waterlily or water-platter *V. cruziana* (sometimes called *V. cruciata*). Hybrids occur where the range of the two species overlaps. The genus was named in honour of England's Queen Victoria who was

*Victoria regia*

monarch at the time when the genus was first discovered.

These rooted aquatics have floating leaves with upturned margins and raised prickly ribs and veins beneath. The flowers open at dusk, close the following morning, open for a second time in the afternoon and finally close the next day, sinking below the surface of the water where the seeds mature. They are white at first, turning pink by the second day and finally changing to red. This colour change is associated with rapid metabolic changes that occur in tropical conditions, and may result from an extremely high level of respiration which also increases the temperature of the flower by as much as 10°C (18°F) over that of the surrounding air.

*V. amazonica* is also known as the giant waterlily because of its enormous circular leaves, usually around 2 m (6.6 ft) in diameter, which are reputed to be capable of supporting the weight of a child (or 40-75 kg/88-165lbs if evenly distributed). Sometimes called the royal waterlily, it is found only in quiet backwaters of the great rivers of Guayana, Bolivia and Amazonia. The fragrance and increased temperature of the 25-40 cm (10-16 in) flowers attract four species of dynastid beetle, which feed on

the starchy appendages of the carpels before leaving with their load of pollen to fertilize another flower. The large olive-green seeds turn black as they mature and are edible if roasted; they are used like maize by the indigenous Indians of the region.

The second species, *V. cruziana*, occurs in northern Argentina, Bolivia and Paraguay. It has smaller leaves with higher upturned margins (12-18 cm (4.5-7 in)) instead of 4-6 cm (1.6-2.4 in) in *V. amazonica*).

### Nymphaeaceae; 2 species

#### VILLARSIA

A genus of perennial aquatic plants, ranging from southeast Asia to Australia, with a single African species. *Villarsia* species have broad thick leaves on long petioles dilated at the base to provide buoyancy, and a loose cluster of flowers arising from the base of the plant.

There are some 14 species in Australia, including the attractive yellow marsh flower *Villarsia exaltata*. This erect marsh plant grows to a height of 30-45 cm (12-18 in) and is distinguished by its tufts of rounded or kidney-shaped leaves and large yellow star-shaped flowers, each about 2 cm (1.8 in) in diameter with five bearded spreading petals. *V. exaltata* is found in

swampy land along the coast of Queensland and New South Wales.

**Menyanthaceae; 16 species**

*WOLFFIA*

This small genus is distributed across the tropical, warm and temperate regions of the world. Its members are minute aquatic plants without recognizable stems, leaves or roots, which rarely flower and are commonly known as water-meal. The most widespread species *Wolffia arrhiza*, which occurs in Eurasia, Africa, America and Australia, is generally considered to be the smallest flowering plant in existence, but even more minute are India's *W. microscopica* and the Brazilian *W. brasiliensis*. The latter is commonly found growing with the gargantuan Amazonian water lily (see *Victoria*) and is distributed in birds' feathers.

Rootless duckweed *W. arrhiza* is nevertheless the smallest European vascular plant. The floating plant body, or thallus, is oval or rounded, less than 1 mm (0.04 in) across, and lacks roots or veins. It has pores (stomata) in parallel rows and a deep reproductive pouch from which new thalloid growths are 'budded off'. Rootless duckweed is entirely vegetative in its manner of reproduction in Europe, where it is possibly

introduced. It is sometimes used in quantitative tests for herbicide pollution of fresh waters in Poland.

**Lemnaceae; about 7 species**

*XYRIS*

A large genus of herbaceous marsh plants of tropical and subtropical regions of the world, especially the southeastern United States, tropical America and southern Africa. Commonly known as yellow-eyed grasses, these perennial plants have bisexual flowers with three yellowish petals fused into a tube and three sepals, one of which forms a hood over the petals. *Xyris* is an ancient name for iris.

*Xyris iridifolia* is a typical North American species which has flat, linear, iris-like leaves up to 80 cm (32 in) long. The flower stalks carry oval heads with reddish brown, scale-like bracts enclosing the yellow flowers, each about 1.3 cm (0.5 in) in diameter. *X. iridifolia* grows in wet peaty or sandy places from North Carolina to Florida and Texas. The smaller *X. torta*, which grows to a maximum of 30 cm (12 in) and has twisted needle-like leaves, is a much more widespread species. Also in North America, the leaves and roots of *X. ambigua* were formerly used to treat colds, while those of *X. caroliniana* were

efficacious in the treatment of skin disease.

One of the dozen or so Australian species is tall yelloweye *X. operculata*, which is distinguished by its rush-like leaves and bright yellow, papery flowers. It grows in swampy land on the coasts of Queensland, New South Wales, Victoria, South Australia and Tasmania. Eight species of yellow-eyed grass are found in South Africa, including *X. capensis*, in which the flowering stem rises high above the basal rosette of narrow leaves.

**Xyridaceae; about 240 species**

*ZANNICHELLIA*

A tiny genus of perennial submerged aquatic herbs with a cosmopolitan distribution. Horned pondweed *Zannichellia palustris* has much-branched, slender stems and narrow opposite leaves, 0.5-2 mm (0.02-0.1 in) wide and 1.5-5 cm (0.6-2 in) long. The unisexual flowers are produced in more or less stalkless clusters in the axils of the leaves, usually one male flower and 2-6 female flowers together in a tiny cup-shaped sheath. Horned pondweed is found in still or slow-moving, often slightly brackish waters throughout the lakes, rivers and ditches of the world.

**Zannichelliaceae; 2 species**

# CHAPTER NINE

# COASTLANDS

A constantly changing frontier between terrestrial and marine environments, the coastline of the world's continents and islands is about 1.5 million km (1 million miles) in length. Along sheltered stretches of coastline the deposition of fine sediments by both tides and rivers creates raised mudflats in the intertidal zone. These mudflats support salt-marsh vegetation between the polar regions and warm temperate zones, and mangrove swamps in a belt around the tropics. Salt-marshes are dominated by succulent annual herbs and woody perennials, particularly members of the Chenopodiaceae and Plumbaginaceae, whilst mangrove swamps are dominated by trees, with few herbs because of the high levels of shade.

On exposed gently sloping coasts onshore winds pile loose sand into parallel ridges of dunes. Here flowering plants are confined to the region above the strand line, out of reach of all but the highest spring tides. The build up of organic detritus along the strand line enables the sea-dispersed seeds of annual pioneer plants to germinate, their roots trapping more windblown sand until a small dune develops. As the dune stabilizes and grows, the characteristic rich and diverse sand dune flora develops, many species of which display drought resistant features to combat the associated lack of water. In other exposed situations ridges of shingle develop, while rocky shores backed by cliffs support plant communities which thrive in the spray lifted by the thundering waves.

Undersea meadows develop below the low-tide mark on soft substrata in the shallow seas surrounding both tropical and temperate coasts. These communities, which thrive at depths of between 6 and 50 m (20-165 ft), depending on the clarity of the water, are home to a few dozen species of flowering plants known as sea-grasses. These are not true grasses but are representatives of several families that have adapted to a truly marine environment, even to the extent of having submarine pollination mechanisms.

The main characteristic linking all species of flowering plants that thrive in coastal habitats is their ability to cope with high levels of salinity. Known as halophytes, these plants must match the external salt concentration to that of their cell sap and so combat osmotic forces that would otherwise prevent their being able to absorb water. In many cases halophytes are succulent plants, retaining a reservoir of water in their tissues for use when uptake from the environment is not possible. Some also have salt glands which enable them to excrete excess salt crystals through their stems and leaves, and many produce seeds that are dispersed by the sea and are able to germinate in saline conditions.

Facing page: dunes, Northumberland, England.

Mangrove swamp, Fiji.

*Posidonia oceanica*

*Glaucium flavum*

Dunes, Coto Donana, Spain.

Red mangrove, Florida, USA.

## ARTHROCNEMUM

A small genus of hairless dwarf shrubs with a cosmopolitan distribution in coastal habitats, especially salt marshes. The opposite leaves are scale-like but dilated and clasping the stem at the base, and where each pair is fused to form a fleshy, cylindrical stem segment. The spike-like inflorescences are also segmented, each flower has four perianth segments and two stamens. There is much confusion over the taxonomic distinction between *Arthrocnemum* and the closely related *Salicornia*, although in general perennial species are placed in the former genus and annual species belong to the latter. The leaves of some species are edible.

*Arthrocnemum perenne*, a plant of salt marshes in southern and western Europe, has short creeping stems that form mats up to 1 m (3.3 ft) across; the stems are green when young, becoming reddish or brownish with age. The similar *A. fruticosum*, essentially a southern European species, is distinguished by its blue-green stems up to 1 m (3.3 ft) long. *A. glaucum* (*A. macrostachyum*) is a sprawling, glaucous shrub of the coastal dunes and salt marshes of southern Europe and the Middle East, the branches turning yellowish or reddish with age.

*A. salicornicum* thrives in muddy littoral habitats in the Middle East and tolerates twice-daily immersions in sea water. It has reddish stems and flowers twice, from September to October and January to February. *A. pachystachyum* grows on the shores of the western Indian Ocean.

**Chenopodiaceae; about 10 species**

## BATIS

This genus contains just two species *Batis maritima* and *B. argillicola* although some authorities consider *B. maritima* to be the sole representative, of both genus and family.

Saltwort or beachwort *B. maritima* is a much-branched shrub with trailing or erect stems and narrow, fleshy leaves arranged in opposite pairs. The axillary inflorescences are cone-like and consist of small, greenish, unisexual flowers, with male and female flowers on separate plants. Each male flower has a two-lipped calyx and four petals (sometimes described as staminodes) which alternate with the four stamens. The calyx and petals are absent in the female flowers, which have a four-seeded ovary topped by a flattened stigma.

*B. maritima* favours sandy shores at the edge of

salt water lagoons throughout the New World tropics, extending to the Galápagos Islands and Hawaii to the West Indies. The second species is *B. argillicola*, a native of New Guinea and Queensland, in which the separate male and female flowers are found on the same plant. The leaves of both species are occasionally used raw in salads and the ash was formerly used in glass and soap-making.

**Bataceae; 2 species**

## CAKILE

A small genus of annual, hairless, glaucous shore plants with succulent leaves distributed around the shores of Europe, the Mediterranean, Arabia, western Asia, Australia and North America. The flowers have four clawed petals which may be violet, white or pink, and six stamens. The seed pods have two segments, both usually containing a single seed. The upper segment is larger and ovoid in shape, the lower top-shaped. When ripe the upper segment breaks off while the lower segment remains attached to the plant: in this way half the buoyant seeds are dispersed by sea and the remainder guarantee the survival of the species on the original site. The distinctive torpedo-like shape of the fruits has given these plants the common name of sea rockets.

*Cakile edentula* is a low sprawling plant with pale lavender flowers and entire, lobed or wavy toothed leaves. It is widespread in North America, growing in sand dunes on both the Pacific and Atlantic coasts (from Labrador to Florida) as well as around the Great Lakes. In addition the range of this attractive annual extends to the Azores, Iceland, the Faeroes, northern Norway and the Soviet arctic. *C. harperi* is another North American species, confined to the east coast between North Carolina and Florida. The tap roots of sea rockets were formerly powdered by the North American Indians and mixed with other flours for making bread.

The very similar *C. maritima* has zigzag branches, deeply lobed leaves and lilac or white flowers up to 3 cm (1.2 in) across. It is a typical European drift line species, ranging north to Finland, Norway and the USSR, south into the Mediterranean and Aegean, and east to the shores of the Black Sea and beyond. It is also naturalized in North America. *C. maritima* typically forms large patches along the drift line on sand and shingle beaches, but is equally at home in salt marshes. The succulent leaves of this European sea rocket are very acrid and are sometimes used as a prevention against scurvy. They were formerly

*Cakile maritima*

prescribed for disturbances of the body's lumphatic system, and to ease the after-effects of malaria. The caterpillars of the sand dart moth *Agrotis ripae* feed on the foliage.

**Cruciferae; 7 species**

### CAMPHOROSMA

A genus of succulent annual or perennial herbs or small shrubs with alternate linear leaves and hermaphrodite flowers, found from the eastern Mediterranean to central Asia. The flowers have four or five perianth segments, of which the lateral segments are larger, four or five stamens and two or three stigmas. Many species thrive in coastal habitats, although saline steppes also provide suitable conditions.

*Camphorosma monspeliaca*, native to southern Europe and western Asia, is equally at home on stony beaches or in dry saline soils away from the sea. It is a tufted perennial which smells strongly of camphor (from which the generic name is derived) and has short, woody, leafy branches at the base and flowering stems up to 60 cm (24 in) tall. *C. annua* is an annual or biennial species of saline habitats in eastern central Europe, while *C. songorica* is a similar plant of salt marshes in central and western Asia.

**Chenopodiaceae; 11 species**

### CANAVALIA

A genus of herbaceous perennial or woody tropical legumes, many of which are associated with coastal habitats. The foliage of some species is used as green manure, while others produce edible beans for both animal and human consumption, although alkaloids present in the unripe seeds render them toxic in large quantities.

Seaside sword-bean *Canavalia maritima* (*C. rosea*) is a typical maritime representative of this genus, a common pantropical beach plant. The climbing or trailing stems may be 10 m (33 ft) long and the trifoliate leaves have elliptic or circular leaflets up to 9 cm (3.5 in) across. The inflorescences are 4-18 cm (1.6-7 in) long, hanging or upright and consist of several showy pink, purple or bluish flowers 3 cm (1.2 in) long and 2 cm (0.8 in) wide.

*C. cathartica* (*C. microcarpa*) is confined to the Old World tropics, particularly in coastal regions. In East Africa and the Seychelles, for example, this climbing herb with its clusters of pink scented flowers and pale brown oblong pods up to 12 cm (4.5 in) long, is typically found on raised coral beaches. The flowers and young seeds of *C. maritima* are eaten as a vegetable, although those of *C. cathartica* are said to be poisonous.

**Leguminosae; 51 species**

### COCHLEARIA

A genus of annual or perennial herbs of northern temperate regions, most of which are associated with coastal habitats, although a few are predominantly

arctic or alpine species. Plants in this genus are commonly called scurvy-grasses because of the high ascorbic acid (vitamin C) content of the foliage; the fresh leaves were much eaten in the past, especially by sailors, as a cure for or safeguard against scurvy. Scurvy-grass ale was once a popular tonic drink especially in the seventeenth century when it was drunk at breakfast rather as orange juice is today.

Common scurvy-grass *Cochlearia officinalis* grows on the coasts of northwest Europe, including the British Isles, as far east as Poland, thriving both in salt marshes and on sea cliffs. Its subspecies occur in the Alps, Pyrenees and Carpathians and occasionally in other inland habitats. One of the larger species, it has stems up to 50 cm (20 in) in height, arising from a rosette of fleshy kidney-shaped leaves. The flowers are 8-12 mm (0.3-0.5 in) across, the white (rarely lilac) petals are two to three times as long as the sepals. Long-leaved scurvy-grass *C. anglica* is locally common in estuaries, saline meadows and on muddy shores around the coasts of northwest Europe. It is a biennial with erect flowering stems up to 35 cm (14 in). The basal leaves are oval or oblong and the white or pale mauve flowers are 10-14 mm (0.4-0.6 in) across.

Danish scurvy-grass *C. danica* is an annual herb of western and northern Europe from the Atlantic coast of Iberia to southern Norway and the Baltic. It grows on sandy and rocky shores and on walls near the sea. The long-stalked basal leaves are heart-shaped, while the stem leaves are often ivy-shaped with 3-7 lobes. The flowers are 4-5 mm (0.2 in) across with mauve or whitish petals about twice as long as the sepals. Scottish scurvy-grass *C. scotica* is a biennial or annual which forms small compact tufts up to 10 cm (4 in) across on maritime sands in northern Scotland, the Hebrides, Orkney and Shetland. The leaves are rather fleshy, the flowering stems are more or less prostrate and the pale mauve flowers are about 5-6 mm (0.2 in) in diameter. *C. aestuaria* is a perennial confined to the Atlantic coasts of France and northern Spain.

Although particularly associated with maritime habitats, several species are confined to the Arctic. Arctic scurvy-grass *C. fenestrata* (*C. arctica*) is a biennial or perennial with heart-shaped basal leaves and white flowers, sometimes tinged with purple, which opens in June and July. The very similar Greenland scurvy-grass *C. groenlandica*, also known as scurvywort, is distinguished by its kidney-shaped basal leaves and smaller flowers. The first year sees the development of a rosette of fleshy leaves, flowers being produced in the second year. After the seed has ripened the whole plant dies. Both species are circumpolar in distribution.

**Cruciferae; about 25 species**

### COREMA

A genus with just two species, one of which, *Corema conradii*, occurs in eastern North America while the other *C. album* is found in the western half of the Iberian peninsula and the Azores. Both species are small evergreen shrubs resembling members of the Ericaceae, with unisexual flowers found on separate plants. The flowers are arranged in small terminal heads when they first open, but in the female plants the flowerhead grows to form a spike as the fruits mature.

*C. album* is a typical plant of maritime sands. An erect shrub with numerous branches, it has tiny linear leaves 6 mm (0.2 in) long and 1 mm (0.04 in) wide and flowerheads with 5-9 blooms. The male plants have straight erect branches, while the female plants have a more tortuous habit. The female flowers are petal-less, with three-lobed reddish stigmas, but the male flowers have pinkish petals 3-4 mm (0.1-0.2 in) long and red anthers. The white or pinkish fruits are berry-like and up to 8 mm (0.3 in) in diameter.

**Empetraceae; 2 species**

*Cochlearia sp.*

*Crithmum maritimum*

## CRITHMUM

The sole member of this genus is rock samphire, or sea fennel *Crithmum maritimum* which grows only in maritime habitats such as shingle, sand, sea cliffs and rocks, from the Canary Islands to the Atlantic coasts of Europe, the Mediterranean and the Black Sea. The name samphire is derived from the abbreviation of Saint Pierre, since this plant is dedicated to the fisherman Saint Peter

*C. maritimum* is a hairless perennial herb, woody at the base, whose clumps of branched stems reach a height of 15-45 cm (6-18 in). The fleshy leaves are triangular in outline, divided several times into linear segments and the minute (2 mm/0.1 in) white or yellowish green, fragrant flowers are arranged in flat-topped umbels of 8-36 rather stout rays. The 5-6 mm (0.2 in) long, rather corky fruits are yellow or purplish with prominent ridges. The whole plant is aromatic and the leaves were formerly used in salads, as a potherb or boiled with vinegar and spice to make pickles, which were sold in the streets of London as 'Crest Marine'.

**Umbelliferae; a single species**

## CYMODOCEA

A small genus of marine flowering plants or sea-grasses (see *Zostera*) from the shallow coastal seas of West Africa and the Canary Islands, the Mediterranean and the Indopacific. They have slender rhizomes and erect leafy branches, the leaves arranged in groups of 2-7 on short shoots. The unisexual flowers are found on separate plants and are solitary and petal-less. The male flowers have two anthers and the female flowers have two thread-like stigmas.

*Cymodocea nodosa*, an essentially Mediterranean species whose range extends to southern Portugal on the Atlantic coast, has leaves up to 40 cm (16 in) long and only 4 mm (0.2 in) wide, with 7-9 parallel veins and toothed or spiny tips. *C. rotundata* and *C. serratula* occur in the shallow tropical seas of the Indian

Ocean, especially around coral islands such as Aldabra.

**Cymodoceaceae; 4 species**

## ENHALUS

The sole member of this genus is *Enhalus acoroides*, the largest of all marine flowering plants, which grows on protected muddy or coral sand coasts near the low-water mark in Indomalaysia, from the Seychelles eastwards and around the coasts of Australia. Underwater meadows of this species provide the chief source of food for the dugong, a rare herbivorous marine mammal of the Indian seas. The seeds are edible and fibres from the leaves are used to make fishing nets in eastern Malaysia.

*Enhalus acoroides* has thick white roots, subterranean rhizomes covered with the stiff, wiry remains of the leaf sheaths, and narrow strap-like leaves up to 90 cm (3 ft) long and about 2 cm (0.8 in) wide. The three-petalled male and female flowers occur on separate plants, maturing at the time of the spring tides. Male plants produce large numbers of small white flowers on hair-like stalks which break easily and allow the flowers, and thus the pollen, to float to the surface and be dispersed by the waves. The green female flowers (which stay attached to the plant) are water-repellent and can float at low tide. The developing fruit is brought down from the surface to the sea floor by its coiling stem.

**Hydrocharitaceae; a single species**

## FASCICULARIA

A small genus of terrestrial bromeliads from Chile. Members of this genus are robust cushion-plants with short branched stems and spiny or toothed leaves in dense crowded rosettes. The inflorescences are stalkless terminal heads surrounded by large spiny bracts. Each flower has three sepals, three petals, six stamens and an inferior ovary.

The best known species is *Fascicularia*

*pitcairniifolia*, whose natural habitat is the spray-drenched rocky shores of central Chile, but which has also become naturalized on maritime rocks on islands off the coast of southwest England and northwest France. It has leathery blue-green leaves up to 35 cm (14 in) long, the innermost of which become bright red on the upper surface when the plant is flowering. The flowerheads are about 5 cm (2 in) in diameter, each flower having whitish erect sepals about 2 cm (0.8 in) in length and slightly longer pale blue petals with turned-out tips.

**Bromeliaceae; 5 species**

## FRANKENIA

A genus of herbs and small shrubs with wiry branches and usually inrolled hairy leaves, characteristic of saline habitats, especially maritime conditions, in temperate and warm regions. The flowers are nearly always hermaphrodite, each having five petals and sepals (rarely four) and usually six stamens arranged in two whorls, the outer shorter than the inner.

Sea-heath *Frankenia laevis* is a typical species commonly found at the landward end of salt marshes, usually on rather sandy or gravelly substrata. It occurs around the coasts of western Europe from the English Channel to southeast Italy, extending to the Canary Islands and North Africa. Sea-heath has heather-like leaves and flowers arranged in small clusters, or solitary, with pink, faintly notched petals.

Other Old World species are annual sea-heath *F. pulverulenta*, an annual with pale or deep violet flowers which grows on maritime sands and shingle and in saline habitats inland in southern and southeast Europe, the Canary Islands and Arabia; *F. boissieri* and *F. corymbosa*, both perennials with purple flowers which thrive in saline places near the sea in Iberia and North Africa; and *F. hirsuta*, a perennial with mauve or white flowers which grows on maritime sands and shingle in southeast Europe and the eastern Mediterranean. *F. ericifolia* is a white-flowered species of Canary Island coasts.

In North America the best known species is undoubtedly yerba reuma *F. grandifolia*, native to sandy habitats and salt marshes in southwestern North America. It is a shrubby plant with tannin-rich leaves used in the treatment of rheumatism and as an astringent remedy for catarrh. The ashes derived from some species of *Frankenia* are a source of salt, whilst others contain medicinal poisons. The Texas species *F. johnstonii* is listed as an endangered species by the United States Fish and Wildlife Service.

**Frankeniaceae; about 25 species**

### GLAUCIUM

A genus of annual, biennial or perennial herbs with blue-green foliage and yellow juice (latex), distributed across Europe and southwest and central Asia. The flowers have four entire petals, numerous stamens and a bilobed stigma, while the seed capsules are linear, two-celled and open from the tip almost to the base by means of two valves. These distinctive capsules have given the plants their common name of horned poppies.

Several species are associated exclusively with maritime habitats, including the sea-poppy *Glaucium flavum*, otherwise known as the yellow horned poppy. This biennial or perennial herb has an erect branched 30-90 cm (12-36 in) stem, lyre-shaped, pinnately lobed basal leaves 15-35 cm (6-14 in) long and stalkless upper leaves clasp the stem. The solitary flowers may be either terminal or axillary and have bright yellow petals 3-4 cm (1.2-1.6 in) long and yellow stamens. The capsules are 15-30 cm (6-12 in) long and often curved.

Sea-poppies are usually found on sandy and gravelly shores in southern and western Europe, their range extending to Oslo in Norway and the Black Sea; they have become naturalized in the eastern United States. The yellow latex is poisonous and was formerly used in medicine while the oil from the seeds was once used in lamps and in the preparation of soap. According to Theophrastus the leaves were used for removing ulcers from sheeps' eyes.

A similar species of dry stony places and beaches in the Balkan peninsula and the Aegean region is *G. leiocarpum*, with deeper yellow flowers and seed capsules not more than 10 cm (4 in) long, which are slightly constricted between the seeds. The more widespread red horned poppy *G. corniculatum*, which ranges from southern Europe into southwest Asia, has orange-red flowers and is more typical of cultivated ground and wasteland.

**Papaveraceae; about 25 species**

### GLAUX

The sole member of this genus is commonly known as sea milkwort or black saltwort *Glaux maritima*. It is a small succulent herb with creeping rooting stems and smooth fleshy entire leaves about 1 cm (0.4 in) long. The lower leaves are arranged in opposite pairs, while the upper leaves are alternate. The petal-less stalkless flowers, which are bell-shaped and about 5 mm (0.2 in) across, are produced in the axils of the leaves. Each has a five-lobed, petaloid, white or pink calyx and five stamens which alternate with the calyx lobes. The flowers, produced from June to August, are usually self-pollinated but are sometimes cross-pollinated by flies.

Sea milkwort is found throughout the northern temperate coastal zone in grassy salt marshes or in rocky places by the sea, as well as occasionally in saline habitats inland. Its succulent salty leaves were formerly pickled for use as a condiment.

**Primulaceae; a single species**

### HALIMIONE

A small genus of annual herbs or perennial shrubs with entire, more or less elliptical leaves, distributed around the shores of Europe and the Mediterranean, into southwest and central Asia.

The best known and most widespread species is sea purslane *Halimione portulacoides*, a very mealy small shrub, growing to an average height of about 80 cm (32 in), which has decumbent and erect stems. The opposite lower leaves are oval with short stalks, while the upper leaves are linear or spoon-shaped. The spike-like inflorescences consist of tiny yellowish green, unisexual flowers and are produced both terminally and in the axils. Male flowers have a perianth of five segments, absent in the female flowers which are enclosed by two persistent three-lobed bracteoles.

Sea purslane is a typical salt marsh plant, where it thrives on the margins of channels and pools inundated at high tide. Its natural range covers the coasts of Europe, from Denmark to the Mediterranean, extending to North Africa and southwest Asia. It has been introduced to similar habitats in North America. *H. portulacoides* is a foodplant for the caterpillars of the sand dart moth *Agrotis ripae*.

The other two species in this genus are *H. verrucifera*, a small shrub very similar to sea purslane which grows in coastal salt marshes and saline soils away from the sea in southeastern Europe and southwestern Asia, and stalked orache *H. pedunculata*, an increasingly rare annual with alternate leaves which thrives on stony beaches, sand-dunes and in the drier parts of salt marshes in

*Halimione portulacoides*

*Glaucium flavum*

northwest and northern Europe and the Black Sea, as well as in saline habitats inland, especially in Turkestan and Siberia. *H. pedunculata* is now extinct in Britain.

**Chenopodiaceae; 3 species**

### HALOCNEMUM

The sole member of this genus is *Halocnemum strobilaceum*, whose distribution ranges from the shores of the Mediterranean to central Asia, particularly around the Black and Caspian Seas. In the southern and eastern parts of its range it provides food for browsing camels and gazelles.

*H. strobilaceum* is a small succulent shrub with grey-green, cylindrical, jointed stems reaching a height of about 50 cm (20 in). The opposite leaves are about 1 mm (0.04 in) wide and the hermaphrodite flowers are arranged in a branched, spike-like inflorescence which appears in late summer or early autumn. Each flower has three perianth segments, a single stamen and two or three stigmas.

**Chenopodiaceae; a single species**

### HALODULE

A small genus of sea-grasses (see *Zostera*) which thrive in shallow tropical seas. The inconspicuous unisexual flowers are produced at the ends of short branches, male and female on separate plants. There is no perianth; the one-stamened male flowers produce thread-like pollen grains and the female flowers have long styles with two or three stigmas.

*Halodule beaudettei* is a Caribbean species that forms meadows in shallow (1-10 m/3.3-33 ft) waters over a wide range of salinities. It produces extensive mats of rhizomes or runners with poorly developed root systems and narrow, flattened, bright green leaves, 4-10 cm (1.6-4 in) long and 2-3 mm (0.1 in) wide. A distinctive feature of the leaves is three small teeth at the tip of the blade. The flowers and seeds have never been found.

*H. wrightii*, which differs in having leaves only about 1 mm (0.04 in) wide with two lateral projections at the tip, is found in the Persian Gulf, the Arabian Sea and the Indian Ocean, while *H. uninervis*, which thrives over a similar geographic range, has two lateral and one central projection at the tip of each 3.5 mm (0.2 in) wide leaf.

**Cymodoceaceae; 6 species**

### HALOPEPLIS

A tiny genus of annual herbs that thrive in coastal habitats in the warm temperate regions of the Old World. Like most maritime chenopods they have succulent segmented stems and fleshy spike-like inflorescences bearing inconspicuous flowers in groups of three. In *Halopeplis* the leaves are alternate, globose and stem-clasping with rudimentary leaf blades and the flowers may be either hermaphrodite or female, each having three perianth segments, one or two stamens and a pair of stigmas.

The grey-green stems of *Halopeplis amplexicaulis* vary from 5-30 cm (2-12 in) in length and are characteristic of salt marshes in the western Mediterranean, southern Portugal and North Africa, while the smaller but rather similar *H. pygmaea* is found in saline habitats in central Asia, including the shores of the Caspian Sea. *H. perfoliata*, distinguished by its red fleshy flower spikes, is typical of damp sandy maritime habitats in the Middle East, especially Bahrain. Its Arabic name of *Khurraiz* translates as 'glass beads', which perfectly describes the appearance of the spherical perfoliate leaves, strung like beads onto the stems.

**Chenopodiaceae; 3 species**

### HALOPHILA

A small genus of marine vascular plants distributed around tropical shores, from the West Indies to the Indian and Pacific oceans. The leaves are opposite and arranged in pairs on shoots produced at the nodes of the slender creeping rhizomes. Male flowers, with three stamens, are found on different plants from the female flowers, which have 3-5 thread-like styles; petals are absent. The pollen grains, which are joined together in chains like strings of beads, are released beneath the surface of the water and are carried to the stigmas by ocean currents.

The Caribbean species *Halophila decipiens* is a small, bright green sea-grass (see *Zostera*) up to 5 cm (2 in) tall which grows in patches up to 1 m (3.3 ft) across in moderately deep waters (to 30 m/98 ft) such as quiet lagoons. It has a network of rhizomes running through the sand or mud which give rise to an opposite pair of translucent oval leaves at each node. The distinctive *H. engelmanii* also grows in the Caribbean, favouring shallow waters less than 5 m (16.5 ft) deep, although in quiet harbours and lagoons it may be found at depths of up to 40 m (130 ft). The erect stalks are topped with whorls of 6-8 narrow, ribbon-like leaves about 3 cm (1.2 in) long. In both species the leaf margins are finely toothed.

*H. hawaiiana* is the only flowering plant able to survive on the tidal flats of the Hawaiian archipelago, while *H. minor* (*H. ovalis*) is a tiny Indian Ocean species with oval stalked leaves about 2 cm (0.8 in) in length. *H. stipulacea* has paired, translucent, oblong leaves about 6 cm (2.4 in) long and grows in submerged sands and muds around the shores of the Red Sea and western Indian Ocean. It entered the Mediterranean Sea via the Suez Canal soon after it was opened in 1869 and appears to be spreading westwards.

**Hydrocharitaceae; 9 species**

### HONKENYA

Just two species belong to this genus, and by far the best known is sea sandwort *Honkenya peploides*, a plant of sandy coasts in the northern temperate region with a circumpolar distribution. A second species is found in southern Patagonia.

Plants in this genus are hairless perennial herbs with trailing succulent stems that root at the nodes and yellowish green fleshy leaves arranged in opposite pairs. The greenish flowers are usually unisexual, with male and female flowers occurring on separate plants. Each flower has five free sepals, five entire greenish white petals and 10 stamens. Although present in female flowers these stamens do not function nor does the one-celled ovary in male flowers. Hermaphrodite flowers are sometimes found, however.

In *Honkenya peploides* the flowers are 6-10 mm (0.2-0.4 in) across and occur singly in the axils of the leaves and in terminal clusters of up to six. They are thought to be pollinated by flies, although hermaphrodite flowers are automatically self-pollinated when they close in dull weather. Sea sandwort can tolerate short periods of immersion in salt water and is a typical species of young, mobile sand dunes, where it may cover large areas. The caterpillars of the bordered straw moth *Heliothis peltiger* and the bordered sallow moth *Pyrrhia umbra* feed on the foliage.

**Caryophyllaceae; 2 species**

### HUDSONIA

The sole member of this genus is beach-heath

*Honkenya peploides*

*Hudsonia ericoides*, a very variable North American species which thrives in maritime habitats on the Atlantic coast. Also known as golden heather or downy false-heather, it is a low, matted, somewhat woody, evergreen plant with tiny scale-like leaves. The numerous sulphur-yellow flowers are about 6 mm (0.2 in) in diameter, each with five petals that open only in sunlight and last for only a single day. Beach-heath is found on sandy shores and in dry pinelands from Nova Scotia and Newfoundland to Delaware and South Carolina.

Some authorities recognize a second species *H. tomentosa* with grey woolly leaves, which is found in sand dunes along the east coast from New Brunswick to North Carolina, as well as on poor soils in the Great Lakes region. A third taxon called *H. montana*, a plant known only from Table Rock Mountain, North Carolina, and commonly called golden mountain heather, is listed as a threatened species by the United States Fish and Wildlife Service (1985) and as endangered in the IUCN Plant Red Data Book (1980).

**Cistaceae; a single species**

### LIMONIASTRUM

A small genus of dwarf shrubs, essentially southern Mediterranean in distribution, with many physical characteristics in common with *Limonium*.

*Limoniastrum monopetalum* is a typical species. A distinctive, silvery glaucous shrub, it has branched leafy stems 50-120 cm (20-48 in) in height and salt glands. The fleshy blue-green leaves are almost spoon-shaped and expanded at the base into a wide stem-clasping sheath. The flowers are solitary or in

*Limoniastrum monopetalum*

pairs, in a spike-like inflorescence 5-10 cm (2-4 in) long. Each flower has a five-toothed calyx enclosed by three overlapping bracts, and a bright pink corolla up to 2 cm (0.8 in) in diameter, the tube corolla as long as the five rounded lobes. *Limoniastrum monopetalum* is a characteristic plant of maritime sands and dry salt marshes in North Africa, the western Mediterranean and southern Portugal.

**Plumbaginaceae (Limoniaceae); 10 species**

### LIMONIUM

A large genus of perennial, rarely annual, herbs or dwarf shrubs with a cosmopolitan distribution. Many species, commonly known as sea lavenders or statices, favour maritime habitats, although others are more typical of arid inland regions such as salt steppes, in the northern hemisphere, especially western Asia.

*Limonium* species have long tap roots, woody stocks and simple leaves, usually confined to a basal rosette. The spreading, branched inflorescences bear numerous short-stalked flowers, usually on one side of the branches only, and each flower has a funnel-shaped calyx and a short-tubed corolla with the stamens inserted at the base. The five styles have thread-like stigmas. The flowers secrete nectar and are visited by insects. The dried flowers of some species are used for decoration as 'everlastings'.

*Limonium vulgare* is a typical species and one of the most widespread. It is a perennial herb which thrives in muddy salt marshes, where it is often the dominant species, in southern and western Europe, North Africa and North America. The flowers are about 8 mm (0.3 in) in diameter, with blue-purple corollas and yellow anthers, and are visited by bees, flies and beetles. *L. carolinianum* has pale purple flowers about 3 mm (0.1 in) across and is a

*Limonium vulgare*

characteristic plant of salt marshes on the Atlantic coast of North America, from Newfoundland and Quebec to Florida and Texas. It is a powerful astringent and was formerly used to treat dysentry.

*L. bellidifolium* has 5 mm (0.2 in) wide pale lilac flowers and grows in drier parts of salt marshes around the Mediterranean and the shores of the Black and Caspian seas, extending into eastern Asia; *L. humile* is a salt marsh species with reddish anthers, confined to northwestern Europe; and *L. binervosum* is a western European species with 8 mm (0.3 in) violet-blue flowers that thrives on maritime rocks, cliffs and stabilized shingle. *L. auriculae-ursifolium* also prefers rocky habitats by the sea. It is distinguished by its larger flowers and occurs in the Channel Islands, France, Iberia and North Africa.

Many sea lavenders have very restricted distributions: *L. transwallianum* and *L. brassicifolium* are native only to the Canary Islands, the latter is also naturalized in southwestern Europe; *L. cancellatum* is confined to the coasts of the Adriatic Sea and western Greece, where it grows on rocks near the sea; and *L. vestitum* is confined to maritime cliffs on the Adriatic islands of Jabuka (Pomo) and Kamik. *L. furfuraceum* grows only on calcareous maritime cliffs in the province of Alicante in southeastern Spain, while *L. lucentinum* is restricted to salt marshes in the same area.

Among numerous species known only from calcareous maritime cliffs in restricted areas are *L. japygicum*, confined to southeast Italy; *L. caprariense*, native of the Balearic Islands; *L. pontium*, restricted to Isole Ponziane, west of Naples; and *L. minutum*, known only from the coast of southeast France.

The giant sea lavender *L. arborescens* is known only from a single locality on the north coast of Tenerife in the Canary Islands and is listed as an endangered species in the IUCN Plant Red Data Book (1980). It is one of 16 species believed to be confined to the Canaries, of which *L. fruticans* and *L. spectabile*, both found only in Tenerife, are also listed as endangered. *L. recurvum* and *L. paradoxum* are apparently confined to the British Isles and are protected by law. *L. recurvum* is confined to a stretch

of about 1,200 m (3,900 ft) on the limestone cliffs of the Isle of Portland in Dorset and is also considered worthy of endangered status according to the IUCN.

**Plumbaginaceae (Limoniaceae); about 150 species**

### NOLANA

A genus of low-growing, sometimes prostrate, fleshy leaved annual or perennial herbs or subshrubs native to western South America, its range extending from northern Chile to southern Peru and including the Galápagos Islands. Many species are fleshy leaved shore plants. Without flowers, plants in this genus could be mistaken for members of the Chenopodiaceae, but the similarity ends with the tubular corollas, topped by five spreading lobes. On floral characteristics it seems that *Nolana* is intermediate between the Solanaceae (potato family), the Convolvulaceae and the Boraginaceae.

*Nolana galapagensis*, confined to the Galápagos archipelago, is a small shrub which thrives in the white sand dunes near the shore. It has erect hairy main branches and many short side-branches crowded with clusters of fleshy club-shaped leaves. The narrow funnel-shaped flowers are white in *N. galapagensis*, but the mainland species *N. paradoxa* has violet flowers with white centres and *N. prostrata* has smaller pale blue flowers which are decorated with black radial stripes.

**Nolanaceae; 18 species**

### OTANTHUS

The sole member of this genus *Otanthus maritimus* is an aromatic perennial herb of maritime sands from western Europe (although now extinct in the British Isles) to the Near East. The plants may reach a height of 50 cm (20 in) and have stout woody stems and fleshy, oblong or linear, alternate leaves with wavy margins. Both leaves and stems are felted with dense white woolly hairs, from which the plant derives its common name of cottonweed. Branched inflorescences bear terminal clusters of near-spherical flowerheads, 8-10 mm (0.3-0.4 in) in diameter. Ray-florets are absent, the flowerheads consisting of

*Otanthus maritimus*

tubular disc-florets only.

**Compositae; a single species**

### PANCRATIUM

A genus of perennial bulbous herbs native to tropical Africa, the Mediterranean and southern Asia. The leaves are strap-shaped with parallel sides and the fragrant white flowers resemble those of daffodils, having a broad corona, or 'trumpet', and an outer ring of six free perianth segments. However, unlike *Narcissus* where the corona consists of appendages of the perianth segments, in *Pancratium* it is made up of the expanded and fused filaments of the stamens. The flowers are arranged in clusters of 3-15 and may be erect or nodding.

The generic name is derived from the combination of two Greek words meaning 'all' and 'strength', in reference to the plants' supposed tonic properties. According to Theophrastus the bulbs are edible and the woolly layer between their outer skin and the interior formerly provided fibres used to weave felt shoes and other items of clothing.

Although most species are found in tropical regions of Africa and Asia, the best known and most widespread species is the sea daffodil *Pancratium maritimum*, which blooms in midsummer in the maritime sands of the Mediterranean. It has twisted grey-green leaves up to 75 cm (30 in) long and 2 cm (0.8 in) wide. The perianth segments of the flowers are 3-5 cm (1.2-2 in) long, while the funnel-shaped corona is about two-thirds the length of the perianth segments and fringed with 12 triangular teeth. The larvae of the southern European moth Brithys Crini feed on the leaves, buds and stems of *P. maritimum*,

*Pancratium maritimum*

also boring into the bulbs.

Other maritime species include *P. illyricum,* which is confined to the western Mediterranean islands of Corsica, Sardinia and Capraia and favours rocky ground near the sea. It differs from *P. maritimum* in having shorter broader leaves and smaller very fragrant flowers that bloom in late spring. The corona, which is less than half the length of the perianth segments, has six pronounced two-toothed lobes around the rim. *P. canariensis* has flowering stems up to 80 cm (32 in) tall and fragrant white flowers in clusters of 5-10. It grows in coastal habitats in Tenerife, Fuerteventura and Lanzarote. The African *P. zeylanicum* is a much smaller species with 30 cm (12 in) stems topped by solitary flowers.

**Liliaceae (Amaryllidaceae); 16 species**

### POSIDONIA

*Posidonia* is the only genus in the family Posidoniaceae and is represented by three species of submerged, marine, perennial herbs with creeping rhizomes and basal, alternate, linear leaves, sheathing at the base. These leaves have numerous dark spots and stripes resulting from the accumulation of tannins. The inflorescences consist of one or more, three- to six-flowered spikes subtended by leaf-like bracts. The flowers are usually hermaphrodite, but may be male. There is no perianth, each flower having three stamens, which produce thread-like pollen grains, and a single carpel. Pollination takes place underwater.

*Posidonia oceanica* is found from the Mediterranean to the Atlantic coast of southwest Europe. It has leaves up to 55 cm (22 in) long and about 1 cm (0.4 in) wide which arise from the nodes of stout subterranean rhizomes. The other two species occur on the southern and western coasts of Australia: *P. australis* has membranous leaves 6-14 mm (0.2-0.6 in) wide, and *P. ostenfeldii* has leathery leaves 1-4 mm (0.04-0.2 in) wide. In all species the pollen grains are discharged at low tide and drift in the shallow waters until they encounter a stigma.

*P. australis* is the source of posidonia fibre, cellonia or lanmar, which is mixed with wool and used for making sacks and coarse fabrics, as well as being used for packing and stuffing. The leaves of all species are often torn loose by the sea, rolled into balls by the waves and washed up on the shore.

**Posidoniaceae; 3 species**

### SABATIA

A small genus of North American and West Indian herbs with pink flowers. The most typical coastal species is the salt-marsh pink *Sabatia stellaris*, which occurs in saline or brackish marshes along the east coast of North America, from Massachusetts to Florida and Louisiana. It has branching stems up to 45 cm (18 in) high, topped by pink wheel-shaped flowers, about 4 cm (1.6 in) in diameter, with conspicuous yellow stamens.

Slender marsh-pink *S. campanulata* has sepals as

*Posidonia oceanica*

long as the petals, while the large marsh-pink *S. dodecandra* grows up to 60 cm (24 in) tall and has flowers up to 6 cm (2.4 in) across. Both species thrive in the damp sands and peat along the coastal plains of the eastern States. American centaury or rose-pink *S. angularis* is another eastern North American native but is now cultivated in the Netherlands to provide cut flowers. It also contains a bitter principle used medicinally as a tonic. *S. elliotii*, from the southeastern United States, is sometimes called the quinine flower because of its antimalarial properties while *S. campestris* is a southwestern species also used as a tonic.

**Gentianaceae; 17 species**

### SALICORNIA

A small genus of annual herbs with a more or less cosmopolitan distribution, excluding Australia. All species occur in saline habitats and it is possible that immersion in sea water is essential for the growth of

*Salicornia stricta*

some. The perennial species formerly regarded as belonging to this genus are now placed in *Arthrocnemum*.

Commonly known as glassworts or marsh samphires, many species are rich in soda and were formerly much used in the making of both soap and glass, as is the case in several other genera of the Chenopodiaceae, notably *Salsola* and *Suaeda*. Indeed, the Bible refers to their use. Glassworts are a favourite food of cattle, because of their salty flavour, and were once widely pickled in malt vinegar for human consumption in areas where rock samphire *Crithmum maritimum* was absent.

The much-branched stems bear succulent translucent leaves, arranged in opposite pairs and joined along their margins to envelop the stem, forming segments. The terminal branched flower spikes bear axillary clusters of three flowers (rarely one), each with an indistinctly three- or four-lobed perianth and one or two stamens. Many species are pigmented, although the typical colour is not fully developed until the seeds are almost ripe, and only then in the absence of shade.

*Salicornia ramosissima* is typically a much-branched bushy species, dark green when young but becoming deep purplish red. It is widespread in the upper parts of salt marshes on bare mud around the coasts of northwest Europe. Marsh samphire *S.*

*europaea* (*S. herbacea*), which is characteristic of open sandy mud in the salt marshes of western Europe and the east coast of North America, turns yellow green with age, later becoming flushed with pink or red, while *S. pusilla*, an essentially British, French and Irish salt marsh species, turns brownish or pinkish yellow.

*S. nitens* becomes brownish purple or orange and *S. fragilis* turns yellowish green. Both species are known to occur in the British Isles and Ireland but are probably also distributed around the coasts of western and southern Europe. *S. dolystachya*, whose mature stems are brownish, is a typical saltmarsh species of northwest Europe, while *S. bigelovii*, usually with unbranched stems, and the creeping *S. virginica* are characteristic of the northern tidal marshes of eastern North America.

**Chenopodiaceae; 13 species**

### SALSOLA

A large genus of annual herbs or dwarf shrubs with a cosmopolitan distribution on sea coasts and in other saline habitats. Many species are essentially Asiatic, extending into southeastern Europe. Members of this genus are rich in soda and were once employed in the preparation of both glass and soap (see *Salicornia*). Large quantities of the ashes of these plants particularly *Salsola kali* and *S. soda* were formerly

*Salsola kali*

imported from southern Europe and North Africa under the name of barilla.

Characteristics of this genus include stalkless, cylindrical or semicylindrical leaves, either alternate or opposite, and hermaphrodite flowers with two conspicuous bracteoles. Each flower has five perianth segments (three outer and two inner) which develop a transverse dorsal wing in fruit, five stamens and two or three stigmas.

One of the most widespread annual species is prickly saltwort *S. kali* which grows on sandy shores and in saline habitats inland across much of Asia, Europe, North Africa, the Azores and North America. It is a sprawling prickly annual with much-branched, pale green, red-striped stems up to 60 cm (24 in) long. The succulent awl-shaped leaves, 1-4 cm (0.4-1.6 in) long, narrow into a spine at the tip and the inconspicuous pinkish green flowers are solitary in the leaf axils. The juice of the fresh plant is said to be an excellent diuretic. The caterpillars of two moths, the sand dart *Agrotis ripae* and the coast dart *Euxoa cursoria*, feed on the foliage.

*S. soda* is a fleshy annual with semicylindrical leaves, which is equally at home on sandy beaches, in dry salt marshes or in saline habitats inland in southern Europe and southwestern Asia. Two perennial species particularly associated with coastal habitats are *S. carpatha*, an erect, grey pubescent shrub confined to calcareous maritime rocks on Karpathos (Crete) and *S. aegea*, a larger shrubby species from similar habitats in the Aegean region.

**Chenopodiaceae; 150 species**

### SESUVIUM

A small halophytic genus of warm and tropical coastal habitats. *Sesuvium portulacastrum* is a pantropical species, *S. edmonstonei* is confined to the Galápagos Islands and four other species are found in the Angola region of Africa.

*S. portulacastrum* is a hairless perennial with sprawling branches up to 30 cm (12 in) long. The oblong or spoon-shaped, rather fleshy leaves are arranged in opposite pairs. They are green at first but often turn orange and then brilliant red in the dry season. The stalkless flowers are produced in the axils of the leaves. Each flower has a tubular pink

calyx with five broad pointed lobes containing numerous stamens with pink anthers; there are no petals. This widely distributed species is native to tropical Africa and America but is naturalized on maritime sands near Lisboa, Portugal. It also occurs in coastal habitats in the Galápagos Islands, Hawaii and the Seychelles. *S. edmonstonei* is distinguished by its white flowers.

**Aizoaceae; 6 species**

### SOWERBAEA

A small genus of tufted herbs with fibrous roots, found only in Australia. The leaves are grasslike and the unbranched rigid stem is topped by an umbel of pink or purple flowers. The generic name honours the naturalist J. Sowerby.

A typical species is *Sowerbaea juncea*, a small rush-like herb of the coastal swamps of Queensland, New South Wales and Victoria. The short narrow basal leaves are 5-15 cm (2-6 in) long and crowned by a more or less globular cluster of delicate mauve flowers, only a few of which are open at any one time. Each flower has three petals and three petal-like sepals and smells faintly of vanilla.

**Liliaceae; 5 species**

### SPERGULARIA

A genus of annual or perennial herbs, sometimes woody at the base, with a cosmopolitan distribution. The genus contains a large number of halophytes and, of these, many species thrive in maritime habitats. Commonly known as sand-spurreys or sea-spurreys, certain species have long been used in the treatment of bladder diseases, especially chronic cystitis.

These often decumbent herbs have opposite linear leaves with silvery scarious stipules (leaf-like appendages) around the nodes. Stems and flower stalks are often covered with reddish glandular hairs. Arranged in loose inflorescences, the flowers have five free sepals, five white or pink entire petals and 5-10 stamens. The one-celled ovary is topped by three styles.

Lesser sea-spurrey *S. marina* is an annual with flowers 6-8 mm (0.2-03 in) across, the deep rose-pink petals shorter than the sepals. It is widespread on coastal salt marshes and inland saline habitats throughout the temperate zone of the northern hemisphere. Greater sea-spurrey *S. marginata* (*S. media*), found in coastal salt marsh communities and inland salt areas of the temperate zone of both hemispheres, has whitish or pinkish flowers up to 12 mm (0.5 in) across, in which the petals are usually longer than the sepals.

Cliff sand-spurrey *S. rupicola* is a perennial herb of maritime cliffs, rocks and walls, more or less confined to the coasts of southwestern Europe from southern Italy to the Inner and Outer Hebrides. It is distinguished by its larger (8-10 mm/0.3-0.4 in) long-stalked, deep pink flowers in which the petals are equal to or slightly longer than the sepals, while *S. bocconii*, an annual or biennial with tiny pale pink or white flowers (about 2 mm/0.1 in. in diameter), is somewhat less common in dry sandy and rocky coastal areas in southwest Europe and the Mediterranean region.

Other maritime species are *S. fimbriata*, from the coasts of Morocco, the Canary Islands and southwestern Iberia; *S. macrorhiza*, found in rocky places by the sea on the Mediterranean islands of Corsica and Sardinia; and *S. heldreichii*, an annual of maritime sands in the Mediterranean region and the Atlantic coasts of southwest Europe.

**Caryophyllaceae; 40 species**

### SUAEDA

A large genus of halophytic annual or perennial herbs or small shrubs, commonly called sea-blites, with a cosmopolitan distribution in coastal areas and inland salt steppes, although less common in the southern hemisphere. The generic name is derived from the Greek word for 'soda', a common constituent

*Suaeda maritima*

of these plants.

The succulent semicylindrical or flattened leaves are usually alternate and the tiny flowers, either hermaphrodite or female, occur singly or in few-flowered inflorescences in the axils of the leaves. Each flower has five fleshy perianth segments, which sometimes develop a small tubercle, horns or a narrow transverse wing on the back in fruit. There are five stamens and two or three stigmas.

Shrubby sea-blite *Suaeda vera* (*S. fruticosa*) occurs in coastal habitats, especially shingle banks, usually above the high-water mark. Its Atlantic and Mediterranean distribution includes southern and western Europe, North Africa, Angola, Madeira, the Canary Islands and St Helena, extending east to the shores of the Indian Ocean in Somalia and southwest Asia. *S. vera* is a small, much-branched, evergreen shrub, 40-120 cm (16-48 in) high, its stems densely clothed with pale green, almost cylindrical leaves 18 mm (0.7 in) long and 1 mm (0.04 in) wide. It is one of the plants burned in southern Europe for the manufacture of barilla (see *Salsola*) and is a favourite food of camels.

Annual sea-blite *S. maritima*, a blue-green or red-tinged plant with leaves 3-25 mm (0.1-1 in) long and about 2 mm (0.1 in) wide is one of the most widespread maritime species and is common in salt marshes and on muddy shores, usually below the high-water mark, around the coasts of Europe, Asia and North America (except the Arctic). It is a foodplant of the sand dart moth *Agrotis ripae*. *S. californica* is a characteristic species of Californian salt marshes.

**Chenopodiaceae; 110 species**

### SYRINGODIUM

There are just two species in this genus of marine plants of tropical and subtropical seas: *Syringodium isoetifolium* from the Indian and West Pacific oceans, and *S. filiforme* from the Caribbean. Both species are unique among sea-grasses (see *Zostera*) in having cylindrical leaves that resemble shoelaces. The flowers are unisexual, naked and arranged in a spike, male and female flowers occurring on separate plants. The male flower has two stamens that produce thread-like pollen, while the female flower has two carpels, each containing a solitary ovule. Pollination takes

place underwater.

Commonly known as manatee grass, *S. filiforme* has runners that form dense mats in fine sediments, such as sands and muds, and the bright green leaves may reach 45 cm (18 in) in length. This species is often found growing with turtle-grass *Thalassia testudinum* in shallow water meadows at depths of between 1 and 10 m (3.3-33 ft). *S. isoetifolium* has shorter leaves (to 30 cm/12 in) and is particularly abundant around islands such as the Seychelles and Aldabra in the Indian Ocean.

**Cymodoceaceae; 2 species**

### THALASSIA

A genus of submerged marine aquatics or sea-grasses (see *Zostera*) capable of surviving at depths of up to 30 m (98 ft). The two species are *Thalassia testudinum* of tropical Atlantic waters, especially the Caribbean, and *T. hemprichii* of the Indian and Pacific Oceans. Both species are commonly known as turtle-grass.

*T. hemprichii* has narrow rhizomes, the nodes of which produce clumps of curved strap-like leaves enclosed in papery sheaths, which may reach lengths

*Spergularia marina*

of 40 cm (16 in) but are usually shorter. This species is harvested in Asia to produce a mulch for fertilizing paddyfields and coconuts.

*T. testudinum* is probably the most abundant marine plant in the Caribbean, forming lush meadows in waters between 1 and 20 m (3.3-66 ft) deep on sandy or sediment bottoms. Colonies of turtle-grass are grazed by West Indian manatees and green turtles, hence the common name. The flattened strap-shaped leaves are 4-12 mm (0.2-0.5 in) wide and up to 1 m (3.3 ft) tall, with 9-15 parallel veins. *T. testudinum* has three-petalled unisexual flowers about 1.3 cm (0.5 in) across which may be greenish, white or pale pink. The solitary male flowers produce pollen grains in chains like rosary beads and pollination takes place underwater. The seeds, which take eight weeks to mature, are pea-like and produced in conspicuous pods. They are highly buoyant and are often dispersed over large distances.

The older blades of *Thalassia* plants are thickly encrusted with marine epiphytes, such as algae and bryozoans, and provide ambush sites for predatory sea horses and pipefish which anchor themselves to the leaves with their prehensile tails.

**Hydrocharitaceae; 2 species**

### THALASSODENDRON

A tiny genus of sea-grasses (see *Zostera*), the most widespread and abundant of which is *Thalassodendron ciliatum*, found from the Red Sea to the western Indian Ocean and the coastal waters of eastern Malaysia and northeast Australia. A second species is confined to the shallow seas off southwest Australia.

*T. ciliatum* has branching rhizomes and long leafy branches up to 30 cm (12 in) long which bear broad, linear, sometimes curved leaves about 1.3 cm (0.5 in) wide and 15 cm (6 in) long. The basal sheath, which is often pinkish or purple, is about 3 cm (1.2 in) long and is shed with the leaves. The flowers are unisexual, found on separate plants and pollination takes place underwater.

**Cymodoceaceae; 2 species**

### ZOSTERA

A genus of perennial submerged halophytes belonging to a taxonomically diverse group known as sea-grasses (see *Cymodocea, Halodule, Halophila, Syringidium, Thalassia, Thalassodendron*), although not related to terrestrial grasses. Species of *Zostera* thrive in the temperate and warm seas of both hemispheres, whereas many other marine flowering plants are confined to the tropics.

The creeping rhizome gives rise to several unbranched roots and a single leaf with a short shoot in its axil at each node. Each shoot has several linear leaves with compressed, sheathing bases. The flower stems are lateral or terminal and carry inflorescences of bisexual petal-less flowers, each consisting of a single ovary with two long, thread-like stigmas and a single stamen. At low tide, when the stems are near the surface, the anthers discharge their pollen in small clouds, the thread-like grains drifting until they come into contact with a stigma.

Eelgrass or grass-wrack *Zostera marina* has leaves up to 50 cm (20 in) long and 5-10 mm (0.2-0.4 in) wide. It grows on fine gravel, sand or mud in the coastal zone defined by the low water neap tide at its upper limit, down to about 10 m (33 ft). It is found only in the northern hemisphere, around most of the European coast from Norwegian Lapland to the Mediterranean, and around western Greenland and the Atlantic and Pacific coasts of North America from North Carolina to Hudson Bay and California to Unalaska Bay.

Less widespread species include narrow-leaved eelgrass *Z. angustifolia*, which has leaves only 2-3 mm (0.1 in) wide and is an essentially northern European species, and dwarf eelgrass *Z. noltii*, with thread-like leaves only 1 mm (0.04 in) wide and 12 cm (4.5 in) long, which is distributed from southwest Norway and Sweden to the Mediterranean Sea. Both species are most common around the low-tide mark, usually in sheltered habitats such as mudflats and estuaries.

*Zostera* beds provide food and habitat for many marine animals and plants and form the staple food of wintering wildfowl in many areas. The dried leaves and stems are used for stuffing pillows and as a packing material, particularly for Venetian glass, and are sometimes mixed with plaster or cement as a strengthening agent.

**Zosteraceae; 11 species**

*Carpobrotus edulis*

# PICTURE INDEX

*Gentiana acaulis*

# PICTURE CREDITS

PHOTOGRAPHY
PLANET EARTH PICTURES: **J. Brian Alker** 104 bottom, 174; **Pete Atkinson** 153 bottom; **A. P. Barnes** 116 bottom; **David Barrett** 2, 51, 192; **Rob Beighton** 10, 98; **Deni Bown** 16 top, 165, 194 bottom left; **J. Bracegirdle** 38 top, 70, 114, 177 bottom; **Jim Bradenburg** 40; **Franz J. Camenzind** 7, 48 bottom, 62, 65, 71, 108 bottom, 110 top, 131; **Mary Clay** 1, 20 bottom, 31, 32, 42 top, 43 bottom, 49 bottom, 181 top; **Mike Coltman** 119 left; **J. A. L. Cooke** 189; **Richard Coomber** 23, 79 bottom, 103 top right, 104 top, 167 left, 191, 211, 205 top; **Sheila Colenette** 135, 136 top; **Mike Coltman** 119 left; **Jack Dermio** 95 top; **John Downer** 27 bottom, 27 top, 185; **Nigel Downer** 18 top, 19, 89, 171 bottom, 177 top left, 183, 186 bottom, 193 bottom, 198, 214; **Georgette Douwma** 4, 5, 76, 96, 97; **Geoff du Feu** 25 top, 72, 85, 105 bottom, 179, 221; **Pieter Folkens** 130; **J. M. Forbes** 29 top, 30, 33, 37 bottom, 44 top, 100, 110 bottom; **David Fox** 218, 220; **Paul Franklin** 187; **Werner Frei** 159 bottom right; **Peter Gasson** 24 bottom, 66 bottom, 67, 84, 91, 180; **J. David George** 74 bottom 204 top, 207; **Nick Greaves** 155 top; **Wayne Harris** 8, 35 bottom, 105 top; **Hans Christian Heap** 15 top, 21 bottom, 78 left, 82, 129 top left, 134, 142 top, 169 top, 190; **John Heap** 81, 106 top, 117; **Terry Heathcote** 186 top; **Philippe Henry** 94; **Antony Joyce** 153 top, 159 top left; **Robert A. Jureit** 144; **Breck P. Kent** 166; **A. Kerstitch** 15 bottom left, 169 bottom; **Richard Kolar** 194/195; **Ford Kristo** 126; **Gwilym Lewis** 64, 83, 156, 168 top; **Dave Lyons** 38 bottom, 139; **Ken Lucas** 145; **Gillian Lythgoe** 25 bottom, 193 top, 209, 222; **John Lythgoe** 14 bottom, 16/17 bottom, 24 top, 34, 39, 46, 49 top, 78 bottom right, 107 top, 128, 132, 138/139, 142 bottom, 147, 176, 199 top, 206, 210; **John & Gillian Lythgoe** 20/21 top, 29 bottom, 35 top, 92, 150, 152, 196 bottom, 215 bottom; **J. Mackinnon** 140, 141, 149; **David Maitland** 146, 173 top; **Richard Matthews** 177 top right, 200/201; **Mark Mattock** 69 bottom, 99, 107 bottom, 181 bottom, 188, 194 left, 197, 212; **Roland Mayr** 80 bottom; **F. C. Millington** 77 left; **David Jesse McChesney** 136/137; **Andrew Mounter** 154 bottom, 161; **Duncan Murrell** 60, 62 top left, 65 top, 68 bottom; **Ernest Neal** 118 top, 129 top right, 205 bottom; **Steve Nicholls** 43 top, 53, 54, 109 bottom; **Raymond Parks** 58 top, 80 top; **J. C. Patterson-Jones** 129 bottom; **C. M. Perrins** 133; **June Perry** 86; **Christian Petron** 204 bottom, 216; **David Phillips** 74 top, 77 top right, 217, 219; **Dr. David A. Ponton** 69 top, 75 bottom; **Mike Potts** 167 top; **Chris Prior** 164 bottom; **Jorge Provenza** 160, 163, 171 top; **Kjell B. Sandved** 170; **Keith Scholey** 26, 37 top, 202, 208; **Alastair Shay** 157 bottom; **Mary Sheridan** 178; **B. Shorter** 36; **William M. Smithey, Jr.** 42 bottom; **Peter Stephenson** 155 bottom; **Spitsbergen Svalbard** 47 top, 48 top, 52, 55-57, 58 bottom, 59, 120; **Mills Tandy** 173 bottom; **P. V. Tearle** 47 bottom; **David Thompson** 172; **Gerald Thompson** 199 bottom; **Nigel Tucker** 68 top, 95 bottom; **John Waters & Bernadette Spiegel** 22; **Margaret Welby** 45; **Babs & Bert Wells** 182; **Alex Williams** 157 top; **April Wilson & Peri Coehlo** 168 bottom; **Joyce Wilson** 148, 158, 162, 164 top, 195 bottom left, 196 top.

ADDITIONAL PHOTOGRAPHY BY Teresa Farino 11-13, 14 top, 15 bottom right, 17 right, 18 bottom, 20 top left, 21 top right, 27 top, 28, 50, 63 bottom, 68 top, 78 top, 87, 88, 90, 93, 102, 103 top left, 103 bottom left, 161 bottom, 108 top, 109 top, 111-113, 115, 116 top, 118 bottom, 119 right, 121-125, 213, 215 top.

224